THE MARKET'S CYCLES 1882–2003

S&P 500 AVERAGE ANNUAL TOTAL REAL RETURN*

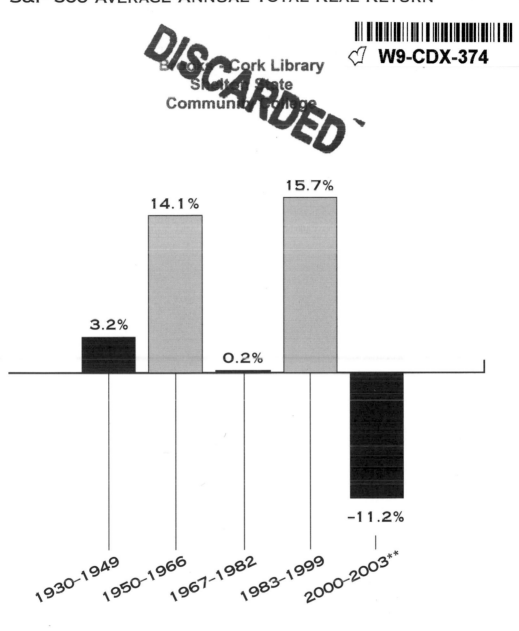

* WITH DIVIDENDS REINVESTED, ADJUSTED FOR INFLATION.

** THROUGH MARCH 30, 2003. ALL OTHER RETURNS ARE CALCULATED ON A CALENDAR YEAR BASIS (JANUARY 1–DECEMBER 31), BEGINNING JANUARY 1882.

SOURCE: GAIL DUDACK, SUNGARD INSTITUTIONAL BROKERAGE; GLOBAL FINANCIAL DATA

BULL!

WHAT DROVE THE
BREAKNECK MARKET
AND WHAT EVERY
INVESTOR NEEDS TO
KNOW ABOUT
FINANCIAL CYCLES

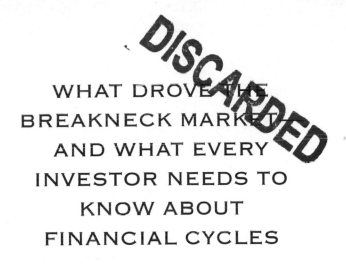

BULL!

A HISTORY OF THE BOOM,
1982–1999

MAGGIE
MAHAR

HarperBusiness
An Imprint of HarperCollins*Publishers*

HarperCollins books may be purchased for educational, business, or sales promotional use. For information, please write to: Special Markets Department, HarperCollins Publishers Inc., 10 East 53rd Street, New York, NY 10022.

Designed by William Ruoto

Library of Congress Cataloging-in-Publication Data
Mahar, Maggie.
Bull!: a history of the boom, 1982–1999: what drove the breakneck market—and what every investor needs to know about financial cycles / Maggie Mahar.
  p. cm.
Includes index.
ISBN 0-06-056413-X (alk. paper)
1. Wall Street—History—20th century.
2. Stock exchanges—United States—History—20th century.
3. Business cycles. I. Title.
HG4572.M245   2003
332.64'273'09048—dc21   2003051131

04   05   06   07   ❖/QW   10   9   8

To Raymond, who believes that everything is possible

— CONTENTS —

THE CAST ASSEMBLES (1990–95)

THE MEDIA, MOMENTUM, AND MUTUAL FUNDS (1995–96)

THE NEW ECONOMY (1996–98)

THE FINAL RUN-UP (1998–2000)

A FINAL ACCOUNTING

— ACKNOWLEDGMENTS —

More than a hundred people contributed to this book, sharing their experiences, their insights, and their knowledge. I would like to thank the many who agreed to be interviewed, often more than once, including Gail Dudack, Bob Farrell, Byron Wein, Henry Blodget, Richard Russell, Steve Leuthold, Ralph Acampora, Jim Chanos, Jim Grant, Jay Diamond, Abby Joseph Cohen, David Tice, Bill Gross, Peter Bernstein, Marc Faber, Jean-Marie Eveillard, Marty Whitman, Ralph Wanger, A. Michael Lipper, Don Phillips, Fred Sheehan, Jeremy Grantham, Maureen Allyn, Mark Headley, Clyde McGregor, Bill Fleckenstein, Martin Barnes, David Shulman, Laurence Tisch, Steven Einhorn, Nassim Nicholas Taleb, John Di Tomasso, Jim Awad, Jim Bianco, Paul Saffo, Robert Shiller, Hank Herrmann, Charles Biderman, Rick Ackerman, Bob Davoli, George Noble, John Collins, Edward Wolff, Bob Nurock, Charlotte Herr, Elizabeth Rivera, Lise Buyer, Jonathan Cohen, George Kelly, Stephen Roach, Neil Barsky, Bill Seidman, Arthur Levitt, Senator Jon Corzine, Joseph Stiglitz, David Ruder, Bert Ely, Harold Bierman, Allan Sloan, Jane Bryant Quinn, Mark Hulbert, Kate Welling, Jeff Madrick, William Powers, Herb Greenberg, Dave Kansas, Jonathan Weil, Ed Wyatt, Steven Lipin, Joe Nocera, Doug Henwood, Shirley Sauerwein, Jim Tucci, Ed Wasserman, Gary Wasserman, and Michael Malone.

Many reporters and financial writers contributed to this book. Since this is both a social history and a financial history, I turned to the media for a record, not just of what happened, but of what investors thought was happening during the Great Bull Market of 1982–99. In many ways, the media served as a mirror for investor sentiment, and sometimes as a lamp, illuminating the facts. I am indebted to the many reporters who kept that record and have tried to acknowledge that debt in my endnotes.

I also would like to thank *Barron's* for giving me the time and space to explore so many aspects of the financial world, in depth and in detail, in the stories that I wrote while working there from 1986 to 1997. During those years I learned much of what I know about both Wall Street and Washington.

I developed many of the ideas in this book in the late nineties while writing for *Bloomberg News* and *Bloomberg Personal Finance.* I especially want to thank my editors at *Bloomberg Personal,* Chris Miles and Steve Gittelson, for giving me the opportunity to explore themes that were not always popular at the time: market timing, bear markets, value investing, the importance of dividends, the dangers of the trade deficit, and the fallibility of the Fed.

From the time I began thinking about this book, Mary Bralove, a former *Wall Street Journal* editor and loyal friend, has proved the best sounding board a writer could have. When I began writing, she became my first reader. Since then, she has read and reread the manuscript, bringing an editor's eye and a reader's ear to the unending challenge of smoothing the narrative while keeping the argument on track. Or, as she would put it, turning spirals into straight lines. I could not have had a better reader.

Gail Dudack also became a collaborator. She provided many of the charts for this book, and her remarkably lucid and often prescient analysis has helped me focus my ideas.

Jim Chanos generously lent me his "New Era" files, a wonderful collection of often funny, always telling clippings that he kept as a personal record of a financial mania.

Susan Chace, Fred Sheehan, Bob Farrell, Gertrude Hughes, Steve Leuthold, Allan Sloan, Gail Dudack, Maureen Allyn, Jeff Madrick, William Powers, and Michael Klotz all read sections of the manuscript and provided valuable suggestions.

Johanna Piazza, Gregg Wirth, Chian Choo, Viken Berberian, Charlie Katz-Leavy, John Giutto, and Carol Dannhauser did an admirable job fact-checking a manuscript filled with facts.

Most of all, I want to thank my family—Emily and Michael and Raymond—for their warm support and absolute faith that I could finish this project.

Last, but far from least, I would like to thank John Brockman, my agent, and Marion Maneker, my editor. Without John Brockman's professional integrity and encouragement I never would have gotten past Chapter 1.

Without Marion Maneker's faith in the manuscript, I never would have arrived at Chapter 21. A writer himself, he is a writer's editor. I particularly want to thank him for the role he played in shaping this story. He recognized, before I did, the importance of financial cycles as the underlying theme of the book. I also want to thank Edwin Tan for smoothing the path to publication with such diplomacy, efficiency, and finesse.

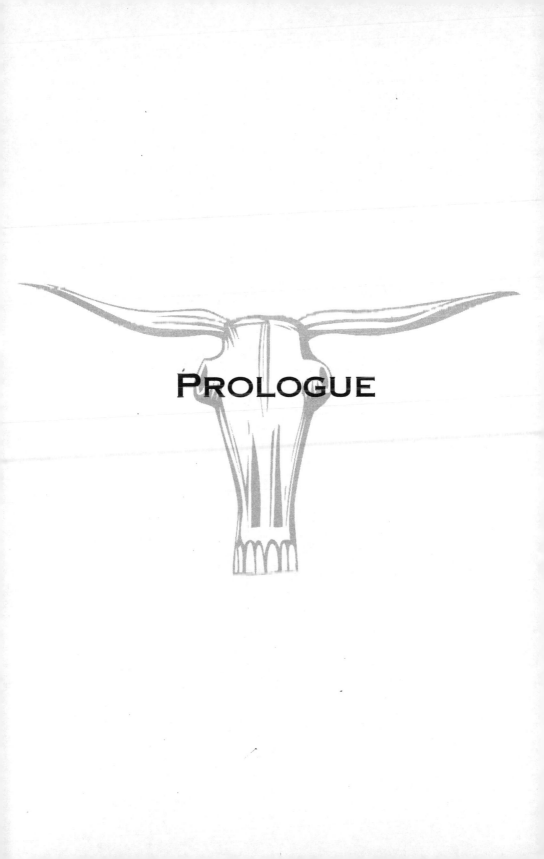

PROLOGUE

HENRY BLODGET

As Henry Blodget rode the elevator to his office in the North Tower of the World Financial Center one morning in the late autumn of 1999, he had no idea that someone had left a message on his voice mail during the middle of the night.[1]

The 34-year-old Merrill Lynch analyst was accustomed to the pressures of his job. In recent years, Wall Street firms had realized the importance of turning their analysts into brand names, and "Blodget" had become a brand. With just a few words, he could send a stock to the moon.

He had made his reputation doing just that, less than a year earlier, by raising the bar for one of the New Economy's most dazzling stars: Amazon.com. Henry Blodget was still a relatively unknown young analyst at CIBC Oppenheimer in December of 1998 when he boosted his forecast for Amazon from $150 to $400 a share. At the time, Amazon was trading at $240; within weeks, it blasted straight through the $400 target.

He was young; he was blond; he was on his way to becoming very rich. Almost immediately, Blodget became a media darling. CNBC's bookers wooed him; USA Today called him the "man of the moment." By the end of 1998 even The Wall Street Journal showcased him as one of a group of "Savvy Pros" who "Had an Early Line on This Year's Biggest Winners."[2]

In February of 1999, Merrill offered Blodget a plum job—first chair on the firm's Internet research team. Before long, the press would be speculating that, in 2001, Merrill Lynch paid Blodget as much as $12 million a year.

Blodget was still amazed by the effect that one call had on his career. The truth was that he had not been entirely comfortable with the $400 forecast, but Oppenheimer's sales force needed a new estimate. When he rolled out his first report on Amazon in October of 1998, the stock was trading well over $80, and he set a target of $150—adding that he thought the stock was worth anywhere between $150 and $500. By December, Amazon had shot past $200, and his firm's sales team began pressing him for a new target. Blodget felt obliged to pick a number. Privately, he was confident that Amazon would hit $400—he just didn't know if he had the balls to say it. But as his very first boss on Wall Street had told him, "You're not a portfolio manager—you're not trying to sneak quietly into a stock before someone else sees it. You're an analyst: your job is to go out and take a position."

So he said it—$400. And Amazon turned out to be a home run. His career had turned on that one call. Three years earlier, he had been a trainee at Prudential. Now, in the small but shimmering pond called the Internet, he stood second only to Morgan Stanley's Mary Meeker, the Internet analyst *Barron's* crowned "Queen of the Net."

Entering his office, Blodget glanced out the window—his office faced uptown, flanked on one side by the Hudson River, on the other side by the World Trade Center. Automatically, he checked his voice mail. As he listened, he recognized the caller—a fund manager who owned some of the stocks that he covered:

"You are *so pathetic,*" said the voice that suddenly filled the room. "I listen to you and I am *disgusted.* You don't own these fucking stocks. *We* own these stocks. You have something to say? *Shut up.* You hear Meeker saying anything negative? *No.* You hear anyone else? *No.*

"Then *shut up.*"

Blodget flushed with anger. The day before, he had said something remotely negative about a stock that the anonymous caller owned. It was not as if he had issued a sell recommendation—he had not even downgraded the stock. But he had not been entirely enthusiastic. The money manager's message was clear: We own the stock. We own you.

This was not the first time that a late-night caller left an intimidating message on Blodget's answering machine. On more than one occasion, he had received physical threats. He knew it was foolish, but the calls rattled him. There were things worth dying for; stock picking was not one of them.

As far as he was concerned, the caller had crossed a line. Blodget understood that the mutual fund managers and other large institutional investors who did business with Merrill were his clients, and he did his best to please them—after all, they had an enormous amount of control over his career. They voted in the *Institutional Investor* rankings that could make his reputation.

Each year *Institutional Investor* (*II*) magazine polled these professional money managers, asking them to rank Wall Street's analysts by sector, and then published the results. Some analysts professed to scoff at the rankings, and a few refused to play the game. But almost everyone who had a shot at the top of the list paid attention. The higher an analyst ranked in *II*'s beauty contest, the bigger his brand name. And the bigger his name, the higher his pay.

Ranking as one of the two or three top analysts in a particular area meant that the analyst could bring in banking—the investment banking business that was the lifeblood of most Wall Street firms. If a high-profile Internet start-up was looking for an investment banker to take it public, its first choice would be a firm where the Internet analyst was a star. Not only could a powerful analyst attract the banking business, his or her word would stir enough excitement among investors to insure that the new offering fetched the highest possible price.

Blodget understood that to Merrill's Internet banking team, he was a key asset. This was no secret. As *The New York Times* pointed out at the end of '99, Merrill had lagged in the race to take Silicon Valley companies public, in large part because it lacked such a star—and this, the *Times* sources suggested, was one reason that Merrill's stock had disappointed investors.[3] Over the course of the year, Morgan Stanley's shares had gained 85 percent. Since going public in May, Goldman Sachs's stock had climbed 53 percent. Over the same span, Merrill's shares had risen just 17 percent. Nevertheless, since hiring Blodget eleven months earlier, Merrill had made progress: it now boasted an estimated 7.8 percent share of all Internet banking business. Admittedly, this was still only half the market share of influential rivals such as Morgan Stanley and Credit Suisse First Boston, but the *Times* noted that by cultivating Blodget, the firm was doing its best to remedy the situation. From the point of view of someone who owned shares in Merrill Lynch, this was good news.

Blodget was under pressure to be a rainmaker for Merrill's bankers. But what many outside Wall Street did not understand was that, for an analyst, the worst pressure often came not from his own firm's investment bankers but from the companies he covered—not to mention the portfolio managers who had bet millions on those companies. Since an analyst's career turned on his *Institutional Investor* ranking, he needed the support of those big institutional investors—money managers at fund companies such as Fidelity and Putnam—to shine. And, you did not make a lot of friends if you downgraded the stocks they owned. Especially if those stocks were volatile.

That was the problem. In 1999, Internet stocks such as AOL took investors on a wild ride, but overall they continued to climb. It didn't matter if the company was any good; if you downgraded it, you were almost certain to be wrong. And, on Wall Street, the reality was that picking a good stock was far more important than picking a good company.

But now, things were getting out of control. At the beginning of '99, while he was still at Oppenheimer, Blodget had told the *The New York Times*, "I don't think there's a sector in history that's been valued at these heights. It's totally frightening."[4] Eleven months later, prices continued to spiral. Then, there were the threatening messages like the one he had received today.

At the end of the year, Blodget promised himself he was going to downgrade the Internet stocks that he covered.

It was a promise that he would not keep.

Over the next six months, the market that had made Blodget's career peaked. The Dow Jones Industrial Average topped out on January 14, 2000, at 11,722.98. Not three months later, on March 10, the Nasdaq index reached its apogee: 5048.6. Two weeks after that, the Standard & Poor's 500 hit its bull market high: 1527.46. Then, the long slide began.

As the market slithered south, Henry Blodget became the poster boy for all that had gone wrong. "Even *60 Minutes* did a story about me," Blodget recalled in a 2001 interview. "I couldn't watch. I hid in the next room, and my wife would come in during the commercials and tell me what they were saying about me."

New York Attorney General Eliot Spitzer launched an investigation. "Why," Spitzer asked, "had Wall Street's top analysts continued to recommend overvalued stocks? Where was the research?" Before long he demonstrated, beyond a doubt, what everyone on Wall Street knew: no one is paid

$12 million a year to do research about anything. Wall Street's premiere analysts had two more pressing jobs: serving their institutional clients' interests and drumming up investment banking business.

Spitzer's investigation took him to Merrill Lynch. There, he began sleuthing Blodget's confidential e-mails, and before long he found what he was looking for: evidence that Merrill's star Internet analyst had doubts about more than one Internet stock. In October of 2000, Blodget sent a message to an analyst on his team, telling him to downgrade Infospace: "Can we please reset this stupid price target and rip this piece of junk from whatever list it is on? If you have to downgrade it, downgrade it."

Two months later, Blodget received an e-mail from a longtime Merrill broker complaining about the firm's rosy forecasts ("We had better stop whistling through the graveyard and pretending we are adding value to our clients' portfolios"). Blodget sent the message on to his colleagues: "Attached, an e-mail from a disgusted Merrill Lynch veteran. The more I read of these, the less willing I am to cut companies any slack, regardless of the predictable temper tantrums, threats, and/or relationship damage that are likely to follow. . . ." By January of 2001, he was getting fed up. When an institutional investor sent Blodget a message asking "What is so interesting about GoTo.com except the banking fees [that Merrill might hope to receive from the company]?" Blodget sent him a one-word reply: "Nothin'." [5]

Clearly, Henry Blodget was becoming uncomfortable in his role as cheerleader. And internally, at least, he was questioning the priorities that firms like Merrill followed when deciding which stocks to recommend. For some time, he had expressed doubts about the sky-high prices assigned to Internet stocks—as early as March of '99 Blodget had been quoted in the newspapers using words such as "bubble" and "euphoria" when talking about the sector. [6]

But Spitzer did not see a closet whistle-blower in Blodget's messages. Instead he, along with most of the investing public, interpreted Blodget's e-mails as a sign of something far worse: cynicism. "Basically, [he] is saying 'Hey, I'm going to threaten you with the truth,'" Spitzer charged. "The brazenness of that, and the insight into what was going on was so overwhelming," he added—as though threatening to use the truth was somehow worse than knowingly concealing it. [7]

At the very end, Henry Blodget was no longer a true believer. By contrast, Morgan Stanley's star Internet analyst, Mary Meeker, maintained her nearly messianic commitment to the Internet. Meeker would not be

hounded by the media or the public—at least not to the same degree as
Blodget. If he had remained deluded, perhaps he, too, might have been for-
given.[8]

In retrospect, Henry Blodget understood the role he had played in the bull
market of the nineties. Sitting in a Greenwich Village café early in 2002, he
reflected on his career.

"Have you ever read John Kenneth Galbraith's book about the history
of bubbles?" he asked, referring to the Harvard economist's *A Short History
of Financial Euphoria.*

"Well, I hadn't—until recently. I just finished it," Blodget admitted,
with a pained smile. "It's amazing how Galbraith spells it all out—what
happens in every bubble, every time. He's almost yawning as he lays it out:
First some new thing comes along and captures the public's imagination.
Then everyone starts making money. After that, some person of average intelligence is held up as a genius."

Blodget raised his hand: "Hi, that was me," he said with a sardonic,
half-embarrassed smile.

Blodget shook his head. "If only I had read that book at the beginning
of 2000. It would have been worth a million dollars to me then." For in his
history of financial manias, Galbraith had predicted Blodget's fate: "The
[public's] anger will fix upon the individuals who were previously most admired for their financial imagination and acuity."[9]

But even if Henry Blodget had read Galbraith's book in 2000, he might
not have recognized the full relevance of Galbraith's story. For as the Great
Bull Market of 1982 to 1999 reached a climax, only a handful of the actors
onstage were ready to acknowledge that the longest bull market in U.S. history was coming to a disastrous end.

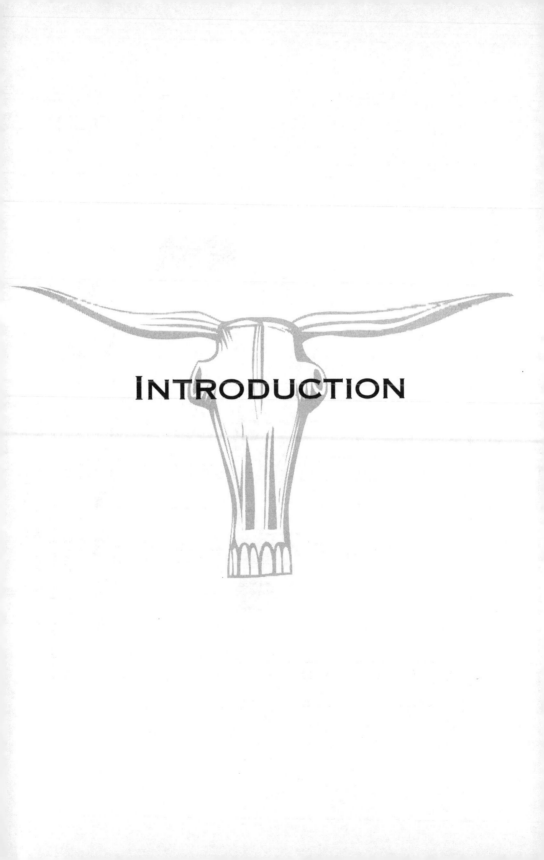

INTRODUCTION

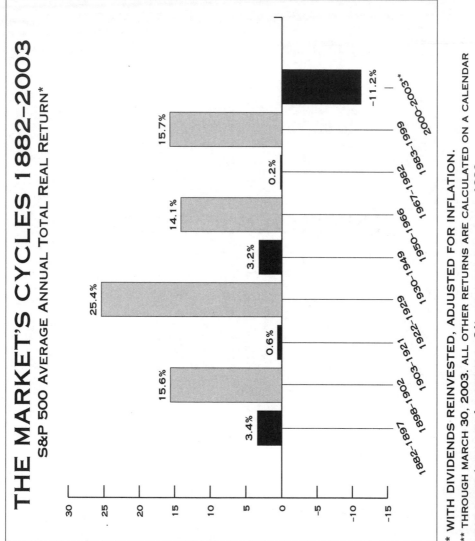

THE MARKET'S CYCLES 1882–2003
S&P 500 AVERAGE ANNUAL TOTAL REAL RETURN*

3.4% 1882–1897
15.6% 1898–1902
0.6% 1903–1921
25.4% 1922–1929
3.2% 1930–1949
14.1% 1950–1966
0.2% 1967–1982
15.7% 1983–1999
-11.2% 2000–2003**

* WITH DIVIDENDS REINVESTED, ADJUSTED FOR INFLATION.

** THROUGH MARCH 30, 2003. ALL OTHER RETURNS ARE CALCULATED ON A CALENDAR
YEAR BASIS (JANUARY 1–DECEMBER 31), BEGINNING JANUARY 1882.

SOURCE: GAIL DUDACK, SUNGARD INSTITUTIONAL BROKERAGE; GLOBAL FINANCIAL DATA

THE MARKET'S CYCLES

January 1975. When Richard Russell squinted, he saw the silhouette of a bull emerging against a bleak horizon. The author of *Richard Russell's Dow Theory Letter,* Russell had been writing his financial newsletter since 1958, and by now he had a wide following—at least among those still willing to read about stocks. Over the past two years, the Dow Jones Industrial Average had lost nearly half of its value.

The Dow had last seen blue skies in 1966 when it grazed 1000. Two years later, it flirted with 1000 again, but in fact, the bull market that began in the fifties was peaking—much as the bull market that began in the eighties peaked at the end of the nineties.

After reaching its apex in the late sixties, the Dow rallied and plunged, rallied and plunged without getting anywhere—until finally, in January of 1973, the benchmark index smashed 1000, setting a new high at 1051.69. It seemed that a new bull market had begun. In fact, the bear was just baiting investors, luring them in so that they could be impaled on the spike of a final bear market rally. What followed was the crash of 1973–74.

When it was all over, in December of 1974, both the Dow and the S&P 500 had been slashed nearly in half; trading volume had all but dried up; mutual fund managers were grateful to find jobs as bartenders and taxi-

cabdrivers, and Morgan Guaranty, the nation's largest pension-fund manager, had lost an estimated two-thirds of its clients' money. As for individual investors, the public was shorn. Between December of 1968 and
October of 1974, the average stock had lost 70 percent of its value.[1]

Nonetheless, at the beginning of 1975, Richard Russell could all but
hear the bull snorting. At last, he believed, the bear market had bottomed.
And he was right, just as he would be in the fall of 1999, when he warned
readers that the first phase of a bear market had begun.[2] By then, *Richard
Russell's Dow Theory Letter* was the oldest and one of the most widely read
financial newsletters in the United States.

Russell based his predictions on "Dow Theory," an analysis of stock
market cycles invented by William Peter Hamilton and Charles Dow. (Cofounder of Dow Jones & Company, Charles Dow also lent his name to the
benchmark stock market index.) At the end of the century many investors
would assume that "market timing" meant day trading, buying and selling
stocks in a matter of hours, days, or, at most, months. But Dow Theory
does not attempt to predict the highs and lows of particular stocks, nor does
it strain to forecast the market's short-term gyrations. Instead, it focuses on
longer trends—cycles that can last for years. Each cycle is the peculiar product of a particular moment in economic and political history, but in Dow's
view the force behind each go-round was the same: human nature.

Most descriptions of investor psychology reduce human behavior to a
series of simple knee-jerk reactions: rampant greed followed by blind fear.
Charles Dow sketched something subtler in *The Wall Street Journal* editori-
als that he wrote between 1899 and 1902. He recognized that investors
do not rush into a bull market, and when it ends they do not swoon in
surrender to the bear. Both bull and bear cycles begin slowly, he observed,
because "[t]here is always a disposition in people's minds to think the existing conditions will be permanent. When the market is down and dull, it is
hard to make people believe that this is the prelude to a period of activity and
advance. When prices are up and the country is prosperous," Dow added,
"it is always said that while preceding booms have not lasted . . . [this time
there are] 'unique circumstances' [which will make prosperity permanent]."[3]

Because human beings are slow to embrace change, these cycles can
run a decade, or longer. In fact, as Gail Dudack, chief market strategist at
SunGard Institutional Brokerage, shows in the table below, the history of
the S&P 500 from 1882 through 1999 can be broken down into alternating "strong" and "weak" cycles that average nearly 15 years. During the

booms, investors who plowed their dividends back into their portfolios reaped returns averaging nearly 18 percent a year—even after adjusting for inflation. During the dry spells, by contrast, average "real" (inflation-adjusted) total returns dropped to less than 2 percent. Without dividends, investors lost nearly 3 percent a year.

In the final third of the twentieth century, the market's returns fit the pattern with ruthless precision: from January 1967 through December 1982, investors averaged 0.2 percent annually—and that was if they reinvested their dividends. Those who became discouraged and stopped plowing their dividends back into the market lost an average of nearly 4 percent a year—year after year, for 16 years. Finally, in 1982, the cycle turned: from January 1983 through December 1999, real returns averaged 12.1 percent. If an investor reinvested his dividends, he was rewarded with annual returns of 15.7 percent.

AVERAGE ANNUAL REAL RETURNS

STRONG CYCLES

	S&P 500 (Capital Gains Only)	S&P 500 (With Dividends Reinvested)
1983–1999	12.1%	15.7%
1950–1966	9.3%	14.1%
1922–1929	19.3%	25.4%
1898–1902	11.8%	15.6%

WEAK CYCLES

	S&P 500 (Capital Gains Only)	S&P 500 (With Dividends Reinvested)
2000–2003*	–12.2%	–11.2%
1967–1982	–3.8%	0.2%
1930–1949	–1.8%	3.2%
1903–1921	–4.4%	0.6%
1882–1897	–1.2%	3.4%

*As of March 2003

SOURCE: SUNGARD INSTITUTIONAL BROKERAGE, GAIL DUDACK

"Few investors realize how much dividends have contributed to the stock market's performance," Dudack observed. "Nor does the public realize that in this century, there have been three separate periods, ranging from 16 to 20 years, when inflation-adjusted capital gains on the S&P have been negative."[4]

Inevitably, any attempt to break the past down into cycles involves choosing beginning and ending points that are, to some degree, arbitrary. Others might well divide the market's cycles somewhat differently. But virtually every market historian agrees on the larger picture: the history of the market is a story of bull and bear markets that take place against a backdrop of much longer waves—weak and strong cycles that last long enough to convince us that they are the norm.

In other words, as James Grant, editor of *Grant's Interest Rate Observer,* put it in 1996, "The stock market is not the kind of game in which one party loses what another wins. It is the kind of game in which, over certain periods of time, nearly everyone may win, or nearly everyone may lose."[5]

The story of the Great Bull Market of 1982–99 needs to be understood in this context. For what was seen, rightly, as the most extraordinary bull run in U.S. history was, at the same time, very much part of a larger pattern.

THE LIMITS AND USES OF CYCLE THEORY— RUSSELL'S RECORD

Charles Dow was neither the first nor the last to note the market's cycles, and he is only one of many who have tried to use a theory of cycles to forecast long-term trends. Some historians emphasize the psychological factors that drive cycles; others focus on economic causes. The most sophisticated recognize that the two cannot be separated.[6] But no system can be turned into a crystal ball. Any scheme that attempts to predict the future based on the patterns of the past is but a grid laid over the messiness of reality. History is ambiguous, and every financial mania is unique, the product of the peculiar folly of its time.

Nevertheless, precisely because such systems are so rigid, they can help steel an investor against his own emotions—giving him the strength to resist bear market rallies, and the faith to get back in at the bottom when everyone else has abandoned the field.

Certainly, over the years, a combination of Dow theory and sharp instinct served Richard Russell well. Even though the final two decades of the 20th century included a 17-year bull market (which should have rendered market timing moot), a subscriber who followed the market timing advice in Russell's newsletter would have earned, on average, 11.9 percent a year, beating a buy-and-hold strategy, on a risk-adjusted basis, for the 21½ years from June 1980 to December of 2001.[7]

But it was in January of 1975 that Richard Russell made what was probably his finest call. With the crash of 1973–74, the market had finally bottomed out. The next bout of prosperity would not begin in earnest until 1982, but Russell was correct: the market had laid the foundation for a new bull run. The Dow was now cheaper than it would be at any time for the rest of the century. Eagerly, Russell trumpeted the good news. It was, he told his subscribers, time to buy stocks.

Then came the hate mail. "I don't want to hear about stocks!" wrote Russell's subscribers in 1975. "How dare you tell us that this is the beginning of a bull market."[8] In fact, an investor who had been patient enough to wait for this final low watermark—and was now both courageous and contrary enough to wade back in—would see double-digit gains for the next two years.

Few were willing to take the wager. It was not just that Russell's readers did not believe him. They were tired of being snookered. When the crash of 1973–74 finally ended, the Dow came to rest at 577—seven points below where it had traded in 1958, some 16 years earlier. No wonder long-term investors felt betrayed.

The long, steep decline broke the spirit of the most faithful investors. "Even if you weren't in the market, there's a good chance you saw someone in your family go through it," said New York money manager Ken Smilen. "Maybe you had an uncle who, say, in 1955 began putting $150 a month into stocks to send his one-year-old to college. Maybe some months he had trouble scraping the money together—maybe one month he borrowed it from your mother. Then, after doing it for 18 years, he finds that, at the end of '74, he's lost all of the appreciation. That's something your family will never forget."[9]

Little wonder that in January of 1975, Richard Russell's readers greeted his "buy" signal with so little grace. "By late 1974 the crowd had not just left the party, it was stoning the host," observed financial writer Andrew Tobias.[10]

Twenty Years Later

July 1995, a sweltering summer on Wall Street, and Ralph Acampora, Prudential's head technical analyst, presented investors with a head-swiveling forecast: by 1998, Acampora declared, the Dow would break 7000. At the time, the benchmark index was trading well under 5000 and Acampora's target seemed, to many, outlandish. Skeptics pointed out that the Dow had already sprinted 900 points in less than eight months—a climb that they called "unprecedented." But the 54-year-old Acampora found precedent in the bull run of 1962–66, when the Dow gained 85 percent in four years. The naysayers were just too young to remember a real bull market, Acampora scoffed: "I have sneakers older than the people who write these articles." [11]

As it turned out, Acampora's forecast was conservative. In 1995, the final leg of the most spectacular bull market in U.S. history was about to begin. The index hit Acampora's target in February of 1997, and at age 56, he found himself a folk hero. He liked to repeat comic Jackie Mason's line: "It took me 30 years to become an overnight sensation." [12]

Ralph Acampora would become one of Wall Street's best-liked seers. The son of a Bronx truck driver, he was a throwback to earlier times on the Street. Although he was a technical analyst who conjured his forecasts from charts and spoke the language of "trend lines" and "60-day moving averages," Acampora was hardly a wonk. Beneath all of the numbers lay an old-fashioned faith in American capitalism. "It makes all the sense in the world that our stock market would go up," he once told a reporter, "because we have more confidence in our way of life." [13]

As a guru, the outgoing, charismatic Acampora was a natural. A showman who thoroughly enjoyed his own show, he brought pizzazz to the otherwise dreary business of technical market analysis. Before long, Prudential's top technical analyst found himself on CNBC. There, the financial network's top anchor, Maria Bartiromo, bestowed a title upon him: "If Abby Cohen is the Queen of the bull market," said Bartiromo, referring to Goldman Sachs's chief market strategist, Abby Joseph Cohen, "you must be the King." [14]

"It played in Peoria," Acampora recalled a few years later. "I had a great time. I got invited to a lot of cocktail parties. My firm gave me a 1962 Roma red Corvette with plates that said DOW 7000. Here I was on a pedestal, driving this little car. I was part of a phenomenon—I think of the whole bull market as a phenomenon. It was exciting. It was real. It was America. But we all got carried away. Now, it's over." [15]

THE SENSE OF AN ENDING

Even Ralph Acampora, the bull market's self-described "raging bull," knew that the Great Bull Market of 1982–99 had to end sometime. In the late nineties, Acampora was still driving the red Corvette his firm gave him when the Dow hit 7000. Nevertheless, he understood what many refused to accept: bull markets cannot continue indefinitely. Acampora, after all, was old enough to remember the crash of 1973–74—and the eight years of drought that followed. As a technician, Acampora saw himself as a historian. Using charts to compare the market patterns of the present to the past, he tried to tell investors when it was time to get in—and when to bail out. Like Charles Dow, he looked at the market's cycles, but unlike economists who attempted to forecast long-term trends, Acampora tried to time both short-term and long-term cycles.

This was why in February of 1998, Acampora called his boss, Rick Simmons, Prudential's CEO, and told him that he wanted to meet him for breakfast. [16] They met only a few times a year, and it was unusual for Acampora to set the time and place. Not long after the meal began, Simmons cut to the chase:

"Why are we having breakfast?" he demanded.

"We have a problem," Acampora replied.

"What's the problem?" asked Simmons.

"I'm too popular."

"Why is that a problem?"

"Abby is the queen," said Acampora. "And I'm the king. The problem is, at some point, one of us is going to blink. You know this market can't last forever. And I'm enough of a competitive son of a bitch that I want to get out before Goldman.

"But if I turn negative," Acampora continued, "people will get very upset. Besides, I'll turn off clients—it will cost the firm revenues."

As Acampora recalled, Simmons told him to stop worrying. It was not Acampora's responsibility to guard the firm's coffers; it was his job to make sure that Prudential's clients bought low and sold high—which meant jumping off the merry-go-round before it stopped.

That Prudential's investment banking business was anemic greatly simplified Simmons's decision. Firms that did a brisk business taking companies public might be loath to announce that the bull market was over: such news would be bound to distress their clients. But Prudential was not a major investment banker: in 2000, the firm handled less than 1 percent of all underwritings. (By 2001 Prudential's new CEO, John Strangfeld, would decide to get out of the investment banking business altogether, "freeing [Prudential's] analysts to call 'em as they see 'em, without fear of alienating potential banking clients.")[17]

The conversation with Simmons was still in the back of Acampora's mind when he took his summer vacation in 1998, going on safari in Africa. When he returned, in late July, the Dow had dropped 500 points in a week, and investors were selling the big stocks—names like Procter & Gamble.

Acampora began to get nervous. *They're shooting the generals,* he thought. Monday, August 3, his first day back in the office, CNBC called and wanted him to appear on air. Acampora was reluctant—he was just beginning to digest what had happened while he was gone. But ultimately he agreed. On air he said, "The breadth is not so good. But if the Dow holds up, we'll be all right."

When he got back to his office, Acampora discovered that the Dow had slid another 90 points. That night he didn't sleep. As he later explained: "I knew that the next day I would have to go into the office and shoot my best friend—the bull."

The morning of August 4 Acampora headed for his office with his forecast written out, ready for broadcast. But when he arrived, the Dow futures looked good. *Maybe I won't have to do it,* he thought. Then, at 10 A.M., the rally died.

A seasoned market watcher, Acampora realized what this meant. He began setting up for the broadcast that he now knew he had to make. "I was two feet off the ground," he remembered, "so agitated that, at one point I nearly ran through the wall of my glass office-within-an-office. Everyone around me knew that something was about to happen."

Finally, at 11:30, Acampora stepped up to Prudential's global in-house PA system: "Ladies and gentlemen," he announced, "I have something very important to say." He knew he had his audience's attention: brokers in Prudential offices around the world were listening. Acampora swallowed, then plunged ahead. Flat out, he uttered the words that, in 1998, no one ever used except in the past tense. "Bear market." The Dow, he predicted, would drop 15 to 20 percent from its summer high.

Acampora half expected the news of his forecast to leak to the media, but it did not. He was glad. "It's only right to get the news out first to our big institutional clients—the money managers who pay for my research—before the rest of the world gets it for free," he thought to himself. The institutional clients were scheduled to phone in at one o'clock that afternoon. In the meantime, the Dow continued to slide. At one o'clock, Acampora repeated his forecast. This time the media picked up the news. Ralph Acampora was calling a bear market.

In fact, Acampora was predicting what economists call a "cyclical bear market," a short-lived affair that would last a matter of months, rather than a "secular bear market," which could last for years. The distinction was lost on the media. The Dow fell another 100 points. By day's end, the benchmark index had plunged 299 points, the third largest one-day decline in Wall Street history. The press blamed Acampora. "Tanks A Lot, Ralph," read the headline in *The New York Post*. Even *Barron's* ran his nickname: "Ralph Make 'em Poorer."

Prudential hired a bodyguard to protect him.[18]

That night, Acampora cautioned those who listened to CNN's *Street Sweep:* "Forget the averages. Look at your portfolio . . . everyone should be sitting down and really seriously going through their holdings, and if there are any stocks in there that look vulnerable—and obviously it's a matter of interpretation—I would sell them."[19] This was not what his audience wanted to hear. Many were outraged. Most still believed that if they just waited—six months, a year, perhaps two years—they would be made whole.

As it turned out, Acampora's intuition on that August night in 1998 was at least half right. It was time for investors to think about cutting their losses. On August 31, the Dow Jones Industrial Average plunged 502 points; in the weeks that followed it continued to slide. By October 8 the Dow had lost 1,900 points. Granted, the bull market had another 18 months to run—and by 1999, Acampora himself was once again a bull.

But in retrospect, it would become clear that the meltdown that began in the summer of 1998 marked a turning point. By the end of that year, the majority of stocks trading on the New York Stock Exchange (NYSE) had peaked, hitting a high that they would not see again for many years. From that point forward, just a handful of stocks would carry the bull market: the broad market lacked support.[20]

As for Acampora, he had learned his lesson. After that, he confided, "Instead of saying 'sell,' I use terms like 'rotation.' I no longer use words like 'bear.' I just say, 'It's too early to pick a bottom.' "[21]

SILENCING DISSENT

What Acampora had learned is that when a strong cycle is peaking, skeptics are shunned. This is part of the process John Kenneth Galbraith outlined in *A Short History of Financial Euphoria*—the book that Henry Blodget finally read in 2001. A bubble, Galbraith observed, is always supported by the belief that there is something new in the world. The history of past cycles is dismissed as irrelevant.

"For practical purposes," Galbraith wrote, "the financial memory should be assumed to last, at a maximum, no more than twenty years. This is normally the time it takes for the recollection of one disaster to be erased and for some variant on previous dementia to come forward to capture the financial mind. It is also the time generally required for a new generation to come on the scene, impressed, as had been its predecessors, with its own innovative genius."[22]

During the period of delirious forgetfulness, no one wishes to think that his good fortune is fortuitous or undeserved. Everyone prefers to believe that it is the result of his own superior insight into the market.

No wonder, then, that during such periods, doubters are silenced. Galbraith recalled the fate of Paul M. Warburg, one of the founding parents of the Federal Reserve System, who tried to warn investors in the winter of 1929 that the current orgy of speculation could lead to economic collapse. At the time, "The reaction to his statement was bitter, even vicious. . . . He was 'sandbagging American prosperity'; quite possibly, he was himself short in the market. There was more than a shadow of anti-Semitism in the response," Galbraith noted. "It was a lesson to all to keep quiet and give tacit support to those indulging their euphoric vision."[23]

The story never changes—just the cast of characters. So, in 1999, as the Great Bull Market reached its climax, even Morgan Stanley's chief domestic strategist, Byron Wein, was beginning to discover what it feels like to be out of step in a parade.

By 1999, Wein realized that a corporation's assets, its cash flow, and even its revenues had little relevance to the total value investors were willing to assign to it. On more than one occasion in recent years a younger colleague had come into Wein's office and told him: "You just don't get it, and you're never going to get it."[74] One scene stuck in Wein's mind: an analyst stood in his office recommending a stock that was selling at over 100 times earnings.

"How do you arrive at your valuation?" Wein asked. "Show me the parameters you're using." The young analyst just stared at the 64-year-old market strategist.

"When you're an older person, and you're cautious, while the market is still going up, you're perceived as out of touch," Wein later recalled. "You think a stock is worth $20; you say that, at $30, it's overbought; then it goes to $40. You can begin to doubt yourself."

But Wein had a corner office with skyscraper views of Manhattan. The young man standing in the middle of his carpet did not. More important, he did not have the thick skin that comes with trying to outguess the market while working your way up to such an office at Morgan Stanley. If Wein doubted himself, he did not show it. He waited for the answer. "The stock is worth what someone will pay for it," said the analyst, stating what seemed, to him, obvious.

The moment crystallized what Wein already suspected: *They're letting the tape tell them what a company is worth.* No wonder, when a stock took a dive, the analysts who followed it were just as surprised as everyone else.

WHAT THE MARKET'S CYCLES MEAN FOR THE 21ST-CENTURY INVESTOR

"Markets go down because they went up," James Grant reminded his readers in the late nineties. "Where the free enterprise system shines is in its treatment of failure," he added. "Individuals as individuals, are always error-prone . . . [they] also make collective mistakes. They overinvest, then underinvest. The underinvestment portion of the cycle is dealt with constructively, with new business formations, bull markets, and initial public offerings. The overinvestment problem is also dealt with constructively, but with the emphasis on demolition: with bankruptcies, bear markets, consolidations, and liquidations. . . . Without miscalculation there would be no price action, no capital gains, no losses and no commissions. Determining the ideal price, the market would sit on it, preening."

Cycles, then, drive markets: three steps forward, two back. Without the alternating rhythms of expansion and contraction, rising prices and falling prices, there would be no movement. In Grant's terms, "A boom is just capitalism's way of setting up the next bust." [25]

This is not to say that booms should be regretted. Often they mark a major technological advance, the discovery of new resources or new lands. But since the limit of the new discovery is unknown, there is no clear way to measure its value. The prospect for profits is open-ended, and lacking a measuring stick, the human imagination tends to err in the direction of desire, envisioning boundless profits. Promoters further encourage imaginative excess, and so, in the natural course of things, a boom can easily turn into a bubble.

Meanwhile, the new technology does change the world, transforming entire industries and raising standards of living nationwide, sometimes even globally. But that does not mean that the investors who bought the pioneers at their peak make money. Great technologies do not necessarily make good stocks.

The great virtue of laissez-faire capitalism, say its staunchest admirers, is that it allows a boom to run its course, and then lets the bubble collapse. With the hissing sound comes a correction: investment mistakes are repriced, and unprofitable companies go bankrupt. "The errors of the up cycle must be sorted out, reorganized or auctioned off," Grant observed. "Cyclical white elephants must be rounded up and led away." [26] Only then can a capitalist economy resume its progress. The correction clears the way for another cycle.

This is "part of the genius of capitalism," declared Treasury Secretary Paul O'Neill following the collapse of Enron in January of 2002. "Companies come and go . . . people get to make good decisions or bad decisions, and they get to pay the consequence or to enjoy the fruits of their decisions." [27]

O'Neill's statement must have seemed unfeeling to the many Enron employees whose life savings were wiped out when that particular white elephant was led away. Unwittingly, and some might say witlessly, O'Neill glossed over the human consequences of boom and bust cycles: the losses are never borne equally. Those who get in early during an upturn—and have the luck or presence of mind to get out before someone shouts "fire"— reap huge rewards. But those who come late to the party, often through no fault of their own, are hammered. Markets do not punish the greedy; nor do they necessarily reward the virtuous and frugal saver. Markets are amoral. "Good decisions" and "bad decisions" play a role in the outcome, but much depends on the wanton accidents of timing—when you get in and when you get out.

Ideally, an investor cashes in his chips when a market peaks. If he holds on, his losses compound. Meanwhile, he loses the opportunity to make money elsewhere, and there is always someplace in the world to make money.

But in any market cycle, those who find themselves losing the game of musical chairs are bound to resist the inevitable. Even drowning victims do not go straight down. If investors who lived through a bear market are slow to recognize an upturn, those who have become accustomed to a bull market fight a downturn tooth and nail. Denial, anger, desperation . . . these are just some of the stages that investors pass through before accepting defeat.

So, even after it became clear to the vast majority of investors that the Great Bull Market of 1982–99 had ended, mutual fund investors stood firm. The mass redemptions from equity funds that many had predicted never took place. As late as March 2003, Gail Dudack observed: "Net redemptions since the beginning of 2002 have been tiny compared with total stock fund assets. The net cash outflow in the 12 months ending March 30, 2003, amounted to 3.6 percent of the sector's assets. Usually, before a new cycle begins, outflows are much greater—as high as 8 percent a year. You need cash to fuel a new cycle," Dudack explained. "Until you get the sell-off that creates liquidity, a new cycle can't begin." [28] (See chart "Mutual Fund Investors Hang On," Appendix, page 462.)

"People have talked about how steadfast the individual investor has been. But I think it's been more paralysis than steadfastness," added Don Phillips, managing director of Morningstar Inc., the Chicago firm that tracks mutual funds.[29] Investors offered various reasons for holding on: "Everything I own has gone down too much—I can't sell now," confided one 401(k) investor. "The market is coming back—this is a buying opportunity," said another.

Ironically, these are the very responses that fuel bear market rallies, making it dangerously difficult to tell when a market has finally scraped bottom. If investors simply bowed their heads and accepted defeat, bear markets would last no more than a few months. Everyone would sell, and that would be that. But human nature, once again, intervenes. Men resist disaster. This is why even the "Great Crash" of 1929 did not happen in a day, a month, or a year.

True, in the fall of 1929, the Dow plunged from a September peak of 381 to a low, on November 13, of 199. But the following spring the market seemed to recover. By April of 1930, the Dow had climbed to 294—up 48 percent.

The bear was playing possum.

The low of November 1929 was a false bottom, the rally of 1930 a sucker rally. In 1930 the bear trap sprang shut. From April of 1930 through July of 1932, the market lost 86 percent of its value. What is commonly called the "Crash of '29" was in fact the crash of 1930–32: that is when the wealth of Gatsby's gilded world was destroyed. It seems that a new market cannot begin until the last bull's heart has been broken, and typically, it takes more than one crash to do the job.

The pattern was repeated at the end of the sixties, when the Dow fell to 631 in May of 1970, rallied to over 1050 in January of 1973, and then took a final, fatal nosedive that ended with the crash of 1973–74. Only then did investors learn not to buy on dips.

It would be another eight years before a new bull market began.

What precisely does this mean for the years ahead? No one knows. But since both human nature and the laws of supply and demand remain more or less constant, there is good reason to expect that past cycles might forecast, at least in broad brush strokes, the shape of the future.

What is certain is that an understanding of the market's cycles is an investor's only defense against becoming a victim of those cycles.

THE PEOPLE'S MARKET

*Each age has its peculiar folly, some scheme, project or phantasy
into which it is plunged, spurred on either by the love of gain, the
necessity of excitement, or the mere force of imitation. . . . Money
has often been a cause of the delusion of multitudes. Sober nations
have all at once become desperate gamblers and risked almost their
existence upon the turn of a piece of paper. . . . Men, it has been
well said, think in herds; it will be seen that they go mad in herds,
while they only recover their senses slowly and one by one.*

—Charles MacKay, *Extraordinary Popular Delusions
& the Madness of Crowds*, 1852

Spring 1998. In a neighborhood restaurant, a waitress confides that she
likes working nights so that she can watch her favorite characters on day-
time TV—Maria Bartiromo and Joe Kernen, the charismatic stars of
CNBC's *Squawk Box*. Though, she confesses, she surfs back and forth between CNBC and Bloomberg Television "because Bloomberg covers the
Nasdaq, and most of my stocks trade there."

"Wouldn't it be fun to set up a pool on when it will cross 9000?" she
adds, turning to the regulars at the bar behind her.

"I thought it crossed today," a man replies, "did it go back?"

No one says, "9000 what?"

As the bull market rolled forward, the financial mania of the nineties
came to define the decade. More and more, the stock market had begun to
take on the aura of a national lottery: as the pot grew, everyone talked about

it. Never before had luck and timing played such a pivotal role in the fortunes of so many Americans. There was a feeling in the air that anyone might get lucky. By the end of the decade, ABC's *Who Wants to Be a Millionaire?* had become the signature show of the era. Coast to coast, Americans answered, "I do, I do."

A history of the Great Bull Market of 1982–99 is more than a financial story. Ultimately, that breakneck ride would mark an epoch in U.S. cultural history. While share prices spiraled, investing replaced baseball as the national pastime. CNBC's stars began to edge the soaps off the screen. The New Economy spawned a New Society, and, as the baby boomers aged, even the symbols of success changed: SUVs trumped BMWs. Trophy mansions replaced trophy wives.

The people's market was telecast as a democracy—though in truth, just over half of all American families owned stocks, either directly or indirectly, through a mutual fund, a 401(k), or some other retirement plan. Still, the share of households with a stake in the market grew from just 19 percent in 1983 to over 49 percent in 1999.[1] And those lucky enough to have the price of admission watched their wealth soar. By '98, the 25 to 30 percent of American families with household incomes north of $75,000 found that since '89, their net worth had increased by some 20 percent. The wealthiest 5 percent watched their retirement funds grow by a dazzling 176 percent.[2] Baby boomers dreamed of retiring at 50 while Gen Xers invented their very own version of the American dream: wealth without working at all.

Financial euphoria cut a wide swath across generations. At one end "the Beardstown Ladies"—a group of Midwestern matrons that included a retired bank teller, a hog farmer, and an elementary school principal— became cult figures after they pooled their pin money, formed an investment club, and wrote a best-seller claiming that over the 10 years ending in 1993, they had reaped returns averaging 23.4 percent a year. At the other end, Ameritrade's punked-out hero, "Stewart," starred in the online broker's television ads, playing a pierced and tattooed Gen X office boy who showed his pudgy middle-aged boss just how easy it is to trade on the Net: "You're ridin' the wave of the future, my man!"

Somewhere in between the retirees and the Gen X investors, graying baby boomers discovered that they had just enough short-term memory left to learn how to use the Internet. With the bits and bytes of information streaming across their computer screens, anything seemed possible. Online, they tapped into a world of virtual knowledge: Wall Street's buoyant estimates of what a business might earn, the company's press release offering its own "pro-forma" version of what it had earned, an analyst's surmise as to what the quarter's profits might augur for the future. . . . It was all there, online, on television, all the time—a beguiling stream of data.

The New Economy ushered in what seemed, to many, a New Democracy. When individual investors found that they could make more in a day online than in a month on the job, they felt the flush of power usually reserved for the very rich. Sometimes the thrill of casino capitalism lent much-needed color to otherwise drab lives: At a social gathering on Manhattan's West Side, circa 1998, a middle-aged woman described her victories trading online. Though, she complained, she dreaded the weekends: "The market isn't open—CNBC isn't even on."[3]

On a larger canvas, the bull market represented a New Era not just of technology, but of hope—and not only in the United States but worldwide. With the fall of the Berlin Wall, U.S. politicians declared the Cold War at an end, and as the nineties unfolded, capitalism seemed to be sweeping the globe. From Bombay to Beijing, a new middle class was assembling. In India, young women wearing saris carried briefcases to work, while in China's coastal cities, newly house-proud couples began renovating apartments that were, at last, their own.

At home, the chief economic problem that had divided Democrats and Republicans for decades seemed resolved. Traditionally, Democrats had worried about high unemployment while Republicans fought rising prices—and virtually everyone agreed that you could not have both high employment and low inflation at the very same time. The nineties proved everyone wrong. When 1995 began, unemployment stood at 5.5 percent, while the consumer price index showed that inflation had fallen to 2.7 percent—"the lowest combined rate of unemployment and inflation in twenty-five years," President Clinton announced in his 1995 State of the Union address.

There had been early warning signs that the Age of Information might come to a bad end. In 1994, the market's promoters trotted out the Beardstown Ladies Investment Club as living proof that virtually anyone willing to do a little research could achieve double-digit returns. Neither special training, nor talent, nor experience was required. But shortly after selling some 800,000 copies of their *Commonsense Investment Guide*, the ladies discovered, to their dismay, that they had made a mistake when calculating their gains. It turned out that rather than clocking returns that averaged more than 23 percent a year, as advertised, they had made only 9.1 percent annually in the 10 years from 1983 to 1993, substantially less than they would have made if, instead of picking stocks, they had invested in a mutual fund indexed to the S&P 500.[4]

The miscalculation—combined with the fact that they seemed not to have noticed the difference between gaining 9.1 percent and racking up returns of 23 percent—might have suggested that not everyman, or everywoman, is cut out to serve as his or her own portfolio manager.

That same year, California's affluent Orange County went under after County Treasurer Robert Citron bought a grab bag of securities that he did not quite understand. Orange County's bankruptcy hinted that listening to the financial experts was not quite a sure bet either, especially when the savants are selling something, which they usually are. Citron, who went to jail, testified that he had relied on his Merrill Lynch broker for financial advice. Merrill did not admit to any wrongdoing, but ultimately the firm would agree to pay over $400 million to settle the case. (Throughout the late nineties, Michael Stamenson, the broker in question, remained on Merrill's payroll at $750,000 a year, spending his time not as a broker but as a prime witness in the ongoing litigation.)[5]

Taken together, the two tales might have sounded a cautionary note. But the average individual investor was innocent, uninitiated, and unscarred. Meanwhile, in 1994, the final leg of the most magnificent bull market the world had ever seen was about to begin. Skepticism seemed out of place. As indeed it was. Over the next four years the bull scaled one barrier after another: Dow 4000 (February 1995), Dow 6000 (October 1996), Dow 8000 (July 1997), Dow 10,000 (March 1999).

Because the most magnificent bull market in U.S. history was a democratic market, stratospheric stock prices seemed to reflect the will of the majority, what James Glassman and Kevin Hassett called "the collective judgment . . . [of] millions of people around the world" in their 1999 bestseller, *Dow 36,000*. Former Citicorp chairman Walter Wriston went so far as to declare markets "global plebiscites . . . voting machines [that] function by taking referenda." *New York Times* columnist Thomas Friedman summed up the spirit of the times as he celebrated the democratization of the financial world: "One dollar, one vote." The market, Friedman declared, had "turned the whole world into a parliamentary system . . . [whose citizens] vote every hour, of every day, through their mutual funds, their pension funds, their brokers, and more and more, from their own basements via the Internet."[6]

The metaphor fueled faith in "the wisdom of the market." Who could question prices set by millions of voters? According to the received wisdom, then, in 1999 AOL was worth 305 times its previous year's earnings, while IBM was fairly valued at 28 times earnings, because more people had voted for AOL.

If investors actually picked stocks while seated in sealed voting booths, one might be able to correct for another's mistakes. But people who buy stocks are social creatures, and be they pros or fledgling 401(k) investors, they are influenced, en masse, by the spirit of the times. As Bill Seidman, CNBC's chief economic commentator and a longtime market watcher, once observed when asked where the American consumer was headed: "You never know what the American public is going to do, but you do know that they will do it all at once."[7]

As the bull market picked up steam, the media fanned the Zeitgeist. The Internet set the pace, CNBC's breathless reports laid down the rhythm, and, to compete, print journalists learned to write in "real-time" prose, leaving little time to dig deeply, or mull over a story. Getting the news first became the priority. On deadline, many reporters simply repeated analysts' estimates, ignoring the fact that valuations had less and less to do with the intrinsic value of a company in the real world (what another businessman on Main Street might pay for it) and everything to do with its perceived value on Wall Street (what another investor might be willing to shell out for the stock).

Old-fashioned value investors such as Berkshire Hathaway chairman Warren Buffett still tried to assess a company's prospects based on its "fundamental" value, measuring and comparing sales, profits, assets, and debt. At the end of the 20th century, however, the popular wisdom said that value was relative. Veterans such as Morgan Stanley's Byron Wein seemed out of touch. On many levels of society, the whole concept of fundamental or "intrinsic" value seemed overly earnest—and by the late nineties, "earnest" itself had become a pejorative term.

But if both Wall Street and CNBC appraised a stock based on what someone might wager the next morning, the mutual fund industry sold shares by appealing to some 70 years of stock market history. "Over the long haul," Wall Street's pitchmen assured investors, "U.S. stocks always outperform other investments, returning, on average, 11 percent a year over ten years." .

Here was the fundamental, largely unacknowledged contradiction that haunted the People's Market: *Stocks were valued for the short term, yet investors were told that they should buy and hold for the long term.*

"BUY AND HOLD"

Newsweek's Jane Bryant Quinn was one of a handful of observers who paused to examine the idea of "the long term," pointing out that the much-touted 11 percent average did not predict what would happen during a specific 10-year period. Rather, it reflected the average annual return if you averaged together all of the 10-year periods from 1926 to 1998.

Since few investors buy and hold for 72 years, the truism had little practical meaning. During any particular 10-year period from 1926 to 1998, it turns out that an investor's chance of averaging more than 10 percent a year was only about 50/50. Contrary to the popular wisdom, he stood a 4 percent chance of making nothing over 10 years—and losing some of his principal to boot. Everything depended on when he got in. And when he got out.

Holding for 20 years, the odds that he would earn the promised 11 percent improved, but still stood at only two in three—far from a guarantee. Even if he did not need to tap his savings for 40 years, his chances of earning over 10 percent rose to just four in five. In 2002, Quinn updated her numbers to include two years of a bear market. Now her results showed that over 20-year periods, chances were one in five that stocks would rise by no more than 7 percent annually. Even over 40 years, chances were almost one in five that an investor would earn no more than 8 percent. In other words, if history is any guide, even the very long term investor should not count on 10 or 11 percent.[8]

Yet the mutual fund industry was inclined to embrace the "buy and hold" philosophy without complication in part because many in the industry believed it, in part because the strategy dovetailed so nicely with its own business plan. By the early nineties, "asset accumulation" was fast becoming the industry's rallying cry. From Boston to San Francisco, marketing a fund became just as important as managing the money.

"Suddenly, at many institutions, you started hearing about 'asset gathering'—bringing new money into the company. Hell, I thought we were in the business of making money for our existing clients," said Clyde McGregor, manager of The Oakmark Equity & Income Fund.[9] But Oakmark, an independent, old-fashioned firm that emphasized value investing, was out of step. The mutual fund business was exploding, and most fees were based on a percentage of the assets a company had under management, or the number of funds that it distributed, not how well it did in protecting those assets. Once a company had an investor's money, it quite naturally wanted to keep it. Besides, if customers withdrew their money every time a fund floundered, it would become all the more difficult to give new funds and new fund managers enough time to prove their mettle. "Buy and hold" made sense for everyone. Or so it seemed.

Thanks in large part to the 401(k)—a retirement plan that allowed workers to control their own investments—the mutual fund industry's efforts at asset gathering succeeded beyond even its own most immodest dreams. In the early nineties, 12-month flows into funds that invested in stocks barely reached $50 billion; by 2001 inflows exceeded $300 billion.[10]

A tidal wave of retirement dollars flooded the mutual fund industry. The 401(k) was invented in 1981, just as the bull market began. By 1998, roughly three of every four new dollars invested in corporate retirement plans were going into 401(k)s. At the end of the decade, two-thirds of all active workers covered by a retirement plan were responsible for directing their own investments. Hands down, they chose stocks. By the end of the millennium, 401(k) investors had stashed 75 percent of their assets in equities.[11] Even older employees preferred stocks: in 2000, 401(k) investors in their 50s had entrusted 49 percent of their savings to equity funds, another 19 percent to company stock.[12]

Struggling to keep pace with a roaring market, fund managers chased Wall Street's darlings. By the end of '98, more than one-third of all diversified U.S. stock funds owned Dell, the best-performing stock of the preceding 10 years. Even so-called value funds were buying the computer maker, despite the fact that by then, investors had bid its share price up to 58 times projected earnings. When America Online was added to the S&P 500 at the beginning of 1999, 20 percent of all U.S. equity funds owned AOL, then trading at 238 times expected earnings.[13]

To keep their jobs, fund managers knew they needed to try to meet, if not beat, the S&P 500. The only way they could hope to keep up with the index's double-digit jumps was by riding the market's leaders. By definition, of course, this meant pouring investors' retirement savings into the market's most expensive shares—often just as they were peaking.

While mutual fund managers chased the hottest shares, individual investors pursued the hottest funds. "The American public was writing endless checks to these funds—and the funds then had to invest the money," recalled George Kelly, an analyst at Morgan Stanley.[14] No matter how high the market climbed, most mutual fund managers were expected to stay fully invested. The only way to dispose of the bags of money piling up at their doors was to pour it into the biggest, most liquid, and most popular names. The buying pressure would push share prices to the moon.

THE UNSUSPECTING

As always, the croupiers fared better than the guests they invited to their tables. David Tice, a fund manager who had founded an independent research firm in 1989, summed up what he had seen when testifying before Congress in the spring of 2001: "The unsuspecting," said Tice, were gulled by "those most skilled at this game of speculation." This, he noted, "was why individual investors wound up owning 75 percent of all Internet stocks—compared to only 44 percent of General Motors."[15] For novices not only bought Internet stocks, they held on to them. More experienced traders were the "price makers"; amateur investors became the "price takers."

At the end of the nineties, "the unsuspecting" became the target market for many initial public offerings (IPOs). Once an IPO like Ariba was in orbit, the investment bankers and other large institutional investors who launched it would begin to lighten their positions, often on the first day of trading, leaving small investors holding the bag.

Within the companies, even novices learned how the game was played. When a 30-year-old attorney left her job at a prestigious law firm to become chief financial officer for an Internet start-up, her mother asked her, "How can you take such a risk? What if the company goes under?"

"Oh," her daughter replied coolly, "I'll be out by then."[16]

Meanwhile, pointless IPOs sucked capital out of the American economy. It was not just day traders, fund managers bucking for stardom, and other amateur plungers who were duped by profitless companies. Billions of dollars that could have been invested in "viable projects" were instead squandered on "massive overinvestment throughout the technology sector," Tice testified. "Do you wonder why our country does not have enough power plants and oil refineries, yet we have a reported 80 to 90 percent overcapacity in fiber optic cable?" he asked the congressmen. "This is a consequence of keeping stock prices artificially high for extended periods while extending credit recklessly in the midst of a mania. . . . As a nation, we are about to pay for this crucial misallocation of capital." [17] Reasonable men might well disagree on where the money should have gone—investment in alternative sources of energy comes to mind. But in hindsight, it was clear to nearly everyone that an enormous misallocation of capital had undermined the economy.

Money flowed, not to where it was most needed, not into the projects with the strongest business plans, but into those with the sexiest "story"—those companies whose backers felt confident that they could take it public, at a premium, in a matter of months.

At Morgan Stanley, Byron Wein saw the waste of capital. "A company would come to us with this new, new thing, and say, 'You've got to take it public.' The new thing might be a little better than the technology that everyone was already using," Wein allowed, "but not that much better. Still, they would say, 'If you don't underwrite it, we'll take it down the street to Goldman.' And we would say, 'Where do we sign?' " [18]

This is not to say that the New Technology was not revolutionary. The Internet, cell phones, and affordable computers would lay the foundation for a New Era in global communication and education that could raise living standards worldwide. But what the New Economy's promoters failed to mention was that major advances in technology usually benefit the consumer—not the investor.

Consider, for example, the auto industry. "If you had foreseen in the early days of cars how this industry would develop, you would have said, 'Here is the road to riches,' " Warren Buffett observed in 1999. "So what did we progress to by the 1990s? After corporate carnage that never let up, we came down to three U.S. car companies—themselves no lollapaloozas for investors. So here is an industry that had an enormous impact on America—and also an enormous impact, though not the anticipated one, on investors. . . . The other truly transforming business invention of the first quarter of the century, besides the car, was the airplane—another industry whose plainly brilliant future would have caused investors to salivate. So I went back to check out aircraft manufacturers and found that in the

1919–39 period, there were about 300 companies, only a handful still breathing today. . . . Move on to failures of airlines. Here's a list of 129 airlines that in the past 20 years filed for bankruptcy. . . . The money that had been made since the dawn of aviation by all of this country's airline companies was zero. Absolutely zero.

"Sizing all this up," Buffett concluded, "I like to think that if I'd been at Kitty Hawk in 1903 when Orville Wright took off, I would have been farsighted enough, and public-spirited enough—I owed this to future capitalists—to shoot him down. I mean, Karl Marx couldn't have done as much damage to capitalists as Orville did." [19]

To its credit, the mainstream press cast a cold eye on many of the more outrageous dot.com stocks: "How Long Will They Fly? A Glut of Net IPO's May Cause Air Sickness for Investors," *U.S. News & World Report* warned in the spring of 1999.[20]

But a profitless IPO was a much easier target than a Tyco, a Cisco, or a WorldCom. These, after all, were companies with real earnings—even if, as investors later discovered, those profits had been inflated by executives who buried expenses, fabricated sales, and made ill-advised acquisitions, all in the name of "enhancing shareholder value."

THE BROAD MARKET

In 2000, many referred to the market's meltdown as the "tech-wreck." The conventional wisdom of the time had it that the excesses of the nineties had been confined to high-tech stocks.

But the mania for Internet stocks turned out to be only the froth on the cappuccino. The larger story was the broad market's giddy climb. From 1995 to the end of 1998 the S&P 500 galloped forward, racking up double-digit returns four years running. Ultimately, the major indices rode on the backs of a few big-cap stocks. Not all were technology stocks—and few were dot.coms. On the Dow, in 1998, the top six belonged to the "Old Economy": Wal-Mart (up 106 percent); IBM (up 75 percent), McDonald's (up 61 percent), UT (up 49 percent), Merck (up 37 percent), and GE (up 38 percent).

On the S&P 500 that year, large-cap technology companies like Dell, Apple, and Lucent were among the big winners.[21] But Providian Financial (up 144 percent) also placed among the top 10, while The Gap, which climbed 142 percent, ranked number 11. By the end of 2000, some of the most wrenching losses would come on established companies like AT&T, Dell, and Motorola, all of which closed the year down more than 65 percent from their 2000 highs.

The Old Economy's stars fell hard. Investors who owned The Gap at the end of 1998 found that by the beginning of 2003 they had lost close to 60 percent of their savings, while those unlucky enough to own Providian Financial were down by more than 80 percent. As for the six companies that led the Dow in 1998, over the next four years only Wal-Mart and UT rewarded investors.[22] Those who had invested in the other four lost money. "Buy and hold," the mantra of the nineties, was beginning to disappoint.

As the market heated up, experienced investors knew, with a sinking certainty, that the big caps were rising too high, too fast. In the three years ending in December 1998, Dell alone shot up 3,197 percent. With the benefit of hindsight, market watchers would point out that the broad market peaked in '98 and that the first phase of the bear market began in August or September of 1999. By the fall of '99, insiders were bailing out en masse.[23] Once again, Richard Russell, editor of *Richard Russell's Dow Theory Letter,* sounded a warning. "Holding for the long term works beautifully in a bull market. In a major bear market, it can be an absolutely disastrous policy," Russell told his subscribers in October of 1999.[24]

THE INDIVIDUAL INVESTOR

While insiders bailed out, most small investors did not sell. They did what they were told, "buy and hold," doubling their bets all the way up. The higher the most aggressive growth funds rose, the greater their allure. In 1999 investors wagered twice as much on these funds as they had in '96 and '97 put together. Even after the Nasdaq began its long slide, investors continued to chase the last best thing: at the end of 2000, individuals were investing in aggressive growth funds at more than twice the rate that they had in 1999.[25]

As always when a bull market ends, those who could afford it least lost the most. In Massachusetts, Sharon Cassidy, a divorced college professor who had single-handedly put her four children through college, began to step up saving for her own retirement in 1990. By then she was 52, and earning roughly $42,000 a year. Listening to the financial advisors who visited her college, she stashed most of her money in broad-based equity funds, and, by the end of 1998, she had managed to accumulate over $350,000. At that point, she felt she was in sight of her goal: retirement in four years, at age 62, with $500,000.

When the market skidded, she held on. "I felt I had no other choice," said Cassidy. Then the bear showed his claws. By the end of 2001, at age 63, she was forced to rethink her life plan. "If I work until I'm 70, I can retire with $400,000," she said. "I'm lucky—I like my work, and $400,000 is a lot more than most people have. But I'm angry, angry at myself and angry at the people who advised me." [26]

As the bear began to loot 401(k)s, even investors who bought "brand name" growth stocks took heartbreaking losses. In August of 2000, James Garfinkel, a 39-year-old investor in Great Neck, New York, was pounding his desk as he talked to *The Wall Street Journal:* "It's just devastating—I'm not a day trader. I did not load up on dot.coms. I picked good, solid blue-chip tech stocks—AT&T Corp., Lucent Technologies Inc., Sun Microsystems Inc., WorldCom Inc. Now, I don't know what to trust." [27]

In Florida, Ed Wasserman took the bait only at the very end of the decade. In the spring of 2000, the 50-year-old business writer finally broke down and invested in a hi-tech fund. "By disposition, I'm a value investor," said Wasserman. "I had a lot of skepticism—but finally, I succumbed. In the spring of 2000, I went into my local brokerage firm and said to these guys: " 'Why did I only make 12 percent last year, when other people are making 40 percent.' And they said, 'We have this very aggressive fund . . .'

"Meanwhile," said Wasserman, "there's a generational squabble between me and my 24-year-old son, who is totally scornful of my reluctance to buy companies that have no profits—no revenues—barely a business plan. I don't think they're sound investments. Yet I'm watching his profits rise while I'm in a ditch with my wheels spinning. I owned a lot of stocks like Time Warner that had been in the mud for years.

"This aggressive fund that my broker is offering puts me into companies like Quest, Oracle, Cisco—these aren't little companies with no revenues—they're blue chips. So I buy in. It was March of 2000."

That month, the Nasdaq began to crater. "I lost two-thirds of the money," said Wasserman. "The market went into free fall. And these guys who I had invested with were paralyzed. I was paying them to manage my money—and they weren't managing. Finally I putted out of that fund on my own." (And what happened to his son? "He got massacred," Wasserman said cheerfully.)

At the end of 2001, Wall Street bonuses were slashed by some 30 percent, but Wasserman noted, "The price of first-tier Bordeaux wines, being casked in 2001, has been bid way up, mainly by Americans. Meanwhile Detroit is preparing a new generation of overweight, $40,000-and-up sports utility vehicles, which, in spite of everything—are selling for 9 percent more than last year.

"And who is buying these top-shelf goodies if not the investment bankers and fund managers?" he asked. "Some of the same people who collected fees for putting my nest eggs in the wrong basket and looking on as they cracked and dribbled onto the ground." [28]

By 2000, many investors began to realize just how long it would take to make up for their losses. Then the recriminations began.

Wall Street's analysts served as the handiest targets. Often, their firms' profits depended on investment banking fees from the very same companies that they covered. No wonder "sell" recommendations were rare. Reporters were quick to point a finger. "Where was the analysis?" they asked. Yet the same question might just as well have been asked of the press. On deadline, few financial journalists did their own research; many took analysts' reports at face value.

Arguably, Wall Street's analysts were served up as scapegoats. Without question, their reports were outrageously optimistic, and their firms' desire to maintain a cordial relationship with investment banking clients drove many a "buy" recommendation. Nevertheless, the analysts were hired by someone higher up on their firms' totem poles, and their superiors made the decision to tie their bonuses to how much investment banking business they brought in. While Merrill Lynch's Henry Blodget and Salomon Brothers' Jack Grubman were pilloried, their bosses were rarely blamed. Nor did the media dwell on how it had showcased the analysts' advice. If the media had not turned Wall Street's seers into stars, their reports never would have carried so much weight.

THE PEOPLE'S CHOICE

Yet whatever sins of omission either Wall Street's executives or the media might have committed, neither made the final decision to buy AOL at 400 times earnings. After an initial round of scapegoating, many observers began to suggest that investors themselves should take responsibility for their investment decisions. It was the same argument that the cigarette industry used, and the analogy was not too far off. Buying stocks and equity funds had become an addiction, but no one had put a gun to the individual investor's head.

Here was the dark side of a democratized market: If the market represented millions of individual choices, then the blame must be laid where it belonged—at the feet of millions of individual investors. Richard Whitney, the fair-haired, aristocratic head of the New York Stock Exchange, gave the same answer in 1932 when Congress questioned him about the cause of the Great Depression: "Ask the one hundred and twenty-three million people in the United States," he replied, with some disdain. Whitney was later sent to jail, a convicted embezzler.[29]

Mark Haines, the outspoken co-anchor of CNBC's *Squawk Box,* was equally quick to turn his own defense into a good offense. "An awful lot of people find it difficult to confront the reality that they screwed up," Haines said in a PBS interview on *Media Matters* in 2001. "Now, they're looking for scapegoats, and the media is an easy scapegoat. But I've got bad news— it was your fault if you lost a lot of money." Investors who didn't understand that the "experts" who appeared on CNBC would be biased were simply "too naïve" to be in the game, Haines declared. "It never *occurred* to us," he added, with a smile verging on a sneer, "that anyone was sitting home, watching this, thinking it was totally unbiased advice."[30]

Even Arthur Levitt, the chairman of the Securities and Exchange Commission, suggested that those who chased high-flying stocks deserved to suffer the consequences. In January of 2000, Levitt appeared on *Wall $treet Week with Louis Rukeyser* along with Prudential's Ralph Acampora. Before the show began, the guests gathered for dinner and, by Acampora's account, he asked Levitt, "Are you concerned about the Internet?"

Levitt responded by talking about fraud on the Net—stock scams and bad tips.

But that was not what Acampora had in mind. He was concerned about the feverish demand for Internet stocks.

"The Nasdaq is heading for 5000 . . . Arthur, they've turned it into Las Vegas!" Acampora exclaimed. "The prices of these stocks . . . look at the Nasdaq, look at the investors—they're all gamblers!

"I'm going on and on," Acampora recalled, "and Arthur Levitt—who is a lovely man—walked over to where I was sitting and put his hand on my shoulder.

" 'Don't worry,' he said to me. 'The market will teach those people a lesson.' " [31]

The problem is that many of "those people" could not afford the lesson. Moreover, they were only doing what they had been told was prudent. Since the eighties, everyone, from Peter Lynch to Merrill Lynch, had been warning baby boomers that they were not saving enough. Social Security was running out, they were told. If the boomers did not want to wind up selling apples on the street, they needed to make double-digit returns. The only way to accomplish that goal, the market's promoters advised them, was by investing in stocks. In the nineties, the typical boomer looked in the mirror and realized that it was all true—or at least the part about growing old.

No wonder middle-class investors sank whatever savings they could scrape together into equities. Much of the money that small investors put into the market of the nineties was what financial consultant and author Peter Bernstein called "blood money." In the past, he observed, the dollars that investors wagered in the stock market was "money that they hoped to get rich on, or play with, or maybe finance a trip to Europe or something." But "with jobs less secure and with the wonderful corporate pension funds gone," small investors were gambling with money that they could not afford to lose—the "blood money" that they had saved for their child's college tuition, or the nest egg they had accumulated for their own retirement." [32]

If at a certain point the bull market became a con, it worked only because investors gave Wall Street their confidence. Still, it would be unfair to say that small investors were done in by greed alone. Many were motivated, not so much by avarice, as by anxiety.

The authorities had assured small investors that they were not gambling. The stock market is a piggy bank, the experts said—not a casino. Unfortunately, the metaphor was a mistake. The stock market is a place to make money, but in a runaway bull market, it is not a place to stash it for safekeeping. As a financier who was buying a house in the Hamptons told *The Wall Street Journal* in 1997, "I have a saying . . . 'Make money on Wall Street, bury it on Main Street.' Take it out of harm's way." [33] But this was not the advice that most investors heard from their mutual fund companies, their stockbrokers, their financial advisors, or the majority of the sages who turned up on CNBC.

To be fair, many of the market's most enthusiastic boosters sincerely believed their own advice. Like almost everyone else, the pros and the pundits were caught up in the myth that the New Economy rendered the old rules of investing obsolete. Journalists could not help but catch the fever: many became true believers. Even Fed Chairman Alan Greenspan cross-dressed as a cheerleader. True, in December of 1996, he spoke of "irrational exuberance," but a month later, when the Fed chairman spoke before the Senate budget committee, what was "irrational" had become "breathtaking." Before long, Greenspan began to proclaim the wonders of a "productivity revolution not seen since early this century" as he made the case for rational exuberance.[34]

In theory, the productivity revolution justified sky-high prices, not just for technology stocks but for the shares of companies using the new technology. By then "everyone knew" that America had entered a "New Era." Yet as Charles MacKay observed in his classic study, *Extraordinary Popular Delusions & the Madness of Crowds,* what "everyone knows to be true" often is made of whole cloth.

MacKay, who was a friend of Charles Dickens, knew that men and women are social creatures. They like to travel in herds. But when they think in unison, they do not always think clearly. In joining the crowd, each has his or her own motive. At the end of the 20th century, some of those who pursued the fin de siècle fantasy of unlimited wealth were spurred on by "love of gain," others by what MacKay called "the necessity of excitement," still others by "the mere force of imitation." Whatever the cause, the outcome was the same: multitudes became gamblers, willing to risk, not just their money, but their happiness, "on the turn of a piece of paper."[35]

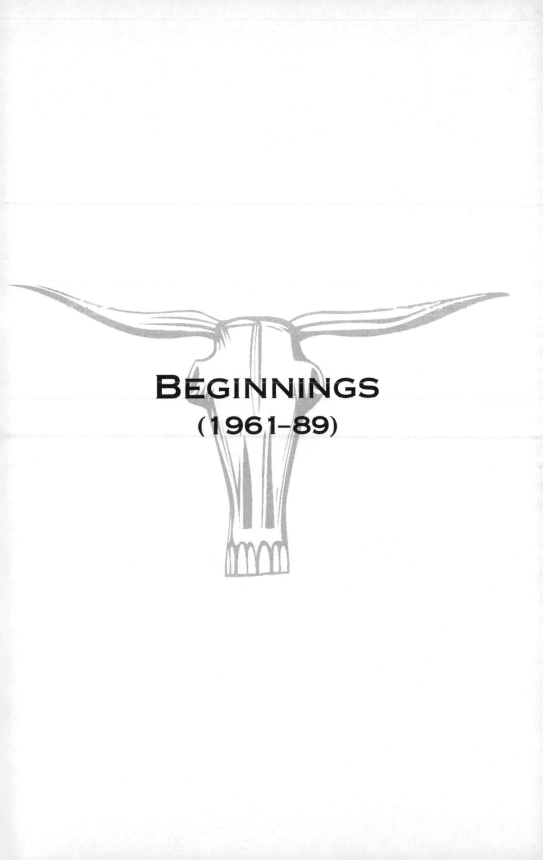

BEGINNINGS
(1961–89)

THE STAGE IS SET (1961–81)

WARREN BUFFETT—THE EARLY YEARS

The received wisdom has it that Berkshire Hathaway chairman Warren Buffett built his fortune by buying good companies and holding them long term. If it were that simple, there would have been many more beatified, balding billionaires residing on the Western Plains at the end of the 20th century. In truth, patience was only half of Buffett's secret. An ace market timer, Buffett knew when to hold and when to fold. Granted, he usually held stocks for long periods of time, but he also realized that the stock market was not always the safest place for an investor to stash his savings. Like Richard Russell or Charles Dow, the Sage of Omaha understood that equity markets, like all other markets, are cyclical, and there can be long stretches of time when a prudent investor should get out—and stay out. And in May of 1969, that is exactly what Warren Buffett did.

He had had a good run. Buffett launched his professional investment career in 1957, when the bull market that began after World War II was still young. It had taken the market nearly 20 years to recover from the Great Crash of '29, but an investor bold enough to take a position in 1948 would find that by 1968 he had more than quintupled his money.[1]

Buffett was lucky enough to set up shop in the fifties. In those early years he managed a pool of money for a group of clients, many of them friends and acquaintances, in his hometown of Omaha, Nebraska, forming what he called the Buffett Partnership. Over the next decade, the Partnership would return a stunning 1,156 percent, leaving the Dow (which gained "merely" 122.9 percent) in the dust.

As the sixties began, however, the bull market of 1954–68 was starting to look frothy. By 1961, IPOs were popping like champagne corks. Even greenhorns like Edwin Levy, who came to Wall Street as a young stockbroker in 1959, were riding high. As a rookie, Levy had little access to the hottest new issues; nevertheless, he was swimming in what seemed to him a sea of cash. At the time, an older broker gave Levy some advice: "You know something, kid," the veteran said, "you ought to buy something you really like, because when this is over, you're not going to have anything." Levy bought himself a Mercedes 190 SL, only slightly used, with an extra top, for $6,100.

"I took his advice," Levy, who went on to form a private money management firm, remembered years later, "and he was quite right." In May of 1962—on a day that would go down in Wall Street history as Blue Monday—the Dow dropped 34.9 points, its largest one-day drop since 1929. "When it was all over, I had $200 and the car," Levy recalled.[2]

In hindsight, the crash of 1962 would be seen as an early warning: investors were beginning to overreach. Nevertheless, at the time the damage was limited. Although the high rollers who had thrown their savings at new issues and hot penny stocks were wiped out, the mutual fund industry, which was just beginning to become a major force in the market, emerged relatively unscathed. The Dow rolled forward, and by the end of 1963 the index hit a new high. In 1964, the U.S. landed a spacecraft on the moon, and the Dow shot for the same heavenly body, crossing 900 for the first time.

The "go-go" market of the sixties had begun.

INVESTING À-GO-GO

On Wall Street, it was a young man's market, and Jim Awad was one of its stars. "I had hair down to here," Awad recalled in 2001, pointing to his shoulder, "rock music in the background—and no business managing money. But I did," added a silver-haired Awad, with something close to a shudder. In fact, he ran one of Wall Street's hottest growth funds.[3]

A graduate of the Harvard Business School, Awad arrived on Wall Street in the sixties, part of the youth revolution that swept downtown Manhattan. The "hotshot" fund managers of the go-go market should be distinguished from the better-known youth brigade that protested the Vietnam War. The protesters made only a guest appearance at the NYSE in 1967 when Abbie Hoffman and his Yippie friends stood in the visitor's gallery, throwing dollar bills onto the Stock Exchange floor. (The Exchange responded by installing bulletproof glass around the visitor's gallery, "thereby seeming to indicate that it considered thrown-away dollar bills to be lethal weapons," noted *New Yorker* writer John Brooks in his history of the era, *The Go-Go Years*.)[4]

Youthful money managers like Awad belonged to a slightly older, more buttoned-down generation. Most attended college in the early or mid-sixties—just before the campus rebellions began. And those few years made all the difference. This, after all, was the cohort that, in the early sixties, voted against coeducation at Yale. In the late sixties, many adopted the mod fashion of the times, growing sideburns and wearing flowered ties, but Wall Street's new stars were not bucking the establishment. They *were* the establishment.

The newcomers were filling a power vacuum. Following the crash of 1929, few young men wished to launch a career on scorched earth. As a result, when the old guard from the twenties retired, they had few middle-aged heirs. Into the breach sauntered the wunderkinds who would lead the bull market of the sixties. By the end of the decade half of Wall Street's salesmen and analysts had been in the market for less than seven years.[5] Like their counterparts in the nineties, they had never seen a bear.

With the youth revolution, a wave of shiny new IPOs came to market early in the decade. Brooks described the issues as "tiny scientific companies put together by little clutches of glittery-eyed young Ph.D.'s, their company names ending in '___onics.' " Thirty years later ".com" would replace "onics" and the IPOs would be launched by little clutches of no-less-bright-eyed business-school dropouts. But Brooks could just as easily have been describing the nineties when he wrote: "It was coming to be believed, in the absence of evidence to the contrary, that almost any man under forty could intuitively understand and foresee the growth of young, fast-moving unconventional companies better than almost anyone over forty."[6]

Financial euphoria achieved a summit in February of 1966 when the Dow reached out and touched 1000—hitting an interday high of 1001.11

to be exact—and staying there almost as long as you could hold your breath. As it turned out, this would be the bull market's high watermark. Nevertheless, the go-go market continued. Now it was a momentum market, driven by "hotshots" like Awad.

WARREN BUFFETT STEPS TO THE SIDELINES

Back in Nebraska, Warren Buffett did not join in the celebration of youth. By 1966, Buffett realized that a bull this brazen was just asking to be replaced by a bear. Stock prices were simply too rich. Worried that he would not be able to find a safe home for fresh money, Buffett closed his partnership to new accounts. Still, the Buffett Partnership flourished, thanks in large part to the bargains Buffett had found earlier in the decade. In 1967 his fund rose 36 percent—more than twice the Dow's advance—and in 1968 the Partnership returned 59 percent. Meanwhile, the market reeled from one rally to the next, "like a drunk intent on finishing the last bottle," said Roger Lowenstein, Buffett's biographer.[7]

"The game is being played by the gullible, the self-hypnotized, and the cynical," Buffet wrote in a letter to his investors in 1969.[8] And in May of that year, he stunned them by announcing that he was liquidating the Buffett Partnership. At the height of a bull market, with his own portfolio soaring, Warren Buffett was cashing in his chips.

Buffett spent the rest of the year selling stocks so that he could return his investors' money—plus the handsome profits their investments had accumulated over a period of years. He advised them that he was putting most of his own money into municipal bonds, while holding on to just two stocks: Diversified Retailing, a small holding company for a dress chain, and a textile company called Berkshire Hathaway. "On the one hand, he didn't think much of textiles; on the other hand, he liked the guy in charge," Lowenstein reported.

Buffett gave his investors a choice between keeping their Berkshire shares or taking cash—making it clear he planned to hold on to his own Berkshire shares. "That's all anybody had to hear if they had any brains," recalled a local doctor who was one of his most devoted partners.[9] Even while liquidating the partnership, Buffett managed a 7 percent gain for '69, then closed his books.

Warren Buffett was not the only professional investor who saw trouble ahead. At Merrill Lynch, Bob Farrell oversaw the firm's market strategists, and in 1969 he, too, turned bearish, causing some consternation at his firm. "Don Regan, who was our CEO back then, had the marketing people poll the brokers in our retail offices to see if my bearishness was hurting business," Farrell recalled more than 40 years later. "But it was okay—they left me alone." [10]

Farrell would continue calling the market as he saw it for the next 31 years. From 1976 to 1992, *Institutional Investor* named Farrell the Street's number one market timer every year save one, and on Wall Street, he became known as an independent, honest voice. Farrell did not claim special courage: "I joined Merrill in 1957, and I grew up with the guys who ran the firm," he explained in a 2001 interview. "They were brokers back when I was an analyst. From that, I had the implicit power to be independent. I was close to the people in charge, so the bureaucrats steered clear of me." It was not until March of 2000 that Farrell, who had been bearish on technology stocks for some time, felt constrained. That spring he got a call from a research director at Merrill: "Bob," he said, "we'd prefer you didn't talk about individual stocks—just stick to general themes." [11] Farrell, of course, had good reason to be skeptical in March of 2000—just as he did in 1969.

In 1969 the market was already set on a crash course that would end, four years later, in the sell-off of 1973–74—a disaster that would rival the Great Crash of 1929.

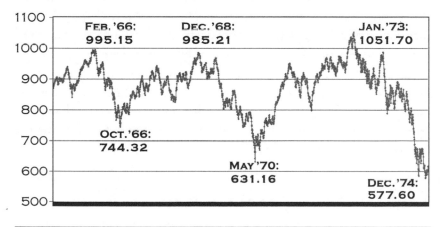

SOURCE: *RICHARD RUSSELL'S DOW THEORY LETTER*

But first, the bear toyed with investors, taking them on a toboggan ride that they would never forget. After grazing 1000 in February of 1966, the Dow slid headfirst, hitting 744 in October, then turned around and headed back uphill, flirting with 1000 a second time at the very end of 1968—before plummeting once again.

By the fall of 1969, investors who had bought the hottest stocks of the go-go market—companies like Litton Industries, Transitron and National General—were decimated. Nevertheless, many a conservative investor still sat on a nice stack of paper gains. The mood in New York remained complacent: "Tables were scarce at expensive restaurants," Brooks reported. "In some areas, a Mercedes was almost as common a sight on the road as a Pontiac; and all that summer and fall, packed airliners departing for or returning from Europe were so numerous at New York City's Kennedy International that they sometimes had to wait hours for clearance to take off or land." [12]

In 1970, the first major crash of the early seventies began: by May the Dow had fallen from roughly 800 to 630, and insouciance quickly gave way to fear. When it was all over, a portfolio made up of one share of every stock traded on the New York Stock Exchange was worth half of what it had been at the beginning of 1969. Small investors took a beating: a 1970 New York Stock Exchange survey showed that fully one-third of all individual investors had bought their first share sometime between 1965–when the Dow stood just under 1000—and mid-1970, when it had fallen to 650. "Exactly how much of the $300 billion overall paper loss in the 1969–1970 crash was suffered by those 11 million new investors is incalculable," Brooks observed. But "it is entirely possible that as of July 1970, [what was then called] 'the people's capitalism' had left at least 10 million Americans, or one-third of all investors, poorer than it had found them." [13]

Financial pundits saw the sell-off of 1970 as a bear market bottom. Loyal investors held on; recovery, they assumed, must be just around the corner. And late in 1970, it seemed that they were rewarded for their faith. Now, the Dow began climbing. It would not be a smooth ride, but over the next two years the index rallied.

THE NIFTY FIFTY

During this period, mutual fund managers looking for safe havens gravitated toward a select group of high-growth blue chips, companies like IBM,

Kodak, Polaroid, Avon, Merck, and Texas Instruments. Dubbed the "Nifty Fifty," these were the Microsofts, GEs, and Ciscos of their day.

Growth was king. "People clung to the belief that if you bought the premier growth companies, they would hold up well, even in a market decline," said Steve Leuthold, a Minnesota-based money manager who in 1969 had already begun to establish a national reputation for his market research. "These were the 'One Decision' stocks of the time. In theory, all you had to do was just buy them and hold them. Everyone knew that the rise of companies like Xerox, Avon, Polaroid, and Digital Equipment marked the beginning of a New Era." [14] Demand sent prices soaring, and when the Nifty Fifty hit its high in 1972, the "One Decision" stocks were trading at 80 times earnings.

Meanwhile, the Dow continued to rise, and in January of 1973, the benchmark index finally smashed through the 1000 barrier, setting a new high at 1071. A new bull market had begun—or so it seemed.

Now, the bear moved in for the kill. What followed was the crash of 1973–74, the most savage mauling investors had endured since 1930. There was no place to hide. The Nifty Fifty sank along with everything else: by 1974, the glamour growth stocks had shed 54 percent of their value. [15] The very stocks that were supposed to sustain investors for the long run betrayed them.

Finally, investors had had enough. In 1970, they had said that it was too late to sell—they would wait for the market to recover. In the rout of 1974, shell-shocked investors raffled off shares for whatever they could fetch.

Jim Awad was one of those trampled in the rush for the exits. Just two years earlier, in 1972, the long-haired 26-year-old Harvard Business School graduate was a celebrity: his small-cap fund was ranked number three in its category by Lipper, a firm that rated mutual funds. "There was a big *New York Times* article—with a picture of me," Awad recalled. There he was, making money to the tune of the Rolling Stones' "Satisfaction." Could life get any better?

One of Awad's favorite stocks was Polaroid. He bet not only his fund's money but his own nest egg on Polaroid, investing $100,000—a fair-sized fortune in 1972. "I ran the $100,000 down to $20,000," said Awad, paling at the memory, more than 35 years later. He could still recall the feeling: "complete humiliation." Investors who bought Polaroid in 1972 still would be waiting to get their money back—without interest—in 1999.

"That was when I grew up as an investor," said Awad. "That's when I learned that managing money isn't just about picking stocks and holding them. It takes a lot of blocking and tackling—disciplined, consistent effort." [16]

Polaroid was not the only disaster. As a group, Minneapolis money manager Steve Leuthold calculated, a portfolio made up of the 25 most popular stocks gained a paltry 2 percent over the next decade—and then, only if the portfolio included Merck, which climbed an extraordinary 382 percent. (Without Merck, a portfolio would have shrunk by 12 percent.) [17]

Leuthold's research contradicted Jeremy Siegel's *Stocks for the Long Run*, a book that many saw as the bible of buy-and-hold investing in the nineties. Siegel, a professor of finance at the Wharton School, used the Nifty Fifty to make the argument that if an investor holds on, over the long haul, stocks outperform all other investments. "Did the Nifty Fifty become overvalued during the buying spree of 1972? Yes—but only by a very small margin," Siegel declared. If an investor bought the Nifty Fifty at their peak in December of 1972, he pointed out, and stood pat until November of 2001, his returns would have averaged 11.76 percent a year.

But Siegel's hypothetical example bore only a tangential relationship to the real world. He assumed that an individual who invested in the Nifty Fifty in 1972 had divided his portfolio evenly among the 50 stocks, putting 2 percent of his savings into each company—and that, as the group plunged, he rebalanced his portfolio each month, for 19 years, taking profits on his winners and putting the profits into his losers, so that each position remained at 2 percent. [18]

As Leuthold pointed out, it was "wholly unrealistic" to imagine that anyone would plow the gains from, say, Merck back into a loser like Polaroid, Burroughs, or Xerox, year after year. After all, from 1972 to 1982 the 10 worst performers in the group lost between 37 and 75 percent. With losses that steep, who would continue to send good money after bad? Indeed, most investors who bought the Nifty Fifty in 1972 became discouraged long before 1993 and dumped their fallen angels, probably at a low point, losing even more than Leuthold's numbers suggested.

BUFFETT TAP-DANCES (1973–74)

Warren Buffett had not been seduced by the rallies that followed his exit in May of 1969. From 1969 through 1973, while the bear played with investors' hopes, Buffett hibernated. Nor was he tempted by the Nifty Fifty. As a value investor, committed to "buying low and selling high," Buffett understood that everything depends on the price you pay when you get in. In that sense, any value investor is a market timer: at the end of a cycle, when prices are highest, he stops buying. And in Buffett's view, in the early seventies prices still were exorbitant.

It was not until 1973, when the Dow went into free-fall, that the market once again commanded Buffett's attention. As he told *Forbes* late in 1974: "All day you wait for the pitch you like; then when the fielders are asleep, you step up and hit it." [19]

Buffett's timing was all but perfect. Of course, one could say that when Buffett abandoned the market in 1969, he was "early." After all, if he had hung on, he could have ridden the Dow to the very top: 1071 in January of 1973. But Warren Buffett was not concerned about catching the top of the wave. He was far more interested in not wiping out. While most investors are motivated by a desire to make money, Buffett focused first on not losing money. In that way, Buffett behaved like Old Money. The majority of investors agonize over the prospect of getting out too early and missing out on the profits that would have made them rich. But the very rich don't fret so much about making money. They have money. Their greatest fear is losing it. This explains why, when the bidding escalates—whether in a stock market, a "hot" real estate market, or at a Sotheby's auction—Old Money tends to step aside, letting New Money carry the day.

When virtually no one else wanted to buy stocks, Buffett went on a buying binge. Corporate America was on sale, and Buffett snapped up one company after another: "National Presto Industries . . . Detroit International Bridge . . . Sperry & Hutchinson . . . U.S. Truck Lines . . . J. Walter Thompson . . . Dean Witter . . . Ford Motor . . . Grand Union, . . ." One day during this period, Buffett's bridge partner, Judge John Grant, mentioned that he had been "having fun trying an interesting case." According to Lowenstein, Buffett's eyes twinkled. " 'You know,' he said, 'some days I get up and I want to tap dance.' " [20]

Because Buffett had sold his positions in 1969, he had plenty of cash when the market began its final nosedive. Like 1949, 1974 was a very good year to begin buying stocks. Most investors were not so lucky. By 1974 they were tapped out, both financially and psychologically. And it would be a long time before they made their money back. Although the market hit rock bottom that year, the Dow would not again cross 1000, and stay there, until 1982—eight long years after the crash. Only then would a new bull run begin.

Buffett made money because he bought at the very bottom. But the majority of investors who remained in the market in the mid-seventies had established their positions in the late sixties or early seventies, when prices were much higher. Following the crash of 1973–74, relatively few investors had the cash or the courage to put new money into the market.[21]

Maureen Allyn was an exception. In 2002, Allyn, who had just retired as chief economist at Zurich Scudder Investments, recalled how she avoided the go-go market of the sixties, not because she was too shrewd to buy into a bubble, but because she was too young.[22]

"I just got lucky generationally—I didn't have any money to invest until the seventies," Allyn explained. "But in November of 1974, I was newly married, and my husband and I decided that we should start saving. So we went to a broker and told him we wanted to buy some shares. I still remember what he said:

" 'I really don't think this is a good idea, a nice young couple like you— you really shouldn't be putting your money into something as risky as stocks.'

"That's how you can tell it's a bottom," added Allyn. "They don't even want to sell you the stuff."

Nevertheless, Allyn insisted. At 29, she had just started a new job as chief economist at Sea-Land, one of the largest shipping companies in the United States, and she was primed to invest. "We bought 200 shares of Rite Aid at $3.50 a share. It was down from $30," Allyn remembered, "and it paid a good dividend. Still, I was terrified. It was $700."

In 2001, Allyn still had a few Rite-Aid shares left. "Today, I may be the only person alive with a capital gain on Rite-Aid," she added dryly, refer- ring to the company's 1999 plunge from $50 to $5 following charges of ac- counting fraud.

But most investors were not lucky enough to get in on the ground floor of the next bull market. Instead, they bought when stocks were hot, in the late sixties, then watched the market move sideways for a dozen years—or more. Indeed, if a buy-and-hold investor committed his savings to the S&P 500 in 1968, his capital gains, over the next 14 years, would add up to exactly zero.[23]

For the majority of investors, however, this was a moot point. In reality, very few were able to hold on to either the S&P or the Nifty Fifty for 14 years. Many needed their money before then. Others simply needed a good night's sleep.

ONLY "OLD FOGIES" BUY STOCKS (1975–82)

From his perch at Merrill Lynch, Bob Farrell watched investors gradually give up. "A downturn normally has two stages, and investor sentiment goes through two fairly predictable phases," said Farrell. "First there's the guillotine stage—the sharp decline. That creates fear. That's what happened in 1974. Then, the second stage goes more slowly—there's the feeling of being sandpapered to death. The investor is whipsawed by a choppy market, and then worn down gradually. In place of fear come feelings of apathy, lack of interest, and finally, hopelessness. That is what happened for the rest of the seventies."

A few nimble stock-pickers made money. "But, except for a very few stocks that benefited from inflation—oil service companies, for example— it was not a buy-and-hold market," said Farrell. "You learned to take your profits when you had them."[24]

Most investors who succeeded in the seventies did it by abandoning U.S. stocks and bonds for other types of investments. Gold, for instance, rose by an astounding 19.4 percent a year from 1968 to 1979; diamonds climbed 11.8 percent annually, while real estate became the favorite inflation hedge among small investors, with the price of single-family homes rising 9.6 percent. Shrewd investors who were in the right place at the right time made money in oil stocks—over the course of the decade oil rose 34.7 percent a year. Foreign shares also offered double-digit returns, with the European Australian and Far East Index (EAFE) averaging more than 12 percent a year from the fall of 1970 through the fall of 1980.[25]

As for the Dow, it remained mired in a trading range. At the end of the decade, the index stood at 831, still down roughly 20 percent from its 1973 high. Many thought the stock market was all but washed up. In August of 1979, *Business Week* sounded the death knell with a cover that proclaimed

"The Death of Equities." Part of the problem, *Business Week* explained, was that younger investors had all but lost interest in stocks: "Only the elderly who have not understood the changes in the nation's financial markets, or who are unable to adjust to them, are sticking with stocks. From 1970 to 1975, the number of investors under 65 who bought equities had dropped by about 25%; meanwhile the number of investors over 65 purchasing stocks grew by more than 30%." They just didn't get it. A "New Era" had begun. *Business Week* ended its story with "a young U.S. executive" asking, " 'Have you been to an American stockholders' meeting lately? They're all old fogies.' " [26]

" 'We have entered a new financial age,' " declared Alan B. Coleman, dean of Southern Methodist University's business school. " 'The old rules no longer apply.' " *Business Week* all but closed the door on the possibility of another bull market cycle: "The U.S. should regard the death of equities as a near-permanent condition. Even if the economic climate could be made right again for equity investment," the article's authors argued, "it would take another massive promotional campaign to bring people back into the market. . . . The range of investment opportunities is so much wider now than in the 1950s that it is unlikely that the experience of two decades ago, when the number of equity investors increased by 250% in 15 years, could be repeated. Nor is it likely that Wall Street would ever again launch such a promotional campaign." [27] The E-trade ads of the nineties were beyond imagining in 1979.

In 1980, the bear, always sadistic, allowed investors a glimmer of hope. That year, the Dow scratched its way back up to 950. Then came the crash of 1980–81. The price of oil had been spiraling, and as a result, by 1980, oil and oil-related stocks accounted for nearly one-fifth of the value of the S&P 500. When they toppled, so did the index, falling 27 percent. To call the crash of 1980–81 the final blow would be an overstatement. By then most investors had fled the market; the bear was now mauling a corpse.

In 1982 the S&P 500 went begging. At its low that year, General Electric traded at $1⅛ (after adjusting for splits), or 10 times earnings; Procter & Gamble changed hands at 8 times earnings; Colgate-Palmolive at 7 times earnings. The auto industry had been savaged: Chrysler, Ford, and General Motors were all lower than they had been 20 years earlier. [28]

Little wonder, then, that on August 23, 1982, when *Barron's* put a bull on its cover, some readers were only slightly less hostile than they had been when Richard Russell called the bottom of the bear market in January of

1975. *Barron's* couldn't help but celebrate; the third week in August had been so sweet. On Tuesday, the Dow gained 38.81 points; on Wednesday, a record 132.69 million shares traded on the NYSE; Thursday was delightful "because it proved that Tuesday was no fluke," wrote *Barron's'* Alan Abelson, and Friday, the Dow rose again, "only 30 points to be sure," he conceded, "but it topped off the week." Nevertheless, cynical readers saw *Barron's'* cover as a contrary indicator: "This sure is encouraging to those of us who regard the upsurge of the past couple of weeks as one big bear trap—an exaggerated version of what happened in November of 1974," wrote one sour subscriber, "he who laughs last . . ." [29]

Barron's itself expressed caution: "Is This Bull for Real?" the cover asked. The economy was far from strong. Unemployment was high, corporate profits unimpressive. The one positive signal: inflation was fading.

Year after year, investors had watched inflation honeycomb their savings while consumer prices climbed: up 6.7 percent in 1977, 9 percent in 1978, 13.34 percent in 1979, 12.4 percent in 1980, and 8.9 percent in 1981. At the beginning of '82, in a letter to Berkshire Hathaway's shareholders, Warren Buffett described inflation as "a gigantic corporate tapeworm" gorging itself on corporate profits. "Even a business earning 8% or 10% on equity has no leftovers for expansion, debt reduction or real dividends," Buffett observed. "The tapeworm of inflation simply cleans the plate." In February of '82, Buffett remained pessimistic about long-term inflationary trends. [30]

But this time, the Sage of Omaha was wrong. In the spring, the tide began to turn, and by year-end, Washington would announce that the consumer price index had risen just 3.8 percent. Stock markets are supposed to anticipate changes in the economy, and the rally that began in August had done just that.

— 4 —

THE CURTAIN RISES
(1982–87)

August 1982, and the curtain rose on the Great Bull Market of 1982–99. Over the next 17 years, the drama would unfold in three acts.

Act I stretched from the summer of 1982 through the end of 1989. First the bull learned to run—by the end of 1985, the Dow had doubled. Then he learned to jump: in 1986, the index gained almost 350 points. But it was not until 1987 that the bull jumped over the moon: Dow 2700. The first phase of the bull market reached a climax that August. Two months later, the market blew up. In one day, the benchmark index plunged 22.6 percent. Despite the shock, "Black Monday," October 19, 1987, proved to be merely an intermission. By the end of 1989, the Dow had made up for its losses, ending the year at 2753.

Act II began inauspiciously, with the recession of 1990–91.[1] Indeed, during the early nineties, Main Street and Wall Street seemed to take separate paths. As the "downsizing" that began in the eighties accelerated, Wall Street celebrated: fewer workers meant lower costs and higher profits for corporate America. On Main Street, by contrast, downsizing meant breadwinners without jobs. Layoffs also put a cap on wages. Insecure workers would not ask for raises—good news for shareholders, bad news for wage earners. Thick-skinned, the bull forged ahead. When this second phase of the bull market came to an end in December of 1994, the Dow stood at 3834—up almost 40 percent in five years.

Act III began in January of 1995, and now the People's Market lifted off. As at any good play, this final act of the bull market of 1982–99 would be met with a willing suspension of disbelief.

HOW IT ALL BEGAN: FINDING A RIDER (1982)

The Dow had been straining to breach the 1000 barrier for some 16 years. Finally, it had succeeded. By May of 1983, the benchmark index had reached 1200. Nevertheless, the Dow still was not worth what it had been when it first brushed 1000 in 1966: Dow 1200 was equivalent to only about Dow 600 in 1966 dollars. If investors looked at their nest eggs in terms of their purchasing power, buy-and-hold investors who purchased stocks in 1966 remained underwater.[2]

No wonder investors did not race to embrace a bull market. True, in 1982, stocks were dirt cheap—but this is only another way of saying that no one wanted to buy them. The Dow was now trading at seven times earnings. In most businesses such a sale would bring customers running. But one of the peculiarities of Wall Street is that buyers shun a bargain.

Indeed, in the summer of 1982, Wall Street's bull resembled nothing more than the mechanical bull in the 1980 movie *Urban Cowboy.* The beast in that Texas barroom would not move until someone fed it cash.

Trouble was, there were not very many cowboys left on Wall Street. The August rally caught everyone's attention—still, many asked, "Is it just another bear trap?" Some labeled the flurry "panic buying" by fund managers afraid of being sacked if they missed the summer surge. Wall Street's pros had been playing defense for so long that they had forgotten what it was like to ride a winner.

Surveying the scene that August, Morgan Stanley's Barton Biggs was reminded of a pivotal moment in World War II. After defeating Rommel in the Battle of Alamein, British Prime Minister Winston Churchill was ready to go on the offensive. "But first," Biggs recalled, "he had to replace his most senior officers: the officers who for so many long years had fought so bravely in rear-guard actions, retreating, containing the damage, conserving their force against . . . a superior enemy, by 1943 they had the wrong instincts trained into them for successful offensive action. They were simply unable to commit troops and boldly exploit victories by pursuing a fleeing enemy. They were too cautious. They always looked for the trap. . . ."

Drawing the parallel to Wall Street, the 50-year-old Biggs observed that "younger money managers . . . who have never run money in a real bull market . . . tend to be skeptical of stocks, and hold the highest short term money positions. I think the era of the old-timers is very close," he added, referring to that small but hardy band of Wall Street veterans who remembered the bull market of the sixties, somehow survived the crash of 1973–74, and lived to manage money another day.[3]

Biggs was right. In '82, there were just enough professionals left on Wall Street to recognize a bull when they saw one. Bob Farrell, Merrill Lynch's top market timer, was one of those veterans. Farrell was the fellow who turned bearish in 1969 (causing some consternation at his firm), and in August of '82, as the rally took wing, he remained cautious. By October, however, Farrell was confident: "The move has good breadth," he told *Barron's*, "and everything's in gear."[4] By the end of the year, the S&P 500 had gained 14.8 percent.

"After that," Farrell recalled years later, "the thing just fed on itself."

But as '83 began, Farrell realized that there was a speculative edge to the stampede. Initial public offerings were hot—too hot. In the first quarter of 1983 corporations floated $8.7 billion of new stock, up 378 percent from a year earlier. The IPO frenzy marked the tail end of a hi-tech boom that began even before the broad market took off, in 1980, the year that both Apple Computer and Genentech, a pioneering biotechnology firm, went public. "At that point, financial institutions were buying the IPOs," Farrell recalled. "But as the quality of the new issues fell, the individual investor came in. As the gains get more obvious and everyone sees how 'easy' it is, the public joins the party. It's all a come-on game."[5] By the spring of '83, high hopes had kited the price of some tech shares to 30 or 40 times earnings.

From that balmy summit, the IPO market plummeted. Over the next few months, many of the new issues were cut in half. By fall, the Nasdaq, the broadest measure of technology stocks, had tumbled 18 percent from its high earlier in the year.[6] Tech stocks had lost their sheen. The sector would not take off again until the end of 1990.

The cause of technology's plunge was clear: excess liquidity. Too much cash had been chasing too few deals. There just were not enough good companies to go around. "The broad market stayed up for the rest of '83," Farrell recalled, "but it stopped making progress. And in '84—it tailed off." That year, the S&P 500 eked out a gain of just 1.4 percent.[7]

Now, the bull looked around for more fuel. But who would stoke the fire? Individual investors were not ready to place large bets. For more than a decade, small investors had been conditioned to be suspicious of rallies, and those adventurous enough to jump into the IPO rally had been badly burned. It would be years before they shifted gears. Three years after the bull market began, individuals still accounted for only 11 to 15 percent of daily volume at the New York Stock Exchange—down from more than 40 percent in 1975.[8]

For 20 years, private pension funds had been driving the market, putting an average of 55 percent of the new money that came their way into equities. But they, too, had turned cautious: in 1982, pension funds invested only 24 percent of their fresh money in stocks.[9] The question remained: Who would provide the liquidity needed to carry the bull market forward?

The answer: corporate America. Every bull market finds a new buyer. In the fifties, the investing public began to step up to the plate. In the sixties, pension funds, mutual funds, and other institutional investors provided the cash. And in the eighties the bull found yet another new customer. Foreign buyers played an important role in the market of the eighties, but the real demand would come from corporations themselves, buying back their own shares or, in the case of takeovers, other companies' shares.[10]

THE TAKEOVER FRENZY

From 1984 to 1987, mergers, takeovers, buybacks, and leveraged buyouts slashed the supply of stock available on the open market by more than $250 billion. By 1988, no less than 121 firms had vanished from the S&P 500. Demand rose while supply shrank. Inevitably, prices soared.[11]

Ironically, it was inflation—the bête noire of the seventies—that inspired the takeover boom of the eighties. While share prices stagnated, inflation boosted the replacement cost of many a corporation's real assets. The land it sat on, the factories it owned, the machinery it used all became more valuable. But at the end of a 16-year bear market, share prices did not reflect the hidden value of corporate America's underlying assets. As early as the late seventies, shrewd investors spied a gap between what the market was willing to pay for a company's shares, and the value of its assets if that same corporation was acquired and dismembered, its assets sold off one by one. At the same time, corporations interested in expanding recognized that it would be cheaper to acquire a competitor rather than to buy the real estate and equipment needed to enlarge its own operation.[12]

In order to raise the cash for mergers, acquisitions, and leveraged buy-outs, corporations issued debt. But interest rates were still steep—even in 1985, 30-year government bonds continued to pay 10 percent. In order to tempt investors, corporations had to offer high yields. Drexel Burnham Lambert's Michael Milken, king of the high-yield "junk" bond, was happy to be of service, and by the mid-eighties, junk bonds were driving the takeover market.[13]

Junk bonds offered investors of the late eighties what they craved: double-digit returns. In return, investors accepted a higher risk that the borrower would default on the loan. Typically, junk bonds were rated "BB" or below, and offered little or no real collateral to back up the loan—no real estate, no equipment, no land. Instead, the borrower pledged to pay junk bond investors dividends as high as 14 percent out of future cash flow.

Junk bonds were used to raise the cash needed for leveraged buyouts—or LBOs. In a classic LBO, insiders, rather than outsiders, took over a corporation. Top executives found a small group of investors with deep pockets, and together they borrowed heavily to buy up the company's shares. When the deal was done, the company's stock had disappeared from the public market: this is what it meant to say that the company had "gone private."

The process transformed the capital structure of corporate America. In the past, just about the only respectable mission for a CEO was to expand. The 1980s introduced a new and radically different goal: shrinking equity while increasing debt. As the new management sold assets and repurchased shares, the equity portion of the total might shrink from 50 percent to a closely held 5 percent (owned by the manager/owners and a select cadre of investors who had helped finance the LBO). Meanwhile, debt exploded.[14]

In theory the debt would serve as a spur, goading the managers to slash costs and generate cash in order to keep up with steep interest payments. In other words, they would be motivated by fear. (In the nineties stock options would be hailed as the new "incentive" needed to motivate top manage ment. Why handsomely paid executives needed an incentive to persuade them to do their jobs—in either decade—was never explained.)

Dealmakers also liked to point out that by taking a company private they freed management from worrying about pleasing and appeasing a horde of outside investors. The senior executives who owned and ran the newly restructured company had to answer only to a handful of outside investors who shared their interests and long-term vision. Rather than fretting over quarterly earnings reports, management could concentrate on long-term strategy. Or at least this was the story.

It all seemed such a splendid idea that from 1981 to 1988 almost 1,550 U.S. companies went private—nearly as many as the number still listed on the NYSE in '88.[15]

A blizzard of buyouts, takeovers, and mergers bid share prices ever higher. Inevitably, as demand mounted, the price paid for many companies exceeded the value of their underlying assets. But behind the deals stood the insatiable egos of the dealmakers. "Hoisted onto the auction block, the company became a vast prism through which scores of Wall Streeters beheld their reflected glories," wrote Bryan Burrough and John Helyar in *Barbarians at the Gate*, a narrative that captures the grandiose madness of the era.[16]

There was just one catch: as the LBO market took off, junk bonds, not cash, drove the market. As investors would later discover, "BB" bonds provided a shaky foundation for a boom.

THE SHORTS—JIM CHANOS (1985)

By 1985, the party was in full swing. Leveraged buyouts, takeovers, and share buybacks were vacuuming up the supply of stocks. As always, while the size and price of the deals rose, the quality declined. In the financial world, "good ideas become bad ideas through a competitive process of 'Can You Top This?'" noted Jim Grant in 1989.[17]

The editor of *Grant's Interest Rate Observer* would become a leading member of the bull market's Greek Chorus—a group that was largely ignored by the investors who drove the plot forward. As the bull market advanced, Grant would play out the thankless role that fate had assigned him, offering his sardonic commentary on unfolding events, often foreshadowing the action to come. This is, of course, another way of saying that he was early.

By the end Act III, however, it would become apparent how often Grant was right—even if his timing was off. "Jim realized what was wrong with Cisco's earnings long before any of us," Byron Wein, Morgan Stanley's chief domestic strategist, pointed out in 2002.[18] But then, a Greek Chorus is always out of synch with the rhythm of the play.

As the buyout binge continued, Grant worried about the debt that was "larding the Forbes Four Hundred."[19] He could see that, just as at the beginning of the decade, there were not enough good deals to go around. For as demand spiraled, supply shriveled: by September of '85, $190 billion worth of stock had disappeared from the open market in just nine months. And the deal making showed no sign of letting up.[20] The market was awash in cash, and the broad index rose with the tide. In early November, the Dow punched through 1400; by the end of '85 the S&P 500 had gained 26.3 percent—31.7 percent with dividends reinvested. (Dividends were still high enough that they made quite a difference.)

Inevitably, such a rich market brought out the "shorts"—investors who make their money by betting that stocks are overvalued. In June of '85, *The Wall Street Journal* reported, the number of shares sold short on the New York Stock Exchange had reached a record 253 million. At that point, the *Journal* decided to launch a three-month investigation into what was seen, in some quarters, as the dark art of short selling: "Loosely Allied Traders Pick a Stock, Then Sow Doubt in an Effort to Depress It—Gray Area of Securities Law," the subheadline read.[21]

The story reflected the mood of the time. Some form of short selling has been around as long as there has been a stock market, but in the tender years of a bull market, "the controversy it generates is becoming increasingly sharp," Wall Street's paper of record reported. By the summer of 1985, Jim Chanos, a 27-year-old analyst and vice president at Deutsche Bank Capital Corp., the New York investment affiliate of Deutsche Bank, had become one of the most visible short sellers on the Street. That made him a special target for the critics who charged that modern short sellers often employed "innuendo, fabrication, and deceit" to swamp a vulnerable stock.

Tall and lanky, wearing wire-rimmed glasses, Chanos looked more like a college professor than a Wall Street sharpshooter. His manner was modest, but he could not help but agree that his reputation loomed large: "People think I have two horns and spread syphilis."

Yet, in his own way, Chanos was simply a value investor: his success rested on his research into the fundamentals of the companies he shorted. The only difference was that while most value investors try to make a profit by buying low and selling high, short sellers reverse the process: their aim is to sell high and buy low.

When a short seller spots a stock that he thinks is overvalued, he borrows a block of its shares from a broker or large institutional investor and then turns around and sells the borrowed shares. He then watches the stock, hoping that it will tumble before he must repay the loan. If he is lucky, and the stock craters, he buys the shares he needs to cover the loan and pockets the difference between what he pays for the new shares and what he made when he sold the borrowed shares. But if the stock climbs, the short seller must pay more to replace the shares, and he takes a loss— sometimes a big loss.

While some shorts attempt to make a living simply by spreading rumors and sowing seeds of doubt, they are not likely to stay in business for long, at least not in a bull market. For one, the institutional investor who lends the shares to the short seller can demand their return at any time. If the short is forced to repay the loan while the stock is still rising, the cost can be enormous. In essence, then, a short seller is placing his faith in a relatively efficient market: he is betting that the market will discover its mistake and correct the price of the overvalued stock before he is forced to repay the loan.

To survive in a bull market, shorts must be right more often than they are wrong. This means being able and willing to do the in-depth research needed to expose slippery accounting—research that most Wall Street analysts have neither the training nor the motivation to do. By default, short sellers frequently become the market's whistle-blowers. While Wall Street's analysts may close their eyes and say a stock is worth whatever the public is willing to pay, shorts have a material interest in doing the hard work needed to get the numbers right.

What made Chanos stand out was both the quality of his research and the fact that he chose his targets carefully. Many shorts take a shotgun approach on the theory that if they short scores of overvalued companies, some of the prices will tumble. Chanos, by contrast, typically spent months researching a stock, and then took a large position for a long period of time.

Nevertheless, few corporate executives appreciated his efforts. "This guy has caused us such grief: we can't stand this guy," the chairman of one company confided in the fall of '85, after acknowledging that his company was part of a group that launched a private investigation of Chanos in hopes of catching him doing something wrong. (Chanos later reported that a maintenance man at his town house saw someone going through his garbage.) Some of his conversations were secretly taped. In the end, the detectives found nothing. One summed up the results: "Chanos lives a nice, quiet yuppy existence." [22]

Chanos himself viewed his situation with some irony. He had, after all, come to the financial world by default. After graduating from Yale in 1980, he cast about for a profession. "I didn't get into law school," he recalled without much regret. "And at the tail end of the bear market, Wall Street was not the place to be. The really good jobs were in commercial banking," he remembered, grinning. "At that point, kids right out of college could get into banking and make loans to Latin American countries," said Chanos— referring to the bad loans that nearly destroyed some of the biggest banks in the United States. "Those were the hot jobs—you got to travel and hand out all that money." [23]

Since Chanos was not able to land one of those plum posts in Latin America, he had to settle for a job as an analyst at Blyth Eastman Webber in Chicago, before moving to Gilford Securities, another Chicago firm. Then, in August of 1982, just two years out of college, the 23-year-old's career caught fire. That year, he spotted trouble at Baldwin-United, a huge life and mortgage insurance company. Taking a close look at Baldwin's financials, he realized that the company's supposed earnings were coming largely from questionable tax credits and complex asset-shuffling among its 200-plus subsidiaries. Chanos urged Gilford's clients to sell the stock. In fact, he had the temerity to go one step further: he advised them to sell the stock short.

Chanos was a maverick. Even in the early eighties Wall Street analysts shied away from issuing "sell" recommendations, let alone "short" recommendations. After all, most worked for brokerages, and their firms made their money by persuading investors to buy. In 1983, major brokerage houses issued 10 "buys" for every "sell," according to Zacks Investment Research. Analysts feared offending the captains of industry. For their information, many depended on tips from executives they had befriended. If they criticized a company, they feared losing access to top management. [24]

Predictably, Wall Street ignored Chanos's warnings. Baldwin-United was a market darling; after the young analyst put out his report, the stock more than doubled. But Chanos knew that the company had "gamed" its books, and for more than six months, the 23-year-old sweated it out.

Baldwin threatened to sue. Gilford Securities' clients got the jitters. Outraged at being found out, Baldwin's president branded Chanos and Gilford "those vultures in Chicago." Finally, in March of 1983, Baldwin-United admitted that it could not repay $800 million of short-term debt. In the months that followed, almost every day brought new revelations of Baldwin's crumbling finances. In August, Baldwin announced that it was filing for bankruptcy. Ultimately, some $6 billion of stock market wealth evaporated, and holders of billions of Baldwin-United annuities were left in the lurch.

Reportedly, veteran analysts had missed the holes in Baldwin-United's accounting because many were "mesmerized by the salesmanship of Morley Thompson," the company's former president. By contrast, Chanos never met with Thompson—and so never risked being overwhelmed by the man's much-touted charisma. It was as if, in 1999, a Wall Street analyst passed up a chance to meet Cisco CEO John Chambers and, instead, decided to study Cisco's books. Using the well-known but tedious technique called cash-flow analysis, Chanos discovered that Baldwin-United was paying out more cash than it was pulling in.[25]

"When Baldwin-United went under, suddenly my whole life changed," Chanos recalled.[26] The media compared him to David, slaying Goliath. Gilford made him a partner. Other major firms made lucrative offers. Before long, Chanos landed the job that he held in the summer of '85, as an analyst and vice president at Deutsche Bank in New York.

At that point, another freewheeling company caught Chanos's attention: Drexel Burnham. It was apparent to Chanos that Mike Milken, the father of junk bonds, had set up a daisy chain of interlocking deals that were close to collapse. Again he issued a warning. But this time, his employer was not pleased. The word came down from management in Germany: "We do business with Drexel—tell him to keep quiet." Chanos was told that if he persisted, his days at Deutsche Bank were numbered.

"I didn't want to keep quiet," Chanos recalled in 2001.[27] "That summer—the summer of '85—I decided to look for something else." As luck would have it, at about that time a client who ran a hedge fund offered Chanos a chance to begin managing a large sum on the short side. In October of 1985, just one month after the *Journal* published its report on shorts, Chanos opened an investment partnership. Its bearish approach would produce compound annual growth, before fees and expenses, of 26.2 percent from its inception, in October of 1985, through June of 1991, handily beating the S&P 500's 17.9 percent return.[28]

When Chanos launched his investment firm, he christened it Kynikos Associates Ltd. He took the name from the Kynikos, a group of ancient Greek philosophers who believed that independence of thought and self-discipline were the way to true light—and whose name became the root of the word "cynic." On his lunch hours, the 27-year-old played basketball at a nearby court.

Seventeen years later, Chanos's name would become known well beyond Wall Street when he blew the whistle on a company called Enron, going public with his information a full year before the energy trader collapsed. Had investors listened, they could have saved millions. But Chanos, like Grant, was part of the Greek Chorus.

On Main Street—
The Individual Investor (1982–87)

On Wall Street, in the mid-eighties, the dealmakers danced while the shorts looked on askance, but, by and large, individual investors stayed at home. Understandably loath to abandon the hard-won lessons of the late sixties and seventies, most small investors were wary of putting money into stocks. Everyone talked about Wall Street, but few participated.

Through most of the eighties, the individual investor would be a voyeur. Although he was titillated by tales of the swashbuckling wheeler-dealers novelist Tom Wolfe dubbed "Masters of the Universe," he did not identify with the high rollers. In the eighties, after all, the average middle-class American did not expect to become a millionaire.

This is why most Americans do not remember Act I of the bull market in great detail. For Wall Street's masters of the universe, the period from 1982 to 1987 marked an era of getting and spending, but relatively few shared in the bounty. From 1981 through the end of 1985, the New York Stock Exchange estimated, the number of individual investors increased by just 6 million.[29] Over the same span, some 10.8 million Americans lost their jobs in plant closings and layoffs while corporate restructuring and mergers eliminated an estimated 600,000 management positions.[30]

In many ways, Wall Street's surge seemed strangely self-contained. Although share prices rose by more than 200 percent, national output increased barely 40 percent before inflation—and only 20 percent after inflation was taken into account. And while companies used their cash and credit to buy back stock, capital spending, adjusted for inflation, increased only modestly. "The stock market strikes me as being all by itself," said Charles P. Kindleberger, who was then emeritus professor of economics at Massachusetts Institute of Technology. "There is no real industrial investment boom behind it. It's a puzzle."[31]

But if the average baby boomer was not participating in the equity boom, he was beginning to think about his future. Anticipating his needs, Wall Street carpet-bombed the populace with financial advice. Tax-deferred 401(k)s and IRAs (individual retirement accounts) were becoming increasingly popular, and newly deregulated S&Ls were learning how to hustle: once staid banks now pasted grocery-store-sized ads on their plate-glass windows: "ONLY 5 DAYS UNTIL APRIL 15. OPEN AN IRA TODAY."

Still, the average small investor was not yet snapping up stocks. Why would he? At the beginning of the eighties, money market funds and bank CDs were paying double-digit returns. Between 1980 and 1985, investors who stashed their money in long-term Treasuries enjoyed returns averaging almost 12 percent. To meet the competition, Wall Street peddled a wide array of new products: Ginnie Maes, REITs (real estate investment trusts), tax-free bond funds, and every possible flavor of money market fund. The hullabaloo created the impression that everyone was investing, though in fact everybody was not investing in equities—they were buying other products. (As late as 1992, the largest share of 401(k) money would still be invested in GICs, fixed income investments offered by insurance companies.)[32]

Granted, mutual fund ownership grew fivefold in the eighties, but for the majority of investors, "mutual funds" were not yet synonymous with equities. Most preferred fixed-income funds that invested in money markets or bonds. In 1983, Peter Lynch's Fidelity Magellan fund returned 39 percent, sealing its 10-year record as the best fund in America, but despite Fidelity's best efforts, mutual fund investors continued to choose dividends over capital gains. In 1986, Americans bought only $28 billion of equity funds—roughly one-fourth of the $120 billion that they poured into bond funds.[33] In fact, from the middle of 1983 through October of 1987, there were just two months when more money flowed into stock funds than into bond funds—April 1987 and August 1987.[34] Unfortunately, those two banner months came on the eve of the bloodiest one-day crash in U.S. stock market history.

BLACK MONDAY (1987–89)

August 1987, and on the 14th of the month, *The New York Times* noted, "The Dow gained, ho-hum, another 22.17 points as Wall Street marked the fifth birthday of the bull market." [1]

The *Times'* comment was but one of many signs of greed sated. Even *The Wall Street Journal* carried a whiff of decadence, telling the story of David Herrlinger, a well-born Cincinnati investment advisor who called the Dow Jones News Service to announce that he was bidding $70 a share for Dayton Hudson.

"Before anyone could confirm that Mr. Herrlinger had neither backing nor funds," Jim Grant reported to the readers of *Grant's Interest Rate Observer*, "the stock levitated."

Asked where the financing for his offer would come from, "Mr. Herrlinger told the *Journal*, 'that's still undecided.' Asked whether the offer was 'a hoax,' he said, 'I don't know. It's no more of a hoax than anything else.' " [2]

Mr. Herrlinger was ahead of his time, his offer a harbinger of things to come. Fourteen years later, widespread confusion about the difference between reality and a hoax would allow AOL to acquire Time Warner without putting down a penny of cash.

In 1987, signs of a top were not limited to Cincinnati. In Florida,

Shearson Lehman Brothers had opened a "money management camp" for 10- to 15-year-olds. For only $500, parents could enroll their offspring in a weeklong investment seminar held at a hotel in the Sunshine State where they could play golf or tennis, confident that their children were learning to read both *The Wall Street Journal* and a balance sheet.[3]

There were other, less local signs that the market was getting ahead of itself. While share prices had climbed 200 percent in five years, GNP rose by just 40 percent, 20 percent after adjusting for inflation.[4] In late August, when the Dow hit a high of 2722, shares were changing hands at 20 times earnings—a multiple not seen since the market's peak in January of '73—just before the catastrophic crash that ended in 1974. And even as stocks became more expensive, Wall Street analysts became more exuberant: for the first time since 1980, more analysts were raising earnings estimates than lowering them.[5]

As might be expected, Warren Buffett cast a baleful eye on valuations created by a market built on LBOs and junk bonds. In the 22 years since Buffett had taken over Berkshire Hathaway (which had become, in effect, his new "investment club"), Berkshire's per-share book value had compounded by an average of 23.3 percent a year. In 1986, the Sage of Omaha enjoyed another incredible year: Berkshire's net worth grew 26.1 percent. But in the spring of 1987, Buffett revealed that he was no longer shopping for new stocks. In his view, the market was overpriced. Rather than buying equities, he explained, he had put some $700 million into medium-term tax-exempt bonds, the "least objectionable alternative" to bloated shares. Indeed, as far as he was concerned, stocks were so overvalued that "there's nothing that we can see buying, even if it went down 10%."[6]

Other seasoned investors sensed that something was very wrong. The nineties had not yet begun, but already investors like Robert Picciotto, a San Antonio, Texas, businessman who had been buying stocks on and off for 20 years, believed that an increasingly volatile market was no longer driven by fundamentals. "I used to think, having looked at this thing in the sixties, that buying equities was a stake in the progress of the economy. If you believed the country would do well, you would do well. Now, it's become a very jerky market driven by people interested in these things as pieces of paper—the financiers," he complained, referring to the buyout frenzy. "How you do with a particular stock has little to do with how the company does."[7]

Harvard economist John Kenneth Galbraith also took note of what he saw as a "speculative buildup," and *The New York Times* asked him to write an article on the subject. "Sadly," Galbraith later reported, "when my treatise was completed, it was thought by the *Times'* editors to be too alarming. I had made clear that the markets were in one of their classically euphoric moods and said that a crash was inevitable, while thoughtfully avoiding any prediction as to precisely when." (After the *Times* turned him down, Galbraith found a home for the piece at *The Atlantic Monthly*).[8]

This is not to say that there was no basis for the boom of the eighties. In the early stages, corporate restructuring *was* boosting the bottom line. As companies "downsized," expenses were cut, along with breadwinners, and earnings per share rose—a persuasive argument that stocks were worth more. Simultaneously, inflation dwindled, and long-term interest rates were halved. Still, if mergers had eliminated redundant vice presidents, these marriages also had pushed corporate debt heavenward. In Washington, the budget deficit loomed large. And the millions of Americans who lost their jobs to plant closings and layoffs would not be buying a second car. There was reason to worry.

Once again, Richard Russell sounded the alert. In August of 1987, he warned his readers that he was downshifting his forecast for the market from "bullish" to "neutral." On Thursday, October 15, four days before Black Monday, *Dow Theory* sent a "Sell" signal. Russell told his subscribers to get out.[9]

Russell was not alone. The small but hardy crew of money managers who had survived the seventies knew a peak when they saw one, and this time they were not inclined to let the bear toss them from the top. "In 1987, there weren't many novices in the market—it was a market run by professionals and at the beginning of the year, a lot of us knew that it was radically overpriced," said Steve Leuthold, who had been managing money since the mid-sixties. "But in the spring, the market broke out, and institutional investors were afraid of being held at the post. They jumped in—it was panic buying."[10]

Leuthold, who ran his own shop in Minnesota, stuck to his guns. When the October crash came, only 16 percent of his model portfolio was committed to equities.[11] But many fund managers were afraid of missing a runup and falling behind their peers. They preferred market risk to career risk.

At Morgan Stanley, Byron Wein, the firm's domestic market strategist, remained fully invested, though he was frankly uneasy: "A number of truly successful investors with long memories have already stepped aside, prefer-ring to be too early rather than face the possibility of having their portfolios abused by a waterfall decline," he candidly told Morgan Stanley's clients in late March. "Others, like myself, are hanging on for the last eighths, confi-dent (alas) that we understand the special forces influencing this bull move. . . ."[12]

The end did not come without warning. The market had been spooked for months. After spiraling to an all-time high of 2722.4 in August of '87, the Dow began to falter, losing more than 13.5 percent of its value in late summer and early fall. Nevertheless, on Thursday, October 15, the Dow still stood at 2355.1. Then, the apocalypse. Friday, the Dow plunged 108 points. Yet on Wall Street, many soothsayers remained sanguine. The mar-ket, they said, was due for a correction. After five halcyon years, they had forgotten the word "rout."

Traders had a more visceral reaction to Friday's plunge. At stock ex-changes coast to coast, they found themselves on the front line of the deba-cle. In Chicago, at 2:45 P.M. central time, Steve Lapper, a 30-something trader on the CBOE (Chicago Board Options Exchange), realized that he could hear the time clock ticking in the trader's pit. Up until that point, the day had been almost normal. True, the market had already slid 100 points, but in an orderly fashion. Then, in just five minutes, the Dow blew up, plunging from down 85 to down 130 points. The silence was abrupt. An eeriness settled over the crowd. "You felt like the plane was losing power—and taking a dive. All the food was on the ceiling," Lapper said later.[13]

On the San Francisco Exchange, Rick Ackerman began to feel a little queasy when the market had lost 100 points and some traders began clap-ping and applauding. Ackerman, 38, had been working the San Francisco Exchange for nine years, and he knew the black humor of the trading pits. He realized that market makers were just trying to keep their spirits up. But Ackerman also knew that some traders weren't taking the slide too seriously. At the end of the day, he found himself sitting between two traders who each had lost a few hundred thousand dollars. Both had been having an ex-traordinary year and weren't too upset. One of them said, "I bet I get back at least a third Monday—on S&P futures." The bravado scared Ackerman. That evening, he called a friend on the East Coast. "This is it," he said. "It's over."[14]

But on the morning of Monday, October 19, Ackerman wasn't yet terrified—just a little edgy. No one knew what was going to happen. "Some expected the market to be blasting up right out of the chute," he said. "They had lost 20 or 30 percent of their capital the previous week, and they were raring to go." What followed was chaos. Some traders couldn't even keep track of their positions. At day's end, the Dow had plunged 508 points, a stupefying 22.6 percent. In Chicago, Steve Lapper lost $1 million in that one day.

On the way out, traders didn't speak in the elevators. Friday, they had chatted, half exhilarated by the action. "But Monday," Ackerman recalled, "people just sort of grunted." As for Ackerman, he had lost about one-third of his capital. His two friends who had been looking forward to the buying opportunities on Monday weren't so lucky. When the crash began they were both approaching two-million-dollar years—but by the end of trading on Monday, both were in the red. In the afternoon one of them turned to Ackerman: "Rick, what do I do? I'm out of the game." He was an excellent trader, a dozen years Ackerman's senior. Normally, he did not ask for his advice. "But this was a guy with kids and a mortgage," Ackerman said later. "He just looked really sick."

A few swashbuckling skeptics had the nerve to short the market. Most were fairly young. Lapper estimated that some of the novices made enough to retire on. He knew one trader, a very smart, very nice guy, 29 years old, who had been short for a month or two. Probably he made millions. But the winners weren't bragging. They looked sheepish. If someone asked, they said, "Yeah, I did okay." Lapper saw only one trader with a giddy look. "He wasn't mature enough to hide the gains on his face."[15]

In Boston, Fidelity, the nation's preeminent mutual fund firm, was coping with its own chaos. The success of funds like Peter Lynch's Magellan Fund—combined with aggressive marketing—had made Fidelity the crown prince of financial service firms. Long before the decade of online trading, Fidelity had made it easy to buy a stock: just dial 800. And while most mutual funds reported their results only once a day, after the market's close, Fidelity offered hourly pricing of its funds—a feature that critics charged appealed merely to the gambling instincts of many of its clients.[16]

On Black Monday that emphasis on instant gratification turned against the Boston firm. Across the nation, mutual fund investors were phoning in to sell—at least if they could get through on the phones. Fidelity's lines were jammed. Meanwhile, fund managers were raising cash to meet the redemptions. Methodically, Peter Lynch began handing out the stocks in the Magellan Fund, in alphabetical order, to his traders. One received companies in the fund beginning with the letters A–D. Another got E–L. Their marching orders: Sell.[17]

Forced sales might have been avoided if Fidelity's fund managers had been able to keep some cash in reserve. But the unspoken rule at Fidelity was that funds must be fully invested at all times. Fidelity chairman Ned Johnson "could have . . . protect[ed] his investors from the full force of the coming crash," Joseph Nocera observed in a *A Piece of the Action,* a book that traces the rise of the mutual fund industry during this period. "He could have let it be known, as the market began to tumble, that it would be all right for the fund managers to shelter some assets in cash. But Johnson did no such thing." [18]

In the end, Fidelity unloaded shares worth nearly $1 billion. So many mutual fund customers bailed out that, at the height of the panic, the firm activated a clause in its funds' prospectuses that allowed it to delay making payments until seven days after redemption.[19] Still, Fidelity Magellan was much better off than many funds because it held so many positions. As a result, it was able to sell a small portion of each stock, without moving the market. More concentrated funds found it much harder to unwind their positions.

Tuesday was little better. In the morning, the Dow shot up 200 points, then spun into free fall. At one point, some Dow stocks could not be traded—there were no buyers. When the day finally ended, the Dow managed to close up 102 points, but investors were shell-shocked. Outside the New York Stock Exchange, a doomsday prophet exhorted the crowd, "People, I plead with you, start reading your Bible." Across the street, a mobile van operated by the Seventh-Day Adventists offered free blood pressure tests.[20] Wednesday, the Dow came up for air and grabbed another 186 points, but on Thursday it sank again, falling 77 points. Friday, the market closed flat. But traders were still dazed. All told, a trillion dollars had vanished into thin air.

As for the individual investor, many bailed out. Those with money in mutual funds began phoning in their orders on Friday, and in the first half hour of trading on Black Monday, Fidelity, the largest mutual fund company in the United States, sold $500 million worth of stocks on the New York Stock Exchange—roughly 25 percent of the Big Board's total volume in that period.[21]

But in the two days following the crash, a giddy public began to rush back in, snapping up bargains. "Anytime the market gets the stuffing beaten out of it, there's a knee-jerk reaction to buy. It's as if Macy's is having a sale—it's unbelievable," marveled Marty Zweig, manager of the Zweig Funds. "Those were the two biggest net-buying days ever," Merrill Lynch's Bob Farrell noted at the time. "Even my 25-year-old daughter in London—who doesn't know anything about the market—called up and wanted to buy a stock." [22]

On Wall Street, the finger pointing began. What had caused the crash? "Program trading" (automatic trades based on signals from a computer program) was a favorite target. In particular, the critics blamed professionals who tried to cushion their portfolios against disaster with "portfolio insurance," a form of computerized trading that involves selling futures contracts when the market begins to fall. As the market plunged, their "insurance" orders hammered futures prices, and share prices followed.

If investors would just realize that "the crash was largely a technical problem, caused by computerized trading schemes, the worst can be avoided," a story in *The Wall Street Journal* declared. [23]

General Electric chairman Jack Welch also took an interest in damage control. "GE had recently bought NBC," recalled Lawrence Grossman, then president of NBC News, "and early in the morning of Tuesday, October 20, I received an angry phone call. . . . Welch was phoning to complain about the way we were reporting the previous day's sudden stock market plunge. He thought our pieces were undercutting the public's confidence in the market, which would certainly not help the stock of NBC's parent company. He felt no qualms about letting his news division know that he thought NBC's reporters should refrain from using depressing terms like 'Black Monday' to describe what had happened to the stock market the day before." [24]

But whatever they were saying in New York, Minnesota money manager Steve Leuthold knew that neither computerized trading nor the media was creating the sell-off. "The market was overvalued—that triggered the program trading. Then mutual fund redemptions added to the pressure. But program trading didn't cause it," said Leuthold. [25] In 1987 the traders were simply the handiest scapegoats.

A close look at the numbers suggested that individual investors contributed to the stampede for the exits. Institutions that use computers to program their trades do most of their buying and selling in "block trades" of 10,000 shares or more, and on October 19, block trading accounted for only about "half of the share volume and 60% of the dollar volume of transactions," Peter Bernstein, a financial consultant to institutional investors, observed in his 1992 book, *Capital Ideas*. "This was only two percentage points above the average for the preceding fifty days, and almost identical to the average for the last fifty trading days of 1986," suggesting that the admittedly savage selling pressure from the institutions was but "a part, and not an unusually large part of Black Monday's sell-off," Bernstein observed. Meanwhile, the volume of transactions below 10,000 shares ballooned on Black Monday, winding up "nearly triple the average daily number in 1986 and well above the previous high." Few, if any, of these smaller transactions would have been triggered by programmed trading; the bulk represented trades by smaller investors.[26]

As for portfolio insurance, while it contributed to the speed of the market's fall, there was little reason to suspect that it *caused* the crash. What is certain is that it played a role in the market's parabolic climb: as prices levitated, those who used the strategy remained complacent: "After all," they said, "if the market collapses, we have portfolio insurance to protect almost all of our gains."[27]

Nevertheless, those true believers who subscribed to the theory that stock markets are efficient had to try to find some external explanation for the crash. According to their theory, the stock market does a nearly perfect job of pricing in all available information about a given stock—in other words, investors weigh the information available to them judiciously and act rationally on it. Of course, the theory's followers acknowledge that individual investors may make errors, but if misguided investors offer to sell a stock for less than it is worth, investors who have paid better attention to the available information will rush in to buy it, quickly bidding up the price. Conversely, if the inattentive offer to pay more than a stock is worth, sellers rush in to meet their orders, and as supply increases, the price falls.

Under the efficient market theory, then, only a sudden turn in the news—an event that has not been priced into the market—could explain such a precipitous plunge. But in the days before Black Monday, there had been no abrupt change in the information available to shareholders: no declaration of war, no oil embargo, no terrorist attack. Then again, "There was no rational case for things being so far up [before the crash]—only romantic reasons," Bernstein noted at the time.[28]

All of this confirmed what heretics, such as Yale economist Robert Shiller, had always believed. To Shiller, Black Monday merely served as further proof that the efficient market hypothesis was "the most remarkable error in the history of economic theory. This is just another nail in its coffin," added Shiller, who would become better known in 2000 after he published his best-selling critique of the nineties bubble, *Irrational Exuberance.*[29]

Why, then, did the market fall in 1987? To say "the computers did it" is too easy—or not easy enough. Gravity is the simplest answer: the market fell because it had climbed too high, too fast.

Markets, after all, are only as rational as we are. Often, they over-shoot—and the result is a boom that leads to a bust as prices revert to a mean. In 1987, stocks were overvalued. Many investors knew it, and once prices began to slide, they headed for the exits. What seemed an irrational sell-off was, in fact, a perfectly reasonable response: when risk becomes too steep, the market has a nervous breakdown.

The crash was not caused by some external event. Booms and busts are built into the system. As noted earlier, without cycles there would be no progress. But not all downturns signal the beginning of a cataclysmic bear market. Sometimes, if prices have not strayed too far off course, the market is able to wring out the excess and move forward within a matter of months. On other occasions, it takes years for the market to retrench and build a solid foundation for a new bull market.

In October of 1987, many believed that Black Monday signaled the beginning of just such a long, bleak bear market. But when Steve Leuthold looked at fundamental measures of the market's value, comparing share prices to earnings and "book value" (the value of a company's assets, minus liabilities such as debt), he was not convinced.

"It's not one of those big bear markets, like 1929–32, or even 1973–74," the Minnesota money manager declared a week after the crash. "It's perhaps more akin to the bear markets that we saw back in the sixties, especially 1962," he added, referring to the blowup that cost Edwin Levy, a greenhorn who had just come to Wall Street, everything except his slightly used Mercedes SL. That crash signaled that the bull was getting giddy, but the long bull market of 1954–66 was far from over. Indeed, it would be 11 years before the crash of 1973–74 brought it to a decisive, disastrous end.

So, in the fall of 1987, Leuthold realized that the bull was not ready to give up the ghost. In the wake of the '87 crash, he acknowledged that the market still looked pricey to investors accustomed to the seventies, a time when many stocks traded at seven or eight times earnings. But Leuthold believed in market history—which meant going back more than a decade to put things in historical perspective. In terms of "intrinsic value . . . the market is really at just about median levels," he observed. "At 14 or 15 times earnings, price earnings ratios are about mid-way in their historical range."

The market might drift to a new low sometime before the end of the year, Leuthold predicted, but he anticipated "nothing that's terribly dramatic." Before long, he expected the bull market to resume, forecasting that in the next leg of the bull market, the Dow could easily climb to 3000.[30]

Most investors fight the last war: their expectations are conditioned by what happened in the preceding cycle. But Leuthold was in a good position to put recent experience into a much broader historical context—he had been investing since the early sixties, which meant that he had already lived through two long cycles.

Steve Leuthold

Steve Leuthold had grown up in Minnesota in the forties. His father, the founder of a chain of clothing stores, wanted him to join the family business, but Steve had other ambitions. When he was 17, Elvis Presley recorded at the Sun Records studio. Bedazzled, Steve and three friends formed their own band, with Steve on vocals and rhythm guitar. In 1958, the group—by then calling itself "Steve Carl and the Jags"—landed a recording contract with Meteor Records and cut a demo. But nothing came of the contract, and Leuthold's career as a rocker fizzled.

After college, Leuthold tried out a second career: law school. Forty years later, he could still recall how much he hated it. "I saw these people grinding away in the law library and I thought, 'Boy, I don't want to do that!' Later, I came to look on lawyers as the sands in the gears of progress—always saying 'You Can't Do That!' "[31]

When Leuthold abandoned law school, he signed on as a management trainee at Cargill Grain Co., where he acquired his first real training in investments and trading. There he became interested in the commodities market. But once again his career was short-circuited; in 1960, he joined the army.

As it turned out, the army became Leuthold's version of Harvard Business School. Because of his background working in his father's clothing stores, he was assigned to supply, handing out clothing to new recruits. But as it happened, the captain of his unit was an avid stock market maven, and when he heard of Leuthold's experience at Cargill, he gave him a job in the company's office.

There, Leuthold's main job was charting stocks for the captain. Sensing that it would be impolitic to disappoint, Leuthold took a correspondence course in securities analysis. He also used his own money to trade soybeans futures.

From the army, Leuthold went to PaineWebber, where, at 22, he became a broker. By 1966, he was running a hedge fund, and in 1969, he set up his own research division at Piper Jaffray. There he began to establish a national reputation for the quality of his research. In 1980 he established his own firm, The Leuthold Group. A year later, he appeared on the PBS show *Wall Street Week with Louis Rukeyser*. Now even Leuthold's mother knew that he had arrived. "Ever since my father's death, I had been managing her money, but she never paid much attention to my recommendations—and always questioned my judgment," he recalled with a grin. "Then she saw me on *Wall Street Week* and never questioned me again. Whatever I said was okay by her." [32]

Throughout the eighties, Leuthold maintained his independence. This was why, in the summer of '87, he was able to call the market as he saw it, advising his clients to move out of stocks. "I could see that we were at the outer limit of all evaluation benchmarks for the stock market—price/earnings ratio, yields, et cetera," Leuthold said. "Unless we'd entered a new era, it was clear that we'd topped out. I've been in the business a long time, and I've heard a lot about new eras, but I've never actually seen one. Someday, there may be a new era. But betting on one is a lousy basis for making investment decisions."

If he had worked for a major Wall Street firm, Leuthold would not have been able to take a stand. But because he worked for himself, "I just do what I want to do," he said in 1988. "I could never do that at an establishment firm. Fortunately, I've never been very security conscious," he added. "I could live just as comfortably on $30,000 a year. I would enjoy life just as much."

Of course, even then, Leuthold earned well more than $30,000 a year. But his success dramatized another of Wall Street's ironies: professional investors who are obsessed with money—or the idea that it makes life secure—are often less likely to succeed. When they are wrong, they have a hard time cutting their losses. Those who realize that investing is a game have the edge. They know that they cannot be right all of the time: the future is, by definition, unpredictable. This makes it much easier to ride a bull. You know that, from time to time, you will be tossed over his horns—and gored. It is part of the game.

The Aftermath: On Main Street (1987–89)

When all was said and done, what was most remarkable about the crash of 1987 was the aftermath. Nothing happened. The economy did not collapse. The first phase of the bull market had reached its climax—the rest of the decade would be denouement.

Old hands like John Kenneth Galbraith and Richard Russell had been right in thinking that the market was getting ahead of itself, but they were wrong on one crucial point: the bull market was not over. Less than six months after the debacle, the Dow was again floating close to 2000—just where it had been a year earlier. As for the S&P 500, it ended 1987 with a 2 percent gain, rose 12.4 percent in '88, and climbed another 27.3 percent in '89.

But while the bull was resuscitated, public enthusiasm for the market did not revive. The fire-sale mood that swept the nation in the days immediately following the crash lasted only a short time. In October of 1987, net withdrawals from stock funds totaled $7.5 billion, and investors continued to pull money out of equities for 15 of the next 17 months—even as the market started to recover. Ultimately, investors withdrew $29 billion—equal to 12 percent of the assets in stock funds before the crash.[33]

In October of 1988, a year after the collapse, Charles Schwab's customers were still holding about $5.5 billion in cash on the sidelines, though Schwab himself took some comfort in the fact that they weren't pulling their money out altogether. They might not be buying stocks, but at least they were keeping the cash in their Schwab accounts. "Black Monday did to investors what *Jaws* did to swimmers," Schwab observed. "They don't want to go in the water, but they still come to the beach."[34]

As the crash of 1987 became a misty memory, history would be rewritten. The revisionists would claim that while professional traders panicked, the small investor stood pat. Tales of the small investors' courage became a cornerstone of the major populist myth of the nineties: that the "little guy" was smarter than the pro. (Warren Buffett "just didn't get it"; the dentist who watched CNBC while drilling did.)

The truth was that a year after the crash, mutual fund investors were still steering clear of stocks.[35] Net sales of equity funds were only a third of what they had been a year earlier. Meanwhile, at Fidelity, redemptions had drained the firm's equity funds: just before Black Monday, funds that invested in stocks boasted assets of roughly $47.6 billion; five months later they had shriveled to $34.8 billion. Of course, some of the shrinkage was due to market losses, but by February of '88 the market was making a nice recovery. Yet assets in Fidelity's equity funds remained down 27 percent from their precrash levels.[36] Mutual fund redemptions did not hold the Dow down, but that was only because mutual fund investors were not major players in the equity market.

As the eighties drew to a close, small investors became even more cautious. Insider trading scandals roiled Wall Street, and by 1989, many were convinced that the market was a game run by people who might be described, most charitably, as "too smart by half." Public participation in the stock market, measured as a percentage of household assets invested in stocks or equity funds, stood far below its 1968 peak.[37] What would it take to revive the people's market of the late sixties?

"It's a peculiar time," Merrill Lynch's Bob Farrell acknowledged late in 1988. "So much publicity is given to people who make a lot of money— whether it's a guy who wins the lottery or an investment banker, and Wall Street has been in the middle of it. *Bonfire of the Vanities* sums it up. Now if the standard of living goes down, or if there is a decline in the value of housing, more people will be looking for a way to 'score.' If the little guy views equities as a speculative game, he may be more likely to play it if he feels that he has to find a way to accumulate wealth." [38]

In other words, it might take hard times to bring small investors back in. Farrell had a point. The second leg of the People's Market would not begin in earnest until 1991, when the economy was in recession and interest rates on money market funds had slipped to well below 5 percent. Only then did individual investors begin to think about buying stocks.

THE AFTERMATH: ON WALL STREET (1987–89)

As the eighties trailed off, a malaise hung over the Street. "No one wants a corner office," confided a young executive at Merrill Lynch. "No one wants to look expensive." [39]

A year after the crash, securities transactions of all types were down 22 percent and some 15,000 Wall Streeters had lost their jobs.[40] The one supposedly bright spot: the merger business continued. In 1988, PaineWebber reported, fully 29.8 percent of the appreciation of the S&P 500 was in companies that were acquired or that carried out major restructuring. But now there was a desperate edge to the takeover game. Wall Street brokerages badly needed the windfall profits that they could reap from a leveraged buy-out. A single deal could generate up-front fees of $50 million or more—enough to save a firm's quarter.[41]

At first, specialized takeover firms had financed most deals, but as takeover fever grew, other Wall Street firms wanted a piece of the action. No longer content merely to collect the fees on the deals, they became buyers. By 1988, Prudential Bache owned 49 percent of Dr Pepper/Seven Up, Merrill Lynch controlled Supermarkets General, and Shearson Lehman Hutton owned Chief Auto Parts.[42]

Because of the astounding returns earned in the past, cash and credit poured into the LBO market, "making it more liquid than a double mar-tini," PaineWebber reported in June of 1989. By then, LBO partnerships and investment banks had roughly $25 billion at their disposal. Mean-while, commercial banks pushed into the LBO area—a survey of 28 major banks revealed that they had $46.9 billion exposed to LBOs—an amount equal to 5.6 percent of the loans, and 67.8 percent of the banks' equity. Jap-anese banks also were lining up to finance LBOs and provided the major funding for the deal that capped the decade: the sale of RJR Nabisco.

Dealmakers scrambled to put the money to work. They had raised a huge amount of capital; now they had to find places to invest. "It is tough for a financier to assemble $100 million in an LBO fund in November and then ring up a client in December to say, 'We've changed our mind. There are no high-quality, reasonably priced deals available right now. We're going to put your money in T-bills until the next recession,'" PaineWebber's Thomas Doerflinger warned clients in June of 1989. "Instead, the finan-ciers did what they were hired to do—deals."[43]

All the while, the junk bond market that financed the LBOs flourished. Junk had plunged, along with stocks, in October 1987, but soon recov-ered—thanks in large part to Mike Milken's talent for peddling old debt in new bottles. The prince of leverage had created a network of buyers. Now he used that network to rescue junk bonds on the verge of default, trading debt that was going sour for new debt that, in many cases, promised even higher returns—which is to say that it was even riskier. Milken had created a pyramid of junk bonds and, like any pyramid scheme, it ultimately would topple under its own weight.

Many of Milken's most loyal buyers were savings and loans (S&Ls). He had helped the banks grow by issuing junk bonds on their behalf, and now they, in turn, bought the junk bonds of his other customers. Meanwhile, Milken arranged for a massive inflow of deposits into the S&Ls, putting them in a good position to suck up huge chunks of Drexel's junk bond inventory. Milken knew the S&Ls did not really have to worry about how risky the junk bonds might be. After all, the banks were using the money that their customers had put on deposit, and those accounts were, in turn, protected by the FDIC (Federal Deposit Insurance Corporation). The upshot: if the bonds went bad, the government would wind up taking the hit. Of course, "the government" meant taxpayers—who else funds the government? At the end of the decade, when the junk bond market crashed, taxpayers wound up holding the bag.

Jim Chanos had been right: even before the '87 crash, Mike Milken's Ponzi scheme was on the verge of collapse. His junk kingdom had been built on air. The junk bonds were "unsecured loans"—the borrower did not put up collateral to back up the loan. Instead, he promised to pay investors double-digit dividends out of future cash flow. If the cash flow proved insufficient, the investor who bought the junk bonds was left high and dry.

And in many cases, this is exactly what happened. For as inflation faded and share prices rose, the gap between a company's share price and the value of its underlying assets shrank. That gap had created the value that made takeovers attractive. Now, as the pool of money available to finance LBOs grew, junk bonds were being used to finance the purchase of mediocre companies at exorbitant prices.

As the game heated up, insiders grew greedier and took greater risks. At the same time, their high-stakes game drew more and more attention from the authorities. By the fall of 1988, the SEC was moving in, ready to close the barn door. Now the SEC accused Drexel and Milken, among others, of insider trading, stock manipulation, and fraud. At year-end Drexel agreed to plead guilty to six felonies and settled SEC charges, paying a record $650 million. In March of 1989 Milken and his brother Lowell were indicted on 98 counts of racketeering and securities fraud.

Without Milken to force-feed bonds to his clients, Drexel found it impossible to roll over weak debt. The first eight months of 1989 saw $4 billion worth of junk bond defaults and debt moratoriums.[44]

In October the junk bond bubble popped. UAL Corporation, the parent of United Airlines, provided the pin by announcing that it would not be able to complete a leveraged buyout that had pushed the company's stock price above $200 a share. "The UAL failure crystallized the symbiotic relationship between the health of the junk bond market and the ability to mount takeovers that had so pushed up prices in the stock market," wrote James Stewart in *Den of Thieves,* a landmark account of the insider trading scandals of the eighties.[45] Anxious buyers were no longer willing to purchase junk bonds, and without junk bonds to support the pyramid scheme, share prices swooned. On October 13, with takeover stocks leading the sell-off, the market lost 190 points. The S&P 500 still ended the year with a neat gain of 27 percent. But junk bond investors were decimated.

When a bubble collapses, it usually gives back not just some, but all, of its gains. Over the course of the eighties, it seemed clear that returns on junk bonds would easily outstrip the profit that a cautious investor might hope to make on AAA government bonds. It was a no-brainer: higher risk equals higher return. What junk bond investors had forgotten is that higher risk does not guarantee higher returns; it merely offers the *chance* of higher returns. When they closed their books on the eighties, they discovered that they had lost the gamble. Over the course of the decade, money invested in the average junk bond grew just 145 percent—substantially less than the 177 percent investors would have earned in U.S. Treasuries, without taking any credit risk whatsoever.[46]

As the eighties came to a close, the curtain fell on the first phase of the Great Bull Market of 1982–99. *Barbarians at the Gate* was published in 1990, and its final pages reflect the sense that an era of excess had come to an end:

"By 1990 Wall Street's party was over, the memories of massive buyouts and takeovers receding each day. . . . With Drexel's demise, and the guilty pleas of financial titans Ivan Boesky and Mike Milken in the insider-trading scandals, popular opinion turned strongly against Wall Street and the unfettered greed of the 1980s. That backlash, combined with deteriorating financial fundamentals, effectively spelled the end to an era unlike Wall Street had ever seen. . . . The Roaring Eighties were a new gilded age, when winning was celebrated at all costs. 'The casino society' Felix Rohatyn once dubbed it." But, "as a new decade dawned," it seemed, to many, that "a new wind was blowing" on Wall Street.[47]

So the nineties began with an illusion—the illusion that the casino society was dead. With the Milkens and Boeskys behind bars, many believed that the financial fraud of the eighties was behind them.

"In the early nineties New York Mayor Rudy Giuliani prosecuted Wall Street's white-collar criminals—he was the sheriff who came in to clean up the town," Jim Chanos recalled in 2001, looking back at how the decade began. "And he cleaned up Wall Street's image. Main Street began to feel better about New York: all of a sudden, New York was a warm and fuzzy place. This, I think, was tied to the increasing credulity about the market." [48] Fear of risk faded, and investors began to believe that the market was not a casino, but a safe haven—a place to stash money that you could not afford to lose.

In fact, the nineties would be an extension of the eighties. Act I of the Great Bull Market of 1982–99 had laid out the plot for Acts II and III: once again, liquidity would send the market skyward, as too much money chased too few good deals.

It was true that LBOs would no longer prop up share prices. The bull needed a new source of cash. But the buyer who would drive the bull market of the nineties was already waiting in the wings: the individual investor.

The crash of 1987 had taught him all he needed to know about bull markets: buy on dips. "People drew the lesson, not because that is what they did in '87," said Farrell, Merrill Lynch's chief investor advisor, "but because that is what they didn't do." Throughout most of 1988, people were still taking more money out of equity funds than they were putting in. [49]

But investors who sold would watch neighbors who bought grow rich. It was a lesson that they would never forget.

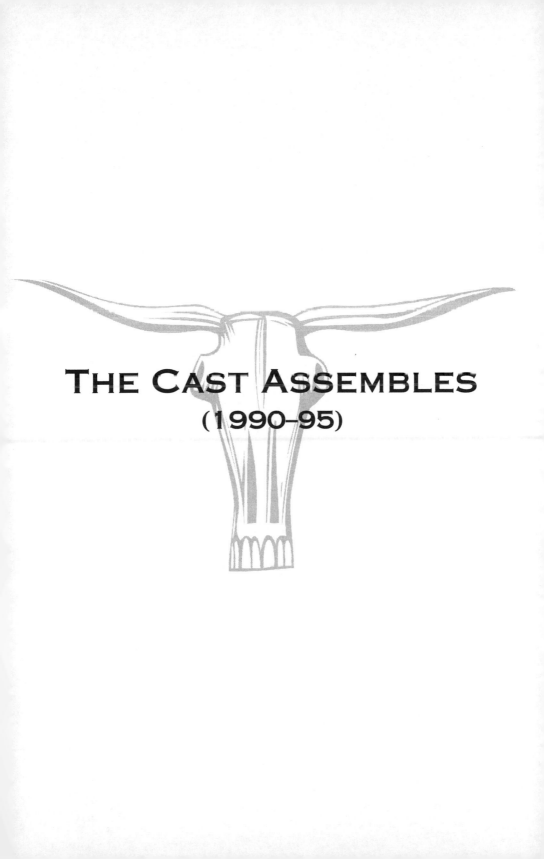

THE CAST ASSEMBLES
(1990–95)

THE GURUS

ABBY JOSEPH COHEN

On an October morning in 1990, a 38-year-old mother of two with a wide-open face and short-cropped light brown hair boarded a bus in Flushing, Queens, en route to her first day at a new job. It was early, about 6:30 A.M. But she knew that if she waited until rush hour, it could take an hour and a half to wend her way to 85 Broad Street in downtown Manhattan. As she stepped onto the bus, she looked like many another Queens housewife, but in fact, Abby Joseph Cohen was on her way to becoming one of the most powerful women in America. If Alan Greenspan would turn out to be the father of the bull market of the nineties—as surely he would—Abby Joseph Cohen, the new chair of investment strategy at Goldman Sachs, would be its muse.

That October day, she was aware that in joining Goldman Sachs, she was joining one of Wall Street's most venerable firms. Goldman was Wall Street's premier investment bank, and well on its way to becoming the most profitable. That year alone, the firm generated some $600 million before taxes, or roughly $5 million apiece for the firm's 128 partners.[1] In Cohen's mind Goldman Sachs & Co. "set the gold standard" for Wall Street's great investment houses.[2] If she was nervous, she would not admit it.

It took more than gilt to define that standard. The "Goldman culture" played a major role in the bank's mystique. At the 121-year-old firm, white shirts were still preferred to blue, and displays of temper were taboo—even partners were expected to keep their egos in check. Modesty was appreciated; publicity was not. Traders learned not to shout. Glitz was out. Bankers at other firms might flash French cuffs, but at 85 Broad Street they were more likely to wear their white sleeves rolled up. Unpretentious, hardworking, and smart, Cohen might not be one of the boys, but she would fit in with the code.[3]

Long known as Wall Street's most genteel club, Goldman was the only major Wall Street firm that had remained a private partnership. By 1990, Salomon Brothers, Morgan Stanley, and Merrill Lynch were publicly traded corporations, while Shearson Lehman and Kidder Peabody had become units of corporate giants. Goldman, by contrast, remained independent: the firm belonged to its 128 partners. When they made a deal, they were wagering their own net worth. Understandably, this led to a certain fiscal conservatism.

As it turned out, Cohen was joining Goldman at a transitional point in the firm's long history. Two months earlier, senior partner John Weinberg (whose father, Sidney, brought the firm back from disaster following the '29 crash) announced that he was retiring. His two top lieutenants, Robert Rubin and Stephen Friedman, would become the firm's co-chairmen. "Our single biggest priority," said Rubin, "is keeping the social fabric together."[4]

Yet that fabric was already showing signs of strain. At the end of the eighties, Goldman—once a bastion of lifetime employment—had caught up with the times, slashing roughly one-fourth of its workforce. There were other signs, too, which hinted that, as it grew, the close-knit firm was changing. In the past, Goldman had been known for its collegial relationships, but in 1989 it hired outside consultants to shepherd its staff into focus groups and probe their concerns. "They've tried to institutionalize all that 'uncle stuff,'" said a disenchanted trader who left the firm. Most shocking of all, interlopers were masquerading as uncles. Traditionally, one became a partner at Goldman by rising through the ranks, but in an about-face, the partnership had begun to take in outsiders.[5]

Cohen, however, was not invited to join the club as a partner, even though her new position as co-chair of investment strategy—a job that she would share with Goldman partner Steven Einhorn—made her one of the bank's most visible seers. But at the beginning of 1990, only one of the firm's 128 partners was a woman.[6] To be fair, it is not at all clear that Cohen's sex was the most important barrier to partnership. With few exceptions, the firm boasted a long tradition of expecting would-be partners to patiently wait their turn. A novitiate needed to demonstrate some capacity for self-effacement if he hoped to achieve Goldman's ideal of egoless team play. Anyone who could not bear the feeling that he or she was languishing on the vine probably would not fit in.

As for Cohen, the brotherhood would not anoint her for eight long years. When it did, she would become all the more famous by continuing to take the bus to work.

If Abby Joseph Cohen were virtually any other Wall Street idol, all of the bus riding might lead one to suspect that she was in training to run for public office. But in Cohen's case, the truth was that she was a creature of habit. Abby Cohen preferred the accustomed track: it appealed to her strong sense of order and tradition. This would be both Cohen's greatest strength, but also, perhaps, her greatest weakness. By the end of the nineties, one might say of Cohen what Fed-watcher Martin Mayer said of Fed Chairman Alan Greenspan: "Here . . . as elsewhere, Greenspan is trapped by his unshakable philosophical bias that whatever is, is right."[7] When it came to the workings of American-style capitalism, they shared a laissez-faire optimism: if it works, don't fix it.

Certainly, Cohen's upbringing provided sound basis for such optimism. Even after becoming a partner at Goldman, Cohen remained connected to that childhood, continuing to live in the Flushing, Queens, neighborhood where she grew up, the child of college-educated Polish immigrants. Her father, Raymond Joseph, was an accountant employed by J.K. Lasser, while her mother, Shirley Joseph, had worked in the financial division of General Foods. Cohen's parents graced her with a sense that, despite the fact that she was a girl, she could do whatever she might set out to do. In 1969, that meant going to Cornell, one of the few Ivy League colleges that accepted women as undergraduates. There, Cohen double-majored in economics and computer science—"which then was called electrical engineering," she recalled. "At that time, we worked on enormous IBM mainframes big enough to fill a room. We programmed them in languages like Fortran."[8] She met her future husband, David, in Econ 101, and after graduating they moved to Washington, D.C., where Cohen worked in the statistics division of the Federal Reserve while earning a masters in economics at George Washington University.

Following a seven-year stint as an economist at T. Rowe Price, the Baltimore-based mutual fund company, Cohen landed a job on Wall Street in 1983 as a portfolio strategist at Drexel Burnham Lambert. Cohen found herself in exactly the right place at precisely the right moment: the bull was just learning to run. Four years later she wasn't quite so lucky: in mid-1987 Drexel named Cohen its chief market strategist—just in time for the October crash.

Some gurus saw the crash coming. In September, for example, Goldman's Steve Einhorn advised his clients to sell stocks and raise cash, suggesting that they reduce their stock holdings to 40 percent of their portfolio, while increasing cash to 35 percent.

Cohen, by contrast, was blindsided. "We did not give our clients suitable warning. The experience showed that my kit was missing a tool," she later confessed.[9] Although she was caught off guard, Cohen did not lose her nerve. In the wake of Black Monday she advised Drexel's clients to buy. For those who had any cash left, it was good advice.

When Drexel collapsed under the weight of a junk bond scandal in 1990, Cohen, who was not implicated, got up, brushed the debris off her skirt, and found temporary shelter as chief market strategist at Barclays de Zoete Wedd, a London-based bank. She had been there only a few months when the call came from Goldman. Once again her stars were aligned: over the next 10 years, Abby Joseph Cohen would become the bull market's preeminent seer, "the mother of all optimists," one London paper dubbed her.[10]

But in the autumn of 1990, Cohen was not yet a bull. One of the lesser, but pointed, ironies of the bull market is that when Goldman Sachs hired Abby Joseph Cohen, she was far from enthusiastic about the market. "According to *The Wall Street Journal,* I was the biggest bear around," Cohen remembered 11 years later, half smiling, half grimacing at the thought.[11] Indeed, in September of 1990, a month before Cohen joined Goldman, the paper had described her as a "prescient bear . . . unmoved by peace, Perestroika, European unity and [other] supposed market panaceas." Instead, Cohen focused on corporate profits: "I think conditions are deteriorating," she told the *Journal.* "The growth rate of profits peaked in early 1988." [12]

Following the October 1987 crash, Cohen believed that the market would bounce back—which it did—but her optimism did not last for long. In June of 1989, she refused to be impressed by a rally that she saw as "a nice little boomlet," nothing more.[13] Roughly a year later, the Dow grazed 3000, but Cohen remained cool, noting that since the beginning of the year, "investors still would have been better off holding 3-month Treasury bills."[14] By then, the economy was sliding into the recession that would cost President George Bush his second term. A month later, Iraq's invasion of Kuwait pushed the market over the edge, confirming Cohen's fears that the rally lacked a solid foundation. By year-end the Dow had tumbled from its July high of nearly 3000 to 2365.

Cohen understood that the bull could not resume his run unless interest rates fell. "If rates were high, companies wouldn't be spending on capital investments."[15] High rates also meant paying the piper for the debt amassed in the eighties, a decade when individual, corporate, and government IOUs spiraled from 140 percent of GDP to 190 percent.[16] But Federal Reserve Chairman Alan Greenspan already had begun trimming. In January of 1989, the Fed funds rate (the rate that banks charge each other on overnight loans), stood at 9.5 percent; by the end of '90 the Fed had brought that key short-term rate down to 8.25 percent. More cuts followed, and by April of 1991, returns on three-month Treasuries had shrunk to 5.7 percent—down from 7.6 percent a year earlier—good news for brokers trying to coax investors into stocks. Meanwhile, in March an easy victory in the Gulf War buoyed spirits on the Street.

At this point, Steve Einhorn, the partner who had hired Cohen to work with him at Goldman Sachs, became openly bullish. In February of 1991, Einhorn announced that Act II of the bull market was in progress. "The single most attractive place to put money now is in the stock market," Einhorn declared, advising clients to put "60 to 65 percent of their assets in stocks"—up from his target of 40 to 45 percent only a month earlier.[17]

While Einhorn took center stage, Cohen, perhaps still chastened by the '87 crash, hung back in the wings. Even when the Dow finally closed above 3000 two months later, she remained cautious: "The P/E multiples [still] don't thrill me," said Cohen in April of 1991, referring to the fact stocks on the S&P were changing hands at 17.8 times earnings—far above the average P/E ratio of 12.6 over the preceding 10 years. But, like Einhorn, she was impressed by Greenspan's continuing cuts: "The Fed stood up and said there really is a recession, and policy has been changed to handle that."[18]

In April of 1991, the Dow stood at 3000—up from 2000 at the beginning of 1987. Not bad: the index had climbed 50 percent in less than four years. But investors could be excused if they had not enjoyed the ride. Since 1987, they had endured the biggest one-day plunge in stock market history, scandal on Wall Street, graft in the S&L banking system, a national recession, soaring white-collar unemployment, and a war that threatened stability in the Middle East. Within a few months, their fortitude would be tested once again: in late November of 1991, the Dow fell 121 points in one day.

Market watchers saw this as a crucial moment. Would investors head for the door? The financial press looked for gurus to say it wasn't so. Finally, Abby Joseph Cohen stepped forward: "What the market is going through now is transitory," Cohen declared. She made it clear that she put her faith in the Fed: "Ultimately the Fed has a significant amount of power to get us out of this malaise." [19]

At that tender point Cohen's faith in the Fed was much needed—and Alan Greenspan lived up to her expectations. At the end of 1991, the Fed chairman lopped a full point off the Federal Funds rate, bringing that key short-term rate to 4 percent—the lowest it had been in 27 years. Wall Street responded in kind: the Dow ended 1991 at 3168.83, a gain of more than 20 percent, while the Nasdaq climbed an astounding 56.8 percent, to 586.34. But even then, not everyone was sure what to make of the rally.

Cohen remained bullish, if cautious: "People must remember that the 1980's were an anomaly," Abby Joseph Cohen warned at the end of 1991.[20] They should not expect another run-up to match the sprint from 1984 to 1990 when returns averaged 15.3 percent a year.

Nevertheless, in the early nineties, she saw the economy improving: "The U.S. was turning a corner: the deficit was getting smaller," she recalled years later. "There was an upturn in capital spending on research and development. And inflation was under control. When it's out of control—and the data is puffed up by inflation—everyone makes very bad decisions." In that context, she decided that stocks were cheap. "Picture a cardigan sweater on sale half price," she urged a visitor in 2001. "It has a button missing—but who cares? Even if you're a little disappointed, there's room for error." [21]

As the bull market picked up steam, Cohen would grow into her role as the market's muse. For the rest of the decade, no matter how high stock prices climbed, Cohen never wavered in her belief in the New Economy.

And it seemed that neither the public nor the press would ever lose its faith in Cohen. As late as August of 1999—just months before the major indices peaked—*Barron's* would tell investors: "Stay Relaxed, Abby Cohen Says There's No Bear in Sight."²² Like Walter Cronkite in the sixties, or Ronald Reagan in the eighties, Abby Joseph Cohen had become one of the most trusted faces on American television.

It was no accident that the most trusted guru of the nineties turned out to be a woman. For in the eighties the bull market had become a rogue's gallery of male exhibitionists. One could argue that Wall Street was always a rogue's gallery, of course, and not be too far off the mark. But in the Greed Decade, even the pros were embarrassed. The barbarians who came through the gate had crossed a line—now some were behind bars. The Street was looking for a new image, not just for the public but for itself. The masters of the universe were about to be replaced with a Jewish mother, a prophet who, as *Business Week* noted approvingly, "wore sensible shoes." ²³

Certainly, the decade ahead would need a calming influence. The bull of the nineties proved a rough beast. As he lurched forward, breaking through one barrier after another, he would take investors on a high-speed ride. Along the way, even momentum investors suffered bouts of anxiety—doubting their good fortune and wondering how long it could last. Meanwhile, value investors began to doubt themselves. The times demanded a soothing, reassuring presence. If CNBC's blow-by-blow reporting sent your blood racing, Cohen's confident composure could settle your nerves. She could not tether the bull—nor did she try—but her genius was that she could make even an irrational market seem perfectly sensible, at least for a time.

IN WASHINGTON—ALAN GREENSPAN

The cast that drove the bull market would not be complete without its crucial Washington contingent. On the hill, senators and congressmen on both sides of the aisle, from Newt Gingrich to Joe Lieberman, extolled the virtues of the New Economy. In the White House, two presidents named Bush, father and son, presided, like bookends, over the beginning and end of the New Era. In between, the Clinton administration paid down the deficit while celebrating an economy that managed to combine low unemployment with low inflation. Along the way, the two-term president demonstrated that he could teach Wall Street's salesmen something about "spin."

But more than any of Washington's elected politicians, it was Alan Greenspan who nurtured the public's faith that however high the market might soar, the people in charge knew what they were doing.

In 1974, Gerald Ford had just moved into the White House when he asked Bill Seidman, his assistant for economic affairs, to talk to Alan Greenspan. "Before Nixon resigned, he had nominated Greenspan to become head of his Council of Economic Advisors," Seidman recalled, "but the appointment had never been confirmed, and now Ford needed to decide what to do." Years later, Seidman still remembered the scene. "After he sat down, Greenspan said to me, 'You know, I'm not a politician, I'm an economist.'

"But I thought he was okay," Seidman continued. "So I told Ford—and Greenspan got the job. Within a couple of months, it was apparent to all of us that he was a much better politician than anyone had guessed—maybe a better politician than he was an economist. And he was a good economist," added Seidman, who understood both economics and Potomac politics better than most.[24]

Heir to the accounting firm Seidman and Seidman, Bill Seidman had come to Washington a year earlier to fill a slot as an undersecretary at HUD. But the summer of 1973 turned out to be Watergate summer. Few presidential appointments would be confirmed that season, and Seidman was about to pack his bags to go home when Gerald Ford, who at that point had just been appointed vice president, asked him to help clean up the mess that a departing Vice President Spiro Agnew had left in his wake. (After being investigated by the U.S. Attorney's office in Baltimore for allegedly receiving payoffs from engineers seeking contracts while he was governor of Maryland, the Vice President had resigned. In his haste to leave town, Agnew left his office a shambles. Not the least of the items to be disposed of, Seidman recalled, were large cases of Scotch whiskey, presented to Agnew by eager supplicants.)[25] Seidman agreed to help out, and when Ford became president, he stayed on. This is when he first met Alan Greenspan.

In the Ford administration, Greenspan was, in at least one important way, the odd man out: "Everyone in the administration played tennis," Seidman recalled, "everyone except Greenspan. He didn't know one end of the racket from the other."

By 1987, however, when both Seidman and Greenspan found them-

selves back in Washington—Seidman as head of the Federal Deposit Insurance Corporation (FDIC), and Greenspan as chairman of the Federal Reserve—Greenspan had learned the game. "All of those years, he had been
taking lessons," said Seidman. And by 1987, at age 61, "Greenspan had become a pretty decent player." At first glance, Alan Greenspan does not appear cut out to be a tennis player. It is hard to imagine his somewhat
ungainly, melancholy figure dancing the baseline or rushing the net. But, as
Seidman observed, "He knew it was important—that's the kind of politician he was."[26]

Alan Greenspan had always learned by watching. When he was five
years old, his parents divorced. According to Justin Martin, one of
Greenspan's biographers, the crash of 1929 had pushed their marriage over
the edge. His mother moved back into the one-bedroom apartment where
her parents lived in the Washington Heights section of New York. There,
Greenspan and his mother slept in the dining room. But the young
Greenspan also spent time with the family of an uncle who was a successful
businessman with a summer home in the Rockaways. There, an observant,
bright child could learn about a more spacious world.[27]

After high school, Greenspan studied at the Juilliard School of Music,
and then went on to play tenor sax and clarinet for the Henry Jerome Band,
a "big band" known for its bebop sound. (Leonard Garment, who would
become President Nixon's special counsel during the Watergate hearings,
was the band's manager. In 1966 Garment introduced Greenspan to
Nixon, then Garment's law partner.) Greenspan was a workmanlike musi-
cian, and good enough to play professionally. But in an era when improvi-
sation was changing the texture of American music, he lacked both the
talent and the temperament to riff. He could only play "by the sheets"—
following the notes on the page.[28]

Already interested in business, Greenspan became the band's book-
keeper and helped his fellow musicians with their income taxes. After a year
he left the band, and in 1945, he began studying economics at New York
University's business school. From there he went on to take graduate
courses at Columbia. But Greenspan was too pragmatic to be interested in
the academic world of economic theory, and before completing a Ph.D., he
left Columbia. In 1953, at the age of 27, he became a partner at an economic consulting firm that counted companies like U.S. Steel and J.P.
Morgan among its clients. As an economist, Greenspan liked to focus on
the basic nuts and bolts of business statistics: inventories, prices, home

sales. He was obsessed with data—but the nineties image of the Fed chairman as a savant would be misleading. Among his peers, acquaintances said he was "about what you would expect from a business economist—nothing more, nothing less." [29] Greenspan would never win a Nobel Prize for economics. Nevertheless, as Bill Seidman observed, "part of his mystique is that he is hard to understand, and that also gives him a certain genius aspect." [30]

Greenspan's speaking style illustrated the limits of his empirical approach to knowledge. Often, the Fed chairman was accused of being opaque—though if you sat down to read his speeches, you would see his meaning was perfectly clear. The problem was that his bristling vocabulary got in the way of communicating. He lacked an ear both for the rhythm of the language and for its nuances. It was as if he had grown up in another country and had studied English from a very large dictionary—but had never heard the language spoken. He knew the notes, but not the phrasing. Yet, the sheer size of his vocabulary, combined with the gravitas of his physical presence, created the image of Greenspan as the wizard behind the curtain.

If Greenspan did not bring genius, he brought a certain moral passion to his post as Fed chairman. In the fifties, while honing his skills as an empiricist and a working economist, Greenspan fell under the spell of Ayn Rand, a utopian libertarian best known for her popular novels *The Fountainhead* and *Atlas Shrugged.* In these novels and in other writings, Rand celebrated individualism and laissez-faire capitalism—the belief that government should keep "hands off" free markets. Her effect on Greenspan would be long lasting. Years later, he told a reporter from the *Times:* "What she did—through long discussions and lots of arguments into the night— was to make me think why capitalism is not only efficient and practical, but also moral." In an article for Rand's *Objectivist Newsletter* written in the early sixties, Greenspan explained the basis for his belief: capitalism "holds integrity and trustworthiness as cardinal virtues and makes them pay off in the marketplace," he declared, "thus demanding that men survive by means of virtues, not of vices." [31]

It was an idealistic but flawed view. Certainly capitalism intends to reward ambition and hard work, but it is not set up to punish dishonesty or penalize a lack of integrity. An industrious robber baron can flourish—as the biographies of both turn-of-the-century rogue capitalists and modern-day adventurers like Enron's CEO Kenneth Lay demonstrate. In the marketplace, short sellers sometimes curtail the career of a rogue capitalist, but American-style capitalism assigns primary responsibility for curbing criminal ambition to government bodies: the SEC, the Justice Department, Congress, and the courts—which is why it is so important that their integrity not be compromised. If they fail, capital flows, not into the projects that might increase the wealth of nations, but into the pockets of those with the greatest clout or the strongest lobbyists.

Nevertheless, Greenspan, like Rand, believed that capitalism was inherently moral, and Rand's teaching stiffened Greenspan's own laissez-faire philosophy: insofar as possible, government should keep "hands off" and let a market that is not only efficient, but moral, have its head.

Meanwhile, during the years that he served as head of Gerald Ford's Council of Economic Advisors, Greenspan built his social and political network in the power corridor that runs from New York to Washington. Before long, he was seen squiring television personality Barbara Walters to A-list social events.[32] "Greenspan's ability to impress influential people, though rarely remarked upon, is in many ways the key to his success," observed *New Yorker* writer John Cassidy in a revealing profile of the Fed chairman. Though Cassidy noted, Ayn Rand was suspicious of Greenspan's social skills: " 'The problem with A.G. [Alan Greenspan] is he thinks Henry Luce is important,' she once remarked, referring to Time Inc.'s founder. On another occasion, she asked, 'Do you think Alan might be a social climber?' "[33]

After Ford was defeated in 1976, Greenspan left Washington, but he continued to cultivate his connections, and in 1981 President Reagan appointed him to his economic policy board. Six years later, Reagan named Alan Greenspan chairman of the Federal Reserve.

Greenspan won the job first and foremost because he was a Republican. His predecessor, Paul Volcker, was "a known Democrat" in the words of James Baker III, the Texas lawyer who served first as President Reagan's chief of staff, then as secretary of the Treasury. Baker lobbied hard to replace Volcker. He wanted a Fed chairman who shared the administration's politics, but even more he wanted a Fed chairman who would cut interest rates. Volcker would go down in history as the Fed chairman who finally broke the back of the double-digit inflation that strangled the seventies, but he had done it in the only, painful, way it could be done: by raising interest rates.

Finally, in 1987, Baker managed to engineer Volcker's retirement. "We got the son of a bitch," he told a friend in New York. "Baker was convinced that Greenspan was the person they needed at the Fed—a team player," political reporter Bob Woodward observed.[34]

On August 18, 1987, Alan Greenspan chaired his first Federal Reserve meeting. After several hours of roundtable discussion, Greenspan addressed the board: "We spent all morning, and no one even mentioned the stock market—which I find interesting in itself," he remarked.[35] With that one statement, Greenspan, however unwittingly, set the tone for Fed policy in the nineties. Wall Street, not Main Street, was now the center of the economy. Greenspan, after all, was from New York, not Washington. From his perspective, the seat of the nation's prosperity lay in lower Manhattan. And during his tenure as Fed chairman, a roaring bull market would convert much of the nation to a New Yorker's view of the world.

But in August of 1987, Greenspan was concerned that the center would not hold. Like many experienced observers, he realized that the stock market was overvalued. Worried that financial euphoria would lead to inflation, he persuaded the Fed board to do exactly the opposite of what Baker had envisioned. One month before the October 1987 crash, the Federal Reserve voted to boost the discount rate—the rate that the Fed charges banks for overnight loans—a full half percent, to 6 percent.

By making it more expensive to borrow, Greenspan hoped to slow the economy. But central bankers have limited powers: he could not forestall Black Monday. Still, he did his best to restore confidence. The day after the crash, the Federal Reserve flooded the markets with liquidity—though, in retrospect, some observers would suggest that the Fed's response may have set investors up for the high-stakes game of the nineties. "The lingering effect of the Fed's timely intervention was to leave investors believing that the markets were less risky than [they really are]," observed Leon Levy, cofounder of the Oppenheimer Funds. "The crash itself was written off as the result of a one-time and unforeseen catastrophe caused by computer selling."[36] The efficient market theory remained intact.

But if Greenspan helped sweep the lessons of '87 under the rug, he did not stop worrying about inflation. As part of his campaign to make sure that inflation was truly dead, he continued to jack up short-term rates, lifting them from 6.5 percent in March 1988 and to almost 10 percent a year later. When the Fed chairman had finished the task, inflation was no longer a threat—if it ever had been. Some economists would say that although the memory of a rising consumer price index still haunted the economy, an era of disinflation already had begun. Over the next decade, consumers could no longer assume that the price of a new car would rise every year. Prices of many items would fall. But it would be a long time before Americans would stop looking over their shoulders for the ghost of inflation—another example of how long it takes human beings to realize that they are in a new economic cycle.

What is certain is that by 1989, the economy was no longer in danger of pirouetting out of control. To the contrary, when George Bush came to the White House in January, he inherited an economy on the verge of a swoon. Greenspan recognized the need for stimulus, and in the spring of 1989, he reversed direction and began cutting interest rates, making it cheaper to borrow money. From 1989 to 1992, the Fed chairman trimmed short-term rates as if he were slicing sushi: swiftly, neatly, methodically—some 24 consecutive times. In the space of three years, overnight rates fell from 8 percent to 3 percent, the lowest rate since the sixties.[37]

Was 24 rate cuts overdoing it? During this time Greenspan pumped cash into the economy, buying Treasuries with Federal Reserve money. Before long the market was awash in cash. As the Fed poured money into the system, it raised the nation's immediate cash supply by over 12 percent in one year—the fastest one-year growth in history.

It was Greenspan's great good luck, observed Fed watcher Martin Mayer, that the people with that extra cash bought stock rather than goods and services. If they had poured the money into new cars, furniture, and clothes, inflation might have heated up. But "instead of consumer price inflation, the United States got asset price inflation": stock prices rose.[38] Asset inflation seemed, to many, benign—at least at the time.

Certainly, the Bush administration did not feel that the Fed was moving too aggressively. To the contrary, the White House agonized over how long the process was taking. The economy had slipped into a recession, and the banking system was beginning to wobble under the weight of bad debts. Throughout the eighties, newly deregulated S&Ls had been swallowing junk bonds whole, while making billions in bad real estate loans, and the failure of the Bank of New England, early in 1991, made it clear just how dire the situation had become.

Once again, it was Bill Seidman, now head of FDIC, who was brought in to mop up a Washington mess. Seidman broke the bad news to the nation in his inimitable, straightforward fashion: "My friends," he said, "there is good news and bad news. The good news is that the full faith and credit of the FDIC and the U.S. government stands behind your money at the bank. But the bad news is that you, my fellow taxpayers, stand behind the U.S. government."[39] The S&L fiasco would cost taxpayers hundreds of billions of dollars, and Seidman's refusal to sugarcoat that fact infuriated many in the White House.

The administration's initial reaction was to try to downplay the seriousness of the crisis. When Treasury Secretary Nicholas Brady suggested that Washington might be able to bail out the S&Ls by charging for FDIC insurance—say 30 cents for every $100 that a bank customer deposited in his savings account—Seidman made it clear that he did not think much of the idea of penalizing savers for the S&L's sins. "It's the reverse toaster theory," he deadpanned. "Instead of the bank giving you a toaster when you make a deposit, you give them one."[40]

The administration did not appreciate Seidman's puckish humor. John Sununu, President Bush's chief of staff, "went ballistic," an interested spectator at the FDIC confided. "The next day, he stormed into a staff meeting and said, 'This proves it. Bill Seidman is not a team player'—he went on and on. . . ."[41] But Seidman knew that the longer the politicians tried to downplay the fiasco by pretending that everything was under control, the more it would cost taxpayers in the long run. And he said so publicly. A straight shooter, Seidman managed to build credibility in Congress, where he was trusted by politicians on both sides of the aisle. In 1990, when the White House tried to oust him, Congress was enraged. It is a tribute to Seidman's skills as a politician that he survived.

In contrast to Seidman, Greenspan was a "team player," and now the Fed chairman rode to the rescue of the banks. The bad real estate loans made by the S&Ls were not the bankers' only problem. Junk bond issuers were beginning to default, while May of 1991 brought news of rising delinquencies in Citicorp's consumer-loan portfolio. In October, Citicorp itself stopped paying a dividend to its shareholders, and in December, the bank's stock closed below $10 a share—for the first time in 11 years. "It was on the day of the low trade in Citicorp, in fact, that the Fed uncharacteristically took a big step instead of a little one," noted Jim Grant in *The Trouble with Prosperity*.[42] On December 20, 1991, the Fed took an ax to the federal funds rate, whacking it by a full 1 percent, thereby bringing it down to 3.5 percent.

By slashing short-term rates, the Fed chairman opened up a gap between short-term and long-term rates that gave banks like Citicorp breathing room. When banks borrow, they pay short-term rates; when they make loans, they typically charge long-term rates. As Greenspan trimmed short-term rates, the spread between short rates and long rates widened, and banks were able to make a nice profit on the difference between what they paid when they borrowed money (for instance, the interest that they paid to customers who deposited money in bank savings accounts) and the rate they made when they lent the money out (mortgage rates, for instance, were often tied to long-term rates).

In Grant's view, "It was a short inferential hop to the conclusion that the Fed was [now] running monetary policy for the express purpose of bailing out Citi in particular, the banking system in general, and Wall Street in toto."[43]

On Wall Street, Abby Cohen and Steve Einhorn began to see hope. On the Potomac, the Bush administration was well pleased with the one-point cut. In Boston, Ned Johnson, the head of Fidelity investments, and daughter Abby, who helped run the family fiefdom, must have been turning somersaults. Lower short-term rates drove small investors out of bank savings accounts—and into the waiting arms of the mutual fund industry. 1993 would be the best year on record for the industry, as some 700 new funds opened their doors.

As for Greenspan himself, he had set a precedent for his tenure as Fed chairman: from now on, he would be the guy who rode to the rescue. So much for his laissez-faire philosophy. When he cut rates 24 times from 1989 to 1992, Greenspan established a pattern. In times of financial crisis, he could be counted on to pump liquidity into the financial system, providing enough cash—and, more important, enough confidence—to assure those who ran the system that they could backstroke their way out of almost any fiscal problem. At least that is what many believed.

The one person Greenspan did not save was President George H. W. Bush. In January of 1992, the president's second term seemed all but sewn up. The election was 10 months away and no one knew the Democratic candidate's name. Certainly, Greenspan had done his best by lopping a full point off short-term rates at the end of 1991. There was just one ominous note: only 50 percent of all shareholders gave the president a "favorable" rating—down from 70 percent a year earlier—while Alan Greenspan, his Fed chairman, won favor from 80 percent of those citizens who bought stock.[44] It seemed that voters still blamed the president for the recession.

Many in the Bush administration would say that Alan Greenspan betrayed them: the rate cuts did not come soon enough. Whatever the case, on Election Day, November 1992, the malaise of a recession still hanging over Main Street, Americans voted with their pocketbooks. Bill Clinton's slogan "It's the Economy, Stupid!" carried the day.

Alan Greenspan, however, did not have to run for office in the autumn of 1992. He would remain chairman of the Federal Reserve, and throughout the nineties, he would manage to maintain Wall Street's confidence.

The Fed chairman's power was manifest when a newly elected President Clinton unveiled his economic plan to a joint session of Congress on February 18, 1993. When the camera panned the House gallery, it found Hillary Rodham Clinton, the president's wife. On her left, Alan Greenspan.

The king is dead. Long live the king.[45]

THE ANALYSTS

The nineties may have cast Abby Cohen as Wall Street's leading lady, and Alan Greenspan as its wiseman, but of course there were other seers. Some tried to resist the role, but the media tended to treat Wall Street pros, such as Morgan Stanley's Byron Wein and Barton Biggs, Prudential's Ralph Acampora, PaineWebber's Ed Kerschner, and Donaldson, Lufkin & Jenrette's Tom Galvin, as clairvoyants. And they were not the only soothsayers who found themselves in the media spotlight.

Suddenly, once-humble research analysts found a star on their dressing room door. In the past they had labored alone, in small cubicles, surrounded by tall stacks of paper. Traditionally, very few women could ever hope to become traders or portfolio managers on Wall Street—who would trust them with all of that money? But an intelligent woman could hope to be hired as a research analyst. That fact alone defined the status of the job.

In the nineties, however, "research analysts" were no longer extras. As the bull market rolled forward, Wall Street firms discovered that their analysts' reports could send an unknown company into orbit. On television, the chattering classes took analysts' "estimates" of what a company might earn as a target—and companies learned to make sure that the target was reached.

A decade earlier, only investment bankers and top traders could hope to take home what Tom Wolfe called "salaries like telephone numbers."

But now analysts such as Salomon Brothers' Jack Grubman, Merrill Lynch's Henry Blodget, and Morgan Stanley's Mary Meeker were seen as the New Era's wheeler-dealers. During Act II of the bull market most investment bankers kept a low profile: the pin-striped players had their fill of publicity in the eighties. Now, the analysts began moving center stage. Grubman, a veteran telecom analyst, reported that his wife called their sudden prominence "the revenge of the nerds." [46]

Mary Meeker

A year after Abby Cohen joined Goldman, the firm that would become Goldman's chief rival in the decade ahead, Morgan Stanley, hired the woman destined to play the ingenue in the drama about to unfold, Mary Meeker. Before the decade was out, the 30-something Internet analyst would be anointed the diva of the dot.com world. When *Barron's* crowned her "Queen of the Net," the magazine explained that in the Internet sector, Meeker was "the ax." In the race to go public, her word decided which new companies made the final cut. [47]

Business Week, which had applauded Abby Cohen for her "sensible shoes," seemed to like Meeker for some of the same reasons. "Raised in rural Indiana, she's plain-spoken and humble. But all that only masks her laser-sharp analytical skills." [48] In other words, she was very smart, but no Martha Stewart. Wall Street liked arrogance only in its men—not in its women.

Nor was she a vamp. Meeker wore little or no makeup and kept her straight brown hair short. She belonged to the generation who played Xtreme Sports in college—sometimes she slipped into surfer talk, calling someone "wicked smart." In other words, she was part of the generation that "got it" about the New Technology. Indeed, in 1995, Mary Meeker and Netscape wunderkind Marc Andreessen estimated that perhaps only 400 people on the planet "really get the Net." Meeker was perhaps the only one of the 400 on Wall Street. "She sees how large the opportunity is—and encourages us to think big," said Amazon CEO Jeffrey Bezos. [49]

Frank Quattrone, perhaps the best known, and certainly the most flamboyant, investment banker of the nineties, recruited the 32-year-old Meeker for her job at Morgan Stanley. No doubt he recognized a kindred spirit. Granted, Meeker came from a small farming community in Indiana, while Quattrone had grown up in a two-story row house in south Philadelphia (a neighborhood best known by non-Philadelphians as the setting for the movie *Rocky*). But both were self-made, and they shared the same drive. "They were each very focused," said a colleague who knew them well. He paused. "Mary is not unlike Frank and Mary and Frank are not unlike Sherman going through Atlanta." [50]

Meeker's interest in the market began early. As a high school student in Indiana, she entered a stock-picking contest and watched her choices double. After graduating from DePauw University in Illinois, Meeker spent two years as a Merrill Lynch broker in Chicago before heading east to earn an MBA at Cornell. At Cornell, Meeker was never very interested in courses that involved crunching numbers, but she was smart—and extremely ambitious. "She knew exactly what she wanted," said Harold Bierman, one of her professors at the time. "And my course in corporate finance—which involved a lot of numbers and a lot of symbols—was not what she looking for. She let me know that.

"My course insisted on the details," he added. "She was interested in more intangible things. She was a visionary, not a number-pusher." Still, he admired her confidence and determination. "With some students, you wouldn't care if they didn't like your course. But she was bright, very composed, very self-confident; she knew what she was looking for, and I wasn't teaching it." When Meeker graduated from Cornell in 1986, she landed her first job on Wall Street at Salomon Brothers in New York. "At that time, we didn't give graduates much help in finding jobs," Bierman recalled, "but I give her credit—she must have really bird-dogged it to get that job." [51]

At Salomon, Meeker found her niche as a junior analyst, working with the firm's senior computer analyst, Michele Preston. When Preston jumped to S.G. Cowen in 1990, Meeker followed. A year later, Frank Quattrone spotted Meeker and offered her the opportunity to become a senior analyst at Morgan Stanley, following PCs and computer software. Before long, she had found two of the stocks that would make her reputation: Dell and AOL. Mary Meeker was on her way, with Frank Quattrone as her guide.

Over the next few years Quattrone built his reputation as the New Technology's top investment banker. By the end of the decade, he would wind up at Credit Suisse First Boston, overseeing his own investment banking fiefdom—and earning a reported $100 million a year. Wherever Frank Quattrone went, he took Silicon Valley's investment banking business with him. After he moved to Credit Suisse, the firm would take more technology companies public than any other firm on Wall Street. When the party ended, some would call him "the nineties' Mike Milken." [52]

"Frank was probably the best banker I've ever run into: incredibly smart, and equally shrewd—which is different," said a colleague at Credit Suisse. "The bad side was that he had only one word in his vocabulary: *more*. 'What have you done for me today? Fine. What are you doing for me tomorrow? Fine. The day after? Fine. The day after that?' He was the kind of guy who could say, 'Great, you've brought in $100 million worth of business this year. But it's December 27. There are four days left in the year—what are you doing *now?*' " [53]

Quattrone had joined Morgan Stanley in 1979, a time when few on Wall Street knew much about what was happening on the West Coast. "High-tech deals were dominated by smaller California firms," said a former colleague. "But Frank was shrewd enough to make the Valley his home. And, when he went to meet with a CEO, he wore a sweater and a polo shirt." Meanwhile, the investment banking divisions of other Wall Street firms were still based in New York. "They would send bankers out here wearing yellow ties and suspenders," recalled one venture capitalist. "Frank, on the other hand, understood that this is not the land of the CEO with a corporate dining room and servers who wear white gloves. Out here, no one asked, 'Where did you go to college?' They asked, 'Where do you work?' In the investment banking world of New York, Ivy League schools and bloodlines were still very important. But here, the college dropout drew as much—or more—reverence than the guy with all the grades. Output was more important than pedigree." [54]

In 1990, Frank Quattrone snagged Cisco as a client and took the company public—a major coup for Morgan Stanley. But in the years that followed, Quattrone did not feel that he was receiving his due. Each time he made the pilgrimage to the bank's Manhattan headquarters, he made clear what he wanted: *more*. More control over the investment bankers who worked for him. More control over the research analysts. More money.

Morgan Stanley president John Mack gave him more, but not enough. On Easter Sunday, 1996, in what insiders at the firm called "the Easter massacre," Quattrone would decamp for Deutsche Morgan Grenfell, taking top members of the investment banking team with him. Once he settled into his new job, Quattrone tried to steal Meeker as well. But, shrewdly, she elected to stay behind.

Meeker would take over Quattrone's job. Her title was still research analyst, but now she was the one who would take the lead on Morgan
Stanley's IPOs. A year earlier, when Morgan Stanley took Netscape Communications public, Meeker was already an important part of the investment banking team. She claimed to have brought the company to
Quattrone's attention—a claim that Quattrone denied.[55] What is clear is
that she felt some responsibility for the fledgling IPO—the first profitless
company ever to offer its shares to the American public.

Its first day out, the stock spiraled. By day's end, the market had decided that Netscape was worth $2 billion. The next morning, *The Wall
Street Journal* insisted that the IPO's "breathtaking rise" was not a red flag
signaling that the market was frothy. After all, it was only one stock:
"Netscape isn't worrisome to the bulls," the paper assured its readers.[56]

While the *Journal* remained sanguine, Meeker was frankly terrified. As
Netscape soared, she stood on the trading floor, amazed. When it hit $72,
someone turned to her to say, "Isn't this exciting?!"

"I just looked at him, and almost started to cry because now I had to
deal with this," Meeker later recalled.[57]

Nevertheless, she was a pragmatist. Once she steadied herself, Meeker
forged ahead, making the most of the opportunity. In 1995, just four
months after Netscape went public, Meeker published a 300-page research
report called simply "The Internet Report." On Wall Street, an eight-page
research report was considered thorough. Her opus made her famous. "At
that point, she went from 0 to 90," said Morgan Stanley partner Byron
Wein.[58]

At Morgan Stanley, Meeker brought in the business. Fledgling companies chose Morgan Stanley over other investment banks because they
wanted Meeker's imprimatur on their offering plan. Many of the firms she
attracted would become the New Technology's blue chips. At the end of
1995, she recommended a portfolio for investors interested in playing the
Internet: America Online, Ascend Communications, Cascade Communications, Cisco Systems, and Intuit. (Morgan Stanley had helped all five
raise cash, either through IPOs or secondary offerings.)[59]

Meeker's loyalty to the Internet companies that she covered would be
nearly messianic: "Mary felt it was her mission to get the word out about
the Internet—that these companies were special—that it was her responsibility to tell the world about them," said a colleague who was also a friend.
When Deutsche Morgan Grenfell analyst Bill Gurley downgraded Net-

scape in 1997, "he saw that the orders were not coming in—and Mary went ballistic. Even after the numbers came out, proving that Bill was right, she was furious. To this day, she blames Gurley for Netscape's downfall. As she saw it, analysts weren't there to investigate and tell the story—they were there to write the story—to transmit the vision." [60]

THE INDIVIDUAL INVESTOR

THE RISE OF THE 401(K)

Over the course of the eighties, employers took one look at a generation of baby boomers treadmilling their way toward middle age and paled. Boomers who had given up smoking before they turned 30 were switching from red meat to fish and replacing Scotch with lite beer. They checked their cholesterol yearly, swam laps weekly, and weighed themselves daily. Appalled at the prospect of supporting a horde of octogenarian vegetarians, corporations began to rethink pension plans that pledged lifetime benefits to all of their retirees.

By 1991, one-third of all retirement plans were 401(k)s.[1] Until then, the majority of all pensions promised a fixed benefit equal to a percentage of the employee's salary during his final years of service. Under these plans, employers agreed to keep the checks coming, year after year, for better or worse, as long as the retiree might live. As a safety net, the federal government set up an insurance pool funded by private-sector employers. In '91, if a company underfunded its pension plan and then went belly-up, the insurance pool covered pensions up to $27,000 a year.[2]

The 401(k), by contrast, avoided commitment. Under the new "defined contribution" plans (which included both 401(k)s and profit-sharing plans), employers promised only that they would contribute a certain amount to an employee's nest egg while he was working. What happened to the money after they parted was the employees' responsibility. How long they lived, and how far their savings stretched, was their problem, not his.

Corporate management feared that long-term liability, not only because boomers could be expected to live so much longer than their parents, but because corporate profits were sluggish. "The 401(k) was the child of a slow-growth period in the American economy," William Wolman and Anne Colamosca observe in *The Great 401(k) Hoax.* "[It was] the years beginning with the OPEC oil embargo in 1973, to the mid-1990s that undermined the old pension system. The 401(k) became the new model, not during a period when American capitalism was enjoying great economic success but rather when the corporations were having a tough time making money."[3] In the meantime, the Employee Retirement Income Security Act (ERISA) passed in 1974 had made it both more difficult and more expensive to run a traditional pension program—a particular problem for smaller employers.

For the employer, then, the advantages of a 401(k) were clear. The new retirement plans offered low-cost marriage and no-fault divorce. From the outset, 401(k)s were far cheaper than traditional pensions: employers saved both the expense of managing the money and the cost of paying the premiums for federal pension insurance. (401[k]s would not be insured.) And, over time, the employer's role in funding the plans would shrink: in 1989, employers contributed roughly 70 percent of the money that went into retirement plans; by 2002, employees' cash contributions outstripped company payments into retirement plans of all kinds—including traditional pensions.[4] Moreover, while employees put cash on the table, employers often matched their money with company shares. In this way, a corporation could mask the expense of funding a pension: accounting rules allowed corporations to contribute stock to a 401(k) without deducting the cost on their income statements.

No wonder so many companies embraced the 401(k). But employees proved almost as enthusiastic. Gamely, the majority accepted the responsibility of managing their own retirements and took pride in their new freedom. Your employer no longer decided how to invest your retirement money—you did.

The new system offered other major advantages. For one, the new retirement plans gave employees a chance to defer paying taxes on their nest eggs—a tax break second only to the deduction for home mortgages. Secondly, the 401(k) was portable. If an employee changed jobs, he could take his retirement fund with him. For an increasingly mobile workforce, the portability of the new plans was essential. Under a classic pension plan, a worker could lose his benefits if he made a move; at the very least, job hoppers saw their benefits diminished. (Because a defined-benefit plan builds up slowly, most of its worth comes in the later years of an employee's career, making it most valuable to the employee who stays for the long haul.)

Labor unions were the only major group to view the 401(k) with mistrust, and they retained power only in the public sector. There, old-fashioned pension plans would remain the rule: in 1998, more than three-quarters of all unionized workers were still covered by a guaranteed fixed payment.[5] But in the nineties, unions held little sway over private-sector workers, who, by and large, embraced the benefits of the new plan. By 2000, less than 30 percent of all U.S. workers covered by a retirement plan could count on a fixed, continuous payout after they retired.[6]

In a single stroke, the risk of saving and investing for retirement flipped from the employer to the employee. It would prove a seismic shift.

The Individual Investor Fuels Act II (1990)

Without the 401(k), it is fair to say, Act II of the bull market might well never have gotten off the ground. The LBOs of the eighties had dried up, and the professionals who oversaw the old-fashioned pension funds of the early nineties still preferred bonds over stocks. But the employees who began managing their own retirement funds in the early years of the decade proved more daring. By 1993, 401(k) investors were wagering more than half of their savings on stocks or stock funds.[7]

New investors poured into the market. Mutual funds marketed to them. Newly launched financial magazines advised them. Financial experts urged them to take more risk, warning that unless they achieved double-digit returns on their savings, they would never be able to retire. With interest rates on both money market accounts and bank savings accounts sinking, equities seemed the new investors' only choice. By 1995, Fidelity Magellan, the king of equity funds, reported that 87 percent of the fresh money flowing into its coffers could be traced to retirement savings.[8]

Of course, not all of the newcomers were buying stocks for a 401(k). But the 401(k) led the way, bringing a new class of investor to the market—one who could ill afford to lose his savings. Some of the newcomers were buying stocks for other tax-deferred plans: IRAs and Keoghs were becoming increasingly popular. Still others, drawn by the sizzle of a market that was making their neighbors rich, bought equities with savings earmarked for college tuition or the down payment on a house. As early as 1992, Americans with incomes under $75,000 owned 42 percent of all publicly traded stocks.[9]

Jennifer Postlewaithe epitomized the individual investor of the early nineties.[10] A tall redhead, Postlewaithe was modeling for clothing catalogues in Chicago in the early seventies when she met her husband, a history professor at a Midwestern university. In the years that followed, she gave up modeling but continued to work part-time in a local clothing store while raising their four children. Their joint income was modest, but both Postlewaithe and her husband were savers, and throughout the eighties they managed to make the maximum contribution to her husband's retirement plan. Like most university professors, he was covered by a version of the 401(k) administered by TIAA-CREF, the world's largest pension fund manager. Under the plan, he could not pick individual stocks, but he was given the choice between putting his money into CREF—which invested the money in a diversified portfolio of stocks—or TIAA, which invested in mortgages, bonds, and other fixed-income investments. Like many academics, he took the path of least resistance, investing 50 percent in stocks, 50 percent in fixed income.

In 1994, Postlewaithe and her husband divorced. They were still putting two children through college, had no savings other than the TIAA-CREF retirement plan, and owed $75,000 on a home worth roughly $125,000. Postlewaithe, who had just turned 51, had no recent work experience except her part-time job at the clothing store, which paid only minimum wage. The one bright spot was that it was an amicable divorce and she and her husband agreed to split their assets 50/50. After selling the house and paying the broker, the closing costs, and the divorce attorneys, she wound up with nearly $90,000—$70,000 of it in an IRA that had been rolled over from her husband's retirement plan.

TIAA-CREF was one of the nation's most respected pension fund managers, but Jennifer Postlewaithe thought she could do a better job of managing her money. For one, she believed that her husband had put too much of their savings into fixed-income investments. "He had no interest in the market—or anything to do with business," Postlewaithe recalled. "If it didn't happen in the 17th century, he didn't care."

The bull market was beginning to roll, and she itched to try her hand at picking stocks. "I had grown up on a farm, and so I was familiar with markets—the whole idea of buying and selling," she explained. "And my mother always had owned a few stocks." In the eighties, Jennifer Postlewaithe's appetite had been whetted by watching her best friend and next-door neighbor play the market. "Vicariously, I followed her investing career." She remembered when her friend bought Apple, and then Microsoft. As she drove her children to school, to hockey practice, to their friends' homes, Postlewaithe started listening to what was said about the Nasdaq on the radio. "It was like following a sport," Postlewaithe recalled. "I didn't have any money to buy individual stocks myself, but it was a game—seeing how much it had gone up—feeling a little depressed if it went down." Meanwhile, her friend's portfolio grew: "She remodeled her kitchen; she and her husband took vacations to Europe—and with all that spending, they still had far more savings than we did."

No longer yoked to her stick-in-the-mud husband, in 1994 Postlewaithe set out to do some research of her own. Following her friend's advice, she went to the library and consulted Value Line, a financial service that produces in-depth research reports. Microsoft was one of her first investments. Then, Dell and Intel.

"I was proud of myself. Here I was, independent for the first time in my life, investing my own money." Before long, her original $90,000 had grown to $150,000 . . . then $200,000. Postlewaithe was elated. She bought AOL and Amazon.com. "I really didn't want to spend any of the money," she recalled. "I just liked buying more shares—and watching my holdings mount. First, I'd buy 100 shares of something, then another 150 . . . often they'd split. And I liked the idea that I would have something to leave to my children—something of my own." By 2001, Postlewaithe was managing a portfolio worth more than $500,000—though roughly a third of that was "on margin," stocks she owned with money that she had borrowed from her online broker.

Jennifer Postlewaithe was just one of many women who flexed their financial muscles in the nineties. Shirley Sauerwein was another.[11] Sauerwein, a social worker in Redondo Beach, California, first dipped her toe into the water in 1991. "I had never considered buying stocks," said Sauerwein. "I didn't understand the market." But one day in August of 1991, the 47-year-old heard a story on her car radio about a local company that had signed a contract with Russia. It sounded interesting. After calling for more information, she set up her first brokerage account and bought 100 shares at $12 each. Eight years later, that company had a new name: MCI World-Com. Sauerwein's original $1,200 investment was now worth $15,000—part of a mid-six-figure portfolio that included Red Hat, Yahoo!, General Electric, and America Online.

Sauerwein's husband, James, who was a program manager at Hughes Aircraft, had a 401(k); in time, she would take a hand in managing that, too. But since her employer did not offer a retirement plan, Sauerwein kept her shares in a taxable brokerage account. Like many American families, the couple now had most of their savings invested in stocks, and in 1999, *The Wall Street Journal* singled out Sauerwein as an example of the individual investor's new power: "Along with Wall Street's heavy hitters, Main Street investors like Ms. Sauerwein have emerged as a powerful financial force in the 1990s, simultaneously boosting their net worths beyond their wildest dreams and helping to propel the market to records. Indeed, individual investors now account for more than 30% of the New York Stock Exchange's trading volume, up from less than 15% in 1989."

By 1999 Sauerwein had cut back her social work to weekends and was spending weekdays trading full-time from home. "I make a few buys and a few sells each day," she said. In one year, she had made $150,000. On the face of it, when *The Wall Street Journal* left her in 1999, Sauerwein sounded like a lamb just waiting to be shorn. But when a runaway market finally hit a wall, she would emerge from the wreck, a survivor.

"I'm not a smart cookie," Sauerwein insisted, yet she turned out to be a very shrewd investor. Throughout the nineties, she never subscribed to the decade's mantra, buy and hold: "I never thought it would last. I just thought, 'I'll get in and buy some tulips,'" she said, referring to the infamous Tulipmania that swept 17th-century Holland.

Shirley Sauerwein combined commonsense savvy with investment discipline. "When I was a little girl my grandmother and I would play the horses on paper," she recalled, "and I found it's a good thing to do with stocks. Before buying a company, I followed it on paper." But she would be the first to admit that luck played a role in her investing career, and her awareness that investing is a game of chance as well as skill protected her against falling in love with her own portfolio. "It is safer to be a speculator than an investor," economist John Maynard Keynes once remarked, "in the sense . . . that a speculator is one who runs risks of which he is aware and an investor is one who runs risks of which he is unaware." [12] Sauerwein knew that she was speculating. It was like playing the horses. As a result, she was humble before the market: "If a stock goes up, it's not because I'm a whiz," she said, "and if it goes against me, I don't stick around. I tried to follow the advice given by *Investor Business Daily's* editor—'sell when it's down 7 percent.' *The Wall Street Journal* never told you that," she added. In general, Sauerwein learned to take the advice served up by financial journalists with a grain of salt: "Whenever I bought anything that *Money* magazine recommended, I lost money."

"WHAT IF THEY GOOF UP?"

In the nineties, Postlewaithe and Sauerwein were just two of the many Americans who ventured into the market for the first time. In 1992, *The Wall Street Journal* published a story that raised a rude but unavoidable question: "By the year 2000, employees will be managing $1 trillion of their own money in 401(k) retirement plans. What if they goof up?" [13]

It was a brave lead. In the last decade of the 20th century, anyone who suggested that individual investors might "goof up" risked being branded an elitist. And in a decade that prized the idea of a democratic market, "elitist" had become a particularly dirty word, observed social historian Thomas Frank. He quoted *Time* magazine contributor William Henry: " 'Sometime in 1992, it dawned on me that the term 'elitist' . . . has come to rival if not outstrip 'racist' as the foremost catchall pejorative of our times.' " [14]

Yet it was only common sense to suspect that an individual investor might well lack the training, the time, and the talent needed to navigate markets: "Many a man or woman who would not expect to be successful as a circus clown, opera singer or grocer, without some kind of preparation or talent, nevertheless expects to be successful right off in the stock market— probably the most intricate and difficult game on earth," warned Fred Kelly, an author and professional investor, in 1930. [15]

Of course, in the nineties, the small investor had far more information at his fingertips than his counterpart in the twenties. But bits and bytes of information can be more dangerous than ignorance. Or, as Malcolm

"Steve" Forbes Jr., heir to the Forbes publishing dynasty, once confessed, "My grandfather told me you make more selling information than you do following it. So let that be a warning." [16]

Later in the decade, 401(k) investors who had been burned by bad information would realize that the traditional pension had offered one major advantage: no matter how well or how badly the market did, the pension promised a check for life. Still, the guaranteed pension checks were usually quite small. And while a small paycheck is certainly better than no paycheck, inflation could easily turn a fixed payment into a pittance, as so many retirees learned in the seventies. Unlike Social Security benefits, pension payments were not adjusted for inflation. By contrast, if a 401(k) investor stashed his savings in stocks, he could keep up with inflation—or at least that was what he was told.

That this had not been the case in the seventies was largely ignored. From 1971 to 1981, inflation averaged 8.3 percent a year, while the total return from equities, even after reinvesting dividends, was just 5.8 percent: in other words, an investor who had entrusted his nest egg to stocks lost an average of 2.5 percent a year, year after year. Over the next 10 years, however, the S&P 500 whipped inflation. By 1991, real (inflation-adjusted) total returns had averaged 13.7 percent a year for a decade.[17] Understandably, small investors wanted a piece of the action—and they were beginning to suspect that the pros running their pension funds lacked the nerve to ride a bull.

Critics groused that the professionals who ran the old-fashioned plans were too conservative. Many of the pros were still haunted by the harrowing market of 1966–82, the 16-year span that began and ended with the Dow at 1000. Even if they had not lived through the market of the seventies, they heard the stories from colleagues who survived. True, a bull market had begun in 1982, but no one knew how long it would last. Some state pension funds were not even allowed to invest in stocks. Pension fund sponsors felt the burden of their fiduciary responsibility: while the market might fluctuate, a pension could not. When the time came, the employer could not tell a retiring employee: "Well, you'll just have to work a few years longer—or get by on a little less." (This, of course, is precisely what many employees would have to tell themselves, a decade later, when they took a look at their shriveled 401[k]s.)

The pros may have had their reasons for erring in the direction of caution, but some went way overboard, putting too many eggs in the bond basket. Until 1990, for instance, 100 percent of New York City's Teacher's Retirement Fund was invested in fixed-income investments. Admittedly, this was an extreme case, but at the end of the eighties the average corporate pension fund allocated only 45 percent of its assets to equities, while public-sector pension funds stashed just 37 percent in stocks.[18]

Observers charged that such a stodgy strategy would never produce the billions needed to support the legions of boomers who would begin retiring in less than 20 years. Already, payouts were pyramiding while contributions were dwindling. By 1991, 20 percent of all corporate pension plans were underfunded according to estimates by the Pension Benefit Guaranty Corp. (PBGC), a federal agency set up to insure private funds.[19]

What no one knew in 1991 was that over the next eight years, both the stock market and the bond market would soar. Arguably, the plush profits of the bull market could have made up for the shortfalls—though slippery accounting makes it difficult to assess just how profitable the nineties were. More to the point, corporate managers had many other uses for those earnings: awarding themselves stock options, buying back shares to offset the dilution of earnings per share created by the options, acquiring other companies in an effort to boost their balance sheets, paying lawyers and bankers for their services as financial engineers. . . . Creative accounting was expensive.

Meanwhile, companies that continued to offer traditional pensions failed to use the boom as an opportunity to build a hedge against the next bust. Rather than piling up a fat surplus, most cut back on their contributions—as if double-digit returns would continue indefinitely. To be fair, many companies had no choice. If bullish projections showed that they were 150 percent funded, they could not add to the pension fund without losing their tax break.[20] When the bear market hit, most turned out to be as unprepared as many 401(k) investors. By 2003, traditional pensions at some of the nation's largest corporations were facing a crisis: employers needed to step up their contributions at a time when earnings were anemic, at best.

Still, by 2003 it was apparent old-fashioned pensions offered many employees better protection than a 401(k). For one, under the traditional pension system, an investor's exposure to his own company's stock was limited. Federal law made it illegal for an employer to invest more than one-tenth of the pension's assets in company stock on the grounds that if both an employee's livelihood and his savings pivoted on his company's financial health, he would be carrying too many eggs in one basket. But the law did not shield 401(k) investors—by 2001, the average 401(k) would have nearly 40 percent of its assets tangled in company stock.[21] Moreover, 401(k)s were not insured. By contrast, in 2003 the federal government guaranteed old-fashioned pensions up to $3,600 a month.[22]

In 1991, the advantages of the 401(k) for both employer and employee had seemed clear. Twelve years later, observers began to ask: Was the 401(k) really such a boon for employees?

The answer would vary widely, depending on who you were, how much your employer contributed to your account, whether he made his contribution in cash or stock, whether you took profits as stocks spiraled— and, above all, how early you got into the bull market of 1982–99. If you were very, very lucky, you were part of the generation that began saving and investing in the early eighties and retired in the late nineties, moving most of your money out of equities and into fixed-income investments, just before the millennium ended. If very unlucky, your prime years of earning and saving coincided with the final years of a bull market that crashed a few years before you retired—while 90 percent of your nest egg was still invested in stocks. As always, in any market, everything pivoted on how much you paid when you got in—and when you needed to cash out.

Gary Wasserman would be one of the lucky ones, not only because he began investing early, but because he had been chastened by nearly 15 years of experience before Act II of the bull market began.[23] Professionals like Bill Fleckenstein, a portfolio manager in Seattle, pointed out that even pros learn how to ride the market only through direct, often sorrowful, experience: "No matter what they tell you on television, information is not knowledge," Fleckenstein warned. "You know what you have to do to be a good investor? Make a lot of mistakes—and learn from them. The market has a lot of tricks and curves, and you have to encounter each and every one of them to learn."[24]

Wasserman, who began his career as an investor in the mid-seventies, had plenty of time to make mistakes. At the time, he was in his 20s, teaching at a college in Brooklyn. Like Sauerwein's husband, he was covered by TIAA-CREF and had the freedom to decide how to divide his nest egg between CREF—the fund that invested in equities—and TIAA, the fixed-income fund that invested in mortgages and bonds. Without too much thought, Wasserman bet $3,000 on bonds and $5,000 on stocks.

On the side, he played the stock market himself—without much success. "I just lost and lost—all of the time," Wasserman remembered cheerfully in 2002. "It was always only a question of how much I would lose. I found that if you lost money on stocks, you got more speculative," he continued. "Rather than buying two shares of a $50 stock, I would get 50 shares of a $2 stock"—a strategy not unlike playing the long shots at the track. "This is how sophisticated I was. Luckily, I didn't have much money, so I didn't have much to lose. It was like playing Lotto. It wasn't investing. I wasn't setting it aside for something in particular. I was gambling."

By the early eighties, Wasserman had moved out of teaching and more or less forgot about his nest egg in TIAA-CREF. "As both the market improved and my own situation improved, I did get a little better at investing. I started putting money into an IRA, and always put it into a T. Rowe Price mutual fund." But, he recalled, this strategy also backfired. The T. Rowe Price family of funds offered the opportunity to transfer between money market funds and stock funds, "and I always switched at exactly the wrong time, investing through the rearview mirror," Wasserman explained. "The problem was that I had too much control over it. That was also a lesson. In the eighties I finally moved to funds that wouldn't let me play games by switching back and forth. To this day, I avoid families of funds."

He had better luck with bonds: "In 1980, I began buying corporate bonds. Pacific Tel, for example, offered a 30-year bond paying around 16 percent. I'd buy them on margin, carry them for nothing, and either sell them or sell part and collect 16 percent on the rest." Unfortunately, he did not collect 16 percent for long: "As usual, you find life intruding. I wound up selling the bonds in '83 or '84—I was starting a satire magazine, and I put the money into that. And of course, lost all of that money. The magazine went under."

By the early nineties, Wasserman, always resilient, had launched a new career as a political consultant and writer in Washington, D.C. He was a success. By then he was married, had a family, had bought a house, and was making good money. Things were getting serious. He began putting the maximum that he could into retirement. In the meantime, Wasserman remembered the nest egg he had left sitting in TIAA-CREF. "In 1989, after 15 years, I finally took a look at it," he recalled. Of the many investment strategies that he had tried, benign neglect turned out to be the winner, hands down: "The $3,000 I put into bonds had grown to $6,000. The $5,000 in stocks had grown to $30,000. And that was it for me. The clouds parted . . . I had a vision. And after that, I put everything I had into stocks."

Fortunately, by now, Wasserman had been weathered by experience. He took a cautious approach and put most of his money in conservative funds such as the Clipper Fund and GMO's Pelican Fund. Although these were not the most familiar names of the nineties, by the end of the decade their total return would outshine many a marquee fund. At last, Wasserman seemed to have found a system that worked. Just one question remained: Would he stick with these choices, or would he, like so many other investors, be seduced by the siren call of high-flying stocks? Wasserman offered one hint: "I didn't buy Internet stocks until 2000." [25]

Nevertheless, Gary Wasserman survived the nineties better than most because he had waded into a difficult market while still very young, wagering small sums. Other investors learned how to invest by reading the generally cheerful personal finance magazines that filled newsstands in the early nineties, and then plunked down most of their life savings. But Wasserman had studied in the school of hard knocks. Gradually, he figured out that he was not Warren Buffett. "It's surprising how long it takes to learn," he said with some irony, looking back over a 25-year investing career.

Among the baby boomers who came to the bull market of the nineties, Wasserman would be the exception. Few members of his generation remembered the frustrating market of the seventies: it was not a young man's market. As for the older investors who suffered through the crash of 1973–74, by the time the next bull market began eight years later, the majority had retired from the field, so badly burned that they would never touch a stock again. As a result, most of the investors who buoyed the bull market of the nineties had never seen a bear. In 2002, fully 56 percent of those who owned stocks or stock funds had purchased their first shares sometime after 1990, while 30 percent of all equity investors had gotten their feet wet only after 1995. [26]

The new investor would be the final, crucial member of the cast needed to stage Act II of the Great Bull Market of 1982–99. Without his enthusiasm, his faith—and, above all, his cash—the bull market could never have spiraled so high, nor lasted so long.

THE NEWCOMERS SWITCH TO STOCKS

As the nineties began, mutual fund companies scrambled to attract the newcomers. By 1992, they were succeeding. That summer, 1 in 10 mutual fund shareholders had purchased his or her first fund in the past 18 months. Nearly three-quarters of the novices snapped up mutual funds that invested in stocks. The median age of the new mutual fund investor was 37, his or her median household income $50,000. Fully 42 percent were women.

Many of the investors who came to the market in the nineties were baby boomers, but others, like Sauerwein and Postlewaithe, were older.[27] Some financial professionals attempted to caution the novices. In 1993, Neal Litvak, head of Fidelity's product marketing, personally manned Fidelity's flooded phone lines for a day and a half each week. Litvak found the vast majority of investors opening new accounts fell into two groups: boomers in their 30s and early 40s, and older bank customers venturing into the markets for the first time. The greenhorns made him nervous. "The truly scary group are the 45- to 65-year-olds who have never touched a stock or a bond before in their lives," Litvak confessed at the time. "We try to get these people to split their CD money between money markets and short-term government bond funds, but when they look at the menu of funds that we offer, their eyes gravitate to the double digits. They think bonds have a yield just like their CD. They think the Magellan Fund has a fixed rate of return. Many have no idea their principal is at risk." The kicker, said Litvak: "These folks represent half of the people coming into mutual funds."[28]

Why were so many so willing to venture into unfamiliar waters? The short answer, both for the boomers and for the older investors, was interest rates below 3 percent—unimaginable just a few years earlier.

Throughout the eighties most Americans chased yield, sinking their savings into whatever bank accounts, CDs, or money market funds paid the highest rate. But during this period, returns on most bonds plunged. From 1989 to 1992, Fed Chairman Alan Greenspan dutifully whittled away at short-term interest rates, and by 1992 CDs and money market funds were paying as little as 4 percent. Municipal bonds had fallen to 6 percent. Thirty-year bonds yielded 8 percent. Such returns seemed measly to investors who clung to fond memories of six-month bank CDs paying 13 percent—and harbored less fond memories of inflation approaching 15 percent. A year later, the federal funds rate stood at 3 percent, the lowest in three decades.[29] Little wonder investors felt they had no choice but to begin buying stocks. "I'm bullish partially out of necessity," explained John Mc-Dermott, a 71-year-old retiree from New Jersey. "Now that I'm retired, the only way I have to increase my income is to get into equities."[30]

Less affluent investors, too, turned to stocks. In 1983 individuals with incomes over $250,000 owned 43 percent of all publicly traded equities. By 1992, their share of corporate America had fallen to 23 percent. Meanwhile, Americans with incomes under $75,000 had watched their stake grow from 24 to 42 percent.[31] Who was coming to the market from 1990 to 1995? A survey of families who owned equities in 2002 would show that only 12 percent of the wealthiest group polled (families with assets of $500,000 or more) bought their first stocks in the early nineties—more than three-quarters of these households already owned equities. By contrast, one-third of families with assets of $25,000 to $99,000, and one-quarter of those with assets of $100,000 to $499,000, made their first purchase between 1990 and 1995.[32] (See table "Who Owns Stocks?" Appendix, pages 463–64.)

"It's just what you're supposed to do with your money. It's what someone tells you to do—it's the responsible thing," said Michael Malone, 59, head writer of ABC's soap opera *One Life to Live*. Still, Malone did not entirely trust the market: "I keep thinking of 1929—and those movies of people jumping out of windows with cocktail glasses in their hands." Malone would have preferred to be living in a world where CDs paid, say, 8 percent. He still remembered, and envied, friends who made 14 percent a year on CDs in the early 1980s. "But I was a novelist then, and didn't have any money. I didn't begin writing for television until '91, and by that time, my only choice was stocks." Though, frankly, he confided, "I'd rather go to the track where you can see the horses, instead of betting on something that is just initials to me. But I don't want to be foolish, and these days, if you talk about putting money in a bank, you're made to feel that's like putting it in a sock under your bed."

Whenever Malone called his broker to say, "Isn't the market getting pretty high—shouldn't I be cashing in?" his broker replied, "Where else are the boomers going to put all of that money? It has to go somewhere."[33] From 1960 to 2000 the boomers' hopes and dreams would drive every trend from the Beatles to Botox. To many, it seemed inevitable that the bull, too, would prance to their drummer.

THE NEED TO "SCORE"

Falling interest rates were not the only reason that investors were willing to wager their savings on equities in the early nineties. One could argue that it took the recession of 1990–91 to push the majority into the market. As the nineties began, many remained leery of Wall Street. True, 1987 had seen a brief blizzard of buying—but then came the October crash, followed by tales of insider trading in Lower Manhattan. If Black Monday didn't take the small investor's money, white-collar criminals like Ivan Boesky took his faith. In the fall of 1988, *Barron's* devoted a cover story to the disappearance of the individual investor: "The Case of the Vanishing Investor: Where'd He Go? Why Did He Leave? When Will He Come Back?" [34]

What would it take to bring the individual investor back into the market? Wall Street asked. This was when Bob Farrell, Merrill Lynch's chief investment strategist, offered the theory that hard times might drive investors back into stocks: "If people feel that their standard of living is going down, or if there is a decline in the value of housing, more people will be looking for a way to 'score,'" Farrell had explained in 1988. "If the little guy views equities as a speculative game, he may be more likely to play it if he feels he has to find a way to accumulate wealth." [35]

As bad luck would have it, the recession of 1990–91 provided the catalyst that Farrell predicted. Baby boomers watched white-collar unemployment climb while job security sank—along with the value of their homes. In some areas of California and the Northeast, housing prices had fallen by as much as one-third from their top a few years earlier.[36] Younger boomers who had been closed out of the housing market during the bidding frenzy of the eighties were still trying to buy their first home. But how could they hope to put together a down payment if savings banks were offering only 3 percent interest on their deposits?

Back to the wall, investors surged into stocks. This is not to say that individual investors suddenly trusted Wall Street. As late as 1993 a Lou Harris poll revealed that only one in three investors believed that a "level playing field" existed between individuals and institutional investors.[37] Nevertheless, they "needed to score." "The funny thing is that anxiety motivates people to take a risk," Peter Bernstein, author of *Against the Gods: The Story of Risk,* observed in a 2001 interview. "You'd think that anxiety would make them risk averse—but it doesn't. They're more risk averse when they have more to protect." [38]

This is not to suggest that the majority of investors felt forced into the market by either low rates or recession. Few would say, "I had no choice. The Fed made me do it." Most enjoyed the illusion, at least, of free will and could give an enthusiastic account of how they were inspired to become investors. In 1991, after all, it looked like the bull was staging a comeback. That year, the S&P rose more than 26 percent. To some, the market looked rich, but investors were primed to take the gamble "despite high price-to-earnings ratios," *USA Today* reported early in 1992.[39]

To many, P/E ratios were meaningless. More to the point, investors saw few alternatives. Guilty boomers knew that they must atone for the shop-until-you-drop eighties, if not by saving more, then by pursuing higher returns. If the seventies was the Me Decade, the eighties had been the Greed Decade. Now, boomers found themselves facing an Age of Anxiety. A 1993 survey of relatively affluent boomers with household incomes of $50,000 revealed that they felt it would take $1 million to make them feel financially secure. Meanwhile, they confessed, they were saving an average of just $6,300 a year.[40] No wonder they craved double-digit returns.

Wall Street fanned their financial anxiety. The Street's advisors admonished boomers that they must save more—but then published projections that suggested that, without sky-high returns, they could never save enough. Gary Wasserman felt the pressure. "At some point at the end of the eighties, I read one of those insurance company projections showing me what I needed for retirement. I thought 'there is no way I can do this.' Of course, the projections turned out to be way off—they assumed much higher inflation. Still, that was one of the reasons that I saved as much as I did—and began keeping all of my retirement money in equities."

In 1994, Merrill Lynch turned up the heat, publishing its second annual *Baby Boom Retirement* report. The results terrified the Pepsi generation: in order to avoid "dramatic declines" in living standards when they enter retirement, baby boomers must triple the amount they save each year, Merrill declared. And that was the best-case scenario. Assuming "even moderate cuts in future Social Security benefits," the study revealed that baby boom households should be saving "more than five times—rather than three times—what they save currently." Stiletto italics drove the point home. Under "worst-case projections," Merrill's estimates suggested "*the baby boomers may be saving less than one-tenth of what is required for a secure retirement.*"[41]

In the early nineties, Wall Street bombarded the boomers with seemingly authoritative projections. The problem was that the charts and tables made assumptions about inflation, future stock market returns, and future bond market returns that were, at best, guesses—at worst predictions designed to stampede investors into taking more and more risk.

Without question, Americans needed to save more, but very few could afford to increase their savings tenfold. In fact, the majority lacked the discretionary income needed to triple their savings. Those who did have the money lacked the desire. Ideally, the invention of tax-deferred retirement plans like the 401(k) would have spurred investors to tuck more money away, but it did not have that effect. In the nineties, Americans spent more and saved less. Their only hope, it seemed to many, was to chase ever higher returns.

In truth, affluent boomers were not that far from their goal. Consider the typical new investor who, according to ICI, was 37 years old in 1992 with financial assets, not including his home or a pension, of $60,000.[42] By tucking that $60,000 into risk-free 30-year Treasury bonds in 1992, he or she could have earned 8 percent a year, year after year—without ever losing a night's sleep—for the next 30 years. (Of course, locking money up for 30 years means taking the risk that inflation will heat up, but historically 8 percent has been a relatively good hedge against inflation. And, over time, if rates moved higher, the boomer would be able to capture the higher rate as he added to his savings.)

At age 67, the boomer who began with $60,000 would have had over $500,000, plus whatever he or she had added to the retirement account over those 30 years. If, as he earned more, he saved, say, just $7,500 a year instead of $6,300, he could easily have built a nest egg of nearly $1.5 million—while averaging "only" 8 percent. In other words, there was no need for these upper-middle-class boomers to chase double-digit returns.

Yet "everyone urged small investors to take more risk—nobody talked about saving just a little more," recalled Peter Bernstein, author of *Against the Gods*.[43] Throughout the nineties, baby boomers would be overwhelmed with financial advice, yet in hindsight, the counsel that the boomers most needed was the simplest: save just a little more, but save consistently. Start early; spread the money out; and avoid large losses by shunning steep risks. Pass by anything that sounds too good to be true, and let the miracle of compounding do the rest. If an investor earned 8 percent over a lifetime of saving, his money would double roughly every nine years.

Buying a 30-year bond in 1992 would not solve the retirement problems of less affluent families, however. With median household incomes at $30,786, the average family simply did not have assets of $60,000 in 1992—or another $6,000 left over to invest each year after paying for the necessaries of life. But gambling on high-flying stocks would not be the answer to their dilemma either. Down the road, what these middle-class families would need—first and foremost—would be a safety net in the form of a stable Social Security system. In other words, they would need a system that did not risk its funds on the uncertainties of the stock market. Secondly, if they had 401(k)s, they would need plans that gave them a much better opportunity to manage risk by diversifying their savings.[44]

But in the early nineties neither Wall Street nor the mutual fund industry had much incentive to urge investors to discover the peace of mind that might come with owning Treasuries. "Wall Street makes far more money if people buy stocks rather than bonds," said Bill Gross, chairman of Pimco, a fund company that specializes in bond funds. For one, an investor who is holding a bond to maturity is not trading in and out of the market. To generate fees, Wall Street needs trades. Secondly, "To sell a product profitably, you need glamour and you need sizzle," added Gross, who, by the late nineties, was generally recognized as the Peter Lynch of bonds. "There is glamour and sizzle in a stock with a potential growth story that bonds simply lack. That is what allows the equity people to charge more. They always earn the higher fees—investors will take the bait."[45]

The media loves sizzle, and in the early nineties, magazines waving the gaudy banner of "Hot Stocks" filled newsstands. Established business magazines like *Fortune* also began putting more emphasis on personal finance. In 1995, *Fortune* published a "Special Double Issue Investment Guide: Getting the Most from Your 401(k)," which exhorted readers to "PICK A WINNING ASSET MIX."[46]

"You know those golden rules for putting together a retirement nest egg—'Take your age, subtract from 100, and put that amount in equities,' and the like? Phooey," wrote the story's author, Richard Teitelbaum. "By that reckoning, just 60% of a 40-year-old's portfolio would be in stocks now, and by the time he or she retired, that share would be down to 35%, an absurdly low percentage. Far better to keep a bare minimum of 80% of your overall portfolio in equities and maintain that allocation up to and even after retirement. Consider this example from Ibbotson Associates, a Chicago research firm. Say you're 40, earn $90,000 a year, make a 10% contribution (which your company matches to 50%), and get annual raises of 4%. By age 65, *assuming a 12%-a-year market increase,* you'd have a nest egg of $2,159,611. That's comfortably ahead of the $1,825,522 you could likely expect if you followed the so-called golden rule."

Teitelbaum did not mention how he knew that the market would average a return of 12 percent a year over the next 25 years.

Fortune's advice was about par for the course. In a 1993 story headlined "Asset Allocation and the Winner Is . . . Stocks, by Several Lengths," *Business Week* quoted gurus such as PaineWebber's Edward Kerschner—who recommended allocating 72 percent of an investment portfolio to stocks— and CS First Boston Corp.'s Jeffrey Applegate—who advocated committing 80 percent to equities.[47]

At *The Washington Post,* James Glassman joined what was fast becoming a pundits' jamboree, with a headline that said: "Playing Safe Will Make You Sorry."[48] Glassman, who would become more widely known later in the decade as the coauthor of a mildly lunatic book, *Dow 36,000,* spooned out a seductive argument: "One dollar invested in stocks at the start of 1926 became $800 by the end of 1993; a dollar in long-term corporate bonds rose to just $28. It's true that in the short run, stocks are far more risky than bonds," Glassman allowed, "but after 10 years or 20 years, there's almost no difference in volatility. . . . Since practically everyone who puts money in a pension plan has a time horizon beyond 20 years, putting nearly all retirement dollars into equities makes eminently good sense."

It sounded so deliciously simple—invest in stocks for the long term and you're home free. On closer examination, Glassman's definition of "long term" seemed a bit slippery. Was he talking about the 66 years "from 1926 to 1993"? Or "10 or 20 years"—and if so, which? True, the stock market's 66-year record looked impressive—but that is no guarantee of how the market would perform over the next 66 years.

Moreover, for the individual investor, "average returns" over 66 or 36 or 26 years are of only academic interest. They do not reveal how any particular investor fared.[49] In reality, few investors have either the emotional stamina or the deep pockets to ride out decades that include bear markets, sideways markets, recessions, and wars. The Rockefeller Family Trust might well persevere in the expectation that, over generations, returns will even out. The investor who expects to spend most of his savings during his lifetime cannot. Ultimately, "average returns" exist only in the abstract. The difference between that average and an individual investor's experience in the real world marks the difference between the best-laid plans and reality.

As Gary Wasserman put it, "Life intervenes." A once-in-a-lifetime bear market, a divorce, a career change, a layoff, triplets, a business opportunity—these are only a few of the contingencies that can determine when an individual investor gets into the market—and when he gets out.

As it turned out, investors who began establishing large positions in the late eighties or early nineties would be the lucky ones. Even if they took heavy losses at the end of the century, they got in while stocks were still relatively cheap. At the time, the conventional wisdom had it that timing no longer mattered. In fact, in the nineties, timing would be everything. At the end of the millennium, your results pivoted on how much you paid when you got in.[50]

At the beginning of the decade, it was not too late to join the party. The curtain had not yet risen on Act III, the dizzying and ultimately disastrous last act of the Great Bull Market of 1982–99. At this point Jennifer Postlewaithe owned both Dell and Microsoft. "I felt that, in a very small way, I was part of the revolution in American technology," she said. By now Shirley Sauerwein was managing a mid-six-figure portfolio. As for Gary Wasserman, he was betting his son's college savings on blue-chip stock funds: "When he graduated from high school in 1995 we had $50,000 in his fund—about half of what he needed for four years. After paying the first year's tuition, I decided to leave the rest in the market," Wasserman recalled.

The midpoint of the last decade of the 20th century would mark a turning point. Early in '95, the Dow broke 4000—and the bull was just hitting his stride. To fully appreciate what happened in 1995 consider this: It had taken the Dow 76 years to reach 1000, a barrier that it breached, for the first time, in November of 1972. Another 14 years elapsed before the index crossed 2000 in January of 1987. Dow 3000 came four years later, in the spring of 1991. Four years after that, in February 1995, the index broke 4000. Of course, the jump from 1000 to 2000 represented a 100 percent gain, while the move from 3000 to 4000 meant a gain of "only" 33⅓ percent. Nevertheless, the 1000-point advances represented important psychological signposts. And the bull was just warming up. Before the year was out, the beast would demolish yet another record, driving the Dow straight through 5000. This time it had taken just nine months.

That might have been a warning, but few saw it as such. One of the peculiarities of the stock market—when compared to the market for virtually any other item—is that, rather than dampening demand, spiraling prices whet desire. In 1995, Shawn Cassidy, a divorced mother of two who had managed to accumulate nearly $200,000, began to envisage becoming part of that privileged circle of people whom she had always thought of as "rich": "For the first time in my life, I imagined, I might wind up with enough money—plenty of money—more money than I need," she said. "I might be one of those people who goes on vacation to Costa Rica." She vowed to double her investments.[51]

BEHIND THE SCENES,
IN WASHINGTON (1993–95)

In the early nineties, two events paved the way for Enron—and
they both took place in Washington. First, in 1993, corporate
lobbyists buried a proposal that would have forced companies to
reveal the cost of the stock options that they were issuing to their
top executives. Then, in 1995, Congress passed legislation that
protected corporations—and their accountants—against being
sued if they misled investors with overly optimistic projections.
After that, the whole system could be gamed.

—Jim Chanos, 2002 [1]

As Senator Carl Levin prepared to testify before the Senate's Subcommittee on Securities on the morning of Thursday, October 21, 1993, he knew that he faced a lonely fight. Then again, the Michigan Democrat was accustomed to tough fights—he had trained in Detroit. A member of the Detroit city council from 1970 to 1978, Levin was known as a civil rights activist. After being elected to Congress in '78, he built his reputation as a liberal on social issues, a conservative on fiscal issues. When it came to reducing the deficit, he was a hawk.

On the Hill, Senator Levin was seen as a workhorse, not a show horse. Although he would serve in Congress for more than 25 years, it was not likely that he would ever make the cover of *Time* magazine. But, unlike many congressmen, the Harvard-educated lawyer possessed both the patience and the skills needed to analyze and absorb vast amounts of information, which meant that when he sank his teeth into an issue, he could be a tenacious opponent.

Today, Levin had come to the Senate Committee on Banking, Housing, and Urban Affairs' Subcommittee on Securities determined to defend the one group on Wall Street that has no lobby in Washington: the individual investor. The issue at hand: full disclosure of executive pay. Few shareholders realized that they were footing the bill for the multimillion-dollar stock options packages that corporations had begun to lavish on their top executives. But now, the Financial Accounting Standards Board (FASB) had proposed a new rule that would force companies to lay bare the cost of those options in a way that any investor could understand. FASB is an independent, private-sector board that is supposed to serve as a watchdog over corporate accounting, and Levin supported FASB's right to set accounting rules. But some of the most powerful CEOs in corporate America had lined up to fight FASB's reform. In Congress the battle lines had been drawn. On one side, Senator Levin was spearheading the effort to support FASB's proposal. On the other side, Connecticut Senator Joseph Lieberman led the charge to quash the new rule. In the wings stood Arthur Levitt, the new chairman of the Securities and Exchange Commission: FASB desperately needed the SEC's support, but Levitt had not yet shown his hand.

In recent years, stock options packages had become an increasingly popular component of executive pay. These options gave insiders the opportunity (literally the option) to buy their companies' stocks at a fixed price—usually the current market price—over a fixed period of time. For example, if a company's shares were trading at $10, a chief executive officer might be given the right to purchase 100,000 shares at $10 sometime over the next 10 years. Typically, he would be required to wait a few years before exercising his options, but in a bull market the delay would work to his advantage: he could expect the stock to be trading well above $10 by the time he exercised his right to buy the shares. By then, the stock might well have climbed to $30, and after making the purchase at $10, he could turn around and sell the shares at $30, pocketing the difference.

Senator Levin's research told him that at the nation's largest corporations, stock options were becoming the preferred form of executive compensation. A year earlier, a *Fortune* magazine survey of 200 of the nation's largest corporations revealed that in 1991, newly granted options accounted for roughly half of the $2.4 million that the average CEO earned.[2]

Nevertheless, the cost of stock options remained hidden. Unlike cash bonuses, options did not have to be shown as an expense, and subtracted from corporate profits. After all, corporate lobbyists liked to explain, when a company gave an executive stock options, no cash changed hands. The options were free. Yet—and this was a contradiction no one seemed able to explain—corporations were allowed to deduct the "cost" of these options as an "expense" on their corporate income taxes.[3] In other words, when the company reported to shareholders, it claimed that options cost nothing; but when the same company talked to the tax man, it subtracted the cost of those supposedly "free" options from its earnings. Levin knew that the IRS was getting the true story: options did carry a very real cost, and it came directly from shareholders' pockets.

Unlike many investors, Senator Levin understood that when insiders exercise their stock options, the new stock issued adds to the number of shares outstanding, undermining the value of the ordinary stockholders' shares. Imagine, for example, that a company has 9 million shares outstanding: a shareholder who owns 1 million shares owns one-ninth of the company. Then consider what happens if the company decides to give each of its top five executives 200,000 options. When they exercise those options, the company will have to issue 1 million new shares, bringing the total shares outstanding to 10 million. The companies' profits now have to be split among 10 million shares—and the shareholder who owns 1 million shares will find that his or her slice of the earnings pie has been cut from one-ninth to one-tenth.

Meanwhile, as the bull market picked up speed, the value of those options was climbing. In 1991, the S&P 500 jumped 26.3 percent, and the next year Disney CEO Michael Eisner realized a stunning $197 million gain when he cashed in his options. That same year, Thomas F. Frist Jr., CEO and chairman of HCA (Hospital Corporation of America), hauled home $127 million, with the bulk of his compensation coming in the form of options. At Primerica, CEO Sandy Weill earned $67.6 million. Options accounted for 96 percent of the total. Meanwhile, Mirage Resorts' casino king, Steve Wynn, cashed in 1 million stock options, raking in a profit of $23.3 million.

Million-dollar windfalls had become the rule, not the exception. By

1993, *Fortune's* survey of 200 of the nation's largest corporations showed that average CEO compensation had jumped to $4.1 million, with options representing an ever-larger share of the total. In the even more elite group of Fortune 100 companies, 29 percent of CEO pay now came from options—up from 17 percent in 1987.[4]

As CEO salaries mounted, so did public outrage. In the early nineties, many questioned whether CEOs deserved such largesse. In 1991, for example, chief executives' pay at the country's 350 largest corporations climbed by 3.9 percent—even while corporate profits at the companies surveyed slid by about 15 percent.[5] National Medical Enterprises (NME) CEO Richard K. Eamer stood out on the 1991 list. Eamer earned the bulk of the $17 million that he took home that year by exercising stock options. A year later, he resigned in the wake of a scandal involving allegedly fraudulent activity at NME's psychiatric hospitals. Meanwhile, shareholders who, unlike Eamer, had not cashed out watched NME's share price plummet by 60 percent.[6]

In '92, U.S. Surgical's Leon C. Hirsch followed Eamer's example, turning a neat profit even while his company turned south. That year Hirsch netted $60.4 million by exercising options to buy his company's stock for as little as $12.25 a share. He then bailed out, selling the shares at prices ranging from $65 to $120. Ordinary shareholders might well have envied Hirsch his good fortune: first, he was able to buy the shares well below market price, and then he managed to get out while U.S. Surgical was still riding high. By 1993, the company's shares had tumbled to $30.[7]

PERVERSE INCENTIVES

Eamer and Hirsch were able to scoop up their profits before their companies tanked because, although there is normally a waiting period before an executive is allowed to exercise his option to buy stock at a fixed price, there is no waiting period before he sells. An insider can exercise his option to buy, and then dump the shares the next day at the current market price, reaping huge gains. As a result, once the window has opened, an insider sitting on a pile of options has a perverse incentive to do whatever might be necessary to goose his company's share price over the short term—even if that means sending it to unsustainable heights. A well-timed press release announcing a new acquisition can do the trick—even if the acquisition turns out to be a lemon. The stock needs to stay aloft just long enough for him to cash in—and cash out.

Those who defended the generous use of options argued that the grants served to align the interests of management and shareholders. In theory, it seemed a marvelous idea, but in practice, managers and outside shareholders often have very different goals. While the typical shareholder invests for the long haul, many executives use their options to score short-term gains.[8]

Critics also noted that options encourage senior executives to take unreasonable risks while trying to boost their company's stock. If the strategy boomerangs and the stock plunges, insiders face no real downside. At worst, their options expire worthless—but then again, they paid nothing for them in the first place. On the other hand, if the gamble works out, and the stock shoots up, their upside is open-ended. No wonder so many insiders preferred options to cash bonuses. As one Silicon Valley banker put it: "Nobody wants cash anymore—it's too final."[9]

But now, FASB, the private-sector accounting board that served as a kind of Supreme Court for accountants, wanted to spoil the party. Under FASB's proposal, companies would have to deduct the cost of options from profits before reporting earnings to shareholders—just as they subtracted the cost of any other form of employee compensation. FASB did not question whether the benefit of distributing large option packages to top executives justified the expense. That was not the accounting board's job. It just wanted companies to make that cost clear.

In the corridors of corporate power, FASB's seemingly modest proposal triggered a violent and vitriolic response: "The first stage I went through was total rage," Raychem CEO Robert Saldich confided to *The Wall Street Journal*.[10]

Accordingly, a legion of lobbyists descended on Washington, intent upon killing reform. Not satisfied to rely on corporate lobbyists to plead their cause, many executives showed up in person. MCI Communications' chief financial officer, Douglas Maine, worked the Senate. Citicorp's chief executive, John Reed, paid a special visit to Arthur Levitt, the newly appointed chairman of the Securities and Exchange Commission, the body that was supposed to enforce accounting rules.[11]

Rumor had it that the SEC had pledged to provide FASB with "political cover" in Congress. But in fact, Levitt—who had arrived in Washington only a few months earlier—had not yet decided whether it would be politic to support the proposed reforms. And the question of what was politic was important to the new SEC chairman.

ARTHUR LEVITT

Silver-haired and soft-spoken, Arthur Levitt was a diplomat who took considerable pride in his powers of persuasion. No ideologue, Levitt had friends on both sides of the aisle. He counted both Alan Greenspan, the Republican Fed chairman, and Alan Alda, the liberal Hollywood actor, as close friends. It was Ronald Reagan who first seriously considered Arthur Levitt Jr. for chairman of the Securities and Exchange Commission, and President Bill Clinton who finally gave him the nod. That he would wind up on the shortlists of two presidents—one a Republican, the second a Democrat, the first a dedicated deregulator, the second an equally zealous reformer—said a great deal about his ability to find common ground. Other SEC officials described their new chairman as "always interested in hearing both sides," "always collegial," and "always civil."

But that very civility was part of what would make the SEC's Levitt a somewhat reluctant regulator: "Every time we create a regulation, somewhere deep inside of me, I feel diminished," Levitt confided during his first months in office.[12] As a rule, he greatly preferred self-regulation to government regulation. Rather than imposing edicts, Wall Street's new top cop favored the more gentle art of moral suasion, hoping to prod, flatter, lead, and cajole both politicians and Wall Streeters into "doing the right thing."

It would be tempting to say that Levitt was naïve, but even a glance at his history belies that proposition. As the son of New York State Comptroller Arthur Levitt Sr., it is safe to say that Levitt Jr. grew up knowing something about both money and politics. He launched his own financial career selling cattle tax shelters in Kansas City before making his way to Wall Street, where he would spend 28 years, winding up as chairman of the American Stock Exchange (Amex). In the course of his career, Levitt also made some money: newspaper reports put the figure at around $30 million, mostly from the American Express stock he received when the financial services company bought Shearson Lehman Brothers, the firm where he had worked before joining the Amex.[13]

During his years on Wall Street, Levitt had ample opportunity to see the Street's seamier side, and he came to the SEC with a clear understanding of Wall Street's culture: "Actually, there were two conflicting cultures," Levitt wrote in his memoir of his tenure as SEC chairman: "One rewarded professionalism, honesty, and entrepreneurship. . . . The other culture was driven by conflicts of interest, self-dealing and hype. This culture, regrettably, often overshadowed the other." [14]

When he was appointed to the SEC, many on Wall Street saw Levitt as their special envoy to the Capitol. Indeed, as he himself remarked, "I feel like the parish priest who has been elected Pope." [15] Nevertheless, he harbored few illusions about the market: "Let's face it—investing is gambling," Levitt said, with a shrug, in 1993. "But don't quote me saying that," he added, careful not to upset any one of his multiple constituencies. [16]

The new SEC chairman also understood Washington's culture. After leaving the Amex in '89, he had purchased *Roll Call*, a Washington newspaper that covered Capitol Hill, and during the four years he owned the paper, he learned, in his words, "how to work the legislative process— where to apply the pressure and how to find common ground with lawmakers, regardless of political party." [17]

Yet, despite all that he knew about both money and power, Levitt came to the SEC convinced that he could regulate with a velvet glove. If he was not naïve—and he was not—perhaps it was hubris, the fatal flaw of many a would-be hero, which made him believe that his powers of persuasion would prevail.

During his first months in Washington, the new SEC chairman set out to "build up political capital," confident that he had "several advantages over the typical CEO type." After all, Levitt explained, "At the American Stock Exchange, I had formed the American Business Conference, a research and lobbying group made up of the CEOs of high-growth companies. . . . I often led the group when it traveled to Washington to meet with members of Congress and cabinet officials. . . . The experience taught me much about the symbiotic nature of Washington. For the CEOs, the ability to have access to and rub shoulders with well-known people who represented America's political elite had an addictive allure. The politicians, in turn, used these meetings as an opportunity to raise funds. And White House officials saw their chance to lobby the business community to push their own policy goals." [18]

In a nutshell, everyone quite graciously scratched everyone else's back. In the summer of '93, when he took up his post as SEC chairman, Levitt felt confident that he could use his considerable social skills to good advantage in these circles where government policy makers, politicians, and the titans of the business community met to exchange favors and set the agenda not only for the business world but, to a large degree, for the nation. When he arrived in Washington, just a few months before the banking subcommittee's hearing, Levitt found himself at the center of a controversy that could threaten his goal of "building political capital" by making friends and forging alliances.

Almost before he unpacked, the new SEC chairman was drawn into the fight over options accounting reform. CEOs lined up at his door, howling for his attention.

In a 2002 interview, Levitt recalled their pleas: " 'Earnings will sink!' . . . 'You'll confuse investors!' . . . 'You could kill capitalism!' " [19] If options had to be set against profits, the lobbyists cried, they would become too expensive, and companies would have to cut back on their options programs.

But in truth, the new accounting rule would not make options expensive: it simply would measure the expense.

Corporate lobbyists liked to pretend that options were more than an executive perk, claiming that millions of middle-level employees benefit from options programs. If FASB's proposal became a final rule, they warned, companies would have to pare back their use of options, and rank-and-file employees would be the first to lose their benefits. The SEC chairman recognized this argument for what it was—a self-serving ruse. The Executive Compensation Report's survey showed that only 2 percent of all companies that issued stock options gave them to all employees. A survey of 350 major corporations by William M. Mercer revealed that less than 6 percent awarded options to even half of their workers.[20] And even in those cases, the majority of employees received piddling packages that would allow them to buy, at most, a few hundred shares. The truly costly packages were reserved for the executive suite.

"The whole thing was ridiculous," said Levitt, recalling the CEOs' arguments. "The cynicism of giving minor amounts of options to junior employees and using that as a cover for justifying huge grants of options to top management. . . . They just wanted an opportunity to pay themselves more." [21]

In his heart Levitt agreed with Carl Levin, the Michigan senator championing FASB's fight for reform: by burying the cost of options, corporations were deceiving their shareholders.

The Meeting

Nevertheless, when Senator Levin appeared at the Banking, Housing, and Urban Affairs subcommittee meeting on that October morning in 1993, he did not know whether he could count on the SEC to support him publicly. Levitt had not yet taken a public stand, and neither Levitt nor any member of the SEC staff would be appearing to testify before the committee. As for the other congressmen who would testify that morning, Levin knew where they stood. Of the dozen senators and representatives present, he alone would speak out in favor of FASB's reform.

The list of those lined up against FASB ran the gamut from liberal Democrats to conservative Republicans, including both Alfonse D'Amato, a Republican from New York, and Bill Bradley, a liberal Democrat from New Jersey; Barbara Boxer, a California Democrat, and Phil Gramm, a conservative Texas Republican; Anna Eshoo, a Democrat from California, and Richard Shelby, a Dixiecrat from Alabama.[22] Leading the opposition, Senator Joseph Lieberman, Democrat from Connecticut. Already, Lieberman had introduced legislation that would bar the SEC from enforcing FASB's proposal if and when it became a final rule.

From the moment that the hearing began, it was clear that many minds were made up. "They just jumped all over him," a member of Levin's staff later recalled.[23]

Senator Alfonse D'Amato led the attack: FASB's reforms, he declared, could "destroy capital formation." After all, if companies had to deduct the cost of options from their earnings, earnings per share would drop, and they might have a more difficult time attracting new capital. New Jersey Senator Bill Bradley followed up on D'Amato's objections and suggested a compromise: expanding the footnotes that provided information about the cost of options. In an ideal world, such disclosure might be sufficient—but only if all shareholders could afford sophisticated financial advisors to read through all of the footnotes in a corporate report and then do the calculations necessary to estimate just how options might affect earnings.[24]

Nevertheless, Senator Bradley opposed showing options as an expense. If companies were forced to come clean on their cost, earnings could take "a large hit," he warned, citing a study that revealed that in the technology sector, if companies charged the cost of options against profits, they would have to admit that their earnings were only about half of what they claimed.[25]

"Better not to let the cat out of the bag" seemed to be the gist of the argument. After all, if one admitted that companies were hiding expenses, share prices might slide. The SEC's Levitt later summed up this circle of reasoning: "The argument that expensing stock options might hurt share prices was akin to complaining that investors would pay less for shares if they knew that profits were inflated. Of course they would! And that was the whole point," Levitt exclaimed.[26]

But Levitt did not testify at the subcommittee hearing in the fall of 1993. Instead, politicians led the discussion, and each brought his or her own political agenda to the table. Some, like California Senator Barbara Boxer, were defending companies in their home states; others, like Senator Bradley, saw themselves as protecting workers and jobs; still others, like Alabama Senator Richard Shelby, believed that they were defending capitalism itself.

No one except Senator Levin spoke for the small investor. "Individual investors do not have a lobby in Washington—what they need is something like the AARP [American Association of Retired Persons]," Arthur Levitt observed in a 2002 interview.[27]

Indeed, Senator Shelby charged that, by trying to champion the rights of shareholders, FASB was turning "antibusiness," making it clear that, from his point of view, the interests of American business were best served by serving the interests of management—and a pox on pesky shareholders who questioned their stewardship.

Texas Republican Senator Phil Gramm spoke next. He, at least, *did* acknowledge that stock options cost something. Options "dilute the wealth of shareholders," he admitted. "[They do] dilute their earnings." Gramm had conceded a key point. When insiders exercised their options, they added to the pool of outstanding shares, shaving earnings per share.

THE COST TO SHAREHOLDERS

But this was only one way that options programs could undermine the value of a long-term investor's stake. As options grants grew, companies would try to offset the dilution by buying back their own shares: Award 10 million options to insiders, buy back 10 million shares, and the cost of options disappeared—or so it seemed. As the bull market spiraled, companies found themselves paying exorbitant prices for their own stock, using capital that could have been used to pay off debt, finance research—or pay dividends to shareholders. Normally, responsible management buys back its company's stock only when it is a bargain. But as share prices climbed, fewer and fewer stocks were undervalued. Many were overvalued—particularly in the technology sector, where options were widely used. Yet to counter the effects of dilution, companies issuing generous stock options packages had no choice but to buy back shares, whatever the price. Often they were forced to take on new debt in order to finance the buybacks.[28]

Options packages also encouraged management to reduce dividends. Typically, share prices drop immediately after a corporation pays out dividends. For outside shareholders, the dividend offsets any slide in the share price. But the insider who holds options does not receive a dividend. The value of his options depends entirely on the share price. This was one reason why dividends were becoming less and less popular. In 1988, companies in the S&P 500 had paid out dividends averaging well over 4 percent; by 1995, the average yield would slip below 3 percent. Meanwhile, share repurchase programs were growing—but not fast enough to keep up with new stock being issued. In fact, over the preceding two years, the net effect of lower dividends, share dilution, and share repurchase programs had a negative effect on the value of shares listed on the S&P 500, reducing an outside shareholder's total return.[29]

Finally, when a company lets an insider buy shares at a discount, it loses the cash it might have raised by selling those shares at full price. Later in the hearing, GE vice president and comptroller James Bunt would breeze past this point. "What is the expense to the company?" he asked rhetorically, then answered his own question: "Actually the company receives cash when employees exercise options." Bunt utterly ignored the fact that if a company sold the same newly issued shares to outside shareholders paying full market price, it would raise far more capital. For example, in the fall of 1998, when Bunt himself exercised the right to buy 35,000 shares of GE at prices ranging from $24.16 to $31.94, and promptly sold 25,000 shares in the open market at $74.31 to $83.70, he took home the roughly $1.25 million that would have flowed into the company coffers if GE had sold those shares on the open market.[30]

But Senator Gramm did not elaborate on the various ways that shareholders paid for options. He simply admitted the obvious point—options cost something—then slid right past it, as if that cost were inconsequential. "The bottom line here is, this is a stupid proposal," Gramm declared.

SENATOR LIEBERMAN

Connecticut' Senator Joe Lieberman followed Gramm. Levin braced himself—he knew what was coming. Already, Lieberman had launched a preemptive strike, introducing legislation that would bar the SEC from enforcing FASB's rule if and when it was finalized. Going a step further, the Connecticut Democrat was threatening to strip FASB of its independent authority.

Lieberman brandished a big stick: FASB's independence was based on the fact that it was funded, not by Congress, but by private contributions and the sale of its publications. These private-sector contributions kept the lights on at FASB's Norwalk, Connecticut, headquarters. The location, along with the independent funding, insulated "the gnomes of Norwalk," as FASB's accountants were known in Washington, from beltway politics. But if Lieberman's measure passed, every FASB decision would have to be ratified by the SEC. Since the SEC was beholden to Congress for its funding, this meant that, for all practical purposes, Congress would have a veto over any accounting reforms that might be politically unpopular.

Lieberman recognized that many congressmen might be reluctant to tell the SEC that it could not implement a rule proposed by a private-sector accounting board. But he had a backup plan: in case his legislation did not fly, he had sponsored a congressional resolution declaring that FASB's proposal would have "grave consequences for America's entrepreneurs." Congressmen who might resist voting for legislation that told the SEC what accounting rules it should enforce would be much more likely to acquiesce to a nonbinding resolution that simply expressed the will of Congress. At the same time, everyone knew, even a congressional resolution would be enough to serve notice that the Hill was dead set against the reform. The SEC would have to pay attention.

It was not clear why Lieberman led the fight. Since options were widely used in Silicon Valley, many saw this as California's battle. But like most senators, Lieberman relied on campaign contributions from a variety of large corporations, whether or not they were headquartered in his home state. Moreover, the accounting industry was an important lobby in Connecticut, and, no surprise, the Big Six accounting firms that depended on consulting fees from the nation's largest corporations sided with the CEOs. Then, too, Wall Street was important to Lieberman: in 2002, when Wall

Street's campaign contributions to the Senate were totted up, Lieberman ranked 13th among his colleagues.[31]

Finally, Joe Lieberman harbored national aspirations. Options reform was an incendiary issue. Anyone who supported FASB could probably forget about a run for the White House. Or, as Arthur Andersen partner Benjamin Neuhausen warned two months later in a letter to Dennis Beresford, FASB's chairman, "This issue is extremely divisive. . . . Some battles are better not fought."[32]

SEC Chairman Arthur Levitt would find himself at the center of Washington's options controversy for nearly a decade, and thus was probably in as good a position as anyone to understand why Lieberman led the drive against reform. In a 2002 interview, he offered his explanation: "Senator Lieberman is"—Levitt hesitated, and for a moment his blue eyes narrowed, then hardened—"pragmatic, extremely pragmatic."

Whatever his private motives, on that morning in October Lieberman based his public argument on the populist line that had become the lobbyists' rallying cry: "The overwhelming number of people who benefit from stock option plans are middle-income Americans, not upper-income Americans."

This simply was not true. Even later in the decade, when options programs had been broadened in an effort to draw attention away from the size of executive pay, only 2 or 3 million Americans received options in a given year, and most were executives. The National Center for Employee Ownership, a nonprofit group based in Oakland, California, that championed options plans, acknowledged that only a tiny percentage of middle-class employees benefited from the programs. When the Center looked beyond the executive suite later in the decade, it found that just 4.2 percent of employees earning $50,000 to $74,999 received options, while only 1.5 percent of those earning $35,000 to $49,999 shared in the programs. Even among employees who earned $75,000 or more, only 12.9 percent of those who were not executives took home options—and most received small grants.[33]

Moreover, by claiming that "the overwhelming number of people who benefit from stock option plans are middle-income Americans," Lieberman was sliding over the real issue. What was important was not how many people received options, but how many options they received, what they cost, and who paid for them. Ultimately, the bulk of all options flowed to the top of what MIT economist Lester Thurow would call the New Economy's "golden pyramid." By the end of the decade, the National Center for Employee Ownership would report that 75 percent of all options were in the hands of executives who ranked among the top five officials in their companies.[34] By then, options grants represented an unparalleled transfer of wealth from shareholders to corporate management.

But Lieberman ignored the cost and shifted the focus from shareholders' rights to employees' benefits. He painted a picture of hardworking Americans depending on options to realize the American Dream: "For these hundreds of thousands of middle-income Americans," he told the committee, stock options "represent the extra bonus, that dividend which will allow them to put down a payment on a house, send a child to college, or begin to put together a retirement nest egg."

But what of the millions of middle-class shareholders who bought stock in these companies, not at a discount but at full market price, so that they, too, could make a down payment on a house or send a child to college?

However, FASB was not asking the senators to choose between these middle-class shareholders and middle-class workers. The accounting board was simply suggesting that shareholders of all classes had a right to know what options cost. This was the point that Carl Levin was struggling to make clear, and now, at last, it was his turn to testify.

WARREN BUFFETT WEIGHS IN

Levin began bravely: "I am not alone," he declared. "There are many in the Senate as a matter of fact that concur with my view that we should not be reversing FASB."

As Levin knew, this was not quite true. When it came to options reform, he had few allies among his colleagues. Yet he did have one very strong ally outside of Congress: Warren Buffett. The chairman of Berkshire Hathaway stood foursquare in favor of FASB's proposal.

By 1993, Buffett was seen by many, not merely as a brilliant investor, but as one of the most ethical voices in the business community. Two years earlier, when Salomon Brothers was caught red-handed in a bond-trading scandal, and John Gutfreund, Salomon's chairman, was driven out of the firm, Buffett was chosen to come in and clean house. Wall Street's cynics called him "St. Warren of Omaha." Nevertheless, when Buffett had finished, the battered bank was once again profitable.

As for Buffett's own company, Berkshire Hathaway, his style of value investing was flourishing: the previous year, investors lucky enough to own Berkshire watched the stock soar 70 percent. Meanwhile, Buffett's own personal wealth had doubled. Three days before the subcommittee hearing, *Forbes* announced that Buffett was now the wealthiest person in the United States—unseating Microsoft's Bill Gates.

Admittedly, Buffett's stand on options invited that special resentment reserved for billionaire preachers: just because he didn't need options, why should he begrudge other CEOs the opportunity to make an extra million or two? But Buffett would demonstrate that he practiced what he preached. Four years later, when he bought General RE Corp., Buffett replaced the company's options plan with a cash-based incentive program—which meant taking a $36 million charge against earnings. In making acquisitions, Buffett almost always chose to cancel the options plan   a costly decision, because it meant taking a hit to earnings. Sometimes the cost was so high it killed the deal.[35]

Unquestionably, Buffett was, as Levin observed, "a pretty powerful voice" on FASB's side. But unfortunately, that voice would not be heard that morning. "He wanted to be here," Levin noted, "but [the subcommittee hearing] couldn't be arranged at a time when he was able to make it." No one explained why the meeting could not be scheduled at a time when Buffett, one of the nation's most respected and successful CEOs, could appear. Certainly, this leading capitalist's opinion as to whether or not FASB's reforms could "destroy capitalism" would be worth hearing. His reckoning as to how much stock options were costing shareholders would be of considerable interest. And without question, Buffett's colorful presence and witty voice would have drawn the media, focusing public attention on what most viewed as a dry and dreary accounting issue.

Perhaps those arranging the committee meeting were reluctant to let such a popular figure weigh in on FASB's side of the fight. Perhaps Buffett was simply too busy to travel to Washington anytime that fall. Senator Levin's staff was not sure. Whatever the reason, he would not appear. Nevertheless, Buffett had submitted written testimony, and now Senator Levin used it to good purpose, quoting Buffett liberally as he made his argument.

First, Levin reminded the committee of the basic contradiction before them: "Stock options are the only kind of executive pay which a company can deduct from its taxes as an expense, but which it is not required [to include] in its books as an expense." This, Levin told the committee, was why Warren Buffett called options accounting "the most egregious case of let's-not-face-up-to-reality behavior by executives and accountants." Buffett noted that FASB's critics argued that options should not be expensed because they aren't really compensation. After all, the Council of Institutional Investors noted, they "aren't dollars out of a company's coffers."

Levin quoted Buffett's reply: "If options aren't a form of compensation, what are they? If compensation isn't an expense, what is it? And, if expenses shouldn't go into the calculation of earnings, where in the world should they go?"

Buffett's common sense cut across the tangle of financial issues: An expense by any other name is still an expense. "Managers thinking about accounting issues should never forget one of Abraham Lincoln's favorite riddles," Buffett advised. "How many legs does a dog have if you call his tail a leg? The answer: four, because calling a tail a leg does not make it a leg. It behooves managers to remember that Abe's right even if an auditor is willing to certify that the tail is a leg."

Levin then turned to the argument that options should not be counted as an expense because it was too difficult to price them. If the company's share price sank, the option might never have any value. If, on the other hand, the stock rose, its value would soar.

Buffett would have none of it: "It is both silly and cynical to say that an important item of cost should not be recognized simply because it can't be quantified with pinpoint precision. Right now, accounting abounds with imprecision. After all, no manager or auditor knows how long a 747 is going to last, which means he also does not know what the yearly depreciation charge for the plane should be. No one knows with any certainty what a bank's annual loss loss charge ought to be . . . Does this mean that these important items of cost should be ignored simply because they can't be quantified with absolute accuracy?" he asked. "Of course not. Rather, these costs should be estimated by honest and experienced people and then recorded.

"Moreover," Buffett continued, "options are just not that difficult to value." After all, FASB's supporters pointed out, the market values stock options all the time. Employee stock options are not, at bottom, all that different from "call" options, which trade in the open market. Like employee stock options, these options give the investor the right to buy shares at a fixed price at some point in the future. The major difference, as Mary Barth, a Harvard accounting professor who supported FASB's proposal, pointed out in her testimony, is that while the investor who buys a call option pays cash to acquire it, employees acquire options by providing services to their company. The options, then, are part of the employee's compensation for those services.

And companies routinely calculate the value of those options in order to explain total compensation to their executives.[36] When an executive accepts stock options in place of a cash bonus, he knows that there is always the risk that the options will expire worthless. This is the same risk that an investor faces when he buys a call option. He does not know how much— or how little—it will be worth in the end. But he does know that even though a profit is not guaranteed, the chance to buy the stock at a fixed price has value. That is why he pays for it.

To underline his point, Buffett issued a challenge "to any CEO who says that his newly issued options have little or no value. . . . I'll make [him] an offer. On the day of issue, Berkshire will pay him or her a substantial sum for the right to any future gain he or she realizes on the option. . . . In truth we have far more confidence in our ability to determine an appropriate price to pay for an option than we have in our ability to determine the proper depreciation for our corporate jet."

Levin then addressed the idea that it is "in the national interest" to let technology companies, in particular, make lavish use of options packages. In truth, Levin declared, options reduced the capital available for research and development: "CEOs exercising stock options drain hundreds of millions of dollars each year from the capital needed to make American companies more competitive. In one case last year, a CEO and his wife exercised options for $84 million, capital which their high-tech company could have used to ease serious cash flow problems," said Levin, referring to the fact that if the company had sold those newly issued shares in the open market to an outsider, they would have fetched a much higher price. Instead, when the CEO exercised his options, he bought the shares at a discount—meanwhile, "cash flow problems [at that company led to] two quarters of losses, extensive layoffs and a slash in stockholder dividends.

"*The Wall Street Journal* reports that more than 9 percent of company stock is now set aside for executive stock options," Levin observed. "That's triple the 3 percent set aside a few years ago. . . . The millions of dollars going to feed the stock-option frenzy are diverting capital from the research and development and capital improvements that companies need to become competitive. So it's not just where the money is going that's the problem; it's also where it's not going. Stock options divert that capital from other productive uses."

Meanwhile, Levin noted, there was very little evidence that stock options boosted a CEO's performance. Just that year, *Fortune's* survey of executive compensation shot a hole in the theory that CEOs who received options would have an incentive to do a better job. Indeed, the numbers in the report showed that executives who received the most generous stock options that year did no better for shareholders than those who received the smallest packages.[37]

In the end, Levin argued, stock options only undermine the competitiveness of U.S. industry. Here he displayed a chart comparing executive pay in America to corporate pay in other countries. "Our corporate pay is twice as much for the same-size companies as corporate pay in Germany and Japan, our main competitors," he observed. "Twice as much. And there is no connection to performance."

He concluded by quoting Buffett: "True international competitiveness is achieved by reducing costs, not by ignoring them."

WHY CONGRESS SHOULD NOT SET ACCOUNTING RULES

As soon as Levin finished speaking, the objections began. Senator Shelby led the hectoring:

"Are you basically against giving executive compensation where people really perform and lead a company?" he demanded.

"Quite the opposite, quite the opposite," Levin replied.

Shelby ignored him. "You're talking about salaries and bonuses in Europe as opposed to the United States. Are you trying to get the government to mandate what private enterprise can pay and should pay?"

Levin tried again. "Quite the opposite. I think government here—"

Shelby cut him off. "It sounds like it. Are you against people making big salaries or making big profits because of stock options?"

"No," Levin replied, "I just want them treated the way the independent accountants say they should be treated . . . so that we have honest financial statements. . . ."

Shelby refused to meet the argument: "You believe the United States should follow Europe as a model, considering what is going on over there?" It was clear where he was heading: at best, Levin was unpatriotic, at worst a Socialist, and probably a Francophile to boot.

Levin tried again. "You know what I think . . . if we have honest accounting standards. . . ."

"Answer my question," Shelby demanded. "Do you believe that the United States should follow the European model to compensate their executives? Do you believe that?"

The comparison to CEO salaries in Europe had become a red herring, and Shelby would not let it go. Levin repeated his arguments about independent accounting standards and honest financial statements, but no one seemed terribly interested.

Barbara Boxer then zeroed in on Levin's claim that less than 2 percent of all U.S. companies give options to all employees. Boxer was skeptical:

"I just want to know where you got this figure," she said, "because what I have been hearing, all over California, at least, is that many, many companies use stock options to pay the lowest level of their employees." Boxer's question revealed the degree to which she, like most senators, was relying mainly on anecdotal evidence supplied by the lobbyists, rather than hard facts and figures.

Levin, by contrast, had the data: "There are two studies: one is the Executive Compensation Report that says of the 1,100 companies that they look at, less than 2 percent give stock options to all employees. And *The Wall Street Journal* reports that less than 5 percent of all U.S. companies using stock options give them to anyone below management."

Boxer pounced on the word "management."

"I think that is an important clarification because when you talk about management, you talk about some pretty mid-level people, even some low-level people. So, I think that is a little misleading.

"In other words, you can have mid-management people who are earning maybe—correct me if I am wrong—you know, $40,000, $30,000 and still be considered management."

Of course—that was it. When *The Wall Street Journal* said "management," it really meant people earning $30,000 to $40,000. Without a single piece of evidence to support her claim, Boxer had made Levin's numbers disappear.

Now Senator Shelby turned on Levin. "Why would you want to take that away from them?" he demanded.

Levin attempted to defend himself: "That is the last thing I would do. The last thing I would do is take it away from them. I want it honestly reported. According to the independent accountants, the only way to honestly report it is to show it as an expense on their books."

Boxer brushed away the whole issue of accurate accounting: "We could debate an academic argument here—accounting principles—[but] if I see an accounting rule that is going to go in and really hurt our job opportunities and our business opportunities, it gives me cause for concern."

In other words, the numbers did not matter; the truth about earnings did not matter, and the cost to shareholders did not matter. In Silicon Valley options were popular, and from Boxer's point of view it was her job to represent what was popular in her home state.

In that moment, Boxer demonstrated why Congress should not be responsible for setting accounting rules. First, most politicians are not mathematicians; they have neither the training nor the inclination to delve into the details of corporate accounting. Secondly, senators and congressmen are elected to represent the financial interests and social goals of their particular states—goals that, however admirable, have little to do with clean accounting.

The gnomes of Norwalk, on the other hand, represented the numbers, nothing more and nothing less. But in the minds of most of the congressmen at the hearing that morning, options reform was not a financial issue, it was a political issue.

THE POLITICAL WINDS

The debate continued for another year. Treasury Secretary Lloyd Bentsen and Goldman Sachs joined Lieberman, rallying around the corporate lobbyists. On the other side, Warren Buffett, *The Washington Post,* and Bill Seidman, the former head of the FDIC who had overseen cleaning up the S&L scandal, supported FASB and Levin. As for the White House, "President Clinton, characteristically, has expressed sympathy for both sides," *The Washington Post* reported.[38]

The SEC chairman remained on the sidelines. "I was careful not to take a personal stand on any of these issues," Levitt recalled in a 2002 interview. "If FASB is going to be independent of politics, the SEC chairman can't be seen taking a stand."

Nevertheless, Levitt was watching which way the political winds were blowing, and privately, he was worried. Seven months after the subcommittee hearing, the resolution declaring that FASB's reform would have "grave consequences" for the economy passed the Senate by an overwhelming margin: 88–9. Six months later, in the 1994 midterm elections, the Republicans took over the House, putting Georgia's Newt Gingrich into the Speaker's chair. "I thought the country was swinging to the right, and the mood was antiregulation," Levitt recalled.[39] He feared that if FASB continued to push for options reform, Congress might well punish FASB by passing legislation that undercut its authority.

Senator Carl Levin continued to stand his ground, but now Arthur Levitt backed down. Privately, Levitt remained convinced that FASB was correct. "Arguments otherwise did not sway me." But "politics did," he admitted eight years later.

Levitt went to FASB and, behind closed doors, urged the private-sector accounting board to back off. "I warned them that, if they adopted the new standards, the SEC would not enforce it." Levitt had pulled the rug out from under FASB. Without the SEC to implement the rule, there was no point in pressing forward. Not long after, FASB agreed to a toothless compromise that required only that companies disclose stock options grants in the footnotes to their financial statements. As long as executives were paid in options, and not in cash, the cost would not be shown as an expense.

In a 2002 interview, Levitt explained his actions. "I was afraid that if FASB continued to fight, Congress might override their authority—and put FASB out of business. In restrospect, I was wrong," he added. "In fact the country had begun to swing back to the center. I don't believe that Congress could have overridden FASB. I misread the political climate."

Yet, even from a political point of view, would it not have been better to force the issue out into the open, and let Congress bring Lieberman's bill to a vote? That way, even if FASB lost a floor fight, the issues would have been laid bare for all to see. In 2002, Levitt agreed. "Yes," he said quietly. "I now think that if I had let FASB bring it to a head, and let them bring the issues out in public, it would have been the best thing to do—even if I thought they would lose a floor fight."[40]

A more proactive regulator might have encouraged FASB to move forward, much as FDA Commissioner David Kessler forced Congress to address questions about the health hazards associated with smoking—what the tobacco industry knew, when they knew it, and whether they hid that knowledge from the American public. Kessler made many enemies, and ultimately, he lost his fight to bring tobacco under FDA regulation. But the firestorm did focus all eyes on the issue.

Confrontation was not Arthur Levitt's style, however. When he came to the SEC his plan was to cajole, to lead, to use moral suasion—to regulate without making enemies. He thought he understood how the game of power politics was played—"how to find common ground with lawmakers, regardless of political party," how to "build political capital."

But, he confessed in his memoir, it was only after he joined the game that he discovered how little political capital an SEC chairman has. "Once I began pursuing my agenda, I saw a dynamic I hadn't fully witnessed before: the ability of Wall Street and corporate America to combine their considerable forces to stymie reform efforts. . . . The two interest groups first sought to co-opt me. When that didn't work, they turned their guns on me."

But in this first round of fighting, it is fair to say that Levitt was co-opted. The political players persuaded him to see the question of options reform from their point of view—not as a question of right and wrong, not, as Warren Buffett saw it, as a fairly straightforward accounting question (If options aren't a form of compensation, what are they? If compensation isn't an expense, what is it?), but as a political question: Which way is the political wind blowing?

Nine years later, Levitt apologized to FASB. "In retrospect, I was wrong. I know the FASB would have stuck to its guns had I not pushed it to surrender. Out of a misguided belief that I was acting in the FASB's best interests, I failed to support this courageous and beleaguered organization in its time of need, and may have opened the door to more meddling by powerful corporations and Congress. The last thing I wanted was to politicize FASB," he added, "which can't function if it must please every last CEO and deal with the whims of Washington lawmakers."[41]

In the years that followed, Levitt would take a more proactive role in battles over corporate accounting. But as early as 1993, Wall Street needed to be reined in. Major corporations were already concealing expenses in order to inflate earnings. And everyone knew it. This is not to say that most congressmen at the hearing understood how the illusion that options cost nothing would corrupt both corporate management and corporate accounting. But just about everyone at that subcommittee hearing did understand—or should have—that options cost someone something, that the cost was not being reported on earnings statements—and that if it was, investors might not be willing to pay as much for shares.

That was their greatest fear: if the expense was shown, earnings would fall. And share prices would follow.

At the end of the decade, some would blame the CEOs who cooked their books for the bull market's sorry end, saying that they caused the market to crash. To the contrary: CEOs who cooked their books caused the market to rise. The higher reported earnings, the more shareholders would ante up for a company's stock. Bogus bookkeeping did not bring the market down; it helped build the bubble.

But in 1994, few fretted that share prices were rising too fast. That year, S&P companies reported earnings up 39.8 percent. Only a skeptic would question whether there might be a difference between "reported earnings" and actual profits.

Warren Buffett was just such a skeptic. In his 1995 letter to Berkshire Hathaway's investors, Buffett quoted Gilbert and Sullivan's *HMS Pinafore:* " 'Things are seldom what they seem, skim milk masquerades as cream.' . . . In the production of rosy scenarios," Buffett added, "Wall Street can hold its own against Washington."

Certainly, as Act II of the Great Bull Market of 1982–99 drew to a close, CEOs at some of America's largest corporations had every incentive to put a little lipstick on their projections. Their personal fortunes turned on double-digit growth. At the end of 1994, Disney's Michael Eisner, for instance, was sitting on options worth $171 million based on the company's share price at the end of 1994. Just behind Eisner on the list, PepsiCo's Wayne Calloway held options worth $64 million, followed by Oracle's Larry Ellison ($60.5 million), Compaq Computer's Eckhard Pfeiffer ($54 million), Reebok International's Paul Fireman ($49.6 million), United Healthcare's William McGuire ($49 million), and Coca-Cola's Robert Goizueta ($46 million). A little further down on the list, Scott Paper's Al Dunlap ($23 million) and GE's Jack Welch ($22.6 million).[47]

One of the year's biggest winners: an up-and-comer in Houston, Enron's Kenneth Lay. In 1994, Lay received $10.1 million in salary plus the option to buy 1.4 million shares. Enron's board gave him 10 years to exercise those options. If Lay could just move the stock's price up by 10 percent a year over those 10 years, the board's gift would be worth $76 million.

THE SAFE HARBOR PROVISION

A year later, the corporate lobby that beat FASB won yet another beltway battle that would encourage "creative accounting." In December of 1995 Congress passed the Safe Harbor Act, a bill designed to shield both corporations and their accountants against shareholder suits if they misled investors about their earnings.

Opponents called it "The Pirate's Cove Act."

Part of the Private Securities Litigation Reform Act of 1995, the Safe Harbor provision was designed to curtail frivolous lawsuits by offering corporate management "safe harbor" when making predictions about a company's products, future revenue, and earnings. "The bill is important," *The Wall Street Journal* explained to its readers, "because class action lawyers often hold companies' forecasts against them, asserting they have defrauded investors by lying to them or misleading them with unrealistically optimistic predictions." [43]

Seven years later, the idea of holding companies responsible for their forecasts would not seem so frivolous. When short seller Jim Chanos testified before the House Energy and Commerce Committee's hearing on the Enron scandal in February of 2002, he pointed to the Safe Harbor Act as a law that "emboldened dishonest managements to lie with impunity by relieving them of concern that those to whom they lie will have legal recourse." Indeed, Chanos declared, "the statute has probably harmed more investors than any other piece of recent legislation." [44]

But in 1995 the *Journal* was expressing the consensus on Wall Street that in an increasingly litigious society, companies needed to be protected against shareholders inclined to believe that life's disappointments are best addressed by calling a lawyer. With that goal in mind, the new law made it much more difficult for shareholders to bring a class-action suit in federal court if a company's forecasts did not pan out—as long as the company's executives surrounded their predictions with "meaningful cautionary statements," identifying "important factors" that might skew results.

"From that point forward," Chanos recalled in a 2001 interview, "at the beginning of every corporate conference call, they read a few sentences of legal boilerplate [to the effect that] any projections about earnings, revenues, or products [contain] forward-looking statements, which are subject to known and unknown risks, uncertainties, and other factors . . .

"What they were really saying," Chanos observed, "was, 'Now we're going to lie to you. But remember, you can't sue us!' After that, the whole system could be gamed." [45]

The bill raised the bar for what investors needed to prove before launching a suit. In the past, plaintiffs only had to prove that there was good reason to suspect wrongdoing might have taken place before proceeding to the "discovery" stage of a case, where the plaintiff's lawyers would be allowed to interview senior executives. But under the Safe Harbor Act, the plaintiff would have to provide specific facts suggesting that corporate insiders knew they were committing fraud before the plaintiff's attorneys could interview them. Finally, the law protected not only corporate officers but accounting firms that might be inclined to look the other way when corporate clients fudged their books. "The change could save the firms staggering sums in the event of a major calamity such as the savings-and-loan crisis, which forced the Big Six accounting firms to pay more than $1.6 billion in damages and settlements to investors," supporters noted. [46]

State securities regulators, consumer groups, the American Association of Retired Persons, the Mayors' Conference, and class-action lawyers all fought the legislation. "If the bill becomes law, investors will be taken back to a world of caveat emptor," declared Michael Calabrese, who monitored congressional affairs for Public Citizen, a consumer-advocacy group. [47]

Both President Clinton and SEC Chairman Arthur Levitt expressed reservations.

But by 1995, Congress was making it clear to Levitt that he was on a very short leash. That year the House and Senate froze the SEC's budget. David Ruder, a Republican who had served as SEC chairman from 1987 to 1989, understood what was happening: "The Republican Congress is dealing with the SEC as though it is the enemy instead of the policeman on the beat." [48]

Still hoping to regulate through compromise, Levitt tried to find common ground with the Safe Harbor Act's supporters. Senator Alfonse D'Amato, the chairman of the Senate Banking Committee, was one of the bill's biggest backers, and Levitt instructed SEC staffers to sit down with Banking Committee staff to work out language that would be acceptable to both sides. Ultimately, they crafted a compromise, and, in a letter to Senator D'Amato, Levitt gave the revised bill his blessing.

Word of the letter leaked to the press, and Levitt's imprimatur was taken as an indication that President Clinton, too, was now on board. Confident of the president's support, the Senate passed the Private Securities Litigation Reform Act of 1995 on December 5, with the Safe Harbor provision intact, by a vote of 65–30. The next day the House sent the bill to the White House with strong bipartisan support, voting 302 to 102 in favor of passage.

But then President Clinton threw Congress a curve. At the 11th hour—just before a midnight deadline on December 19, 1995—Clinton vetoed the legislation.

The bill's backers were fit to be tied. Congressman Christopher Cox, a Republican from Newport Beach, was the bill's principal supporter in the House, and he denounced the presidential veto: "President Clinton has turned his back on everyone who owns a mutual fund, participates in a pension plan or has a job at a public company."[49]

It might seem curious to suggest that Clinton had betrayed investors by scotching a law that limited their right to sue when they were misled by corporate management. But in 1995, many truly believed that, because so many executives were themselves shareholders, the interests of corporate management and investors were aligned. What was good for one group was good for the other. At the time, few stopped to consider the crucial difference between insiders and outsiders: insiders were in a much better position to know if earnings projections were over the top, and so better positioned to bail out, before the balloon popped.

Following the veto, Clinton tried to defend himself: "I just didn't want innocent people to be shafted." Although he acknowledged that dubious lawsuits posed a threat to business ("There have been examples of frivolous lawsuits filed which really have been unfair to people in California and elsewhere"), Clinton argued that the Safe Harbor provision of the Reform Act went too far in the other direction. "I would ask the American people to remember there have been a lot of examples in the last 15 years of people who have been ripped off to a fare-thee-well, who didn't get all their money back but at least got some of their money back because they could go to court."[50]

Congress was not impressed. The next day the House voted 319 to 100 to override the president, the very first time that the House overturned a presidential veto on Clinton's watch. Two days after that, on December 22, the Senate joined the House, with a vote of 68 to 30.

A sign of the times, *The Wall Street Journal* headline four days later: "Congress Sends Business a Christmas Gift."[51]

The Media, Momentum, and Mutual Funds
(1995–96)

THE MEDIA: CNBC LAYS DOWN THE RHYTHM

*They saw whither led the torrent of the public will; and it being
neither their interest nor their wish to stem it, they allowed
themselves to be carried with it.*

    —Charles MacKay,
        Extraordinary Popular Delusions & the Madness of Crowds[1]

1995, and the theme—on Wall Street, on Main Street, and in the media—
was *speed:* In just nine months the Dow catapulted from 4000 to 5000.
Ralph Acampora predicted that Dow 7000 was within reach. IPOs doubled their first day out. And on CNBC, a breathless Maria Bartiromo reported from the floor of the New York Stock Exchange.

That year, Richard Russell surveyed the scene: "The Dow has not experienced a 10 percent decline within a single calendar year in four years—
unprecedented. Twelve years have now gone by without the Dow breaking
below the low of a previous year—unprecedented . . . This is a market
that's been feeding on itself, and the feeding has evolved into a frenzy. In
fact the frenzy is now rubbing off on global stock markets, and with interest rates declining worldwide, markets everywhere have headed higher. The
whole situation is turning into the party of the century."

What was driving the market? Russell offered his readers an anecdote:
"As a young man back in 1958, in New York City, I used to frequent the
boardrooms. During the explosive up-year of 1958, I asked one crusty old-

timer why, in his opinion, stocks were surging higher day after day. He looked at me with palsied eyes and replied, 'More buyers than sellers.' " [2]

It was that simple: demand was sending stocks to the moon. The third and final phase of the bull market had begun.[3]

Now, middle-class Americans began to pile in, pouring their savings into stocks and mutual funds that invested in stocks. Wealthier Americans already owned equities: a 2002 survey of households with over $500,000 in financial assets revealed that more than three-quarters of these households made their first purchase sometime before 1990.[4] Over the next five years, less affluent investors began to edge into the market—the same survey showed that one-third of households with financial assets of $25,000 to $100,000 bought their first stock or stock funds sometime between 1990 and 1995.[5] But many middle-class investors did not join the party until the second half of the decade. Indeed, 40 percent of those with financial assets of $25,000 to $99,000—and 68 percent of those with less than $25,000—reported making their first purchase after January of 1996.

By then, the stock market was hosting the party not just of the century but of the millennium. Everyone wanted to attend. Seemingly overnight, over 3,000 equity funds had materialized to escort each and every individual investor to the ball. By 1996, investors were pouring $235 billion into stock funds—nearly double the dollars invested a year earlier.[6]

Broadcasters and business journalists covered the heady goings-on. Each stock tick was noted, every earnings whisper reported, and personal fortunes were charted on a daily basis. By 1996 the trading was raucous. In that year alone, 22 brand-new business magazines hit the newsstands; CNN launched its own financial news network, CNNfn; AOL opened its own mutual fund center, and TheStreet.com debuted online.[7]

The market was going up because people were buying stocks. People were buying stocks because the market was going up. The mutual fund industry's superb marketing fed the momentum. Individual investors provided the cash. The media covered it all. It was impossible to say who or what drove share prices. Everyone was involved. Few dared question the fundamental values of the market. It was now running on its own momentum.

In 1995 even a skeptical Richard Russell urged the readers of his *Dow Theory Letter* to hold on: "True valuations are absurd, bullishness is rampant and every magazine and newspaper lets you in on which mutual fund to buy," he acknowledged. "But this bull market has developed a tremendous upside momentum, and upside momentum does not die quickly."[8]

CNBC

The financial world was well on its way to becoming part of pop culture, and nowhere was this more apparent than at GE's cable network, CNBC. General Electric bought the bankrupt Financial News Network and folded it into its own Consumer News and Business Channel (CNBC) in 1991. But it was not until 1993 that CNBC began to find its true audience.

Someone had to figure out how to bring production values to the People's Market, and Roger Ailes, who came to CNBC that year, turned out to be the perfect fellow for the job. A political strategist who had orchestrated winning campaigns for Presidents Richard Nixon, Ronald Reagan, and George Bush, Ailes turned his talents to drawing out the personalities of CNBC's on-air talent. On Ailes's watch, the network's profit soared from a paltry $8 million to $50 million in just two years.[9]

CNBC simultaneously fed and reflected the market's frenzy. In 1995 the network launched *Squawk Box,* its pregame show. Each morning, before the market opened, Mark Haines, the show's host, Joe Kernen, CNBC's on-air stock editor, and David Faber, the network's Wall Street correspondent, traded wisecracks while they revved up viewers for the action to follow. When the market opened, the cameras turned to Maria Bartiromo, reporting from the New York Stock Exchange.

Buffeted by a sea of men, shaking her shiny black hair out of her eyes, Bartiromo was the first television journalist ever to report from the trading floor of the NYSE. Some fans compared Bartiromo to a young Sophia Loren. Without question, she was both charismatic and gutsy. Ignoring the swarm of white shirts that jostled her, Bartiromo held her own on the crowded floor, breathlessly rattling off the tips and touts circulating on the Street that morning, her voice growing hoarse as she shouted into a camera that seemed to hang far above her—making her appear all the more vulnerable, and all the more brave, as she struggled to bring her viewers breaking news of what stocks Wall Street's brokerages were promoting that day.

Bartiromo worked hard to get access to the "morning calls" at the major Wall Street houses, bringing her viewers the highlights of the confabulations that Wall Street firms hold, each day, on their "squawk boxes"—the intercom systems that connect them with brokers across the nation, and, in some cases, around the globe. These conference calls give the firms an opportunity to share new information before the market opens, telling their salesmen which stocks their in-house analysts are recommending that day.

The brokers who hear the pregame report are then unleashed on their clients to talk up the in-house choices. "And if, say, Merrill Lynch is pushing Global Crossing, or Lehman Brothers is talking up cell-phone makers Nokia and Motorola—well, you can bet that such information will have an impact on the stock prices of those companies in the first half hour of trading," *Fast Company,* a fast-track New Economy magazine noted in a largely admiring profile of CNBC. Of course, the information discussed during those morning calls falls into an odd category, *Fast Company* acknowledged: "For one, it's more opinion and analysis than news." [10]

In other words, much of the brokerage house's "morning call" consists of hype, designed to get a sales team moving. But after all, "opinions move stocks too." Indeed, if 10,000 brokers are telling their clients something while the tip is simultaneously broadcast on CNBC—all before the market opens—the morning call is likely to become a self-fulfilling prophecy.

How long the stock flies is quite another matter. But since CNBC operated in "real time," all that mattered was knowing what was going to happen that day. Tomorrow would bring a new story.

While Bartiromo broadcast live from the floor of the NYSE, Haines, Kernen, and Faber reported from the CNBC studio in Fort Lee, New Jersey. There, the trio created a locker-room atmosphere that delighted fans. Richard Hoey, director of equity research at Dreyfus, compared *Squawk Box* to a "bull market frat-house party," and it was that frat-house feeling that suddenly made financial news fun for so many viewers.[11] Indeed, the *Squawk Box* team resembled a trio of high school buddies spring term of senior year.

Each adopted an on-air persona founded on his area of expertise. Haines, a fellow who, in the words of *Fast Company*'s Charles Fishman, "looked more like a butcher forced to wear a suit than a television anchor," was cast as the show's prosecutor. Indeed, *Fast Company* described him as Perry Mason: "a gruff, jowly fellow with a didactic, inquisitorial style, [Haines] is approachable but skeptical—and definitely hard to impress. His mind is as sharp as his physical appearance is, at times, rumpled."

In truth, although Haines had a law degree, the inquisitorial manner was not a style that he had honed through years of courtroom experience. Before joining CNBC, Haines had spent roughly 20 years as a local news anchor in Philadelphia, New York, and Providence, Rhode Island. In the eighties he decided to change careers, earning a law degree at the University of Pennsylvania, but then underwent a change of heart. "Law school was great, but who the hell wants to practice law? You gotta spend all your time with lawyers," Haines complained.[12] So in 1989, he returned to television and joined CNBC. Although he passed the New Jersey Bar, he never practiced law.

Nevertheless, Haines relished impersonating a prosecutor: "My job is to find the negative story My job is to figure out if you're lying. . . . I used to be an investigative reporter, and I'll make 'em squirm if I have to," he declared, referring to the CEOs who appeared on the show. "They come in with great confidence," he added with a chuckle, "but sometimes they don't leave that way."[13]

Still, when Haines interviewed celebrity CEOs such as Ariba's Keith Krach, Sunbeam's Al Dunlap, or Enron's Kenneth Lay, he rarely seemed to find the holes in their stories.[14] Indeed, in Lay's case he handed him his lines.

In October 2000, Haines began an interview with Enron's chairman by announcing, "Enron has the power." His first question to Lay: "So you are an old economy company using the new economy to great effect?" His second question could have been written by Enron's public relations department: "I imagine that the additional revenue pretty much goes straight to the bottom line. I mean, once you have got it set up, there is very little incremental cost, right?"

Haines was almost as helpful when he interviewed Enron's president and CEO Jeffrey Skilling in April of 2001—just seven months before the seventh largest corporation in the United States filed for chapter 11. This time, Haines began with Enron's earnings report—"Energetic earnings from Enron . . . Is Enron en route to greater earnings?" he asked hopefully.

But before posing that question to Skilling, Haines dropped a quick bombshell: "And in fair disclosure terms, I will say that I own shares of Enron and have for quite some time, more than a year." (In other words, Haines owned Enron when he interviewed Lay in October.) Without missing a beat, Haines then handed Skilling his cue: "Mr. Skilling, so what is driving your business here? Is it primarily the energy shortage in the west?

"No, Mark," Skilling replied. "What's going on just in general is we have a tighter electricity and natural gas market than we have had really in the last decade. What Enron sells is reliable delivery and predictable price, and so the value of the product we sell is just going up right now." In truth, of course, what Enron sold was neither reliable nor predictable. What it sold was hype.[15]

To be fair, Haines was not cast as CNBC's investigative reporter. That role was assigned to David "The Brain" Faber. "David Faber likes to think of himself as the Seymour Hersh of financial journalism," Morgan Stanley's Byron Wein remarked with a smile, referring to the Pulitzer Prize–winning investigative journalist who uncovered the My Lai massacre in Vietnam.[16]

Telegenic, polished, and confident, Faber dressed for success. When asked to name "the best perk of being a TV talent," he replied, "Saks does our clothes. I go to Saks and someone walks around with me, and I get to pick anything I want."[17] Natty in jacket and tie, Faber served as a visual foil for his sidekick and sparring partner, Joe Kernen: Faber, the urbane hunk, Kernen, in shirtsleeves, the rumpled everyman.

Faber, who had worked for seven years as a reporter at *Institutional Investor*'s newsletters, took pride in scooping the competition—especially when reporting on upcoming mergers. Yet, while he often nailed the news, his fleeting television reports left little time for in-depth analysis of why the companies were merging: Would the merger add fundamental value? Or was Company A simply looking for a way to inflate its earnings by "pooling" two balance sheets?

But reporters who cover mergers and acquisitions quickly learn that if they criticize the deal, their sources may dry up. "If you're a merger and acquisitions reporter, the reality is that if you scrutinize the deal too closely on day one, next time, your competition is likely to get the tip instead of you," confided *Wall Street Journal* reporter Jonathan Weil. "That's why I would hate to be an M&A reporter. They're in a tough spot."[18]

Steve Lipin, who covered mergers and acquisitions for *The Wall Street Journal*, agreed that some sources tried to apply pressure. "In 1996, I helped write a story about how more and more companies were shunning investment bankers 'going it alone'—negotiating and completing mergers on their own," he recalled. Needless to say, the story was not wildly popular among the bankers: "I was on vacation when the story ran, and I got a call from one of them." It was a short message: " 'Don't bite the hand that feeds you'—Click. But," Lipin added, "I had to call them as I saw them."[19]

Nevertheless, as the number of news outlets multiplied, "the flood of news forced all media to be more aggressive," Lipin recalled. "And as a mergers and acquisitions reporter, there was an immediacy to my job. Company A may be buying Y. You don't want to be irresponsible, but you don't want to be beaten by the competition either. Do I wish I had been more skeptical? Given that all of the acquirers have blown up and half of them are in jail? Yes. But at the time, when you're covering daily events, you can't always sit back and reflect. In retrospect, should we have done more of those reflective stories? Maybe. But rightly or wrongly, we also took our cue from how the market reacted to the deals."

At CNBC, Faber competed with Lipin. As a television reporter, Faber's primary focus was on getting the news first—which can be different from investigating a story. For example, in June of 2002, when CNBC took credit for "breaking" the story of "massive fraud" at WorldCom, the stock was already trading at 61 cents. Faber was the first to report that World-Com was ready to admit to wrongdoing by restating its earnings, but he did not uncover the financial chicanery that led to WorldCom's collapse.[20]

"That's the difference between being an investigative reporter and getting scoops," explained Herb Greenberg, a financial columnist for both *Fortune* and TheStreet.com, who had been questioning WorldCom's finances since 1997. "Getting scoops is being a newsperson, a news hound. I've done it," added Greenberg, who had been a beat reporter in Chicago before he began writing his investigative columns. "It's a lot of fun—it gets your adrenaline going. When you're an investigative reporter, though, it's different. Rather than breaking the story that there is an SEC investigation, you're digging out the stuff that might lead to an SEC investigation."[21]

But Faber concentrated his energies on getting what his viewers wanted—the scoop, not the scandal. When asked why the financial press failed to uncover Enron's financial chicanery, the CNBC reporter was quick with an explanation. "As a journalist, when you pursue a story, you look for feedback and you look to see what is the response. . . . When you break a big story, for example, about fraud at a Waste Management or a Cendant or a Rite Aid or an Oxford Health, the response wasn't necessarily as encouraging as you might have expected."[22]

Jeff Madrick, a financial columnist for *The New York Times* and frequent contributor to *The New York Review of Books,* challenged Faber's explanation: "I don't think it is a good enough defense to say we weren't encouraged by our audience when we reported on these events. They didn't like it. That's the very point," said Madrick. Of course investors did not want to hear that a company they owned was cooking its books, but they needed to know. "I don't think there was ever a golden age in financial and business journalism," Madrick added. "But I think once business journalists looked on themselves as public watchdogs. They were skeptical by nature. . . . What happened to journalism somewhere along the line, I think more so in TV, but certainly in print as well, is that they began to worry about the readers' reaction, the audience's reaction, the corporate reaction."[23]

But on television, at least, ratings were all-important. So, perhaps inevitably, David Faber became an investigative reporter with one eye on the applause-o-meter.

While Faber tracked mergers, Joe "The Big Kahuna" Kernen specialized in explaining medical breakthroughs. CNBC's stock editor had earned a master's in molecular biology from MIT, and his colleagues often referred to his degree when asking him to explain a pharmaceutical breakthrough or a new biotech product. Even CNBC's website made a point of mentioning that after receiving a B.A. from the University of Denver, Kernen spent two years at MIT, where he "worked on several cancer research projects."

As it turned out, just as Haines had never practiced law, Kernen never became a scientist. After leaving MIT, he spent nine years as a retail broker, at E.F. Hutton, Lehman Brothers, and Merrill Lynch, before joining CNBC, making him perhaps the only cancer researcher to wake up one morning and say, "I'd rather be making cold calls."

"I made hundreds and hundreds [of cold calls] a day," said Kernen, recalling his career as a broker.[24] He offered this partial explanation for the turn in his career: "In my last semester [at MIT] I got a C," he confided, "because I was too busy playing the stock market. My dad gave me $5,000 and a guy turned me on to options trading. I was bitten by the bug."[25]

As CNBC's stock market editor, Kernen sat just off the main stage, surrounded by seven computers in a set that vaguely resembled an airplane cockpit. There, he tracked the market like a bomber pilot: "What's up? What's down? What's moving today?" As CNBC's day progressed, Kernen hosted a segment called "Winners and Losers," highlighting any stock that had moved up or down by more than 2 percent.[26] Since most of CNBC's guests advised investors to buy and hold for the long term, it was not clear how Kernen's report that an obscure company was up by 2.5 percent at 10 A.M.—or down by 2.5 percent at 2 P.M.—served his viewers' financial interests. But how else could a financial news network hope to fill 14 hours of airtime, day after day, week after week, for 52 weeks a year?

The fact that Kernen worked in shirtsleeves, his tie loose, his hair slightly disheveled, added to his credibility. Matt Quayle, the show's 30-year-old producer, hit upon the format by accident. One morning, Kernen showed up so late for work that there was no time for him to take his place on the main set. Instead, the camera had to cut to him at his desk. His jacket was off, his hair was askew, and he was reading from his computer screen. "We were, like, wow!" Quayle recalled. "The perception was that Joe was reading news as it was actually happening." [27]

In fact, nothing was happening. The market had not yet opened. But CNBC was based on the illusion that something was happening—every minute. Don't touch your dial—your financial future hinges on what happens next.

Clearly, the only way to keep listeners riveted to the screen all day, five days a week, was to focus on the speed of the game. Should you have a hard time keeping up, *Fast Company* assured investors, the network offered "a charming and instructive tape on how to watch CNBC, narrated by *Jeopardy!* host Alex Trebek. The tape was titled: 'Watch and Make Money.'"

Little wonder, by the mid-nineties, a survey showed that when Americans were asked what role investing played in their lives, the majority labled investing "recreation." [28]

REPORTING IN REAL TIME

By 1996, individuals were putting an average of $25 billion per month into stocks, directly or through retirement plans—equivalent to nearly $100 per citizen. [29]

As public enthusiasm grew, so did the public appetite for financial information. The media met the demand. Electronic news was coming into its own. Six years earlier, Michael Bloomberg created *Bloomberg News,* an online financial news service designed to compete with Dow Jones and Reuters; by the mid-nineties, thousands of chat rooms, financial websites, and bulletin boards had come online, all vying with the news services for investors' eyeballs.

To compete in this high-speed Age of Information, print journalists needed to learn how to write "in real time." In 2001, Dave Kansas, a *Wall*

Street Journal reporter who went on to become editor of TheStreet.com, described the challenge in a piece that he wrote for *The New York Times:* "While the Internet has secured its position as a legitimate news medium, there are reasons for concern. The biggest may be speed. . . . People want news faster than they did ever before. . . . By requiring a writer to show his or her hand earlier and earlier, the Internet has helped expose the raw nature of the news-gathering process. And often, that early hand is imperfect. . . .

"Historically, print reporters have looked down on their broadcast cousins with modest disdain," he acknowledged. "The distillation of complex issues into a 30-second broadcast report makes the print journalist think electronic journalists lack analytical heft. But this disdain can make it difficult for the print people to appreciate the most important skill an electronic journalist possesses: real-time decision making."

Kansas got his start in journalism at the NBC Radio News network, and "when the hourly newscast started, it started," he recalled. "Decisions had to be made by the time the light came on. In print, the deadline is seldom as immediate. Ideas can be mulled and debated." But the line between print and electronic journalism was blurring: now everyone was becoming part of "the media." Many newspapers published an online edition, and print journalists had electronic responsibilities. As a result, Kansas declared, "Print journalists involved with Internet distribution must learn to fuse their traditional strengths with the skill of real-time decision making."[30]

In the end, Kansas suggested, the responsibility lies with editors to balance priorities: "Print journalists face many more pressures than 10 years ago—the drumbeat of news is more intense, and a lot of the pressure is driven by the public being eager to get news as quickly as possible. But while you have to cover the news as it occurs—and break the stories—editors also have to have the discipline to pull reporters away to take the longer look."[31]

Yet, as print journalists raced to keep up with the immediacy of electronic news, many began to narrow their focus to blow-by-blow reporting. The pressure to compete in real time could be felt in stories that mimicked the pulsing, telegraphic rhythm of the Internet: "How much did the market rise today?" "Why?" "Where is it going tomorrow?"

"The trouble is that investing doesn't lend itself to play-by-play reporting," observed Bill Fleckenstein, a Seattle hedge fund manager. "Speculating does, but investing doesn't."[32]

For the investor, what matters most is the primary trend, not the market's day-to-day action. "If you stand on the shore and gaze at the ocean it's impossible to tell, at any given moment, whether the tide's coming in or going out," Richard Russell told his readers in 1995. "By the same token, watching the action of the stock market on any given day, it's equally difficult to determine whether it's a bull or a bear market. But the fact is that the tide of the market is always either coming in (a bull market) or going out (a bear market). It's the determination of the major trend which is so difficult. Yet that determination is critical." [33]

Nevertheless, as financial news became more immediate, "scoops" of all kinds tended to replace analysis that looked backward and forward in time. The spotlight was on the moment. The bull market's rise was presented in the context of no context. To many investors, history seemed unimportant. Sometimes a magazine would print what looked like a lengthy timeline unfolding across the bottom of two pages. But closer inspection would reveal that it tracked the market for, perhaps, three years. Occasionally, a story included a chart that looked back to the sixties, but for the most part, a timeline meant to show the market's history went no further back than 1982—leaving the bull market in splendid isolation. [34]

References to past bear markets provided only snapshots of a cycle. Investors were told, for example, that in recent history, there had been just two long-lasting bear markets: the 42.1 percent collapse that began in January of 1973 and ended in November of 1974, and the 22.3 percent plunge that extended from November of 1980 to August of 1982. But very few stories connected the dots. What happened in between the meltdown of 1973–74 and the crash that came in 1980? In fact, both crashes were part of a much longer cycle where the primary trend was negative: after peaking in 1966, stocks zigzagged for the next 18 years, but the S&P 500 made no headway. Indeed, from 1971 to 1981 the real return on the S&P was negative—even if an investor faithfully plowed all of his dividends back into his stock portfolio. [35]

QUARTER BY QUARTER

But the pointillist perspective of most real-time reporting ignored the market's longer cycles. Instead, the media monitored the Dow's daily performance, while the press tracked both earnings and mutual funds, quarter by quarter.

Quarterly mutual fund reports tried to keep up with a market that never looked back. By the mid-nineties, the press had replaced annual scorecards with reports that appeared every three months. The change spurred investors to chase performance, rushing to buy the funds at the top of the charts, just when they were most expensive—and often shortly before they peaked. Ed Wyatt covered mutual funds for *The New York Times* and he recognized the dilemma: "No matter how much we tried to stress long-term performance at the beginning of the reports, inevitably, quarterly reports focus attention on the short term." [36]

Yet mutual fund reports brought such lush advertising revenues—particularly from mutual fund companies—that the temptation to publish at least four times a year proved irresistible for virtually any magazine or newspaper that followed the mutual fund industry. And without question, the press was responding to its readers' most immodest desires for the timeliest information. Before long, *The Wall Street Journal* would be feeding the lions a *monthly* mutual fund edition.

In search of ever-higher returns, mutual fund investors were beginning to "churn" their own accounts. In the sixties, investors sold only about 7 percent of their stock fund holdings each year, suggesting a typical holding period of 14 years. By the end of the nineties, they were turning over 40 percent of their stock funds annually—which meant investors were holding their funds for an average of just 30 months.[37] Fund supermarkets like Schwab's "One Source," which offered investors one-stop shopping for a wide range of funds, made it easy to skip out of last year's winner and into this quarter's hotshot. Inevitably, investors pursuing "The Best Mutual Fund Now" wound up buying not "The Best Fund Now" but "The Last Best Fund"—the fund that topped the charts in the previous 6 to 12 months. "This was why, although many mutual funds made great gains, most mutual fund investors did not," observed Wyatt.[38]

As the public's attention narrowed, so did the scope of the mutual fund reports. Increasingly, quarterly reports focused on just that—the performance in a particular quarter. A fund's one-year and three-year record often appeared only in year-end rankings. The effect on mutual fund managers was predictable. They knew that they were now operating in a very narrow window. Short-term success was everything. Long-term strategies could kill a career.

In corporate boardrooms across America, executives were equally aware that in an age of up-to-the-minute information, they were only as good as their last three months' performance. "CNBC helped promote the

Wall Street game, 'Beat the Number,'" observed Seattle hedge fund manager Bill Fleckenstein, referring to CNBC's relentless emphasis on whether or not a company had beaten analysts' earnings estimates in a given quarter. "If a company had a $100 stock price and was supposed to make one penny and then made two, it was a big deal. So how can 8 cents of annualized earnings support a $100 stock?" he asked. "They were pouring gasoline on a lit fire."

CNBC producer Bruno Cohen's defense stunned even Fleckenstein: "The fundamentals about a company back then [at the height of the boom] tended to be momentum," he explained. "You could understand a company by understanding whether or not it was on the move or the stock price was on the move. A lot of people thought that's all you needed to know. . . . Now you have to understand who its leadership is," he explained in 2002— "how's its balance sheet, what's its business plan."[39]

The perennial problem for the media is that balance sheets do not fluctuate on a daily basis. Once a reporter has laid out a company's assets and debts, how does he fill the news hole the next day? Only by tracking the market's daily performance.

Trouble is, there is usually nothing meaningful to say about a market's day-to-day moves. "When markets are discussed daily, news becomes chatter," Fred Sheehan, a director at John Hancock Financial Services in Boston warned his clients. "The terms of the discussion are set by CNBC, investment websites, investment magazines, and the previous day's market summaries in the morning newspapers. The daily debate is captured in such phrases as 'we're testing new lows,' or 'the earnings surprises are coming to an end' or 'Greenspan will have to ease now,' or 'the market is 15% undervalued.'"

In other words, the news was becoming noise. "It must have been a similar string of babble," Sheehan concluded, "that prompted the Nobel-laureate physicist Wolfgang Pauli to say of a colleague's paper 'This isn't right. This isn't even wrong.'"[40]

JAMES CRAMER

Ultimately, James Cramer would come to personify the Age of Noise. A fund manager turned financial pundit, Cramer became a ubiquitous multimedia presence in the late nineties. He could be found online, on CNBC, on *Good Morning America*—almost any day, any time. Frequently, he popped up in the pages of *GQ* or *New York* magazine. After 11 o'clock, he might turn up as a guest on Public Broadcasting's *Charlie Rose*. Cramer even modeled for a Newport Shoes ad. Meanwhile, he managed some $300 million of other people's money.[41] "By Wall Street's standards, this is an insignificant amount," observed one longtime market watcher. "Cramer was a small money manager with a sideline in journalism whose influence was way inflated because he had been on the *Harvard Crimson,* and therefore knew people like Mark Whitaker of *Newsweek* and Walter Isaacson of *Time*—all of whom rose rapidly to the upper echelons of the media elite."[42]

Cramer also became cofounder of TheStreet.com, a website that provided a wide range of investment analysis—some of it shrewd and insightful, some of it hype. A media personality, he was a creature spawned by the bull market's cascade of information. And he believed in using the torrent. In his autobiography, *Confessions of a Street Addict,* Cramer described how he used Wall Street's information machine to make money for his hedge fund by becoming, in his words, a "merchant of buzz."

"We developed a style that consisted of figuring out what would be hot, what would be the next big buzz," Cramer recalled. The strategy consisted of "getting long stocks and then schmoozing with analysts about what we saw and heard was positive. Or we would get short stocks and talk to analysts about the negatives."

By Cramer's own account, a colleague trawled for stocks "likely to move quickly on good news." Another member of Cramer's team would then "go to work calling the companies to find anything good we could say about them. I would call the analysts to see if they were hearing anything." When his team found an unrecognized stock that looked ready to move, Cramer explained, "We would load up with call options [which gave him the right to buy the stock at a set price] and then give the news to our favorite analysts who liked the stock so they could go do their promotion. . . . We knew that Wall Street was simply a promotion machine," said Cramer. And once the analysts got the "buzz" going, "we would then be able to liquidate [our] position into the buzz for a handsome profit."[43]

Who would buy the stocks that he sold? Cramer urged individual investors to trade on the buzz. With all of the information available on the Internet, the individual investor "has a veritable trading desk at her fingertips," Cramer told the readers of *Worth* magazine. Investors should "pull some of [their] money out of mutual funds, and begin running it [themselves]. Just try it out—it has never been so easy to have control over your own monetary destiny." [44]

Certainly, it was not Cramer's intention that small investors buy the stocks he was unloading. But inevitably, those who read the news buy stocks from those who "manufacture" the news. (Wall Street has a long history of promotion: always, the promoters who spread the tips sell to those who consume them.)

Cramer helped fan the frenzy. Perhaps one way to sum up the difference between the bull market of the nineties and the market of the eighties would be to consider the contrast between Jim Cramer and Peter Lynch. The eighties gave us Lynch, the "Father Knows Best" of those early years, a solid, reassuring presence telling us that investing was easy—"just buy what you know." The nineties brought us Cramer. Sweating, screaming, eyes bulging, he seemed the perfect guru for what was fast becoming an obsessive-compulsive cult of investing. During the final blow-off, Jim Cramer would upstage even Abby Cohen.

TRUE BELIEVERS

By 1996, a nearly fanatical belief in equities swept the nation. Many members of the media, like the citizens they informed, became true believers. The majority had never seen a bear market, and many younger reporters knew little of the stock market's history. It just was not fashionable to talk about market timing or market cycles.

To others, past bear markets seemed simply irrelevant. It was, after all, a New Era. Headlines trumpeted the good news: "The Triumph of the New Economy" (*Business Week*, December 30, 1996); "The One Stock You Should Buy Now" (*Smart Money*, November 1, 1996); "U.S. Rides a Wave of Economic Stability: Recession No Longer Seen as Inevitable as Nation, Policymakers React Quickly to Changes" (*The Washington Post*, December 2, 1996).

Investor's Business Daily captured the spirit of the times with a jubilantly circular headline: "Overvalued? Not if the Stock Keeps Rising." The story began by paying homage to Just for Feet Inc., an athletic shoe retailer that "might have looked pricey by some standards" in the fourth quarter of 1994, when USAA Aggressive Growth Fund bought the $4 stock at 396 times the previous year's earnings, but the newspaper reported, "Investors who limit themselves to common measures of value, such as trailing p/e's [price/earnings ratios], would have missed Just for Feet—and just about every other leading growth stock."[45] It seems that the company's earnings had sprouted wings, and it was now selling for "only" about 58 times earnings at $28 a share. Of course, an investor who wasn't nimble might be crushed: three years later, the shoemaker had tumbled head over heel and was trading for less than $1.

Ultimately, the media's effect on share prices was, as always, temporary. In the end, intrinsic value would out. But good press can help keep the shares of a company like Just for Feet—or Enron or Tyco—flying high on a hope and a promise for months or even years, long enough for investors to lose billions of dollars.

In truth, the press was only mirroring the public's enthusiasm. Yet the bubble might never have grown so large, nor lasted so long, if the media had not promoted hot stocks, anointed gurus, marginalized "the naysayers," and substituted "good news" for analysis. The cult of personality was key. Chief executives became "celebs" while Wall Street analysts were treated as shamans. You do not ask a celebrity hard questions, and you do not question a shaman at all.

William Powers, a media critic who began his career as a financial reporter at *The Washington Post,* marveled at the effect the bull market had on the media in a column that he wrote for *The National Journal:* "For almost a decade, journalists did something quite out of character: We accentuated the positive. Over the years, we had acquired a reputation, largely deserved, for loving bad news. . . . The age-old complaint about the media, in letters to the editor and in polls, was that we were unrelentingly negative. We laughed it off, but we knew it was true. The bull market changed all that. We stopped enjoying the bad news, and got addicted to the good. A trade that had once searched high and low for negative stories about Wall Street and Big Business, devoted most of its energy to positive ones, and the touts were our best sources."

Most telling of all, Powers noted, was the fact that journalists hardly ever asked, "What are you selling?"

"What are you buying now?" or some variant of that question, was one of the most frequently uttered sentences on CNBC, on *Wall $treet Week with Louis Rukeyser,* and all the other TV and radio shows on which touts appeared," he reported. "*Money, Smart Money,* and other financial magazines were obsessed with stocks and funds we should be buying right now.

The buy focus spilled over into the general media: the big newspapers and networks . . . They almost never spoke of selling. . . . And we almost never asked. It was rude to bring it up, like walking into a wild party and talking about death."

Yet of course, unless a company was issuing new shares, every time someone bought a share of stock, someone else was selling it. "In order for a lot of people to obey the touts and purchase Amazon.com at more than $400 a share, a lot of other people had to sell the stock at the same price," Powers observed. "Who were those people? Why didn't we cover them as assiduously as we covered the touts? Because the sell story was bad news, and we'd lost the taste," he concluded.[46]

Powers felt that the very best print journalists were more likely to look under the rocks: "At *The New York Times* and *The Wall Street Journal,* you have some excellent reporters doing very fine work," he said in a 2003 interview. "The problem is that financial investigative journalism is time-consuming and requires specialized knowledge. Only the biggest news organizations can afford to pay a reporter to spend so much time on one story, and if their best financial minds don't look into a particular story, odds are nobody will. The media are full of people with the ability and willingness to do investigative work on the government, but there are too few investigative journalists reporting on business."[47]

Powers did not blame individual reporters. "Daily beat reporters can't be expected to be crusading investigators, too," he noted. "All their sources would dry up."[48]

Powers's comments underlined the problem implicit in the "beat" system of reporting. Each reporter is assigned a particular industry, and like the cop with a beat, he gets to know the people in the neighborhood. But the danger is that he begins to feel that he is part of that industry. The PR people and Wall Street analysts who promote that industry become his sources. Over time, some may become his friends. In any case, to gain access to corporate executives he needs their goodwill. This puts a damper on investigative reporting.

"During the bubble, many reporters just weren't doing their own critical thinking. They outsourced it to Wall Street analysts—dial-a-quote reporting," explained Jonathan Weil, the reporter who flagged Enron in September of 2000, writing a critical story for the Texas edition of *The Wall Street Journal.*[49]

The *Journal* did not publish the story in its national edition. "That article is an example of what my late broker used to call truffles lying on the forest floor," noted *Newsweek* and *Washington Post* financial columnist Allan Sloan.

This is not to say that no one tried to caution investors. In 1996, *Fortune,* for example, ran a story that asked, "Market Mania? How Crazy Is This Market?" As 1997 began, *Forbes* published a story headlined "Reality Check: What Could End the Bull Market? A Crash in Tech Stocks. Don't Rule It Out." [50]

But the fact that the bull market lasted so long presented problems even for the most skeptical reporters. "You can only say that price/earnings ratios are too high so many times," reflected a business writer at *The New York Times.* "Eventually, you lose credibility." Weil agreed: "There was widespread thinking among skeptical financial writers—this can't go on— but it has. What are we supposed to do about it? How many times can you say it? The problem is, if you're a daily newspaper, you have to come up with something different to say every day." Moreover, "in a public marketplace, if you write a story that doesn't resonate with the marketplace—you have to question the story," said *The Wall Street Journal*'s Kansas. "Reporters can get hesitant about their own convictions." [51]

Meanwhile, "journalism changed," said Mark Hulbert, a financial columnist for *Forbes* and, later, for *The New York Times.* "Publishers and editors started talking to each other. In the past, publishers worried about what readers wanted to hear, and editors worried about what they needed to know." [52] Another Chinese Wall was falling.

For newspapers, the bull proved to be a cash cow. By 1997, the financial services industry accounted for an estimated 30 percent of national newspaper ad revenues. [53]

At the same time, "there is more and more emphasis on selling the product—which means telling people what they want to hear," Hulbert continued. "Why did CNBC and *The Wall Street Journal* focus on information that has no statistical significance?" he asked, referring to the media's focus on the short term. "The answer is that they can't afford to focus on things that have statistical significance. Those things don't change. But in order to get advertising," Hulbert explained, "they need to send the message that this is a publication you need to read every day." [54]

It was not a new problem. "The function of the press in society is to inform, but its role is to make money," media critic A. J. Liebling wrote in 1981. [55] But by the mid-nineties, some observers felt that the good news was getting out of hand. "I've been watching the stock market (blush) since 1945, I've never seen anything like the current market super-hype," Richard Russell told his readers at the end of 1996. "Magazines, newspapers, TV, radio, books, all extolling the wonders, indeed the absolute necessity, of being invested in common stocks or mutual funds." [56]

SWIMMING AGAINST THE TIDE

Allan Sloan, a financial columnist at *Newsweek* and its sibling *The Washington Post*, agreed with Russell. In 2001, Sloan won the Loeb Award for Lifetime Achievement—the Pulitzer of financial journalism—and in his acceptance speech he was forthright. In the nineties, said Sloan, too many journalists "pandered," not only to their sources but to their readers:

"Instead of doing our job and being observers and analysts and truth tellers, we started to identify with our sources," Sloan declared. "It is not our job to kiss up to CEOs, to kiss up to mutual fund managers, especially not to kiss up to analysts." But in the nineties, he suggested, too many journalists were "running scared, and trying to give our readers what we thought they wanted—instead of sucking up our gut and maybe sacrificing a few short-term ads and readers by doing what's right. And telling them things they may not want to hear, but should hear." [57]

Why were so many journalists caught up in the mania? "Because it was fun," Sloan said in a 2002 interview. "It's fun to have access. It's fun to be part of the new thing. It attracted readers. It attracted ads. It created buzz. It made you hot and trendy." [58]

By 1996, however, Sloan was not feeling hot and trendy. He was feeling old and a little cranky—or, at least, alarmed. In May, he directed his readers' attention to a recent stock offering by Berkshire Hathaway, Warren Buffett's company. For weeks before the offering, Buffett had warned investors that the stock was overpriced, and that they should not buy it. "He practically put a skull and crossbones on his prospectus," Sloan wrote. "So what happened? The more Buffett bad-mouthed his stock, the more people lusted after it. Investors bought $500 million worth—five times what Berkshire originally offered to sell." [59]

Perhaps Warren Buffett was using a little reverse psychology to drum up interest in his offering? No, in fact, by March of 1996 Buffett believed that the market as a whole was rising without rhyme or reason: "This was a

year in which any fool could make a bundle in the stock market," he noted
in his annual letter to investors. "And we did. To paraphrase President Kennedy," he added slyly, "a rising tide lifts all yachts." [60]

Buffett made it clear that, in his view, Hathaway's shares were overvalued, along with everything else: "Though the per-share intrinsic value of
our stock has grown at an excellent rate during the past five years, its market
price has grown still faster. The stock, in other words, has outperformed the
business.

"That kind of market overperformance cannot persist indefinitely, neither for Berkshire nor any other stock," he added. "Inevitably, there will be
periods of underperformance as well. The price volatility that results,
though endemic to public markets, is not to our liking. What we would
prefer instead is to have the market price of Berkshire precisely track its intrinsic value." [61]

Why, then, was he offering new shares of Berkshire? Buffett had been
backed into a corner by two promoters who had devised a scheme to peddle
Berkshire stock to individual investors. Since Berkshire was trading at
$35,000 a share, few small investors could afford to buy it directly. Enter
the promoters who created "Affordable Access Trust." They planned to sell
units to individual investors for $1,000, charge a fee, and use the money
that was left over (after they took their fee off the top) to buy Berkshire
stock. When Buffett heard of their plans, "he went ballistic," Sloan reported. "Buffett felt the trust would gouge small investors [with its fees]
and hurt Berkshire's good name. Buffett resents people poaching on his
fame and expertise and he was clearly worried that the trust's buying would
[further] artificially inflate the price of Berkshire's stock." When the promoters refused to abandon their project, Buffett resolved to sell Berkshire
shares to small investors himself. He did this by creating B shares of Berkshire equal to one-thirtieth of a regular share, which he sold at $1,100
apiece in May of 1996.

Sloan understood why Buffett issued the shares, but he did not understand why investors bought them, flying in the face of Buffett's warnings
that Berkshire's shares were bloated.

"Think about it," Sloan wrote. "Investors disregarded stock-picking
advice from the person to whom they were entrusting money to pick
stocks. Hello? And then the stock ran up 8% in its first two days of trading." He titled the column "The Baby Berkshire Frenzy May Reflect a Market Gone Mad."

THE RISKIEST TIME TO BUY STOCKS

A financial journalist since 1969, Sloan understood the market's cycles. Indeed, only a month earlier, he tried to share a little financial history with his readers by recalling the seventies, a decade when buy-and-hold investors were sandpapered to death:

"I still had hair and was writing about stocks for the first time," he recalled. "Many of today's money managers were in grade school. . . . Owning stocks then was water torture—prices kept falling drop by drop. . . . Back then, it took real courage to buy stocks," he explained. "Now, in the longest-running bull market ever, it has taken courage to stay out of the market. . . . Many people have come to believe that baby boomers will pour their retirement money into stocks forever, propping up stock prices forever," Sloan added, "but investing on this basis is a good way to spend your retirement living on Hamburger Helper and day-old buns." [62]

Sloan recognized a truth that would seem, to most people, counterintuitive: the riskiest time to buy stocks is during a roaring bull market. Because when prices are highest, the downside is steepest. Meanwhile, the upside is founded on hope, and hope alone. By contrast, once a bear market has scraped bottom, stocks are cheap, the downside limited.

Late in 1996, by contrast, the downside was enormous. An investor was buying into a market that had doubled in roughly five years. When the market reverted to a mean, he was positioned to lose a large chunk of his savings. And over time, markets do tend to revert to a mean—a midpoint between the high prices of strong cycles and the rock-bottom prices of weak cycles. Historically, at the mean stocks have fetched roughly 15 times earnings. Over a long period of time, the mean may move; 25 years from now, the mean price/earnings ratio might well be higher or lower than 15. Much depends on economic conditions, global politics, and investors' expectations. But there will still be a mean, and it will still be safer to buy stocks when the market is trading below its past averages than when it is trading above them.

In April of 1996, Sloan stressed that each investor had to assess his own situation, based on his age, risk tolerance, and how much he could afford to lose. But "if you can't afford a 20 percent or 30 percent loss," he advised, "you might want to take some of your winnings off the table." [63] Investors who heeded his advice, and stashed some of their winnings in plain-vanilla 10-year Treasuries at the end of the first quarter of 1996, would watch that money grow by 78 percent over the next seven years. If, on the other hand, they decided to ride the S&P 500 all the way, they would take a round trip that left them with total capital gains of just 31 percent. Even if they faithfully reinvested dividends, their total return over seven years would equal just 46 percent—32 percent less than Treasuries.

THE INFORMATION BOMB

By the mid-nineties, investors were riding a wave of information, a never-ending tsunami of news and numbers. No one could resist or stem the explosion of financial information—it became part of the cultural landscape. After all, the bull market of the mid-nineties, like the go-go market of the sixties, was a People's Market, and the democratization of information was part of the process.

As CNBC's Maria Bartiromo put it, "Why shouldn't Joe Smith who works at a deli have the same information as Joe Smith who works at an investment bank?"

The answer: absolutely no reason why he shouldn't. There was just one question: what good would it do him?

As information flooded the marketplace it became more difficult to assemble the bits and pieces into a coherent pattern. Ultimately, the bull market of the nineties was all about excess capacity: too many microchip factories, too many wireless carriers, years' worth of fiber optic capacity in the ground. The excess extended to the information industry.

"The enormous flow of information that we have today doesn't necessarily reduce uncertainty," observed Peter Bernstein, the economic consultant who authored *Against the Gods*. "My favorite example is that on the morning of September 11, 2001, my wife and I were packed to go to California. We were in Manhattan, waiting for the limo to come. We had a lot of information—it was a lovely day, the limo was on time, the flight was scheduled to take off on time. . . .

"But you never know. With all the information you can possibly get, you never know whether it's sufficient."[1]

The problem is that much of the information that investors want—and think they need—is just that, "information," not knowledge. Knowledge comes only through time. It dawns on us gradually, as we digest bits of information, reflect on them, and rearrange them, revising and refining our interpretation. But the New Age of Information aimed to collapse time. An investor no longer had to wait for tomorrow's newspaper to hear the news: the future was *now*.[2]

That explosion of information can mask the few facts that are truly important. "Rarely do more than three or four variables really count. Everything else is noise," Marty Whitman, manager of the Third Avenue Funds, confided. As a long-term value investor, Whitman paid virtually no attention to whether a company beat Wall Street's quarterly earnings estimates. Ignoring the chatter, he zeroed in on a company's balance sheet. There he found less transient numbers—a summary of the company's assets and liabilities. "For many—if not most—companies, analysis of the amount and quality of resources that a management has to work with is as good or an even better tool for predicting earnings per share than past earnings growth," Whitman remarked. It was a method that worked: over the 10 years ending in January of 2003, his Third Avenue Value Fund rewarded investors with returns averaging more than 10 percent annually.[3]

But as the market heated up, the emphasis was on speed, and investors addicted to a constant stream of information came to prefer the *illusion* of knowledge spun from the tips and tidings that came to them with the absolute speed of electronic impulses—online, on television, all day, every day.

Trouble is, that stream of information is always changing. Today's numbers will be revised tomorrow: this quarter's reported earnings; analysts' estimates for the next quarter; the results of this week's poll of 50 economists . . .

The critical process of analyzing that stream of imperfect information, sorting out what is relevant, checking the accuracy of the facts, and then synthesizing the bits of data into a meaningful context is labor intensive.

This makes it expensive.

BEHIND THE NUMBERS

Throughout the nineties, some of the very best financial research was being done, not on Wall Street, but by independent research boutiques. Savvy professional investors knew this and were willing to pay for it. Some paid as much as $10,000 a year, for example, to subscribe to David Tice's newsletter, *Behind the Numbers*, a report that offered in-depth analysis of corporate earnings.

In the late eighties, Tice had noticed that Wall Street analysts were no longer writing "sell" recommendations, and the 33-year-old Dallas money manager set out to fill the gap. A certified public accountant, he knew how to do the nitty-gritty detective work needed to pierce the veil of corporate accounting, and in 1987 he founded his own independent research service, David W. Tice & Associates. Tice started his research boutique at home; his only "associates" were his wife and a wailing baby in the next room.[4]

Dressed in jeans and an open-necked shirt, Tice did not look like a CPA. Rather, he looked like the Texan that he had become—though in fact, he had been born in the show-me state, "home of Harry Truman," as he liked to point out. In the late seventies Tice earned an MBA in finance at Texas Christian University. But MBA programs do not teach financial analysts what they need to know to sleuth phony books. Tice earned his stripes by going to work as an internal auditor, first at Atlantic Richfield, then at ENSERCH, a diversified energy company where he evaluated potential acquisitions. In those jobs, he developed the skills that so many Wall Street analysts lacked, learning how to scour balance sheets, income statements, and cash flow statements with a fine-tooth comb.

Tice had not always been a bear. In the early eighties, at the very beginning of the bull market, he left the energy industry and went to work for a Dallas financial advisor. While there, he urged wealthy clients to move their money out of oil and gas and into stocks. But as the mania for growth grew, he became queasy about equities.

Tice recognized that "the most reckless fund managers, the most reckless auditors, the most reckless investment bankers, the most reckless corporate officers made the most money. So you had greater and greater incentives to promote the most reckless guys." Meanwhile, "the most reckless CEOs hired the most reckless CFOs [chief financial officers]." As the bull market unfolded, Tice watched hundreds of companies buying back their own shares at stunning prices, "and taking on massive debt loads—

even while their business prospects deteriorated." In his view "a culture of growth with no regard to risk had permeated the economy."[5]

Tice's research filled a niche. Before long, a "Who's Who" of institutional investors were buying his newsletter. His often scathing reports became popular because they served as an early-warning system for savvy investors, alerting them to the dangers of overly aggressive accounting at companies such as AOL, Sunbeam, Lucent, TWA, Providian, Gateway, and Tyco. "We're that little voice in the back trying to point out the potential problems that the bulls overlook," Tice said in 1994.[6]

In the meantime, Tice became one of the better-known shorts on Wall Street. In 1995, he launched the Prudent Bear Fund—a fund that was able to short stocks, giving small investors an opportunity to share in the fruits of his research.

Tice's hard-nosed fundamental analysis drew scorn both from Wall Street's boosters and from corporate chieftains who howled when they were caught. Nevertheless, by the middle of 1994, nearly 60 percent of the stocks Tice had flagged since he founded his business six years earlier had underperformed the S&P, while 46 percent had declined in price. Not a bad record, given that over the same period, the S&P as a whole had risen from 247, at the beginning of 1988, to 457, in June of 1994.[7]

It is worth noting that many of the companies Tice shorted belonged to the Old Economy. At the end of the century, some observers would blame the excesses of the bull market on the Internet—as if seedy accounting was limited to dot.coms and telecoms. In truth, bogus bookkeeping was pervasive. The problem in a runaway bull market is that too much money (and too much credit) is chasing too few stocks in virtually every sector of the economy. And whenever there is too much money on the table, the crooks come out of the woodwork. In the nineties "creative accounting" became an accepted management technique in even the most old-fashioned industries. Sunbeam, a maker of small appliances, stood as a homely example.

Sunbeam came under Tice's microscope in 1995, and at the time, he put his finger on the company's essential problem: Sunbeam was in the business of making toasters, blenders, and electric blankets, a market where competition was intense and growth slow. Meanwhile, Tice noted, Sunbeam already had done all it could to boost its earnings with "liberal accounting" and "one-time events." (For example, the appliance maker had eliminated medical and life insurance for retirees eligible for Medicare.)

Before long Sunbeam's CEO, Roger Schipke, was ousted, and Al Dunlap took his place. Known in the corporate community as "chainsaw Al"— a reference to his reputation for slashing jobs—Dunlap was brought in to turn the company around. Investors impressed by Dunlap's press ignored the numbers. But those who had read Tice's careful analysis in 1995 would recognize that Dunlap had little hope of success.

As Tice put it when he wrote about the company again in December of 1996: "Wall Street will probably be 'snowed' for a while longer by the turn-around plan, but we believe the current euphoria has given investors a great second chance to get out of this stock. [Dunlap] still has to overcome the inherent problem that everyone already has a toaster and an electric blanket." [8]

Tice quoted one of Sunbeam's competitors: " 'All consumer appliances cost what they did 20 years ago. We wish we could raise prices like the automakers. But we can't.' " At the 1996 International Housewares Show, one marketing executive displayed a 1950s advertisement for a toaster that cost $15.99. "Today, 40 years later, a toaster still costs $10–$20," he observed.

Dunlap arrived on the scene with a much-ballyhooed restructuring plan that included cutting the number of products Sunbeam manufactured, eliminating "non-core" items such as outdoor furniture and decorative bedding, which once accounted for about one-quarter of total sales. [9] But, Tice pointed out, "The key theme to keep in mind is that the restructuring will put even more emphasis on small appliances." Meanwhile, the small-appliance industry only had unit sales growth of 0.7 percent in 1995. "It is difficult to grow a non-growth business," Tice concluded.

This was the essential fact to understand about the company: it made small appliances, and it had no pricing power. No matter how you cooked the books, you could not get past that fact.

But once Dunlap came on board, a blizzard of press releases tried to obscure the limits of Sunbeam's situation, and the media picked up on the news: "Dunlap Makes Plans to Shine Up Sunbeam: A $12 Million Ad Blitz, Focus on Home Products May Spruce Up Image"; "Sunbeam Plugs into Overseas Market"; "Sunbeam 3Q—Better Times Seen Ahead Under Dunlap"; "Sunbeam Profit Seen on Slimmer Product Line." [10]

Meanwhile, analysts began upping their estimates: "Goldman analyst Elizabeth Fontenelli raised her 1997 earnings estimate on Sunbeam to $1.45 a share from 90 cents," Dow Jones News Service reported in November of 1996. "Fontenelli said she's a 'true believer' in Albert J. Dunlap." [11] Fontenelli was only one of many analysts who upgraded the stock.

Not everyone swallowed Dunlap's story whole. In April of 1997, four months after Tice's second Sunbeam report, *Fortune* columnist Herb Greenberg quoted Tice's charges that "the stock is being driven by 'misunderstood hype' and by analysts living under the 'Dunlap spell.' " The headline on his column: "Sunbeam Is Toast." [12]

Two months later, *Barron's* published a story that questioned Dunlap's restructuring and the quality of Sunbeam's earnings in greater detail. [13] Trading at $39, Sunbeam-Oster now fetched more than triple the price it drew a year earlier when Dunlap took the helm. Readers who took either Greenberg's or *Barron's* warning to heart still had time to get out. But buy-and-hold investors—not to mention momentum investors who continued to buy on the way up—would be Osterized. [14]

Sunbeam offered a clear case of how too many estimates and too many projections could obscure the few facts that were important. Dunlap's larger-than-life personality also helped overshadow the company's story. A West Point–trained former paratrooper begged to be profiled. Not everyone admired Dunlap; his ruthless job-cutting drew fire from many reporters. But there was no question that he was a personality, and "in order to engage people in business, you need personalities," CNBC's president Bill Bolster explained. "It's no longer Sunbeam; it's Al Dunlap. It's no longer IBM; it's Lou Gerstner." [15]

In October of '97, CNBC would provide a showcase for the Dunlap personality, giving the CEO an opportunity to announce that Sunbeam had hired Morgan Stanley to explore the possibility of a merger, an acquisition, or a sale. Sunbeam's shares bounced on the news.

At the end of the interview, *Squawk Box* host Mark Haines did raise a prickly question: "According to Standard & Poor's research, cautious investors should steer clear of Sunbeam shares, given the risk inherent in failing to meet rather lofty expectations." Then he handed Dunlap an easy exit: "I take it that would not be the advice you would give investors."

Dunlap's answer: "It's total bullshit." Apparently Haines deemed it a sufficient response. He did not ask a follow-up question. [16]

A few months later, charges of accounting gimmickry finally caught up with the stock. In the spring of '98, Sunbeam was still trading well over $50; by June, the shares had plunged to less than $9 on reports of an SEC investigation. That year, Dunlap was fired. Three years later, Sunbeam declared bankruptcy. A year after that, Dunlap agreed to pay $500,000 to settle SEC allegations that he used improper accounting to produce "materially false and misleading" results while at Sunbeam Corp. Dunlap did not admit to wrongdoing, but as part of the settlement, he agreed to a permanent ban on serving as an officer or director of a publicly traded company.

Tice pointed out the hole in Dunlap's story in December of 1996, more than a year before the stock tanked. The irony was that in an Age of Information, Tice's reports rarely trickled out into the mainstream media. This was not because he was unwilling to share his ideas. Tice was quoted, from time to time, in publications such as *Barron's*, *The Wall Street Journal*, *The New York Times*, and *Bloomberg Personal Finance*.

But at many publications, journalists were warned to steer clear of the shorts. Columnists like Greenberg were the exceptions. "I think it's easier to use shorts as sources if you're a columnist than if you're a beat reporter covering a particular industry," said Greenberg. "When you're a beat reporter specializing in an industry, you know management, or you need to talk to the PR people—and you're afraid of getting frozen out. If you talk to the shorts, and write negative stuff, the company won't talk to you. In my old days as a beat reporter, in the early to mid-eighties, I was looking for scoops, I was looking to beat the competition, and often you got the scoops from the PR people. So, back then, I needed them." [17]

Even as a columnist, Greenberg took heat for listening to the contrarians. Critics insinuated that he was acting as a "foil" for the shorts. "You're always going to be accused of being a tool of the shorts," said Greenberg, "because that's what people want to think." He addressed the issue directly in his column:

"Regarding whether my pans come from professional shorts or my own research: Honestly—usually professional shorts. No secret in that. I talk to loads of short sellers. Their research is usually far superior to longs in the same stock, and they can point me or any other reporter in the direction of the facts the longs have overlooked, usually hidden in public documents. I then take it from there—usually adding my research to theirs. Often, I dig up info even they don't know. I take tips whenever and wherever I can get them—and then I check them out myself." [18]

"You Get What You Pay For"— Wall Street Research

David Tice's *Behind the Numbers* was not the only place where investors could find cutting-edge independent research. Steve Leuthold, the Minneapolis money manager who honed his analytic skills while charting stocks for his army captain in the early sixties, and Peter Bernstein, an author and economic consultant based in New York, each produced in-depth analysis for institutional investors. Other research boutiques flourished around the country, selling their work to a mostly small, elite audience. Sophisticated investors subscribed to newsletters such as Fred Hickey's *Hi-Tech Strategy* letter, *Richard Russell's Dow Theory Letter, Grant's Interest Rate Observer,* Marc Faber's *Gloom, Boom and Doom Report,* or *welling@weeden,* a newsletter that began circulating in 1999, featuring interviews with some of the best minds in the financial community.[19]

On Wall Street, a small cadre of analysts and market strategists continued to offer insightful commentary. But independent analysts were much freer to throw a spotlight on corporate America's inflated earnings. By 1996, Fred Hickey, for example, was warning investors about the outlook for companies like Micron Technology, AOL, IBM, and Compaq. Both the consumer and the business market for PCs were approaching saturation, he cautioned, and analysts were lowballing earnings estimates in order to make sure that companies would be able to "beat" the numbers. Later in the decade, Jim Grant would call attention to Cisco's "imaginative" accounting.[20]

Few on Wall Street offered the same combination of critical thinking and forensic accounting. The reason: no one was paying for it. In 1975, deregulation turned the economics of Wall Street research upside down. That year, brokerage commissions were thrown open to competition. For the small investor, this was seen as a boon: discount brokers and low-cost online trading followed.

But in the past, brokers' commissions underwrote Wall Street's research. Mutual fund companies and other institutional investors rewarded brokerage houses that produced the best research by directing their business to those houses—buying the stocks that the firms' analysts recommended and paying steep commissions on huge orders. With deregulation, commissions fell precipitously. In 1976, brokers had to move an average of $77 worth of stock to earn $1 of commissions; 10 years later, they needed to peddle $216 worth of stock to make the same dollar.[21] The firms had to find another profit center.

In the eighties, investment banking fees from leveraged buyouts, mergers, and acquisitions helped pay the bills; during that span Wall Street firms also began to focus on trading for their own accounts. In the nineties, IPOs propelled profits at many houses. Wall Street's top firms were no longer in the brokerage business; they were in the "deal" business. And without cushy commissions to line their coffers, they desperately needed that business.

Small wonder, the analyst's function changed. Brokerage fees no longer supported the research effort. Inevitably, analysts realigned their priorities: those who helped bring in the business—and place the IPOs with large institutional investors—drew the top salaries.

For the individual investor, this change carried enormous implications. On the one hand, he no longer had to fork over steep commissions each time he traded. (This, of course, encouraged more trading, making low commissions a double-edged sword for all but the most nimble short-term traders.) At the same time, he could no longer expect objective Wall Street research designed to help him make the best possible trading decisions. He wasn't paying for in-depth, labor-intensive stock analysis—and neither was anyone else.

So analysts like Salomon Brothers' Jack Grubman focused on becoming experts in an industry: "No one knew as much about telecommunications as Jack," said one of his colleagues. Even his critics agreed. Grubman knew the business inside out and used his expertise to advise investment banking clients such as WorldCom. His first allegiance was to the companies he covered, and to the mutual fund companies and other large institutional investors who owned large blocks of WorldCom's shares. As the late-night caller had warned Henry Blodget, these investors did not want an analyst to question the earnings of a company they owned.[22] Mutual fund managers had followed WorldCom to the top of the cliff. Once there, they had taken large positions: if Grubman downgraded the stock, they would have no way to rappel safely to the ground without being crushed in an avalanche of selling.

Looking back on the bull market in 2001, *The New York Times'* chief financial correspondent Floyd Norris summed up the shortcomings of Wall Street research: "You Get What You Pay For." Despite all of the talk about reforming Wall Street's research departments, "the real problem," Norris observed, "is money. With commissions on share trading continually falling the money comes from investment banking fees, and the companies that direct those fees want praise, not criticism. Investors who want good research will have to pay for it," Norris warned. "Until a mechanism is devised to pay Wall Street for quality advice, no new rule is likely to produce it."[23]

Still, the question remains: How much should that research cost, and who should pay for it? Research on many subjects is supported by universities, the government, or private foundations and is disseminated, freely, among interested parties. On Wall Street everything is for sale, including ideas. Yet the notion that the knowledge needed to trade successfully is available only to those who can afford it undermines the notion of a transparent—not to mention a democratic—market.

INFORMATION AND THE 401(K) INVESTOR

The sophisticated investors who went off Wall Street to buy the crème de la crème of independent financial research realized that they needed unbiased analysis. "But the average investor didn't," acknowledged columnist Herb Greenberg. "Our original goal at TheStreet.com was to level the playing field, but ultimately I think we realized, you can't give it away. Our company wanted to stay in business." In 2003, for example, TheStreet.com moved Greenberg's column from its "RealMoney" website—a site that charged subscribers $225—to "Street Insight," a site aimed at professionals that charged $2,200. "I said, 'Why are you moving me?' I had a larger audience on RealMoney," Greenberg recalled. "But management had decided that the information I reported was worth more than $225."[24]

This is not to say that there is not some excellent information available, at no cost, on the Net. But because there is so *much* information online—some of it inaccurate, much of it irrelevant—it is difficult for any but the most astute investor to sort out the gold from the dross. "People will pay for the stuff that's good," added Greenberg, "but unfortunately, only the people who know why they're paying buy it. The average guy doesn't. He doesn't understand that it's a part of the cost of doing business."

The average 401(k) investor does not think of himself as being in business, even though in fact he is running a very small mutual fund—his own nest egg. Yet in 1996, the average 401(k) account balance totaled just $30,270.[25] The typical individual investor could not afford the cost of buying expensive research, even if the best of it was well worth the price. Nevertheless, "to get really skilled analysis, you have to pay," insisted Peter Bernstein. "There is no free lunch. A small investor can get access to the Value Line Investment Survey at a reasonable price," he added, "and it has a very good track record." [26]

Bernstein had a point. While an annual subscription to Value Line cost $598 in 2003—a large sum for an investor trying to decide how to allocate, say, $5,000, to a 401(k)—many public libraries carry Value Line. Still, the question remained: How many investors would make the trip to the library to study Value Line's recommendations?

The dilemma underlines the problem inherent in the 401(k)'s basic mandate: do-it-yourself investing. Many investors have neither the time, nor the money, nor the training needed to take advantage of the best research. Of course the 401(k) investor has the option of entrusting his money to a mutual fund, with the expectation that the fund manager will do the research for him. Certainly a mutual fund company running billions in assets can afford whatever research it needs. But this is not to say that the average fund manager is likely to step out of the box to read the challenging, in-depth analysis that someone like Hickey, Grant, or Bernstein offered. Or that he would feel free to follow that advice.

After all, portfolio managers also lived in a society where most people truly believed that stocks could only go up. Deviations from the conventional wisdom could kill a career.[27]

Moreover, even if an individual investor could count on his mutual fund manager to take advantage of the very best research available, the small investor still needed help in picking funds. How much should he allocate to a bond fund? To foreign stocks? To technology? To health care? Within each sector, which funds should he choose?

MUTUAL FUND REPORTS

The financial press made every effort to provide the information mutual fund investors needed to make their choices. But despite the reams of paper devoted to mutual fund scorecards, the data did not lend itself to prophecy. No matter how carefully the numbers were sliced, diced, and sifted, it often was difficult, if not impossible, to know what they might mean for future performance.

Most mutual fund reports focused primarily on the funds' quarterly, one-year, and three-year returns. Sometimes the scorecard looked back five years, though as one magazine editor explained to a reporter in the mid-nineties, "No one really cares about what happened further back than three years."

Yet history suggests that a fund's returns over three- and five-year periods offer little insight into how it is likely to perform going forward. In fact, a fund's one-year performance might serve as a better short-term indicator, observed Mark Hulbert: "Funds that own a given year's top performing stocks have a good chance of outperforming the next year too. It has nothing to do with the manager's ability. It's the momentum effect—the wind at your back," Hulbert explained. "If you had a bunch of monkeys running the funds, the ones that did best for the previous 6 or 12 months would be likely to outperform the next year. But the effect is short-lived; in the third year they would do no better than the average fund. Investing based on a fund's one-year performance works only if you're a short-term player." [28] And of course, when a bull market ends, momentum goes into reverse: the funds that owned the top technology stocks of 1999 were doomed to plunge in 2000.

"At the other end of the performance spectrum, long-term performance can tell you something about a fund manager's ability," Hulbert explained. Just how long a track record is needed to predict future performance? "At 5 years, the predictive value is minuscule," Hulbert acknowledged. "Based on my own research tracking roughly 160 newsletters, I've found that a newsletter's 15-year record was four times better at predicting future rankings than a record based on just 3 years."

Mark Carhart, head of quantitative research at Goldman Sachs, has done extensive research on mutual fund performance, and his work shows that "for your average fund manager, in order to get results that are statistically significant—results that allow you to say with some certainty that his active management has added value to the returns you would have gotten in an index fund—you might need 64 years of data. On the other hand, a 10-year record might be enough for you to say 'I can't project statistically that he's a star, but I feel pretty confident that he's a star. I think I'll give him some of my money.' The problem with past performance," Carhart added, "is that there is always so much noise in it." [29]

What seems clear is that a three-year record, by itself, is virtually worthless: "It's too long to capture the momentum effect, and too short to capture the manager's ability," said Hulbert. "I think this is one reason why rating services like Morningstar have been so disappointing despite their use of methods that otherwise seem eminently reasonable. Even though Morningstar looks at 3-, 5-, and 10-year returns, they heavily weight 3-year returns. Basically they've got the opposite of the sweet spot—they've got the sour spot. If they only looked at 10-year performance they would do better. But of course, most funds don't have a 10-year record. If they limited themselves to that group, they would rate many fewer funds. By focusing on 3-year returns, it seems to me they've made a marketing decision [to cover more funds.]"

Given the inadequacy of 3-year track records, it should not be surprising that Morningstar's top-rated equity funds have lagged the market by a wide margin. According to Hulbert's research, after deducting fees, Morningstar's top-ranked equity funds underperformed the broadest market index, the Wilshire 5,000, by an annualized average of 5.5 percentage points from the beginning of 1991 through May 31, 2002.[30]

A. Michael Lipper, founder of Lipper Analytical Services, agreed that when it comes to telling the difference between luck and talent "you're moving [away from the science] and into the 'art' of mutual fund analysis." Unlike Morningstar, Lipper's rankings did not give more weight to three-year performance. Nor did they try to rate funds with a star system. "We called our analysis 'rankings' rather than 'ratings'—all we were doing was showing an array, we were not casting a judgment," Lipper explained in a 2003 interview.[31] "Ultimately, you want to look at what *created* the performance," he emphasized. "In many cases, you'll find that a few very good or quite bad decisions made all the difference. For many fund managers, the good ones came early in their career—and if people lengthened the time period they were looking at, the good performance at the beginning would carry the long periods. What you want to do is look at the manager's performance period by period—and try to assess how repeatable it is.

"To me, the managers who showed repeatable results during the bull market were Peter Lynch, John Templeton, and John Neff," Lipper added.[32] "Over the years, they succeeded while investing in different securities. By contrast, a number of managers did well by investing in the same 100 stocks for 30 years, 60 of them at a time. They weren't finding new names," making it harder, Lipper suggested, to assess their talent as stock pickers. Maybe they just got lucky when they first chose their stable of stocks.

Even over long periods of time, virtually everyone who has tried to analyze investment talent agrees, it is impossible to know how much of a mutual fund manager's success is due to skill, and how much is what options trader Nassim Nicholas Taleb calls "survivorship bias."

"We look back at investors who have made a lot of money and we tend to think 'they made it because they were good.' Perhaps," Taleb observed, "we have turned the causality on its head: maybe we consider them good just because they made money."

In *Fooled by Randomness: The Hidden Role of Risk in the Market and in Life,* Taleb offered a wonderfully ghoulish example to illustrate his point: "Imagine an eccentric and bored billionaire who offers you $10 million to play Russian roulette. He gives you a revolver with six chambers, a bullet in only one of those chambers, and challenges you to hold it to your head and pull the trigger. Chances are five in six that you'll come away with $10 million; chances are one in six that you won't come away at all. In other words, there are six possible paths that your story will take—but after the fact, we'll see only one of them." And if you survive, Taleb observed, "you may be used as a role model by family, friends and neighbors." Indeed, if the Russian roulette player was a mutual fund manager, some journalist might well put him on the cover of a magazine ("Savvy Risk-Taker Beats Index").[33]

Of course, Taleb conceded, if the roulette-betting fool kept on playing the game, the alternative story lines would be likely to catch up with him: "Chances are, he wouldn't survive to his 50th birthday. But when we look at the stock market's stars we're looking at the survivors from a very large pool of players. Imagine that there are thousands of 25-year-olds willing to play Russian roulette, playing each year, on their birthdays. At the end of say, twenty years, we can expect to see a handful of extremely rich survivors—and a very large cemetery.

"But that small group of survivors would be hailed as winners—the alternative possibilities of what might have happened to them would be ignored."[34]

Yet maybe they were just lucky—after all, someone had to wind up in the top percentile. This applies not only to mutual fund managers but to the funds themselves. For instance, imagine that in 1987 there were 30 mutual funds in the United States devoted to investing in technology, and that over the next 15 years, 6 of the original 30 produced average returns of more than 12 percent a year. Meanwhile, the other 24 funds averaged less than 5 percent and either were closed or folded into other funds. We would look at the 6 that survived and say that investing in technology funds is not so very risky: after all, on average, technology funds with a 15-year track record returned 12 percent from 1987 to 2002.

That said, Hulbert's research suggests that information about a stock picker's performance over a very long period can be valuable. Taleb agreed. If an investor flourished over a long period of time, surviving more than one cycle, it is fair to presume that more than luck was involved. "George Soros, for example, succeeded, not only in very different cycles, but in very different markets—trading not only U.S. stocks, but currencies and foreign equities," Taleb pointed out. This makes it more likely that his success was due to skill. But, "you cannot be certain," Taleb added. "You can only make the presumption that it was more skill than chance." [35]

Information is, in the end, always imperfect. No matter how much data an investor has, he never knows what piece might be missing. And in the mid-nineties, the available information about the talents of individual mutual fund managers was far from complete. Indeed, very few fund managers had been on the job for 15 years.

BRINGING INDEPENDENT RESEARCH
TO A WIDER AUDIENCE

As the market lifted off, the Age of Information seemed to be failing the small investor, providing an embarrassment of information—and too little knowledge. Some would blame the investor himself. After all, if thoughtful financial analysis drew a wider audience, it might well be less expensive, and therefore more available to small investors. No doubt, many of the best newsletter writers of the nineties would happily have published their reports more widely, at a lower cost. But the truth is that the majority of investors preferred the lighter fare to be found in the mainstream press—or in popular newsletters such as Louis Rukeyser's *Rukeyser Report*, which offered generally upbeat, easily digested commentary at an affordable price.

Others would argue that if the best research were more widely read, it would, almost by definition, become less valuable. Those who read it would no longer enjoy an "edge" over other investors. But this is true only if one assumes that the most valuable information consists of "tips": buy X, or sell Y. In this case, whoever gets the news first winds up the winner.

Ideas, on the other hand, have a much longer shelf life. Tice's analysis of Sunbeam, for instance, was far more than a sell recommendation. He drew a portrait of the company in the context of both the small-appliance industry and Sunbeam's own past performance. This was not a "tip" or a "scoop"—Tice simply analyzed publicly available information. What made the report so valuable was his ability to synthesize that information, ignore the noise, and underline what was most important.

Investors who had access to his report did not need to act on it immediately. They simply needed to do what Tice had done: think about it. Four months after he issued the report to his own subscribers, Tice shared the essential information about Sunbeam with Herb Greenberg—and at that point, it was just as valuable to an investor who read Greenberg's column in *Fortune* as it had been to Tice's subscribers. Sunbeam's shares were still flying high—and would climb higher. Investors had more than a year to act on Tice's warning.

Over the long run, the market may be efficient, but often it takes months—or even years—for the stock market to absorb the implications of publicly available information. This is why the best investment research tends to have lasting value, not just to the investors who get the news first but to anyone willing to reflect on it.

To their credit, some in the mainstream press tried to bring first-rate financial analysis to a larger audience, publishing the independent views of seasoned market observers such as Russell, Grant, Hickey, and Tice— picadors who challenged the bull and threatened to prick the bubble.

But as the bull barreled ahead, critical thinking became less welcome, not only on Wall Street but on Main Street. More often than not, the press conferred authority on the bulls, quoting Abby Cohen, Ralph Acampora, or Salomon Brothers telecom analyst Jack Grubman as "experts" in front-page news stories. For balance, many newspapers and magazines made room for a bearish voice, but the skeptics' arguments were usually consigned to op-ed pieces, columns, or "Q&A" interviews—bracketed in a way that made it clear that the views expressed were the opinion of just one dreary man.

After all, the bull market of the mid-nineties was a democratic market. Any publication that questioned the market's rise was questioning the collective wisdom of its readers—the individual investors who were pouring their retirement dollars into stocks and stock funds. "Our new-found faith in active, intelligent audiences made criticism of the market philosophically untenable," wrote social historian Thomas Frank.[36] Skeptics came to be seen as cynics—doubters who dared to question the judgment of millions of individual investors.

How the Conventional Wisdom Absorbs Information

In truth, however, those individual investors were not making separate judgments. The vast majority were swayed by the same headlines: sound bites that were, at best, incomplete—at worst, hype. Yet precisely because everyone shared the same information, investors enjoyed a false sense of security: "Everyone knew" that, over time, stocks always went up. Ergo, if you just bought a good company and held on, you would make money—no matter what price you paid for the stock.

This was the conventional wisdom of the time. Such truths seemed self-evident. Similarly, in the late seventies, "the death of equities" was the headline that summed up the prevailing view.[37] "Everyone knew" that real estate was the best hedge against inflation. And, for a time, that would be true.

The problem is that as circumstances change, so does the conventional wisdom. Yet at any given cultural moment, we accept it as absolute truth.[38]

Even in an Age of Information, we make the facts fit the conventional wisdom. The trade deficit has broken yet another record? In a bull market, this is assimilated as good news: "The consensus among economists is that the trade gap is a reflection of the U.S. economy's position as the strongest in the world," *Bloomberg News* reported.[39] Price/earnings ratios have hit an all-time high? This was taken not as a warning that stocks might be overvalued, but as further proof that the old rules no longer applied.

Particularly in the midst of a financial mania, the received wisdom creates the illusion that there is safety in numbers. So, in the late eighties, Japanese investors buying near the peak of their own bull market liked to cite a popular Japanese saying: "If we all cross on the red light together, there's no need to be afraid."[40]

In a sense, they were right. For the moment—and at the time, the moment was all that seemed to matter—momentum was on their side. This is why, late in 1996, Richard Russell advised his readers that the bull market still had legs. "Once in every decade or so we see a market move that seemingly has taken on a 'life of its own.' We are seeing one such move now. . . .

For the first time in history, the capitalization of the U.S. stock market is greater than the entire U.S. Gross Domestic Product (the stock market is now valued at 101% of GDP; for comparison, the average in past history is 47.9%)." This bull, Russell knew, would not turn on a dime. It would need to make a long, extended top—even though many stocks were already grossly overvalued.

"In this business, it's easy to be fascinated with what 'should' or 'should not' happen," Russell cautioned. "The reality is that the Dow and the broad S&P have set new record highs. The rise has been confirmed by the advance-decline ratio on the New York Stock Exchange [which showed that the majority of stocks were still rising] and led by my Primary Trend Index." Russell could see that the underlying trend continued to be strongly positive. The tide was still coming in, even though it was sheer momentum, rather than value, that was driving the market.

But Russell also knew that, in the long run, everything depends on value: the price you pay when you get into the market. So, while he urged readers who already were in the market to ride the wave, he warned that prices were now so high that it was too late to join the party:

"If you're out of stocks, stay out; it's too late to be a hero, but it's not too late to be a loser." [41]

AOL: A Case Study

By the fall of 1995, America Online's shares already had taken wing—up 2,000 percent since the company's initial public offering just three years earlier. In a market driven by momentum, AOL was a star. But Allan Sloan realized that AOL's continued success depended upon its ability to stay a step ahead of the shorts. By Sloan's reckoning, the company was running a cash deficit of about $75 million a year. Meanwhile, the company was covering its financial shortfall with perfectly legal—but misleading—accounting techniques.

In other words, AOL was gaming its books. Everyone on Wall Street knew it, but most investors were content to ignore it. After all, in the first nine months of 1995, AOL had shot up 135 percent. Who wanted to quibble about bookkeeping?

Sloan wanted to make sure that his readers understood the risk: "Look closely and you see that AOL is as much about accounting technology as it is about computer technology," he wrote in October of 1995. "So make sure you understand the numbers before rushing out to buy AOL."

That fall, AOL was trying to paper over its cash deficit by issuing more and more stock. "If AOL can't sell stock, it's got big trouble," Sloan warned his readers. "At the least, it would have to drastically scale back its expansion plans."

Just as the operator of a pyramid scheme needs to continually bring in more customers, AOL needed to keep on issuing and selling new shares to keep the cash flow coming. Without the fresh money, the pyramid would collapse. This put AOL in a precarious position: "On Oct. 10 AOL raised about $100 million by selling new shares. The company sold the stock even though its shares had fallen to $58.375 from about $72 in September when the sales plans were announced," Sloan noted. "Most companies would have delayed the offering, waiting for the price to snap back. AOL didn't, prompting cynics to think the company really needed the money." [1]

Sloan had hit the nail on the head. AOL was papering over what should have been reported as losses with accounting tricks while covering its cash flow deficit by selling stock. Meanwhile, AOL tried to keep the dollars flowing in by charging up to $9.95 monthly for just five hours of Internet access—plus $2.95 for each additional hour online. But AOL executives knew that game could not go on forever. Already, a price war had begun. Six months earlier, one of its chief rivals, Prodigy, had announced a plan offering 30 hours of service for a flat fee of $29.95.[2] By 1996, AOL's competitors would offer unlimited use, at least during off-peak hours, for $19.95. But AOL resisted the notion of unlimited access for a flat fee.

AOL dragged its feet because it needed the revenues that it racked up from customers who used its chat rooms—online forums that allowed a freedom of expression that its biggest competitors, Prodigy and Compuserve, eschewed. On AOL, "sex chat" dominated many conversations. AOL users could take online aliases and roam unchaperoned chat rooms where it was easy to attach graphic files, making the site a convenient place to display porn. Members could even create their own chat rooms, with names like "submissive men" (as well as private rooms that a subscriber could enter only if a like-minded user had given him the code). AOL did not police the private rooms, and there, pornographers could flash their wares with impunity.

Not surprisingly, sex chat proved addictive. AOL's $2.95 per hour charges added up. In *aol.con.*, Kara Swisher, who covered the company for *The Washington Post* and, later, for *The Wall Street Journal,* reported that "chat," of all kinds, accounted for fully one-fourth of all member hours online, and some AOL users would spend more than 100 hours a month online.

" 'That's why AOL had eight million members and Prodigy has faded to a shadow of its former self,' " grumbled a high-ranking executive at

Prodigy. By 1996, AOL's "heavy users" accounted for just one-third of its subscriber base but counted for 60 percent of online hours. *Rolling Stone* magazine reckoned that, assuming half of AOL's chat was sexually oriented, the company now was raking in up to $7 million a month from "sex chat" alone. In the same article, Steve Case estimated that less than one-half of all chat was sex related.[3]

AOL was not alone in relying on pornography to generate traffic. "Porn was also very important for Yahoo!" said an analyst who covered the company in its early years. "It got the hours up—and no one talked about it."[4]

But sex chat alone was not enough to keep AOL in the black. To conjure up profits, AOL relied on a form of creative accounting that CUNY accounting professor Abraham Briloff would describe as "in-your-face arrogance." Two months before Sloan published his 1995 story, Briloff delivered a scalding paper at the American Accounting Conference revealing what short sellers on Wall Street already knew: AOL did not subtract the cost of marketing its product from its annual profits. Instead, the company categorized the millions it spent while recruiting customers as "deferred subscriber acquisition costs," and booked the expense as an "investment" to be paid for over a period of years.

In other words, AOL treated the costs of marketing the way a manufacturing company might treat an investment in factory equipment. Such investments are subtracted from profits over a period of years. The difference is that five years later, the manufacturer would still have the equipment. By contrast, in 2000 AOL would have relatively little to show for the advertising dollars it spent recruiting customers in 1995: five years later, many of those customers would have moved on to a different service.

And AOL's marketing costs were staggering. For AOL was all about marketing. After all, the company's chief executive, Steve Case, had learned how to sell a product at the Harvard of marketing: Procter & Gamble. Straight out of college, Case began his career promoting hair-care products at P&G (where he contributed the phrase "Towlette? You Bet!" to the English language), then moved to PepsiCo, where he worked on the Pizza Hut account. Case was not with either company for long, but he learned the basic strategy of introducing a product. He also understood that if you give the American consumer something for free, he might be so pleased that he would spend money to use it. Thus, in 1994, AOL began its campaign to win its way into the wallets of America's Great Unwired by giving away hundreds of millions of free floppy disks.[5]

AOL carpet-bombed America with the disks needed to use its service: flight attendants handed them out on American Airlines. They came packaged with flash-frozen Omaha steaks. You could find them on your seat at a football game. Yet the cost of the marketing extravaganza was not subtracted from profits on AOL's annual earnings statement. Instead, it was labeled an "investment"—as if AOL had invested in new equipment.

AOL justified postponing showing the expense: the company argued that the new subscribers would be with the company for 41 months. Sloan asked the obvious question: Of AOL's current customers, "How many have been around for 41 months?"

"Almost none," conceded Lennert Leader, AOL's chief financial officer.

"AOL had signed up most of its customers in the previous 36 months," Sloan explained. "Leader said the 41-month average life number comes from projections."[6] AOL's projections were, to say the least, rosy: at the time Jupiter Communications, an Internet research and consulting firm based in New York, reported that commercial online services usually lost 40 percent of their customers each year. Before long, AOL's "churn" rate would be even higher.[7]

The short sellers were onto the accounting scam: David Tice was among those known to be shorting the stock. But the shorts were taking a drubbing: in the six months ending in November of '95, investments representing a bet against America Online had lost around $400 million, according to Laszlo Birinyi, who tracked money flows for Birinyi Associates.

Small wonder. While the shorts sold AOL, mutual fund managers were scooping up the shares. "No one came close to forecasting how fast America Online would grow," Lise Buyer, a fund manager at T. Rowe Price Associates, said in the fall of '95. "What the shorts can't understand is that Wall Street, witnessing such growth, is willing to overlook the company's losses and well-known aggressive accounting methods."[8]

But the "growth" she was talking about was a growth in the number of subscribers, not a growth in earnings. The cost of acquiring those customers was so high that AOL had not, in fact, yet turned a profit—though thanks to its creative accounting, it was *reporting* profits.

Sloan continued to track the stock. By May of 1996, it was clear that AOL had a new and formidable rival: the Internet. In the past, the company's promoters claimed that the key to AOL was content, pointing to websites such as "The Motley Fool," an online forum for financial news and gossip available only to AOL customers. But those days were gone. Now, anyone could access The Motley Fool on the Net.[9]

In the seven months since Sloan had last reported on the company, AOL's books had deteriorated. "By my math, AOL ran through $185 million in the nine months that ended on March 31," Sloan observed. Yet it was still sweeping promotional costs under the carpet—putting off the day when it would have to subtract them from profits. Sloan calculated that the hidden pot of deferred expenses now totaled $315 million.

Meanwhile, the customers AOL paid so dearly to acquire were whirling through a revolving door. In the March quarter, AOL added 2.2 million new customers—but lost 1.3 million old customers. And now AOL was succumbing to the rate war, announcing that in July, it would begin offering 20 hours for $19.95—cutting a 20-hour user's bill by almost 60 percent.[10] Nevertheless, when Sloan interviewed AOL's Steve Case that spring, Case appeared unperturbed.

It was not, after all, Case's style to emote. Calm, even placid, and always dressed for his Gap ad—khakis, polo shirt, and sneakers—the moonfaced Case appeared unflappable. He had no edge—or so it seemed. One colleague described him as "catlike   always sitting in the back of the room, and watching everything going on. But you couldn't draw him out. Thoughtful? Yes. Charismatic? No. There was no output."[11]

True to form, in the interview Case could not be drawn into argument. He brushed aside questions about profits: "Only 11 percent of U.S. households are on-line," he pointed out. "Why aren't the other 89 percent? They think it's too hard and too complicated, and they're right." Without AOL, he seemed to suggest, Americans would never be able to figure out how to log on to the Net.

When Sloan wrote about AOL in May, the stock had just lost 25 percent of its value, down from an all-time high of $71 earlier in the month. Long-term buy-and-hold investors had reason to worry. Meanwhile, Sloan reported, Case himself already had cashed in $19.7 million of AOL options. This is not to say that Case was unconcerned about the slide. He still had the company's future to think about—plus options and stock worth another $100 million.

That summer, the pressure was mounting. In June, William Razzouk, a veteran FedEx executive who had been brought in to help steady the ship, quit as president and COO after only four flabbergasted months on the job. (A southern gentleman with a penchant for order, Razzouk had not fit into the company's freewheeling culture.) Razzouk might also have been perturbed that the Federal Trade Commission was looking into AOL's billing practices amid class-action suits charging AOL with overbilling.[12] Granted, Mary Meeker was still loyal—she had just raised her rating on the stock from "outperform" to "strong buy." But in August, a service blackout infuriated customers—America Online was on its way to becoming known as America Onhold. Meanwhile, Case knew that the new rate of 20 hours for $19.95 was only the first step on the slippery slope to unlimited access for a flat fee.

Desperate to maintain its cash flow, AOL began to actively research how it might generate more revenues from "adult content." According to Swisher, the notion was that AOL would create an optional "adult only" channel directly on the service; users would pay a surcharge to be linked to "adult" material culled from the Internet. The question was how to turn porn into profit without undermining AOL's apple pie image. In August, a month after cutting its rates, the company went so far as to conduct focus groups testing the idea. According to a confidential memorandum, dated August 7, 1996, "After much thought and discussion," the response in the eight focus groups was "resigned disappointment."[13] Ultimately, however, management dropped the idea.

In the meantime, the company tried to pump up subscriptions, sending two demonstration trucks on a 30-city tour of downtown shopping malls and fairs across the United States, showering the nation with millions of free disks. The cash expense of the campaign: $240 million to $300 million that summer and fall—twice as much as the two major presidential campaigns were spending, according to USA Today.[14]

In November of '96 Sloan wrote about AOL again—for the third time in 12 months.[15]

His AOL stories had not been well received. "I was in serious disfavor where I worked," he recalled in 2002. "It became more and more of a struggle to get these stories into the magazine. You'd think I was criticizing God. I just kept writing it because I felt I really needed to do it."[16] Sloan was not the only journalist to question AOL's numbers, but, in the mainstream press, he was the toughest and the most persistent. And his analysis carried a punch: it was written in a way that individual investors could understand.

AOL continued to mask the size of its expenses. "In the twelve months ending June 30 of 1996," Sloan reported, "AOL spent some $363 million on promotion—a third of its total revenues. However, AOL charged only $126 million of promotional costs against its profits. The difference of $237 million," Sloan observed, "was lots more than the $65 million pretax profit AOL claimed." Indeed, over the years, he calculated, AOL had inflated its profits by some $885 million—"us[ing] these nonexistent profits to bill itself as a money-making company." [17]

On Wall Street, AOL's aggressive accounting had been an open secret for years. But by the fall of 1996, the pot of deferred expenses had become difficult to ignore. At about the same time, AOL realized that as rivals moved to unlimited access for a flat fee, it could no longer rely on hourly fees for earnings. It needed a new profit center. Now AOL turned its attention to courting advertisers.

Enter Bob Pittman, who stepped into the job Razzouk had fled. A media-savvy promoter best known as one of MTV's founders, he came on board with good news: AOL was not an Internet company. It was a media company. Advertisers would provide the revenue it needed to keep going.

Pittman slashed AOL's swollen marketing budget and helped refocus AOL's strategy. In meeting after meeting with analysts, Pittman "repositioned" AOL as a burgeoning media empire. A *Harvard Business Review* study praised Pittman for the way he "laid siege at once to analysts and investors specializing in cable TV and other mass media and set out to educate them. He held analyst meetings at AOL's corporate headquarters every six months, conducted an ongoing road show for the financial community for more than three years, invited key analysts to meet one-on-one with himself and Case, and directed AOL's investor relations staff to work closely with analysts' assistants."

The case study wound up by congratulating Pittman for his handling of both Wall Street and the media: "During Pittman's first full year as president . . . AOL held twice as many analyst conference calls and received ten to 20 times the coverage in media and entertainment publications as any other company in its then peer set, which included Yahoo! and Lycos." [18]

Pittman's goal was to "brand" AOL. "Pepsi won all the taste tests," he liked to point out, "but Coke had the brand name." When asked whether that meant that American consumers could be brainwashed into buying inferior products simply because advertising has reached Orwellian levels of effectiveness, his reply suggested just a tinge of contempt for the consumer:

"The consumer is not a scientist. The consumer is not willing to spend the time it takes to do a research project to compare everything feature for feature." [19]

Ergo, the package was all-important. The consumer would not take the time to check the contents. Indeed much of the unique "content" that AOL had to offer the public was, like the Motley Fool's investment advice, of questionable value. But in an age of supersonic information, a company's product was like its stock: as things speeded by, appearance was everything. Questions of intrinsic value fell by the wayside.

Certainly, Pittman was right on the main point: AOL was a media company. It had virtually nothing to do with technology, everything to do with gathering eyeballs and trying to sell them something. Brian Oakes, an analyst for Lehman Brothers, translated the new business model for Wall Street: "In the future, the company will generate the majority of its profits from advertising and transactions. While these revenues make up only 13% to 17% of total revenues, they will contribute 70% of the profits." [20]

How did Oakes know advertising would contribute 70 percent? Why not 60 percent? Or 75 percent? No doubt, it was a "projection." At this point many of the numbers that passed for "information" were simply judgments—and biased judgments at that.

As AOL redefined its business model in the third quarter of 1998, Case finally responded to pressure from critics who questioned the company's bookkeeping. From that point forward, he announced, AOL would deduct its promotion expenses from earnings as it spent the money—"the way a normal company does," Sloan remarked. It also would take a charge of $385 million to write off a portion of the marketing investments it had already made. The $385 million, Sloan explained, was "the money AOL had spent but hadn't charged against profits, and [instead] counted as an asset." In the same press release, AOL announced that it was introducing flat-rate pricing. [21]

Incredibly, AOL's admission that for years it had been, in effect, lying to investors about its profits did not seem to chill their enthusiasm. On the news of the accounting changes, the stock jumped 12 percent in two days. After all, AOL explained to its many admirers, "it's just bookkeeping."

Back at *Newsweek,* Allan Sloan was rubbing his eyes. He could not quite believe investors' willingness to forgive and forget the $385 million. That special charge "wiped out most of AOL's net worth, plus all the profits it claimed to have made in its entire 11-year history," he wrote. "But guess what? Wall Street loved it. This despite the fact that neither the financial re-booting nor AOL's hiring of the highly touted Bob Pittman, a cofounder of MTV, solves AOL's crucial business problem: how to make money online when the Internet offers so much free stuff."[22]

Eventually, Sloan was worn down. It was not just that his bosses objected to his constant carping about AOL's numbers. In the nineties, few readers appreciated a Woodward and Bernstein approach to financial reporting. Indeed, a year later, *Time* magazine would be lauding Steve Case's "visionary" skills in an article headlined "How AOL Lost the Battles but Won the War."[23]

"I knew I was right, but whenever I published one of these stories, everyone would carry on," Sloan recalled. "Finally I just gave up. I shouldn't have, but I did. There are only a limited number of swings you can take—eventually you look like a crank."[24]

Nevertheless, Sloan's view of AOL would prove prophetic: "The bottom line: I think AOL's stock market value of $6.8 billion is way too high," he wrote in May of 1996. "Then again, I thought its $4 billion valuation seven months ago was too high. Even Steve Case's best scrambling can't prop up AOL's stock forever. Someday, he's going to have to score by showing real profits or pull off a financial Hail Mary miracle play by selling AOL. Know a good, hungry phone company?"[25]

No, but four years later, Case would find a good, hungry media giant. And in January of 2000 he would pull off his Hail Mary by announcing that he was passing the ball to Time Warner's shareholders just minutes before the clock ran out. (Actually, he was three months ahead of the clock: the technology meltdown would not begin until March.) Over the next two years, AOL Time Warner shareholders would watch the media marriage of the century crumble while charges of flimflam accounting mounted.

In 2002, Lise Buyer, the mutual fund manager who had explained that the shorts "just didn't understand that Wall Street was willing to overlook AOL's aggressive accounting," looked back on AOL's rise. By then, Buyer herself had become disillusioned with Wall Street and had gone west to become a venture capitalist. Yet, she still tried to rationalize the way AOL conjured up profits in the mid-nineties: "Maybe you could say that, by cooking the books, they saved the company?"[26] The question mark in her voice belied her words. It seemed that Buyer herself did not truly believe her own halfhearted explanation.

What some liked to refer to as AOL's "accounting shenanigans" had represented more than a onetime attempt to paper over an earnings gap until the fledgling company could get on its feet. People who cheat once cheat again. And again—and again. The saga of AOL's bookkeeping would prove another example of how, in a market driven by momentum rather than value, the more you lie, the more you have to lie, to keep the merry-go-round turning.

No surprise, then, that in 1997 the SEC once again caught AOL in a compromising position. Just a year after supposedly cleaning up the questions about those marketing expenses, AOL reported that now, at last, it could report true profits. It seemed a key turning point for an embattled company. But within months, AOL had to retroactively erase that quarterly profit. The SEC told AOL that it had prematurely booked millions of dollars of revenue from a major deal.[27]

As the next century began, AOL would still be restating its revenues. In 2000, the company agreed to pay a $3.5 million fine to settle charges that it used improper accounting during the mid-1990s to report profits when it was actually losing money. Two years later, AOL Time Warner found itself in the embarrassing position of restating its financial results for the past two years, reducing revenues by $190 million, as the company disclosed it had uncovered more "questionable advertising transactions" at its troubled America Online unit.[28] In 2003, the SEC reported that not only had AOL been cooking its own books, it had been helping other companies to cook theirs.[29]

But then again, how did you think that AOL "courted" all of those advertisers? This would become yet another subplot in the story of the bull market's rise and fall.

MUTUAL FUNDS:
MOMENTUM VERSUS VALUE

Imagine a country, a fundamentally prosperous country, where a network of brilliant people decides daily how resources get moved around. These people—not a cabal, but a decently spread-out group—determine the nation's savings, its spending, its capital budgets. They make rational decisions based on what the world will look like far in the future. They work with the tacit approval of government and industry. Though the sometimes brutal decisions they make may not always represent the best possible allocation of the country's resources, they come pretty close. And, when they make a mistake, they are replaced by abler, more aggressive people. What is this wondrous kingdom? . . . It's the United States in the nineties. And the wizards who rule so benevolently are identified by the somewhat banal title "mutual-fund manager."

—James Cramer, October 1996[1]

MOMENTUM PLAYERS

When James Cramer penned his paean to mutual fund managers in October of 1996, he was exaggerating their power—but not too much. The mutual fund industry now commanded roughly 15 percent of the market, up from 7 percent in 1990. In another two years, the industry would boast assets equal to three times the federal budget.

The mid-nineties had marked a turning point for the individual investor. In 1995, for the first time in decades, Americans reported that they had more of their savings stashed in the stock market than in their homes.[2] But the stampede into mutual funds that invested in stocks was just beginning: that year equity fund sales reached an all-time high of $306.7 billion, up 13 percent from the 1994 record of $270.8 billion.[3]

Cramer was right: the financial "wizards" he described would indeed play a major role in deciding how to allocate the nation's assets—though not everyone would agree that they made "close to the best possible decisions."

In 1996, the mutual fund managers who topped the charts chased growth, not value. Cramer praised "a new generation of fund managers" for their courage and vision. "These aggressive growth managers pay little heed to book value or balance-sheet considerations," he wrote. "These managers don't even care if the product works yet. If it fails the next one might not, and it might be another Cisco. . . . They are believers. And they bet that way."[4]

Cramer singled out "momentum players" such as Garrett Van Wagoner, manager of the Van Wagoner funds. While value investors try to buy low and sell high, momentum fund managers buy stocks that are already airborne, hoping to buy high, and sell higher. According to Cramer, this new generation of momentum players favored stocks "with promising names like Ascend, Cascade, Avanti and Pure Atria." As an example of the type of company that they sought, he highlighted Komag, a hard-disc manufacturer that "old-line managers would never have bet on. For one, they wouldn't have understood what the company was talking about. . . . But these new managers know this stuff."

Once again, Cramer was right: old-line value managers would not have looked high enough to find Komag. Value investors search for what Allan Sloan had called truffles on the forest floor, buying what others may overlook. They care about price. They also care if the product works. Momentum investors, by contrast, are surfers: they ride a stock while it is rising, buying it all the way up, then jumping, just as it crests, to catch the next wave. Or, at least, that is their goal.

In its own way, momentum investing (aka "chasing a stock") is a little like falling hopelessly in love. The further the object of desire recedes into the distance, the faster the momentum investor runs.

In the normal course of things, higher prices dampen desire. When lamb becomes too dear, consumers eat chicken; when the price of gasoline soars, people take fewer vacations. Conversely, lower prices usually whet our interest: color TVs, VCRs, and cell phones became more popular as they became more affordable. But when a stock market soars, investors do not behave like consumers. Rather, they are consumed by stocks. Equities seem to appeal to the perversity of human desire. The more costly the prize, the greater the allure. So, at the height of a bull market, investors lust after the market's leaders. (Conversely, when the prize is too ready at hand, investors lose interest. At the bottom of a bear market, when equities are bargains, they go begging, like overly earnest, suitable suitors.)

And so, in the fall of 1996, the momentum players were buying Komag. By the spring of 2002, its shares would be changing hands for less than a penny. As for Van Wagoner, in March of 2003, he would liquidate three of his funds—over three years, all had fallen by more than 90 percent. That spring he also disclosed that the SEC was investigating whether his firm had overstated the value of some of its holdings. The company denied doing anything wrong.[5]

In 1996, however, momentum funds were red-hot. And Gary Pilgrim's PBGH Growth Fund was leading the pack. In 1990, Pilgrim had $12 million under management; by 1996, he was running $5 billion. In the middle of that year, PBGH Growth boasted the best 10-year record of any small company stock fund. All the while, Pilgrim made headlines as he snapped up companies with fast-growing profits, frankly unperturbed by questions of price or value: "Some are underpriced and some are overpriced; we don't try to figure that out," he modestly explained.[6]

To Pilgrim, high growth did not necessarily mean technology. In 1995, two of his favorites were consumer stocks: Bed Bath & Beyond and Callaway Golf. By June of 1996, Corrections Corporation of America, a leader among for-profit prisons, rounded out a portfolio that reflected the values of the New Economy's New Society. By then, Corrections traded at 146 times trailing earnings.[7]

The aggressive fund managers of the mid-nineties did not confine themselves to small-cap stocks. Large-cap growth stocks also were coming into their own, and Cramer credited this new generation with creating "great wealth" for the nation by pouring investors' savings into winners such as "Intel, Hewlett-Packard, Microsoft, Motorola, Oracle, Sun Microsystems." And, last but not least, "Cisco."

Cisco

In the six years from 1990 to 1996, Cisco's share price snowballed, gaining over 10,000 percent. With a market capitalization of $40 billion, it was now bigger than Maytag, Phelps Dodge, Alcoa, Whirlpool, Bethlehem Steel, Woolworth, and Westinghouse combined. "This," Cramer noted cheerfully, "despite the fact that . . . it will make much less money this year than those old-line companies."[8]

But fund managers looking for momentum did not care so much about actual earnings as the rate of quarterly earnings *growth,* the percent by which earnings grew—or were projected to grow—every three months. Their focus was short-term, their object: speed. As Cramer observed, "Cisco owes its phenomenal rise to its ability to please mutual fund managers, quarter after quarter."

The nation's fund managers could not have worked the "economic miracle" Cramer celebrated without a little help from Wall Street. "As companies like Cisco continually met or exceeded their targets," he explained, "analysts from these brokerage houses raised estimates and mutual fund managers bought more and more shares."

In just one sentence, Cramer had summed up how Wall Street and the mutual fund industry worked hand in hand to stoke the fire: Higher earnings estimates spurred fund managers to pay a higher price for Cisco's shares; in turn, the fact that fund managers owned the shares encouraged analysts to boost their earnings estimates.

After all, analysts had an incentive to raise estimates on the stocks that fund managers favored. The fund managers' votes determined an analyst's ranking in *Institutional Investor*'s annual poll, with the highest-ranking analysts commanding enormous salaries. Moreover, a mutual fund was most likely to buy huge blocks of stocks through a particular brokerage if its analysts smiled on the fund's stocks. "Any analyst can tell stories of downgrading stocks to something as innocuous as a 'Hold' rating and being barraged with calls from clients, irate that a holding is falling," *Barron's* Michael Santoli reported in 2002.[9]

From one perspective, their ire was understandable. Mutual fund managers could not afford a downgrade. As millions flowed into their funds, they had no choice but to take huge positions in individual stocks. If an analyst lowered his earnings estimate by a few pennies, a fund manager could lose a small fortune. Well aware that they themselves were being rated on a quarterly basis, fund managers put enormous pressure on both the companies they owned and the analysts who covered those companies to make sure that both earnings and earnings estimates climbed, like clockwork, quarter after quarter. Such uncannily consistent performance came to be known as "managed earnings," not just at Cisco, but at blue chips such as GE and IBM.[10]

At the end of the decade, the authorities would point to analysts, investment bankers, and corporate executives as the main culprits behind the market hype. But the mutual fund industry played a critical role. "Mutual-fund strategies that gained favor in the nineties shaped analyst priorities and behavior," Santoli reported. The rise of momentum investing "led analysts to pump companies for each incremental bit of positive information that could be passed along to investors in the form of 'whisper numbers.' "[11]

With a little help from Wall Street, Cisco's share price skyrocketed—growing far faster than the company itself. "In 1990, Cisco was selling at 20 times earnings—with revenues growing at a triple-digit rate. By the time we got to the mid-nineties, if you looked at a graph of the share price, the line was turning vertical—it was going straight up," observed George Kelly, a Morgan Stanley analyst who helped take Cisco public. "The stock was trading at 80 times the next year's earnings. Meanwhile, Cisco's growth had slowed from over 100 percent to 30 percent. By any traditional valuation techniques, the rise was totally irrational."[12]

Irrational or not, Cisco CEO John Chambers took the ball and ran with it, using the inflated shares to compensate his people "with an abnormal amount of stock options," and to go on a shopping spree, buying "dozens" of companies. "Capitalism," said Cramer, "never made more sense."

Unerringly, Cramer put his finger on two of the tools that Cisco used to meet or exceed analysts' estimates, quarter after quarter. By rewarding its engineers with shares rather than cash bonuses, Cisco avoided having to subtract the full cost of employee compensation from its earnings. And by using its bloated shares to purchase other companies, Cisco was able to go on an acquisition binge, boosting its earnings—at least on paper. "To report its progress, Cisco ignored generally accepted accounting principles (GAAP) and developed its own style of bookkeeping: accounting standards that it believes more accurately reflect [its] performance (and coincidentally add more lilt to the stock price)," Jim Grant would report to his newsletter's readers a few years later.[13]

Like many of the mutual fund industry's favorites, Cisco became a serial acquirer. Over the course of the nineties, it would use a combination of cash and its own overvalued shares to scoop up some 70 firms. Often, it bought companies that were not publicly traded, making it all but impossible, Grant noted, to determine the true value of those acquisitions. By 2002, however, it was becoming clear that the majority of the companies Cisco had bought were worth less than it paid. Many of the top talents at the companies Cisco collected had left.[14] Meanwhile, Cisco's own share price had fallen by 80 percent.

But for a time, momentum kept the game going: mutual fund managers piled into growth stocks, analysts raised estimates for future growth, fund managers bought more shares, and corporate executives did whatever was necessary to create the appearance of earnings that matched Wall Street's expectations. Cisco was hardly alone. Deal-happy companies such as Tyco and WorldCom shopped until they (or their share price) dropped. In many cases, they used their own overvalued stock—what some on Wall Street called "vapor money"—to finance their purchases.

Ignoring any questions about the intrinsic value of the companies acquired, Wall Street viewed these purchases as a further excuse to hike earnings estimates. The higher estimates, in turn, led to higher share prices—creating more vapor money to fuel more deals. In this way the average acquisition price rose 70 percent over the last five years of the decade. Of course, as the acquirers grew, it took larger and larger deals to show impressive percentage gains in earnings.

In the end, it would turn out that those gains were not quite what they seemed. "Deals give companies more ways to play with their accounting," Robert Willens, an accounting expert and managing director at Lehman Brothers, pointed out in 2002. Perhaps this explains why, when the game finally ended, the biggest acquirers of the late nineties took a bigger fall than most large caps. In 2002, a study by *The Wall Street Journal* revealed that the top 50 acquirers had plunged three times as much as the Dow.[15]

"IF YOU WANT MOMENTUM, BUY AN INDEX FUND"

In the summer of 1996, the tailwind that had been propelling some of the hottest momentum funds began to peter out. After making $1.3 billion in five good years, Gary Pilgrim lost $900 million in a mere seven weeks. He was not alone. Over the next year, many momentum funds fizzled, and disillusioned investors began to withdraw their money, pulling $468 million out of AIM Aggressive Growth Fund, $206 million out of Twentieth Century Vista, and $125 million out of Van Wagoner Emerging Growth.[16]

But while these momentum funds faded, "momentum investing" never died. Individual investors continued to pursue the double-digit returns that, to many, now seemed the norm. With that goal in mind, they flocked to index funds and large-cap blue-chip funds.[17] In essence, these had become the new momentum funds. For by now, the benchmark indices, and the brand name stocks that drove them, were on a roll. In 1995, the S&P 500 jumped 37.5 percent. In '96, it gained another 22.9 percent. By year-end, the S&P was trading at more than 20 times the previous years' earnings—25 to 30 percent above its historic average. As *Barron's* put it early in '97, "If you want momentum these days, buy an index fund." [18]

The popular wisdom of the time had it that if an investor stuck to index funds, he reduced risk by spreading his money around. What the received wisdom ignored was the price of the index. When the S&P is driven by highfliers, an investor who buys the index is, by definition, buying high.

Boston money manager Jeremy Grantham had pioneered the very idea of an index fund at Batterymarch Financial Management in 1971, before launching his own money management firm, Grantham, Mayo, Van Otterloo & Co., but unlike other indexers, Grantham never believed that the market was either consistently rational or efficient. Experience had taught him otherwise. In 1968, a self-described "gun-slinging nitwit," fresh out of Harvard Business School, Grantham played the go-go market at its peak. By 1970, he had lost all of his money. "I like to say I got wiped out before anyone else knew the bear market started," Grantham recalled years later. As a result, he knew that indexing makes sense early in a bull market cycle, not at the end. "Indexing in the long run is sensible," said Grantham in 1999. "In the short run it can be lethal, particularly now." [19]

THE NIFTY FIFTY

At the end of the decade, many would try to redline the bubble, pretending that it had been limited to that racy district known as the Nasdaq. In fact, the chimera later known as "the bubble" began to form in the mid-nineties, and it was inspired not by dot.coms but by the meteoric rise of some of the most reputable names trading on the NYSE. By August of 1996, the blue-chip favorites included Time Warner (trading at 85 times earnings), Microsoft (46 times earnings), Coca-Cola (39 times earnings), Gillette (36 times earnings), Cisco (33 times earnings), Oracle (32 times earnings), Pfizer (31 times earnings), Lilly (31 times earnings), Warner Lambert (30 times earnings), and Boeing (29 times earnings).[20] The difference between a "momentum fund" and a fund that invested in the large-cap growth stocks was narrowing.

In Minneapolis, Steve Leuthold realized that he had seen this movie before: "The 99 stocks most favored by large institutional investors are selling at price-earnings ratios 25% to 50% over historical averages," he warned. "This group has the potential to behave like the Nifty Fifty," he added, referring to the brand-name growth stocks that became the fund managers' favorites at the tail end of the go-go market of the sixties—companies such as Polaroid, Xerox, and Avon.[21] As the hotshot fund managers of the sixties crowded into these stocks, they bid price/earnings ratios to un-heard-of heights. Within a few years, the darlings of that decade would plummet, losing 45 percent of their value in the crash of 1973–74.

Nearly 25 years later, the mutual fund industry was assembling another Nifty Fifty. Even if the large caps were pricey, portfolio managers had ample reason to pile in. As the S&P 500 took flight, fund managers had been struggling to keep up. In 1995, just 16 percent of diversified U.S. stock funds beat the S&P 500. 1996 proved almost as discouraging: at year-end, Lipper reported that only 25 percent of the group had paced the index.

At that point, a fund manager's only hope was to buy the market's leaders. From his perch at Merrill Lynch, Bob Farrell continued to keep a sympathetic eye on the human drama created by bull and bear markets, and he understood the herd instinct: "They're buying what's working," he remarked in 1996. "Most managers have lagged the market, so even though big stocks are over-extended, the managers keep buying them out of fear of falling further behind."[22]

THE MUTUAL FUND INVESTOR

While mutual fund managers pursued the hottest stocks, individual investors panted after the hottest funds. Spoilsports suggested that the United States was turning into a nation of gamblers: in 1995, more of its citizens visited casinos than theme parks.[23] In truth, while some 401(k) investors enjoyed the thrill of betting, others simply felt that they had no choice. Interest rates remained low, and by now, investors were convinced that if they earned anything less than 10 percent they would never be able to retire. As Peter Bernstein had noted, few gurus advised saving just a little more, investing conservatively, and settling for, say, a relatively safe 7 percent. Nor did they talk much about the risk that came with double-digit returns—the chance of losing a large chunk of your principal.

Many investors were just plain scared. "I'm 58, I earn $47,000 a year, I finished putting my fourth child through college just six years ago, and now I've managed to save $200,000," confided Sharon Cassidy, a divorced college professor in Massachusetts. "I've looked at the tables that tell you how much you need to save—and I know that if I want to maintain my standard of living when I retire in six years I should have $500,000. I also know I won't have it. But I could have $400,000 if my account keeps on earning more than 10 percent. That's why I've been having the maximum taken out of my paycheck each week, and I'm putting it all in stocks. I know that's dangerous at my age," she added. "The market could crash. But it's the only way I can hope to have even $400,000, which still won't be enough."[24]

Others were spurred on by what one fund manager called "the politics of envy": "One of my partners heard again and again from clients who were infuriated that younger family members—for whom they had almost no respect—were now worth 20 or 30 times more than they were," he recalled. "They felt a tremendous need to catch up with the nieces, the nephews, even their own children, who were now fabulously wealthy, driving the Ferraris—and 'didn't deserve it.' We were too conservative for them. Eventually they withdrew their money and took it elsewhere to play a high-stakes game."[25]

Trouble is, "momentum investing" works only in bull markets. When the cycle turns, momentum reverses, and investors quickly discover that last year's high-risk winners are this year's high-risk losers.

But in 1996, few mutual fund investors worried about the cycle reversing. That fall, a Lou Harris poll showed that 84 percent would hold their funds or buy more shares if the fund dropped 20 percent in value. Not that they expected a downturn: only 15 percent of mutual fund investors thought that stock prices might fall over the next six months, while more than half (56 percent) truly believed that over the next 10 years, the stock market was likely to match the 14 percent annual return of the preceding

10 years. In fact, nearly a third (29 percent) dreamed of egg in their beer, predicting that over the next decade, the market would return *more* than 14 percent a year.[26]

VALUE VERSUS GROWTH

As the indices levitated, "growth managers," who favored airborne stocks, took home the trophies, trouncing "value managers" who scrounged for bargains. Late in 1995, *Barron's* reported that funds willing to pay top price for high earnings growth were up some 40 percent for the year—while the average value fund had gained just 22.4 percent.[27] Far from a pittance, but investors who saw their neighbors making 40 percent felt cheated.

"I think it's much harder for many investors to make 10 percent when others are making 40 percent than it is to lose 10 percent," confided Mark Hulbert. "When everyone else is cleaning up and you're not . . . most people can't stand that. On the other hand, when they lose 10 percent, they become philosophical—as long as everyone else is losing 10 percent too."[28]

The basic truth—that everything turns on the price an investor pays when he buys a stock—was falling out of fashion. "This is when the value strategy began to be discredited—it got worse in '97, '98, and '99," recalled Jean-Marie Eveillard, a veteran value investor who ran the SoGen funds.[29]

Traditionally, value investors aim to buy $1 of growth for 50 cents. But cheap alone is not enough. "There is a misperception that value investing is cigar-butt investing—buying the moribund leftovers of the market," observed Christopher Browne, a directing manager of Tweedy, Browne Company, an 80-year-old investment firm. "In fact, we're the best growth investors around. Growth funds report an average annual turnover of 120 percent; ours is 10 percent. We thought the idea of buying a growth business was to buy something you could hold on to," he added mildly. "After all, management is compounding value."

Growth investors flip stocks like houses in the Hamptons "because they're interested in short-term results, and the illusion of control," Browne suggested. "They're like the guy you see on the turnpike weaving in and out of lanes. He gets ahead of you. He gets behind you. He gets ahead of you." And if he's investing, he pays taxes on short-term capital gains.

In a hefty report to clients, Tweedy Browne's directors quoted Pascal: "All men's miseries come from their inability to sit quiet and alone."[30]

Every investment strategy carries its own risk. For the value investor, the risk is time. Sometimes, he may have to wait years for a holding to pan out. But he can afford to wait. Typically, he buys a company early in its cycle, while it is still cheap. When an investor gets in on the ground floor, buy and hold makes sense.

When Bill Miller, manager of Legg Mason Value Trust, bought Dell "at around $1.25," for example, his downside was limited, the upside steep. Once the stock became pricey, he backed off: "We haven't bought Dell . . . in years," Miller revealed early in 2000. How was he able to guess at Dell's "intrinsic value" at such an early stage in the company's development? "If an investor is buying tech stocks," Miller stressed, "he must thoroughly understand both the economics of the business and the technology." In other words, the investor needs to understand how the company makes its money. For a value investor, a stock is more than simply a piece of paper trading in the pits, or a symbol flickering along the bottom of CNBC's screen. It is a share in a business that exists in the real world—with products, profit margins, debts, and rivals. Without understanding it in that context, an investor is making a blind bet.

JEAN-MARIE EVEILLARD

A value manager could not hope to outrun the bull that had taken charge of the market in the mid-nineties. He had just two alternatives: hop on the bull's back and let that wild beast take him (and his client's money) where it would, or stand his ground and stare it down. The second course of action required equal parts conviction and discipline. Of those who succeeded, Jean-Marie Eveillard would prove one of the most stubborn.

Eveillard was a survivor: by 1996 he had been steering the SoGen International Fund for some 18 years. During that time, the fund lost money only once: in 1990, it fell by 1.7 percent. But what was remarkable was not just that Eveillard avoided losses: in the 19 years ending December 31, 1997, the fund returned, on average, 16.20 percent a year. Over 10 years, the fund averaged 11.99 percent. When its 10-year record was adjusted for risk, that translated into 18.62 percent.[31] In other words, Eveillard was that rare animal—an equity fund manager who endured both the late seventies and the crash of 1980–81 and emerged with double-digit returns.

Born in France in 1940, Eveillard took a longer and more philosophical view of time and change than many younger, American-born fund managers. Although he had been in the United States since the sixties, Eveillard still spoke with a mild Gallic shrug more than 30 years later: "All markets are cyclical," he said, accepting the inevitable. "This means that, by definition, all value investors are market timers. We refuse to participate in the last few years of a long bull market because those last few years are when you get a speculative bubble." [32]

Granted, an investor did not have to be French to appreciate the role of cycles in stock market history—and the risks inherent in investing toward the end of a strong cycle. Eveillard belonged to a small, international circle of experienced investors who would refuse to be seduced by the bull. By 1996, many realized that valuations were growing far faster than value: share prices reflected earnings estimates that outstripped the profits that the market's favorites could realistically hope to earn. One clue that something was amiss was the fact that share prices were now beginning to grow *faster* than the gross domestic product (GDP). Since the growth of the stock market reflects the growth of the economy, it was clear that this situation could not continue indefinitely. In fact, history shows that over time, earnings growth lags real growth of GDP. [33]

"First the bubble came in large-cap growth stocks—stocks like Coca-Cola—and then later, in '97, '98, and '99 in technology, telecom, and the media," Eveillard recalled in 2003. At the time, he realized the hazards of investing in a market where prices are set by true believers. (If you are going to play cards for money, you do not want to play with lunatics. It is too difficult to guess what they might do next.) "The market had been going up for more than 10 years, and psychologically, the longer it goes up, the more people believe it will go up forever. That's not the way the world works," he added. "If you look at history you know everything runs in cycles. But that's the way psychology works." [34]

By November of '96, Eveillard was pulling back, trimming his position in U.S. equities to just 22 percent of SoGen's International Fund, while allocating 33 percent to foreign stocks, 23 percent to cash, 15 percent to U.S. and foreign bonds, and 7 percent to gold-related securities. "We don't appeal to aggressive investors," he acknowledged at the time, "because we're not aggressive ourselves. We only appeal to defensive investors, people who are more worried about losing money than they are eager to make as much money as possible." [35]

In the summer of 1988, Eveillard had withdrawn from Japan, for many of the same reasons that he pulled back from U.S. equities in 1996. "Everything was atrociously expensive [in Japan in 1988] and accordingly we didn't belong there anymore." This is what Eveillard had meant when he said that all value investors are, by definition, market timers.

But Eveillard was not trying to time the market in the sense of predicting when the Nikkei would peak. He realized that was a rube's game. "Over the next eighteen months the Tokyo stock market managed to go up another 20 or 25 percent," he recalled. "But, our attitude is, we'll play our game, and if it's no longer our game, we won't play." [36] In retrospect, he had few regrets. The Japanese market reached its summit in 1989, then plunged, entering a bear market that still had not ended 14 years later.

In the United States, just as in Japan, Eveillard realized that there was no telling how long the bull would reign. He just knew that he wanted no part of an overvalued market. "There is the historical knowledge that, at some point, the bubble will burst. If I participate in what I think is a bubble, I would expose the shareholders in my fund to undue risk. At some point," he added, "you have to decide in your own mind whether you see yourself as the steward of the customer's savings or whether you see yourself as an asset-gathering machine. In the nineties I think most large mutual fund organizations saw themselves as asset-gathering machines." [37]

Of course, on paper, many investors made money in the second half of the nineties. But in reality, only those who cashed in their chips sometime between 1996 and the fall of 2000 took their winnings home. The vast majority of mutual fund investors held on—as they had been told to do, by the press, by their brokers, by the gurus. "I don't know anyone who got out with massive amounts of money, except some corporate insiders," noted Clyde McGregor, manager of Oakmark's Equity and Income Fund. [38]

In 1996, however, many of Eveillard's investors were displeased, and they began to take their money elsewhere. "From the spring of 1995 to the spring of 2000—that was our crossing of the desert," Eveillard later recalled. "We were still returning double digits in 1996, and yet they were not happy with us." [39] Indeed, beginning in the fall of 1997, Eveillard's investors began to desert him. By 2000, more than half of his clients had jumped ship, even though the fund managed to return 8.5 percent in 1997 and 19.6 percent in 1999, with just one losing year—1998, when it lost 0.3 percent.

Eveillard began to feel isolated. "It is warmer inside the herd; it is terribly lonely to be a value investor," he noted in 1996. [40] A few years later, a discouraged Eveillard asked: "If no one else cares about intrinsic value—how do I invest?" It seemed, for a time, that there were neither buyers nor sellers who played his game. In truth, the problem was not that no one *cared* about intrinsic value. Rather, by the late nineties it seemed that few even believed in the concept.

"Almost everyone was abandoning us," Eveillard later recalled. "I don't mind seeing professional investors I respect do better than me. To see people I did not respect doing better than me—this was truly discouraging.

"But," Eveillard added, "as one of my partners said at the time: 'At least we lost half of our shareholders—rather than half of our shareholders' money.' "[41]

It would take seven years, but Eveillard would be vindicated. As of the end of the first quarter of 2003, SoGen International (now renamed First Eagle SoGen Global) was beating the bear. Over the preceding five years, loyalists who stuck with the fund had reaped returns averaging more than 10 percent a year. Since its inception in January of 1979, the fund had averaged 14.56 percent annually. In 2002, after reviewing the performance of some 372 diversified foreign stock funds, Morningstar named Jean-Marie Eveillard, along with comanager Charles de Vaulx, International Fund Managers of the Year.

THE MUTUAL FUND MANAGER: CAREER RISK VERSUS INVESTMENT RISK

The stock market is a no-called-strike game. You don't have to swing at everything—you can wait for your pitch. The problem when you're a money manager is that your fans keep yelling, "Swing, you bum!"

—Warren Buffett,
1999 Berkshire Hathaway Annual Meeting

ACCUMULATING ASSETS

In many ways, Eveillard was lucky—he ran his own shop. Had he worked for a large fund company, he might not have had the luxury of choosing whether or not to participate in the run-up. "At the large mutual fund firms there was an institutional imperative to play the game, and the game meant that you had to have 35 percent of your portfolio in big cap stocks," said Oakmark's Clyde McGregor.[1]

Big-cap stocks drew customers, and as the largest fund companies vied to divide the pie, many became what Eveillard called "asset gathering machines." After all, in most cases a firm's profits turned on how many dollars it had under management, not how well it managed those dollars. At some firms, managing the portfolios seemed almost a second priority.

This is not to say that performance was irrelevant to a mutual fund company's earnings. Far from it: research showed that investors rewarded those that ranked at the top of the charts by pouring new money into their funds. But while investors were likely to chase a fund that outperformed, they were much less likely to punish a fund that lagged. Sheer inertia, coupled with an instilled belief in buy-and-hold investing, made the mutual fund investor of the nineties loyal. Once a fund company had won his or her assets, it was likely to keep them.

"You had to have some reasonable numbers," A. Michael Lipper, founder of Lipper Analytical Services, allowed in a 2003 interview. But in a market that was going up by more than 20 percent a year, that was not too difficult. Most funds were making money, and most investors would stick with them.

As early as 1987, Lipper suggested that in a burgeoning mutual fund industry, marketing accounted for "about 60 percent of what it takes to succeed." Another "30 percent" of a firm's success might be attributed to "customer service," he said. That left 10 percent for picking stocks and managing a portfolio. "Just generating a good performance record . . . may no longer ensure a manager's success," said Lipper. In fact, mutual fund operators that sold on the basis of performance could be asking for trouble, since "investors who buy performance are often heavy redeemers." [2]

The fund companies' marketers began to take over the industry. Questions about either market fundamentals or corporate balance sheets gave way to more urgent queries: What sector is hot? What's moving? What can we sell today? "When a company opened a new fund, the idea came from the marketing guys, not from the portfolio managers," confided a manager chosen to start an Internet fund at a large Wall Street firm. "I thought Internet stocks were overvalued by then, and that an Internet fund was a bad idea. But that didn't matter. They knew they could sell the fund." [3]

SHIFTING THE RESPONSIBILITY

Meanwhile, sector funds were expected to stay fully invested in their industry—not only in the mid-nineties but later, in the middle of a bear market. "Right after September 11, 2001, I bought a couple of defense contractors, and a couple of health care names," recalled a technology fund manager, "and in the following weeks, these stocks had positive returns. Nevertheless, I got a call from our firm's risk management guy, from my boss, and from the chief investment officer. All the while, tech stocks are imploding. But I had to write four memos, explaining over and over again why I wasn't buying pure tech plays. And I still got heat."[4]

On the face of it, it seemed logical that a technology fund should be required to invest exclusively in pure technology stocks: after all, the investors who put their money in that fund had made a decision to allocate a certain percentage of their assets to that sector. Leaving aside the question of how many mutual fund investors actually had the time or inclination to study both asset allocation and the technology industry—and how many put new money into technology simply because the sector was rising—the fact remains that they had invested in a mutual fund because they wanted a professional to manage their money. They expected the manager to use his knowledge, experience, and best judgment to watch over their capital. This is what Eveillard called being a "steward."

As technology shares rose to unreasonable heights, a steward's best judgment might well tell him that he should look elsewhere for value. "In any sector there are times when you don't want to be buying—the sector has been a favorite for a long time, and now, it's overpriced," the technology fund manager explained. "There are no good values. But if new money is coming in, and everyone expects you to be fully invested, you have to buy. If I had a choice, I wouldn't run a sector fund again unless I could also short the sector, or at least go into cash."[5]

What many mutual fund investors did not realize was that it was up to them to decide when a sector was overpriced. "For an experienced investor who has enough knowledge and time to do the research needed to allocate his own assets, sector funds are fine," said Don Phillips, Morningstar's managing director. "But they're not in the best interest of all investors. I remember, during the bull market, hearing many investors say, 'If we move into a bear market I just hope my fund manager is smart enough to go into cash.'

"They didn't understand that when you invest in a sector fund you're taking on the responsibility of deciding when you no longer want to be fully invested in that sector," said Phillips. "And if you take on that responsibility, you have to take it seriously. The fund manager isn't going to go into cash—his mandate is to buy stocks in his sector."

Phillips himself wanted a steward: "I keep all of my own IRA money in the Clipper Fund—a fund that can go into bonds or cash if stocks seem too expensive," he confided. "It's a fund that lets the manager go where the best opportunities are. He does the asset allocation for me."[6]

MORNINGSTAR'S STARS

By 1996, individual investors could choose among more than 6,000 funds. The variety was dizzying, the raw performance numbers confusing. To help investors make choices, Morningstar and Lipper Analytical Services ranked the funds.

Predictably, the mutual fund industry seized upon the rankings, turning them into marketing tools. Morningstar's stars seemed particularly well suited to tub-thumping. "The genius of Morningstar was the stars; it was a wonderful graphic," said Lipper. "And there was enough mystery behind it that people took it as a judgment call."[7] Lipper's rankings also figured in many a mutual fund ad, but the stars had a special appeal. They suggested that the mutual fund rating service was handing out grades: five stars equaled an "A," four stars a "B," three stars a "C."

That was not Morningstar's intention. The company insisted that the stars were not buy and sell recommendations. "The stars are just a starting point," said Morningstar's Don Phillips. "If a fund receives five stars for ten years of performance, you next want to check to see how long the current manager has been running the fund. If he started just last year, the stars reflect someone else's performance."

Morningstar's critics suggested that when a new manager came on board, the slate should be wiped clean. The rating service should wait and see how the new manager performed before awarding stars. But in the nineties, fund managers came and went with such regularity that if Morningstar waited until a manager had even two years' experience under his belt, the rating system would cover fewer funds. A huge number of five- and ten-year rankings would have disappeared altogether: managers seldom stayed with a fund that long. So when a new manager took charge, Morningstar let the fund keep its stars, leaving it to the investor reading Morningstar's report to click on "fees and management" in order to discover that the stars said nothing about the current manager's talent. Once again, the burden was on the individual investor.

"Before making a decision, an investor also should look at the fund's year-by-year returns," Phillips added. After all, a five-star fund's performance could turn on just one or two outstanding years—something that an investor would see only if he went beyond the first page of the online report to look at the year-by-year breakdown of the fund's total returns. "That is what I look at. I want to see consistent returns," says Phillips. "But," he acknowledged, "people do gravitate to shortcuts." In other words, they count the stars.[8]

The mutual fund industry also counted the stars—and, in many cases, paid its managers accordingly. "The rankings became far too important," confided a manager at one large Wall Street brokerage. "Our organization, and many organizations, managed their managers, and compensated their managers, for being in a certain place in the Morningstar or the Lipper pecking order, rather than on their absolute performance. If you made 15 percent—but other funds in your category were willing to take greater risks and made 20 percent—you might earn four stars that year instead of five. As a result, your bonus would shrink—even though your investors had made 15 percent. On the other hand, if you lost 10 percent—but other funds in your category lost 20 percent—you might well pick up a star, and get a raise. Your Morningstar rating could determine your entire bonus."

Perhaps inevitably, money managers began to let the ratings shape their investment decisions. "Once a week we would get a memo from our boss about how our fund's ranking stacked up against the weekly Lipper rankings," he continued. "Sometimes, you made stupid investment decisions—buying a stock that was hot—just to raise your short-term rating. And I did this," he added ruefully, "even though I had all of my own savings in my own fund."[9]

Meanwhile, the marketers learned how to tool the stars to fit their ads, boasting, for example: "42 of our 66 rated funds received an Overall Morningstar Rating of four or five stars." The ad was worded carefully: "of our rated funds" was the key phrase. Typically, not all of a company's funds were rated.

"Often a fund would use its own money to start four 'incubator funds,'" Mark Headley, president of Matthews Asian Funds, explained. "If one of the four flourished, the firm would quietly close the other three. The one that survived would be rated. Investors saw only the survivors."[10]

Even after a fund was established, if it flopped, it could be discreetly buried. Often a lemon was merged into another, larger and more successful fund that could "absorb" the losses. "They ended up merging my fund into our global fund," recalled the manager of a failed sector fund. "This took some time. You had to have a shareholder vote—send everyone a proxy. Most people, when they get a proxy, it goes right in the garbage can. It wasn't that people didn't want to merge—they were just apathetic. At the same time, the brokers at our firm who had put the clients into the fund in the first place weren't too enthusiastic about calling their clients and saying, 'You know that fund I recommended—well, we need to deep-six it, so if you could just fill out that proxy . . .' The whole process took about a year," he recalled.[11]

While investors in the so-called vanishing fund may have felt that they had been rescued from a desert island, "the fact remains that they end up with a fund and manager they didn't choose—the equivalent of buying a Ford and finding a Chevy in the driveway one day," pointed out *The Wall Street Journal*'s Ian McDonald. As for investors who owned the larger, more successful fund, when they finally inherited the loser, tax law forced their manager to hold on to one-third of that fund's positions for at least one year.[12] The only clear winners in the process: the marketers, who emerged with a cleaner record for their ads.

THE COST OF MARKETING

As the mutual fund industry grew, so did the cost of promoting its funds. Who footed the bill? Mutual fund investors. "12b-1" fees were created specifically so that existing investors could underwrite the expense of bringing in new investors. Incredibly, even when a fund was closed to new customers, Morningstar reported that as many as one-fourth of those closed funds continued charging 12b-1 fees.

Some financial publications tiptoed around their mutual fund advertisers. To its great credit, *Smart Money* asked the obvious but no doubt unwelcome question: "How do these closed funds justify charging a marketing fee?

" 'We're not interested in talking about that,' [replied] Mainstay Funds' spokeswoman Diane Kagel. William Shiebler, senior managing director at Putnam Investments, which had several closed funds that charged 12b-1 fees, was more expansive: 'They're paid to the brokers so that they have a continuing interest in the fund,' he explained.

"In other words," *Smart Money* concluded, "the mutual fund companies are using shareholders' money to pay off brokers who sold the funds (and thus earned a healthy commission) in order to keep them from moving their clients' money elsewhere."[13]

An investor might well assume that most of his 12b-1 fees pay for glossy magazine ads. In fact, the lion's share of the money that mutual fund companies spend on marketing is funneled to brokers and financial planners. "Only a small portion of the fund business advertises. Most marketing has to do with relationships through the broker distribution system, and to a lesser degree the financial planners," Michael Lipper explained. "Some financial planners take fees only from their clients. But they are the minority, because they can't live on fees unless they have extremely wealthy clients with huge accounts." Do most individual investors realize that their financial planner may receive a fee for recommending a particular fund? "They've been told," said Lipper. "But I don't know if they know." [14]

Certainly, few investors realized that the mutual fund industry paid brokerages such as Merrill Lynch and Citgroup's Salomon Smith Barney to move their merchandise. In what is euphemistically called "revenue sharing," mutual fund companies such as Franklin Resources, Putnam Investments, and AIM Management Group were shelling out princely sums to the brokerages—*above and beyond the commissions paid to brokers when they sold a fund*. These are fees that the fund companies pay directly to the brokerage itself, in return for special access to the firm's brokers.

By the end of the decade, fund companies were forking over as much as $2 billion (in what a cynic might call kickbacks) according to *Institutional Investor*, citing estimates by Boston-based Financial Research Corp., a strategic consulting firm. By comparison, FRC reckoned that mutual fund companies spent just $515 million on advertising. From 1996 through 2001, FRC estimated that the cost of "revenue sharing" had doubled.

By paying off the brokerages, fund companies could gain a place on a short, confidential list of "preferred" fund providers that most brokerages maintain. The investor who buys the fund almost never knows about the list. Sometimes even his broker is unaware of the fund's special standing, though he might well figure it out. For a preferred provider is more than a salesman with a foot in the door—he enjoys easy access to a firm's brokers. [15] That access gives him the opportunity to wine and dine a broker even after he has sold a fund. This is what Putnam's Shiebler meant when he explained that mutual fund companies paid 12b-1 fees to brokerages "so that they have a continuing interest in the fund." After all, if the payments did not continue, the firm's brokers might decide to switch their clients to another fund.

FINDING A HOME FOR THE MONEY

In the eyes of some equity fund managers, the marketers succeeded all too well. In 1996, a record $208 billion flooded into stock funds—up more than 60 percent from the previous record of $129.6 billion in 1993, the year when investors began to shift, in large numbers, from fixed income and money market funds, into equities.[16]

Now portfolio managers had to contend with the avalanche of money landing at their doors. "Dozens of portfolio managers would tell me that when they opened the mail in the morning, there would be another $100 million," said George Kelly, a technology analyst at Morgan Stanley. "Meanwhile, their bylaws often mandated that they stay fully invested. They had to buy stocks. And there was some urgency—there might be another $100 million in the afternoon mail." Under the gun, "they usually bought stocks that they knew, stocks that they already owned," Kelly explained. "Generally that meant they bought large-cap, highly liquid stocks." And so the new Nifty Fifty was canonized.[17]

As retirement dollars poured into stock funds, managers did their best to put the money to work as quickly as possible, and by and large, they succeeded. In 1996, the average equity fund held only 6.2 percent of its assets in "cash or its equivalent" (safe, short-term instruments such as Treasury bills)—down from almost 13 percent in 1990. This meant that if the market turned sour, and investors suddenly decided to cash in their chips, fund managers would be forced to sell stocks—even though prices were falling— just as Fidelity Magellan's Peter Lynch had been forced to sell during the October '87 crash. In the past, fund managers had kept a cash cushion to try to avoid such forced sales, but as the bull market heated up, the cushion shrank. By March of 2000, the average equity fund held just 4 percent of its assets in cash. Even during the bear market that followed, fund managers remained close to fully invested: at the end of 2002, the average equity fund held less than 6 percent cash.[18] (See chart "Equity Mutual Fund Cash Ratio" on page 461 of the Appendix.)

Yet even while portfolio managers struggled to find a home for their investors' money, more than a few began moving their personal nest eggs into bonds and cash. Robert Marcin, manager of the $2.3 billion MAS Funds Value Portfolio, was candid. In December of 1996, he told *The Wall Street Journal* that he had cut back on the stock holdings in his personal portfolio, even while keeping his clients' money fully invested. In fact, Marcin confided, he was "bending" his usual investment rules to pump up the mutual fund's stock holding. "He is slower to sell issues that have risen sharply, and hurries to invest new money," Wall Street's paper of record reported. After all, "investors expect funds to stay fully invested," said Marcin.[19]

Meanwhile, out-of-breath fund managers still struggled to keep up with the Dow and the S&P. As the benchmark indices levitated, a manager's only hope was to invest his clients' money in the index leaders—in other words, the market's most expensive stocks. The investment risk inherent in buying the highfliers was evident. But in a runaway bull market fund managers had to worry about another type of risk: career risk. If they could not match the index, they could forget about fat bonuses. Indeed, in some cases, they could forget about their jobs.

"Even the administrators in charge of corporate 401(k) plans were telling you how to invest," groused a manager who ran a fairly conservative growth fund. "You might be making 11 percent—but they would say, 'Look at Janus, they're making 22 percent. Why can't you do that?' If your returns didn't equal those of the high-growth funds, they would drop you from their plan. They wanted all jazz, all the time. The system was stacked in favor of fund managers who took the greatest risks—at least until they blew up."[20]

With higher rewards comes higher risk. A portfolio manager who chased returns of 20 percent or more faced a greater chance of blowing up. But if he took a more cautious course, he could scuttle his own career. Laurence Siegel, director of investment policy research at the Ford Foundation, spelled out the dilemma in an interview with Kathryn Welling, editor of *welling@weeden*:

A money manager is judged by his results, and those results break down into four categories, Siegel explained. "You can be right and with the crowd—which is fine. . . . You can be right and alone—and then you are a hero. You can be wrong and with the crowd, which isn't actually so bad. When everyone else is down it doesn't hurt [the fund manager's career] to be down. Or you can be wrong and alone and then you really look like an idiot." This is the ignominious fate that a career-conscious fund manager strives to avoid at all costs.

When younger fund managers, "under the age of say, 45 or 50," make investment decisions, "job-protecting behavior . . . dominates," Siegel observed—a fact of life he described as "understandable, even if it is not good for the client. This is called the principal-agent conflict," Siegel added, summing up the relationship between investors and portfolio managers. "Preserving purchasing power and earning a return on capital is good for the client. Minimizing the risk of being wrong and alone is good for the managers."[21]

In other words, it is in the fund manager's interest to follow the herd—even if he thinks the herd is wrong. In the worst-case scenario, he will go down in flames along with everyone else. No one will blame him. Alternatively, if he dares to think outside of the box, and do what he believes is in the best long-term interest of his clients, he takes the chance of being "wrong and alone." Not surprisingly, as the market climbed, most managers chose investment risk (for their clients) over career risk (for themselves).

In 1996, a portfolio manger who had any doubts about which course to take need only glance over his shoulder to glimpse the ghost of Jeff Vinik. The image of Vinik, Fidelity Magellan's former manager, would be sufficient to remind him that in a market driven by momentum, his position was only as secure as that quarter's returns.

"FORGET JEFF VINIK"

When Jeff Vinik took the helm of Fidelity's flagship fund, Fidelity Magellan, in the summer of 1992, he shocked some investors by dumping the then-popular consumer stocks that Magellan's founder, Peter Lynch, had favored, replacing them with stocks in less popular sectors: energy, technology, and heavy industry. To some, it seemed a reckless and irreverent move.

A year later, *Barron's* declared Vinik a "winner." As he had predicted, semiconductor, oil-service, and natural-gas shares were leading the market, "while the favorites of yesteryear, the peddlers of brand-name goods," were down by about 10 percent.

"Jeff will buy what he wants to buy," John Rekenthaler, editor of Morningstar Reports, said at the time. "He's never had a taste for growth stocks. He likes buying stocks with below-market multiples," he added, referring to Vinik's preference for what he called GARP—"growth at a reasonable price." Even at the end of the decade, Vinik avoided the price/earnings ratios of 30, 40, or 50 that had become commonplace in the large-cap universe. "For a company that's growing 15% or 20%, [I might pay] 12 times earnings," he confided. "For a company that's growing 40%, it might be 25 times earnings."

In 1993, *Barron's* noted, "Vinik's distaste for traditional growth stocks is ironic considering that Magellan is supposed to be a growth-stock fund. But," the magazine acknowledged, "it's hard to argue with his results."[22]

For the moment, Vinik was allowed his head. At the time, Fidelity's stars were given a fairly free rein to invest as they saw fit. In the early nineties, for example, when Vinik was steering Fidelity's Growth and Income Fund, he had tucked 40 percent of its assets into cash, saving investors from the worst effects of the recession. But when Vinik managed the Growth and Income Fund, he was not in the media spotlight. Fidelity Magellan, by contrast, was the world's largest fund, and the financial press kept him in its sights.[23]

All went well until the fall of 1995. That was when the 37-year-old portfolio manager began to slash Magellan's technology holdings. In October, 43 percent of the fund's assets were committed to technology stocks; by the end of November, Vinik had cut the $53 billion fund's position to less than 25 percent. Vinik thought the technology sector had become too speculative, and he continued to pare his holdings: by the spring of 1996, a mere 3.5 percent of Magellan's assets were committed to tech. In the fund's annual report, Vinik explained that he thought bonds would outperform stocks "over the next year or two." With that in mind, he put 11 percent of Magellan's funds into cash, and 19 percent into bonds, mainly long-term Treasuries.[24]

In one stroke, Vinik had violated the three articles of blind faith that drove the bull market:

- Over time, stocks always outperform bonds.
- You can't time the market.
- Just buy a good company and hold it, and over the long haul, you'll make money.

Unfortunately, his timing was off. Over the short term, the market moved against Vinik. Interest rates rose and Treasuries plunged. Meanwhile, technology stocks continued their climb. As a result, early in 1996 the fund's three-year record of returns dropped below the S&P 500's returns over the same span. (In 1995, Magellan had earned 36.8 percent, but, with dividends reinvested, the S&P did slightly better.) Magellan's management fees fluctuate based on performance, and at this point, fees fell—from 0.73 percent to 0.47 percent. For Fidelity, that added up to a $130 million decline on a $50 billion portfolio.[25]

Few were willing to wait even a year to see how Vinik's strategy worked out—despite his strong long-term record. The media turned on him. "The knives are out for Jeffrey N. Vinik," reported *The New York Times*.[26]

In the spring of '96, Gail Dudack understood why Vinik was pulling back. As chief market strategist at Warburg Dillon Read, Dudack was responsible for advising mutual fund and pension fund managers at firms like Fidelity and Merrill Lynch Asset Management on where to invest the billions piling up at their doors. Her job put her backstage on Wall Street, and by the spring of 1996, she knew that many portfolio managers were buying stocks, not out of choice but out of necessity. Vinik was one of her clients, and she respected the calm, bespectacled young fund manager's quiet, intense intelligence. She also admired his independence and integrity.[27]

Moreover, by August 1996, Dudack herself was beginning to turn bearish. At the end of the year, Richard Russell would quote her in his newsletter: "We've shifted to a market that's being driven by liquidity and emotion instead of valuation. Once the market drops valuation as a benchmark, it has lost its rudder." [28]

A petite blonde baby boomer with a B.A. in economics from Skidmore, Dudack had come to Wall Street in 1970. At the tender age of 25, she appeared on *Wall $treet Week with Louis Rukeyser.* Before long, she became a regular on the show. Unlike many of the pros who survived the hair-raising bear market of the early seventies, Dudack remained an optimist. In the summer of 1983, sweaty-palmed veterans still traumatized by the bear were reluctant to recognize the beginning of a new cycle. They warned that the market was rising too high, too fast. But Dudack, then a senior vice president at Donaldson, Lufkin & Jenrette's Pershing Division, warned against playing contrarian in such a strong market, predicting that the Dow would punch through 1300 before year-end.

Dudack's target was a little high, but she was right about the market's direction, as she would be again in the spring of 1994, when she said that despite an 8 percent correction, the bull remained on track. That spring, Richard Russell was concerned that the market's primary trend might be shifting, but Dudack, who by then had become the chief market strategist at S.G. Warburg, remained confident that the tide was still coming in.[29]

By 1996, however, she was worried. Dudack realized that, by insisting that their equity funds remain fully invested, the Fidelitys of the world were forcing their money managers to buy stocks that were, at best, fully valued, at worst overvalued. Some of Dudack's clients were beginning to chafe under the pressure. Jeff Vinik had rebelled.

From the fall of 1995 through the spring of 1996, the Magellan Fund trailed the competition. The media narrowed its scrutiny, and things quickly turned nasty. As Vinik's reputation faltered, some newspapers began to question his integrity. Reporters seized on allegations that Vinik had publicly touted Micron Technology, calling it "relatively cheap," while he quietly sold the stock. *The Boston Globe* made the attack personal.

"Mrs. Vinik, please don't punch us in the nose," began a *Globe* story in January of 1996. "But we have doubts your husband, Jeff, was telling us the truth about all those billions he had invested in technology stocks. The issue, of course, is Vinik's rosy public musings on tech stocks in early November, about the same time his giant Fidelity Magellan mutual fund started selling those same investments to the tune of $10 billion."[30]

Rumors circulated that Vinik had become "a public relations problem" for his firm. Fidelity chairman Ned Johnson offered what might best be called lukewarm support. When asked about the allegations that Vinik had touted Micron, Johnson told *The Wall Street Journal* that Vinik "did nothing wrong to my knowledge, but I cannot tell you what went on inside his brain cells."[31] Ultimately, the SEC would find no basis for the allegations.

Nevertheless, an individual investor who alleged that Vinik manipulated the price of Micron Technology by saying that the stock was "reasonably priced"—while he was in fact selling shares—filed a lawsuit. In response, Fidelity Magellan banned its fund managers from making public comments about individual companies.

In May of 1996, Vinik left Fidelity, his reputation temporarily sullied. *Barron's* "Trader" column summed up the Street's response: "One of the big lessons of the Vinik affair is that bonds are for losers."

"Vinik's dead man's portfolio suggests a burnt-out case," *Forbes* declared.[32]

"Forget Jeff Vinik," wrote Jim Cramer in his hymn to a new generation of fund managers."[33]

Gail Dudack, however, was not so ready to forget Vinik. She felt that he had gotten a raw deal at Fidelity, and that he had been "slaughtered" by the press. "What people don't realize," she told friends, "is that money managers like Jeff Vinik are put in an impossible position. Their firms want them to wear two hats: they're expected to market the firm by giving media interviews, and at the same time they are supposed to manage money."[34] It was yet another sign that the marketers had taken over the mutual fund industry. Even a mutual fund manager running billions of dollars was expected to spend part of his time talking to reporters.

Inevitably, they would ask questions about the stocks that Vinik might be trading. What could he say: "Actually, I'm thinking about selling it over the next three weeks?" If he did, "he would be violating his fiduciary responsibility to the fund's investors," said Dudack. On the news that the world's largest mutual fund was trying to lighten its position, the stock would plunge, long before he had a chance to get out.

Dudack recognized that the real reason that both the media and the public turned on Vinik was not because he failed to announce that he was going to sell technology stocks, but because he had sold them at all. By selling stocks and buying bonds, Vinik had signaled that he thought the market was overpriced.

Vinik's "resignation/firing" sent a message to other mutual fund managers. "In the future . . . few major mutual funds will have the courage to reduce risk by raising cash or holding significant treasury note or bond positions," wrote Ned Davis of Ned Davis Research, an independent technical-analysis firm founded in 1980.[35] Davis would be right. Even after the Nasdaq cracked in the spring of 2000, the vast majority of fund managers felt that they had no choice but to remain fully invested. (See chart on page 461 in Appendix.)

Years after he left Fidelity, Vinik would be remembered as the Magellan Fund manager who tried to time the market—with disastrous results. By 2002, however, it was becoming clear that an investor who moved out of technology and into Treasuries and cash in 1996 had made a shrewd move. He would miss the Nasdaq's peak, of course, but he would also miss the wreck that followed.

If investors had been patient, Vinik's market timing might have worked after all. Over the next seven years, an investor who switched to bonds at the end of March 1996 would have done far better than someone who stuck with the S&P 500. And he would have avoided the gut-wrenching swings of the equity market. "Few investors noticed the fabulous performance in bonds during the nineties," said Dudack in a 2003 interview. "In the last seven years [ending in March 2003], both corporate and treasury bonds outperformed stocks. On a total return basis, 10-year Treasuries returned 78 percent, AAA corporate bonds returned 85 percent, while the S&P 500 returned 46 percent—and that is with dividends reinvested. Capital gains on the S&P totaled a paltry 31 percent."[36]

"In some respects Jeff was a better strategist than Peter Lynch, in the sense of seeing things further ahead than most," observed Michael Lipper, who considered Lynch one of the best investors of all time. "Vinik went to extremes—his timing was slightly off—but the thought patterns were correct."[37]

Nevertheless, in 1996, everyone was in a rush to become a millionaire. That spring, Vinik's performance fell short. In the six months ending in May of '96, Magellan had produced a total return of 0.25 percent, including dividends, trailing the S&P 500's 10.3 percent return.[38] In a market that focused on the moment, the last six months was all that counted. No matter that on Vinik's watch, Fidelity Magellan had returned 84 percent in four years.[39]

Ultimately, Vinik would be vindicated. After leaving Fidelity, he went on to set up his own hedge fund, raising $800 million from the likes of Donaldson, Lufkin & Jenrette (the Wall Street firm invested clients' capital in Vinik's fund) and Jeff Feinberg, chairman of the $1 billion JLF Asset Management hedge fund (who invested a portion of his personal portfolio with Vinik). These investors did not fidget. They were not in a rush to get rich. They were already rich. (The minimum investment needed to participate in Vinik's fund was $2 million).

Their fortitude was rewarded. By the fall of 2000, Vinik Partners had racked up a total return of 646 percent in just over four years, handily beating the S&P 500's return of 110 percent over the same period.

And in 2000, Vinik made the best market timing decision of his career. He retired, with a peerless record. Over the course of his 12-year career, Vinik had clocked returns that averaged 32 percent a year—nosing out even Peter Lynch, who averaged roughly 29 percent in the 13 years that he ran Fidelity's Magellan Fund.[40]

The Power of the Individual Investor

It is easy to blame mutual fund firms for forcing their managers to buy into the bubble. It is somewhat more difficult to blame the portfolio managers for not rising up and quitting, en masse—though it certainly would have been preferable if a larger number took Jean-Marie Eveillard's point of view that he would rather lose his clients than lose his clients' money.

But the hard fact is that both the firms and their fund managers were doing what most investors wanted them to do—or *thought* they wanted them to do. On the one hand, investors assumed that professional managers would use their best judgment when watching over their money. But they also wanted the 14 percent annual return that many had begun to think of as their due.

Anyone who doubted investors' desires need look no further than the story of Foster Friess, the highly respected manager of Brandywine's funds. A year after Jeff Vinik left Fidelity, Friess's funds topped the charts, returning more than 30 percent annually in the three years ending September 1997. Friess's talent as a stock picker matched his skill as a market timer. In 1990, just as Saddam Hussein invaded Kuwait, Friess predicted that the stock market would fall, and in just three days, he sold 80 percent of the stocks in the Brandywine Fund. As a result, his investors were spared the ravages of the 1990 recession—a year when the S&P 500 lost 6.6 percent. Nimbly, Friess jumped back into stocks in time to take advantage of the rally that followed.[41]

By the end of 1997, Friess Associates was running some $12 billion—up from $1 billion in 1990. Sir John Templeton, founder of the Templeton Funds, numbered himself among Friess's clients.

Late in 1997, Friess began to suspect that his holdings had peaked. He ordered his analysts to complete a "bottom-up" review of every company in the Brandywine funds—and told them to get rid of any that looked iffy.

Following the review, traders worked 12- to 15-hour days to unload stocks. Over 10 days, the Friess team sold about 40 percent of the stocks in the two funds. They broke only for Christmas Day. By the end of the month, they had unloaded most of the stocks both in Friess's mutual funds and in the private accounts he managed.

By mid-January, the market was climbing once again. At the end of the month, the Brandywine Fund had tumbled from among the top performers to a rank of 820 out of 1,011 comparable funds tracked by Lipper Analytical. The reaction from investors was swift and brutal. "People screamed and hollered," Friess recalled. They began withdrawing millions from his funds.

In March, Friess started to move back into stocks. "I'd like to think all this pressure wasn't an influence," he said later. "So what, that 50 million bucks a week is leaving? I'm going to do what I'm going to do, because the pressure is irrelevant. But in my gut, it probably wasn't." [42]

As it turned out, Friess had moved back in at exactly the wrong time. By August, the market for the mid-cap stocks he had been buying blew up. Irate investors began pulling more and more money out of his funds.

"He had so many redemptions, his fund started melting down," Ralph Wanger, founder of the Acorn Funds, recalled. "His staff started defecting—they could see the whole thing was caving in.

"The fact is if you look at the market's advance/decline line, you'll see that he wasn't wrong," Wanger continued, referring to the line on a graph that shows the percentage of stocks that have risen, versus the percentage that have fallen. "Take a look at when the average stock peaked out," Wanger added. "He had it pretty well taped. But I can tell you, his investors were furious. I was on a finance committee of an institution here in Chicago that had his fund—and the finance committee was incensed.

"Friess didn't have the guts to tough it out," Wanger continued, "and I don't blame him. With the withdrawals, his funds were melting down. It was just awful. So finally he had to reinvest his cash—in the middle of '98—and of course he managed to reinvest just as most stocks peaked. In the end, Friess sold his business.

"Every other fund manager took careful heed of this. Everyone realized at that point that as a fund manager, you were basically just a purchasing agent. As a purchasing agent, it was your job to put the money that showed up in whatever stocks your fund was supposed to invest in—large-cap growth or technology or whatever. If you're a purchasing agent, price is not the issue," said Wanger, "you're like the produce manager at the supermarket—you have got to have lettuce on sale the next day. No matter what the price. Maybe you can decide to buy the curly lettuce instead of the romaine. But the equity fund manager has to have stocks. You have limited control over what you're doing.

"You really couldn't go to 50 percent cash and stay there," Wanger concluded. "Your shareholders wouldn't let you. The few guys who tried it were wrecked."[43]

The Individual Investor Takes Charge

Without fully realizing their power, individual investors had taken charge of the market. "As strange as it may seem, by writing all of those checks to these mutual funds, the American public was setting price levels," said George Kelly, a technology analyst at Morgan Stanley. "The market's own pricing mechanism was breaking down. The public was setting the valuation of these technology companies—without any understanding of the underlying fundamentals."

"It was a totally mechanical process," he added. "They sent the money in, the fund managers invested it, the stocks went higher. Fund managers would say to me, 'This is totally nuts.'"

Cisco was one of the Nifty Fifty, and Kelly, who had helped take the company public, continued to recommend Cisco to fund managers even though he considered the company's share price completely out of line with its earnings growth. "I remember hearing another analyst say, 'The stock is overvalued—and it's going higher.' That summed up the problem," said Kelly. "As an analyst you're trying to be right about where the price is going—here is Cisco, which, by any traditional metrics, is worth about half of its current price, but it's still rising. Do we say sell?"

The truth is that the analysts like Kelly were trapped in a catch-22: if they recommended overvalued stocks, they were wrong, but if they downgraded those same stocks, they would also be wrong—at least for as long as the market continued to rise. "Given the inflows of money into these mutual funds, we thought stocks like Cisco were going to continue to climb, so we told investors to buy," Kelly explained.[44]

Put that way, his "buy" recommendations sound neither deceitful nor cynical. In truth, most individual investors were far more interested in where a company's share price was headed than in the intrinsic value of the business. They just wanted to know what the next fellow might pay for the stock. And from 1996 through 1999, the next fellow was probably prepared to pay through the nose for large-cap growth stocks.

Incredibly, individual investors were now running the show.

"THIS MARVELOUS DANCE"

Mutual fund investors provided the cash to fuel this final leg of the bull market. But this is not to say that individual investors bore sole, or even prime, responsibility for turning the boom into a bubble.

"Everyone was involved—all in this marvelous dance. It is very hard to say anyone was guilt-free if they were involved in the market at all," said Acorn Funds founder Ralph Wanger.[45]

The mutual fund companies that put asset gathering ahead of conserving their customers' assets, the brokerages that put mutual funds on a "preferred" list if they shared revenues with the brokerage, the analysts who upgraded their recommendations to justify the prices fund managers were paying, those journalists who "outsourced" their critical thinking (and published mutual fund scorecards without warning investors that three-year records told little about a fund manager's talent), the 401(k)plan administrators so dazzled by momentum that they forgot about diversification, and, last but not least, the 401(k) investors who complained bitterly if their plan was *not* stacked with high-growth choices—they were all part of the dizzying dance.

Yet they were not the whole story. Like society itself, the bull market depended on a web of relationships, and that web stretched all the way to Washington.

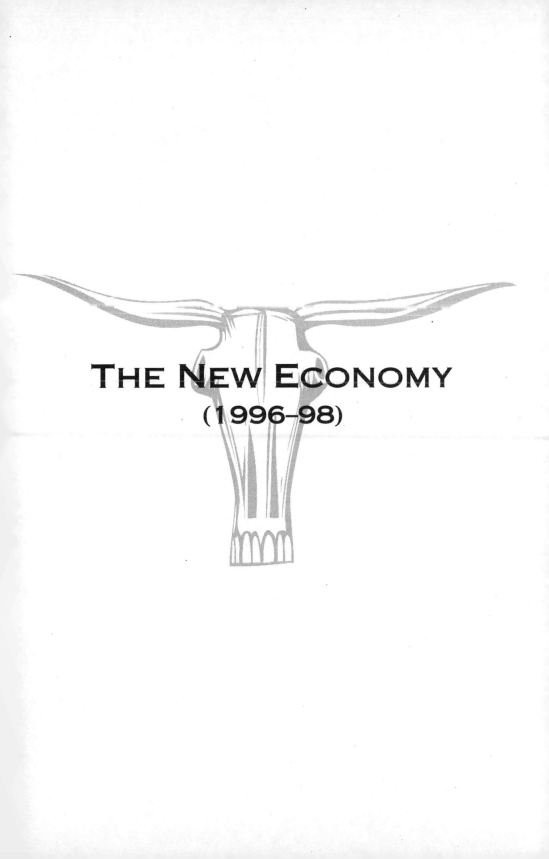

THE NEW ECONOMY
(1996–98)

ABBY COHEN GOES TO WASHINGTON; ALAN GREENSPAN GIVES A SPEECH

"STEP ASIDE, ELAINE. NOW, THE BIG NAME IS ABBY"

November 16, 1996. The Dow appeared headed for yet another record close when the rumor slithered across Wall Street that Abby Joseph Cohen was about to alter her bullish stock market forecast. As it happened, Cohen was not in New York. Instead, she was attending a conference, along with a few hundred other senior Goldman executives, in Westchester County, just an hour's drive from Manhattan.

As Cohen listened to a speech by Goldman CEO Jon Corzine, someone tapped her on the shoulder. "There's an emergency," she was told. "You must call the office." Cohen's first thought was that one of her daughters was sick.[1]

When Cohen reached Goldman's hotline, her assistant was apologetic: "They made me call." She was referring to Goldman's traders. The Dow already had fallen 60 points—and in 1996, 60 points was still a stomach-turning plunge. Soon, she was patched through to the intercom system linking Goldman offices around the world.

On the trading floor in New York, the very sound of Cohen's voice calmed the room. She made it clear that she had *not* changed her position—and hundreds of traders picked up their phones to spread the word. The market began climbing. At the end of the day, it closed up 35 points.

Such was Abby Joseph Cohen's power. She had not sought the notoriety. (If she had, her colleagues at Goldman Sachs, a firm that prided itself upon its reputation for discretion, would have been appalled.) But the media needed a leading lady to star in the bull market, and it had chosen Cohen.

Abby Joseph Cohen was replacing Elaine Garzarelli, the Shearson analyst who came to fame by predicting the October 1987 crash. In the early nineties, Garzarelli remained a name in the financial press, but by November of '96 a *Business Week* headline announced that the media was passing the baton on to Cohen: "Step Aside, Elaine. Now, the Big Name Is Abby."[2]

The two could not have been more different. Garzarelli personified the eighties: "Slim, lively and high-strung, Garzarelli favors sheer white silk blouses and suits by Tahari," *Smart Money* gushed in '88. "She is at once tough and sexy. Witnesses to a panel discussion a few years ago remember her seductively nibbling on her pearls."[3]

But the flamboyant, long-legged Shearson analyst was never wholeheartedly accepted by Wall Street—especially after she appeared on television in pantyhose ads. By 1996, the Street had made its choice clear: the financial world of the nineties wanted a wise mother, not a financial femme fatale.

To imagine Abby Cohen nibbling on her pearls is to imagine Alan Greenspan clad in black leather. As noted earlier, Wall Street trusted Cohen, in part, because she was a woman who "wore sensible shoes." " 'When I go home, I still have to do the cleaning and the laundry,' " she told *Business Week.* " 'Actually I like doing the laundry,' " she added, " 'it's cathartic.' "[4]

But the bedrock of Cohen's credibility was her consistency. The doyenne of the bull market, Cohen was always bullish, yet never exuberant. Serene and wise, she simply insisted that, despite the day-to-day volatility, the larger trend was positive. At the end of 1996, she wrote an op-ed piece for *The Washington Post* that laid out the backbone of her argument for the New Era: "The U.S. economy has re-established itself as the world's strongest," Cohen declared. "Our workers are the most productive, our businesses are the most profitable, and we are investing in new technologies and creating new jobs at an unrivaled pace."

Cohen acknowledged that "with the bull market entering its seventh year, stocks are no longer undervalued and prices have become more volatile. Our recommended portfolio for professional investors now suggests putting 60 percent in equities, compared with 70 to 75 percent in late 1994 and 1995." Yet, she stressed, "we believe that further stock price gains will be soundly based on the slower-moving but more durable economy." [5]

In the future, Cohen would describe that "durable" U.S. economy as the "supertanker" of the world economy—"not fast, not showy" but, like Cohen herself, "hard to knock off course." Her optimism seemed closely tied to her belief in the United States as a nation, her rhetoric laced with a patriotism that, while genuine, also could become dangerous. If you questioned the New Economy, were you questioning the ingenuity and productivity of the American worker?

But if Cohen seemed, to some, Panglossian in her confidence, her optimism appeared well founded. In the summer of 1996, while some pundits predicted a downturn, Cohen forecast Dow 6000. She was right, as she would be, throughout the nineties, proving, in Michael Lewis's words, that "no matter how rich you are, your mother is smarter than you are." [6]

WOMEN ON WALL STREET

While Wall Street embraced Cohen as its maternal muse, Goldman Sachs still had not made her a partner. In 1996, only 18 of the brotherhood's 285 managing directors were women. Just 11 of the 18 had been tapped to be full partners. Asked about Goldman's decision not to make Cohen a partner in its last round of appointments late in 1996, Linda Strumpf, a money manager who used Cohen's advice to help steer the Ford Foundation's $8.5 billion investment portfolio, answered, "Please, that's a very sore subject." [7]

Nevertheless, it must be acknowledged, women on Wall Street had, as they say, "come a long way." Thirty years earlier, women were not even allowed to lunch on the Street. As New Yorker writer John Brooks reported at the time, not only were women barred from Wall Street's private lunch clubs, "most astonishing . . . was the fact that many of the public restaurants in the area did not take advantage of the situation by encouraging women, but rather fell in line with the clubs by banning them. . . . Without a reservation or a long wait, a woman could scarcely get a decent lunch anywhere in the area at any price."

Nor could a woman aspire to stardom. Of the thousands of women who got off the subway at Broadway and Wall each morning, the vast majority were secretaries or clerks. The most ambitious might hope to become research analysts, but only because "the ladies doing research could be kept hidden in a back room," Brooks explained. As late as 1965, "professionally, prejudice against women in the financial business was wide, deep and largely unquestioned." Wall Street was still an all-male bastion, a stony labyrinth of canyons created by narrow streets and gray buildings where "even in summer, the air lies heavy, dank and sunless" and "pretty women seemed flesh without magic." [8]

In 1996, sunlight still rarely pierced Wall Street's winding alleyways, but women had made notable progress. Not only were the ladies allowed to lunch, more than a few had been anointed as seers.

Abby Cohen and Mary Meeker stood out. Each possessed what was needed to become a guru on Wall Street: conviction. In Cohen's case, her optimism was grounded in her faith in the American economy. Meeker's millennial outlook, on the other hand, was founded on a nearly religious belief in the promise of the Internet.

But it hardly mattered what served as the anchor for their confidence. More than anything, Wall Street craves certainty.

Few investors, be they professionals or amateurs, wish to believe that the market is as irrational or imperfect as they are. Enter the wizards, with their charts and their numbers, their smoke and their theories. Some of these are very fine theories—and sometimes they work. But the very best of the oracles know very well that prophecy is part luck. Ultimately, the future is unknowable.

Investors, however, have little time for seers who dwell on the contradictions and inconsistencies of the marketplace. At one point, *The Wall Street Journal* complained that Bob Farrell, Merrill's top-ranked technical analyst, was not quite, in the reporter's view, "first tier," because he "usually writes reports that are dense with hedges, conditional clauses and predictions going in several directions at once. Elaine Garzarelli," the *Journal* noted, "doesn't have that problem." [9]

Like the market itself, investors abhor ambiguity. They want a seer who comes with a system for counting the cards. Like Dorothy in Oz, investors invent wizards to give them courage. Financial gurus exist because they satisfy Wall Street's need to believe that "the market" is rational, efficient, and above all predictable—that "the market" is not us, but a higher, separate power, and that Wall Street's shamans are in touch with that power.

On that score, investors were reassured by the fact that corporate earnings were growing so very smoothly, year after year—an important part of the illusion that markets and economies are predictable.

Cohen genuinely believed those earnings reports. In a 1997 debate with Jim Grant, she rested her argument on the superiority of American accounting practices.

"I get a little concerned when I see technology companies paying their officers with options," Grant ventured. "To the extent that they treat this as a balance-sheet rather than an income-statement item, they are overstating earnings. If and when these stocks come down and these companies have to pay cash compensation, it will instantly show up in the income statement."

In Grant's view, prosperity made investors gullible: "Bull markets have many great uses but they don't produce much in the way of vigilance and skepticism," he suggested. "I don't think the Street is doing as good a job as it might in analyzing companies. . . . A case study in how people forgot to look under the hood is Centennial Technologies, which had a $1 billion market cap and was the New York Stock Exchange's top-performing stock in 1996. The former CEO is now in jail, and the Feds are trying to figure out if any of the sales the company reported were real. This kind of thing happens because, in a rising tide of prosperity, skepticism doesn't pay," Grant added. "That being the case, I think you have to expect that many companies are guilty of shading and trimming earnings these days."

Cohen would have none of it: "We have just done an exhaustive study that concludes that the quality of earnings is actually superb," she replied crisply. "Accounting standards are tougher. The FASB has annoyed corporations for years and has forced them to adopt more conservative accounting. . . . Does this mean there's no flexibility for companies to do things to their reported earnings? No, but on average the quality of what's being reported is better now than it has been anytime in my professional lifetime." [10]

How, without being rude, could Grant possibly counter such rectitude? By 1997, Cohen would become known as "the soothsayer who never blinked." [11]

GREENSPAN WAVERS

Abby Joseph Cohen might be the most trusted voice on Wall Street, but the guru of all gurus still resided, not in Lower Manhattan, but in Washington. "In Greenspan We Trust" read the headline on *Forbes* cover in March of 1996.

While the nation trusted in Greenspan, by 1996, the Fed chairman was not so sure that he trusted in the market. A transcript of a Fed policy meeting in September revealed his anxiety over the market's rapid rise: "I recognize there is a stock-market bubble problem at this point," he allowed. Moreover, he seemed to know what he could do to deflate that bubble: "We do have the possibility of raising major concerns by increasing margin requirements," he observed, referring to the fact that if investors were required to have more capital before buying stocks "on margin" (borrowing money from their broker to buy) that would be a signal that the Fed was concerned. Indeed, Greenspan seemed certain on this point: "I guarantee that if you want to get rid of the bubble, whatever it is, that will do it," he declared.

But instead of stiffening margin requirements, the Fed decided to "sit on the sidelines as mere observers of the Great American Asset Bubble," said Morgan Stanley economist Stephen Roach, after reading the transcript six years later. Roach believed that the Fed's reluctance to raise margin requirements reflected Greenspan's concern as to "what else [raising margin requirements] will do." So rather than acting, the chairman decided to "keep an eye on" the bubble.[12]

By November, the Dow had climbed 15 percent in two months, Citicorp's shares had gained 28 percent since Labor Day, and IBM's shares were up 40 percent. "The sort of historical data on stock prices and profits that Fed economists examine suggests the market may be overvalued as much as 20%," observed *The Wall Street Journal* in a story that began: "If you were United States Federal Reserve Chairman Alan Greenspan, wouldn't you be worried about the soaring American stock market?"

Greenspan, however, seemed to be keeping his concerns under his hat: "The watchword among Fed officials is: Don't use the words 'stock' and 'market' in the same sentence. No one wants the blame for a crash," wrote the *Journal*'s David Wessel. Nonetheless, he noted, a summary of the Fed's deliberations just six months earlier showed that Fed officials "questioned the sustainability of the performance of the stock market." Since then, the industrial average had added 700 points. *"One headline-making Greenspan speech about 'speculative excess' would shatter the market's complacency,"* Wessel added, with remarkable prescience (emphasis mine).[13]

Greenspan would make that speech in less than two weeks. But first, he summoned a small circle of the financial world's best and brightest to Washington.

THE MEETING

December 3, 1996: Abby Joseph Cohen, Morgan Stanley equity strategist Byron Wein, David Shulman (Wein's counterpart at Salomon Brothers), Yale economist Robert Shiller, and Harvard economist John Campbell trooped down to Washington to attend a private meeting with the chairman of the Federal Reserve. Each would be asked to outline his or her view of the market. Of the group, Cohen was the one bull you could count on. (She was also the only one who would be invited back.)

Wein came to the meeting in a bullish frame of mind, but only six months earlier, he had been a bear. This is not to say that Morgan Stanley's chief strategist for domestic equities was mealymouthed. To the contrary, Wein took definite stands, and as a forecaster, he had been on a roll for two years. After calling 1994's brief bear market, he predicted that the Dow would sprint to 4500 by the end of 1995. Some in the industry scoffed at his sudden change of mind, even calling his forecast "irresponsible." In fact, the Dow broke 5000. "I wasn't irresponsible enough," said Wein.

At the beginning of 1996, however, Wein's analysis told him that the market was likely to top out by midyear. In May, he predicted a 1000-point drop on the Dow. By the summer, it looked as if his forecast was coming true. In June and July the Dow sold off. The Dow did not fall as far as he expected, however, and by October, he realized that his 1000-point decline was not going to materialize. "I underestimated the market's inherent momentum," Wein confessed. "Maybe I'm a year early, but unfortunately, I don't have too many years left."[14]

Accounts vary as to how and why Wein changed his mind. "By late September the rebounding market made his position difficult. At the end of September he said, 'I can't stand it anymore,' " said Thomas McManus, an equity strategist and principal at Morgan who worked with Wein.

Certainly, it was getting more and more difficult to be a bear on Wall

Street. "I have the hoof marks of the bull all over my back," said Salomon's David Shulman, one of the most vocal bears on the Street, a few days after meeting with Greenspan. "It requires company to be bearish," he added, "and there are still very few people willing to take that view."

A year earlier, Shulman had tried to come in from the cold. "Lone Bear on Wall Street Joins the Herd," read the headline in *The Wall Street Journal*. But as share prices continued to climb, Salomon Brothers chief equity strategist found it hard to turn off his mind: it seemed to him obvious that share prices were outstripping realistic expectations for earnings growth. By the time he met with the Fed chairman in December of 1996, Shulman was once again advising clients to trim their stock holdings back from 50 to 45 percent of their portfolio.[15]

David Shulman did not share *Forbes*'s faith that the Fed chairman would be able to ensure a "soft landing" for either the market or the economy: "Very simply the economy is too big and complicated to be piloted by a few central bankers sitting in Washington and other world capitals," Shulman explained. "The bulls seem to envision them in an airplane with an electronically controlled cockpit, steering us through a fog of economic statistics. I see the bankers riding in a bumper car in an amusement park. The link between the steering wheel and the front axle is loose."

Despite his contrarian views, throughout the mid-nineties Shulman continued to be one of the most respected strategists on Wall Street.[16] Nevertheless, in January 1998, when his firm merged with the Smith Barney unit of Travelers Group, Shulman himself would be "trimmed" from the herd. "Many of Smith Barney's clients were individual investors—a bearish chief equity strategist wasn't going to help the firm sell stocks," a colleague explained.[17]

By contrast, economists Robert Shiller and John Campbell were free to speak their minds without fear of putting a crimp in their careers. Their bearish views would not affect either Yale's or Harvard's revenues. This is not to suggest that Wall Street's market strategists should be tenured—a chilling thought—only that everyone who listens to them needs to understand that Wall Street exists to sell investments. From a business point of view, no one on Wall Street has any earthly reason ever to suggest that the market is overpriced.

Shiller's work was based, in part, on his analysis of market psychology. Since the 1987 crash, he had been polling investors every six months, and by 1996, he saw unnerving parallels between investor sentiment in the United States and the views expressed by Japanese investors in 1989—just as that market was peaking.

Investor sentiment was not the only warning sign. In 1996, after reviewing historical data comparing earnings and stock prices, Shiller and Campbell projected that the reward for investing in the U.S. stock market over the next decade, after adjusting for inflation, would be roughly zero.

At the time, their forecasts sounded outlandish. But unlike many academicians, Shiller and Campbell put their theories to work in the real world. By the beginning of '97, Campbell had bought futures to hedge his entire stock exposure (an alternative path to selling the stocks, which would have triggered capital gains taxes). Shiller also confided that he had pulled most of his own money out of the stock market, though he added, "I'm not completely out. I don't have complete confidence in this. . . . So many people may be willing to put money into the stock market that it will keep rising." [18] As it would, at least for a few years.

There was no question that Greenspan had assembled a skeptical group—another sign that he was concerned about the market's meteoric rise.

As the five seers laid out their positions, "the chairman said very little," Byron Wein later recalled. "But when he got to me, he implied that the market was overvalued. I told him that I disagreed. According to my valuation model stocks were 7 to 10 percent undervalued. I explained my model—I said this is just a tool, but it had stood me in good stead for many years.

"I left the meeting thinking that I had convinced him," Wein added. "And that's what I told people at Morgan Stanley when I got back to New York." [19]

Two days later, Wein traveled to Houston to give a speech for the Juvenile Diabetes Foundation. Early Friday morning, he was sound asleep in his room at the Four Seasons Hotel when the phone rang.

"You idiot," shouted the voice on the other end of the line. It was a Morgan Stanley trader.

To his chagrin, Wein discovered that he had been dead wrong. He had not convinced Greenspan. In fact, the night before, the Fed chairman uttered the words that would roil markets around the world: "irrational exuberance."

In New York, the stock futures market opened down its limit and was not allowed to drop further for fifteen minutes. Because Morgan Stanley's traders had listened to Wein, they were totally unprepared.

THE SPEECH

Thursday, December 5, 1996, and the chairman of the Federal Reserve stood up at a black-tie dinner and asked what could be construed as a perfectly reasonable question: "How do we know when irrational exuberance has unduly escalated asset values, which then become subject to unexpected and prolonged contractions as they have in Japan over the past decade?" The Fed chairman did not attempt to provide an answer. There was no need. Just by posing the question, he had done what he no doubt intended to do: he had, ever so carefully, raised a small but pointed red flag.

The phrase was buried on page 14 of an 18-page speech that the chairman was delivering that evening at a dinner sponsored by the American Enterprise Institute, a conservative think tank. But Greenspan had chosen his words carefully.

Bob Woodward would later report that after reading a draft of the speech, Alice Rivlin (the former budget director who had become a member of the Fed board), had come into Greenspan's office and asked, "Do you really want to say that?"

"I think I do," he replied.

According to Woodward, by December of 1996, not only the Fed chairman but Treasury Secretary Robert Rubin had been troubled by the market's parabolic climb. "Rubin couldn't believe how high the market had gone. Never in his lifetime had he seen anything like it, and he was deeply worried. People had lost their discipline in making financial decisions. . . . Did Treasury and the Fed have an obligation to do or at least say something?

"Both Rubin and Greenspan knew that the Treasury secretary could hardly speak out against the stock market and issue a warning," Woodward wrote. "The White House would have to be involved, and the president's political advisers considered the bull market a badge of honor. Several times, somebody at the White House had proposed that the President [Clinton] should ring the bell at the New York Stock Exchange, and Rubin had to go to the battle station to stop it." [20]

That only Rubin understood just how unseemly it would be to have the president of the United States join CNBC's Maria Bartiromo to ring in another day at the races on the trading floor says something about how little Washington understood about Wall Street. Few of the beltway's policy makers seemed to recognize that the market was, after all, a casino. Rubin, by contrast, had been a trader; he knew the risks of the marketplace all too well. He also knew that if the market went down, the film clip of Clinton launching the *Titanic* would haunt him forever.

When asked later in the decade whether he thought it would be a good idea to invest some part of the Social Security fund in the stock market, the Treasury secretary blanched ever so slightly. "No," he replied. Why not? "The market is too . . ." Always circumspect, Rubin searched carefully for a word other than "irrational." "Psychological," he said finally. "The market is too psychological." [21] In other words, the market is us.

From the beginning of the administration, according to Woodward, "Rubin had told Clinton, 'If the economy does well, you ought to talk about it—but if the markets do well don't use that as your credential because markets go up and markets go down.' " [22]

Nevertheless, the Treasury secretary could not be the one to issue a warning to the public. So it was left to Greenspan to raise that tiny red flag in the midst of the long, dry after-dinner speech that he gave on that December night.

Almost as quickly, he lowered it: "We as central bankers need not be concerned if a collapsing financial bubble does not threaten to impair the real economy, its production, jobs and price stability," he added. "Indeed, the sharp stock market break of 1987 had few negative consequences for the economy."

After delivering the speech, Woodward reported, "Greenspan returned to his table, where his girlfriend, Andrea Mitchell, was also seated.

" 'So what was the most important thing I said?' he asked her.

"She looked perplexed, not at all sure."

THE MORNING AFTER

Greenspan's words rippled round the globe. Markets in Tokyo and London plunged. In New York, some observers predicted that when the market opened, the Dow would shed 300 points. In fact, the benchmark index did lose 145 points in early trading. But by midday, panic gave way to pragmatism: "Money managers showed themselves unexpectedly reluctant to sell, possibly for fear of pushing the prices of their remaining holdings lower as well as damaging their 1996 performance results only weeks before the end of the year," observed *The Wall Street Journal*.[23] Once again, careerism won out over caution.

By Monday, the market had shrugged off the chairman's warnings: that day the Nasdaq posted its second-largest point gain in the history of the index.[24]

Nevertheless, Wall Street's paper of record reacted sharply to what it considered the Fed chairman's faux pas: "Financial markets figured out quickly enough that Alan Greenspan didn't mean it," *The Wall Street Journal* declared in Tuesday's "Review & Outlook." "But we hope the Federal Reserve chairman and those around him take a moment to ponder the world-wide turmoil following his Thursday night mumblings."

Normally viewed as pearls of wisdom, the chairman's words suddenly had been reduced to the "mumblings" of an old man.

As for the danger of a financial bubble, the *Journal*'s editorial dismissed the very idea: "An irrational bubble, if indeed any such animal has ever been identified, will by definition go away of its own accord." The paper's editors did not dwell on the cost to investors when bubbles "go away." [25]

Even Senate Majority Leader Trent Lott felt free to publicly rebuke the Fed chairman on nationwide television. "He probably shouldn't have done that," said Lott. "The next morning markets dropped all over the world. . . . I've always been a little nervous about the Fed," Lott added. "They focus too much on one side of the equation rather than the broader basket." Lott also offered his counsel on monetary policy, suggesting that the Fed should lower rates.[26]

Meanwhile, the *Journal*'s "Heard on the Street" column provided a window on how Wall Street's analysts were coping with the crisis. It seemed that a bank analyst at Merrill Lynch had recently put out a report showing that, based on standard methods for calculating bank stocks, the banks he covered were fully valued. "But instead of cutting bank-stock ratings and sending a sell signal, Mr. Kraushaar chose to change his valuation methods," E. S. Browning reported dryly.[27] Everyone, it appeared, was doing his best to counter any loss of confidence brought on by the chairman's unfortunate remarks.

THE CHAIRMAN RECANTS

Less than seven weeks later, Greenspan tried to assuage any fears that his words might have stirred. Testifying before the Senate Budget Committee, the Fed chairman gave a speech that Edward Yardeni, chief economist at Deutsche Morgan Grenfell, summed up neatly as "the case for rational exuberance."

"His comments indicate that he is very pleased with the performance of the economy and sees no reason to either raise or lower interest rates at this time," noted Yardeni. "I believe that his analysis of the economy's recent performance is especially bullish for stocks. In his formal presentation, there was no mention of 'irrational exuberance.' He simply observed that the stock market continued to climb at a 'breathtaking' rate." [28]

From "irrational" to "breathtaking." It was not just an about-face; it was a pirouette.

In March, the Fed lifted interest rates by a quarter point—a small but important move. Reportedly, Fed Governor Laurence Meyer considered this a "brilliant" stroke on the chairman's part. "Here is Greenspan, the poster boy for the New Economy, playing the Old Economy inflation hawk card. The chairman was keeping a foot in both camps, both the New Economy/higher productivity school and the Old Economy/inflation-fighting school. It was a masterly management of the process," Meyer concluded. [29]

But neither Wall Street nor Washington welcomed the tightening, and Greenspan would not lift rates again until June of 1999. In the interval, he cut interest rates three times.

In the spring of '96, Greenspan also publicly repudiated the idea of raising margin requirements. Once again testifying before Congress, he rejected the notion as an "anachronism," recalled Morgan Stanley's Steve Roach—"and this was just six months after declaring that if the Fed wanted to pop the bubble 'I guarantee, that would do it.'"

In retrospect some would claim that even if the Fed had made it more difficult to borrow in order to buy stocks, studies show that raising margin requirements would have little effect. Roach disagreed: "No one *knew* what effect it would have—they hadn't touched margin requirements since '75," he said. Moreover, any action by the Fed would have had a psychological impact. "As a signaling mechanism, lifting margin requirements could have been very powerful," Roach observed in 2003. [30]

For by now, the bull market had become a confidence game, and Greenspan had the nation's confidence. As noted, the Fed chairman's power was, to a large degree, psychological. In the past, "the Fed exerted control by regulating the dollars called bank reserves. Figuratively speaking, Citibank (to name one of the central bank's charges) was a dog at the end of a leash. The Fed was the master and the leash was the monetary transmission mechanism," noted James Grant. "Nowadays, in a freer environment, Citi may be thought of as a cat. No longer inclined to walk at heel, it can lend and borrow without undue reliance on these Fed-supplied balances."[31]

Moreover, by the nineties, four-fifths of the working capital used to finance industry and commerce came, not from the banks the Fed supervised, but from the market itself. As a result, the chairman's power was greatly circumscribed, observed Martin Mayer, the author of a seminal study of the relationship between the Federal Reserve and the New Economy, *The Fed: The Inside Story of How the World's Most Powerful Financial Institution Drives the Markets.*

True, the Fed could pump liquidity into the economy—as it did in the early nineties when the Fed bought up so much Treasury paper that the nation's immediate cash supply (cash plus balances in checking accounts) rose by more than 12 percent in one year. And the Fed could create abundant credit by lowering short-term interest rates—as it would, most fatefully, in 1999. But the Fed chairman's ability to direct the economy was greatly exaggerated both in the media and in the mind of the public: "The Fed is always in the news, as if it alone holds the key to prosperity," as if "minor changes in interest rates and liquidity . . . will decide economic growth rates, employment levels, inflation, deflation or stability," Mayer noted. But, he added, "this certainly is not the case."

Yet, there was no doubt, Greenspan's words could move markets—sending "a frisson through the markets and then the media" simply because so many people believed that Greenspan's was "the most authoritative and thus predictive voice." No matter that the Fed chairman's power was largely a matter of what Mayer called "custom, belief, and the power of theatre." Economics could not explain it: "We just don't know how it happens—or why it sometimes doesn't happen."[32] In other words, like many psychological phenomena, the chairman's power remained both inexplicable—and unpredictable.

The wizard behind the curtain, Greenspan was left in a nearly impossible position. On the one hand, he was expected to manage the bubble—but he was never, ever, to suggest that there *was* a bubble. This would upset the people who believed that he could manage it.

Moreover, even if he wanted to let the air out, the truth is that there is no way to prick a bubble without running the risk that the thing will splatter all over the room. Better to leave it alone. Better yet, announce that what looked like irrational exuberance is in fact justifiable euphoria.

Before long, the Fed chairman would be singing with the choir. And the excesses that the bubble had created would have a new name: "The New Economy."

THE MIRACLE OF
PRODUCTIVITY

In July of 1997, *Business Week* announced the Fed chairman's conversion: "The staunch conservative who once personified industrial-era economic thinking has turned into the avant-garde advocate of the New Economy."

What the magazine called "Alan Greenspan's Brave New World" was built on the premise that the United States was undergoing "a productivity revolution not seen since early in the 20th century." When output was compared to hours worked, American workers were producing more goods and services per hour. Admittedly, the Bureau of Labor Statistics reports on productivity showed gains stuck at around 1 percent, but, *Business Week* explained, Greenspan believed that "statistical distortions are understating efficiency gains."

"The suspected productivity payoff is also making Greenspan more sanguine about the rising stock market," the magazine reported. "When he raised his famous concern last December about whether stocks were in the grip of 'irrational exuberance,' the Fed chief was worried that corporate profits couldn't keep pace and that a steep correction might ensue. But margins have been rising smartly—faster than Greenspan can ever recall. His only explanation: 'productivity.'

"So confident is Greenspan of his argument, that he has required researchers to make a second productivity measure by 'zeroing out' any industry sector—such as health care—where statistics show falling productivity. Reason? In this cost-cutting era, he can't fathom any sector becoming less efficient. Still, these exercises drive researchers nuts. 'A lot of the staff are skeptical of overmining the data,' said Fed Governor Susan M. Phillips. 'They'll complain about it, but in hindsight, it has made a lot of sense.' "[1]

As anyone who has ever started with a high concept and then worked backward to find numbers to fit the theory knows, it is not unusual for the theory to make a lot of sense "in hindsight."

Somewhat belatedly, the chairman of the Federal Reserve was falling in line with *Business Week*'s own assessment of the economy. No wonder the magazine was impressed. Seven months earlier, *Business Week* had heralded "The Triumph of the New Economy," explaining how the new technology was driving American workers to new heights of productivity: "Business investment in computers and communications hardware has soared by 24% over the past year alone, accounting for almost one-third of economic growth. From the Internet to direct-broadcast television, new companies are springing up almost overnight to take advantage of cutting-edge technologies.

"GREEN LIGHTS," *Business Week* proclaimed. "The stock market's rise is an accurate reflection of the growing strength of the New Economy. Productivity growth, although understated by official statistics, is rising as companies learn to use information technology to cut costs, a necessity for competing in global markets."[2]

Like most supernatural events, the "productivity miracle" depended, to a fair degree, on blind faith.

A CLOSER LOOK AT THE NUMBERS

When economists talk about "productivity," they are referring to the amount of goods and services the nation produces per hour of work. In theory, when businesses produce more per worker, they increase profits and raise wages. The growth of gross domestic product (GDP) is the sum of increases in productivity and the labor force. In other words, when more people work more hours, GDP grows. But everything turns on how you measure the value of those goods and services.

Not surprisingly, as long as the market rose, the optimists carried the day. The government reported that productivity had grown nearly 2.9 percent a year from 1995 to 2000—double the 1.4 percent rate of growth from 1973 to 1995. In the cold light of 2001, however, the government would be forced to revise its numbers. "Overestimates of computer software sales and consumer spending" had inflated productivity gains, explained *New York Times* columnist Jeff Madrick. Now, it became clear "how thin the new-economy thinking has been all along. Those gains turn out mostly to have been the product of a counting error."

In the late nineties, the Fed seized upon government reports that productivity was beginning to soar as proof of a *structural* change in the economy. But then the government began revising its numbers. "The 2.6 percent growth rate in 1999 was cut to 2.3 percent, and the stunning 4.3 percent rate in 2000, which converted many a skeptic to the new-economy cause, was cut to 3 percent," Madrick reported. "This is hardly a deepening computer revolution." Madrick, an economist and author of *Why Economies Grow: The Forces That Shape Prosperity and How We Can Get Them Working Again,* calculated that from 1990—the start of the cycle—to 2000, productivity rose by less than 2 percent a year.[3]

Indeed, even before the government revised its figures, research by Harvard economist James Medoff, published in *Grant's Interest Rate Observer,* suggested that the only real gains in productivity were limited to the computer industry itself. And even there, the industry's predilection for creative accounting made it difficult to be certain.

In the end, the problem is that it is very difficult to assess the value of the new technology. "Until it is set to profitable employment, a computer is a piece of furniture. Like a piano, its utility depends on the individual at the keyboard," Grant observed. "He may play 'The Moonlight Sonata' or 'Happy Birthday.'" When the New Economists estimated the value of the computers produced by the New Economy, they assumed, Grant suggested, "that the U.S. workforce studied at Juilliard."[4]

PRODUCTIVITY AND PROFITS

But what of the Internet? Throughout the late nineties, the digerati would give the Net much credit as the catalyst for the boom—though again, it was hard to find concrete proof.

This was because, as a study released by McKinsey & Company in

2002 would reveal, total productivity gains after 1995 could be explained by the performance of just six sectors: retail, wholesale, securities, telecom, semiconductors, and computer manufacturing. "The other 70% of the economy contributed a mix of small productivity gains and losses that offset each other," the study reported.

Moreover, of those six, only one sector benefited from the Internet: brokerages that sold securities to individual investors. Once again, the croupiers were the big winners: By the end of 1999, nearly 40 percent of retail securities trades were performed online—a huge boon to discount brokers such as Charles Schwab.

A close look at how much computers did for banking told another story. Despite generous spending on personal computers and software, retail banks, for instance, saw their productivity rate decline during the late nineties. "Banking was an example of an industry that spent on technology simply because it could," McKinsey's James Manyika explained. "It will now spend less." [5]

Ultimately, "productivity statistics mistook a spending spree for increased efficiency," declared Leon Levy, founder of the Oppenheimer Funds, and one of Wall Street's shrewdest investors, in 2002. "With seemingly insatiable consumers willing to buy higher-priced goods, those selling the goods looked more efficient because their revenues were rising without any increase in their workforce." [6]

Sales rose, but what about profits? The proof of productivity gains should be seen in earnings.

1997—A TURNING POINT FOR PROFITS

In fact, 1997 would turn out to be a watershed year for the New Economy, but not in the way that the New Economists expected. Corporate profits hit a wall: "According to government statistics, overall corporate profits grew rapidly between 1992 and 1997," Princeton economist Paul Krugman observed, "but then stalled; after-tax profits in the third quarter of 2000 were barely higher than they were three years earlier." Meanwhile, the "operating earnings" of the S&P 500—the profits companies reported to investors—showed 46 percent growth during those three years, thanks, largely, to "accounting gimmicks." [7]

In reality, profit margins for the S&P 400 stopped expanding in 1996, according to a study by Sanford Bernstein, one of the few Wall Street firms that did not mix investment research with investment banking. After cleaning up the numbers, Bernstein discovered that from '76 through 2000, the "exceptional performance" of operating margins in the second half of the nineties "disappear[ed] entirely." [8]

How could this be? In theory, the more corporate America spent on information technology, the more efficient its workers would become— leading, inexorably, to higher profits. "Trouble is, productivity can have very little to do with profits," noted Jeremy Grantham, the Boston-based money manager who pioneered the index fund. In two sentences, Grantham summed up the flaw in the New Economists' theory: "Imagine what would happen if you lay a lot of cable, and it turns out to have five times more carrying capacity than before. It's wonderful for productivity, and devastating for profits." [9]

EXCESS CAPACITY

While more spending on technology can boost capacity, increased capacity does not necessarily mean higher earnings. To the contrary, when businesses sink billions into technology willy-nilly, more capacity can quickly become excess capacity, and as supply swamps demand, profits plunge.

By 1997, this is precisely what happened in some of the hottest sectors. Investors eager to buy technology stocks financed the boom in capital spending, and the Fed did its part by keeping interest rates low. Borrowing to build another factory seemed a bargain. "Presented with the financial means to build the extra semiconductor fabricating plant or the marginal personal-computer manufacturing plant, the world's high-tech manufacturers have not hesitated," Jim Grant noted in October of 1997. "A huge expansion of manufacturing capacity is under way—in chemicals, paper, aircraft, autos, commercial banking and high technology. . . . The result is a boom in productive capacity—and a collapse in the prices of memory chips and personal computers, the most basic commodities of the information age. Even Intel has lately been forced to cut the prices of its microprocessors. And the hottest new computers are the ones that sell for less than $1000." [10]

Meanwhile, tech shares headed for heaven. In 1996, semiconductor shares rose 80 percent, computer hardware makers climbed 41 percent, and software companies rose 36 percent. Ten of technology's blue chips—IBM, Oracle, Cisco Systems, Motorola, Hewlett-Packard, Sun Microsystems, Intel, Texas Instruments, Micron Technology, and Microsoft—boasted a combined market value of nearly $500 billion at the beginning of 1997, up a staggering $196 billion in fifteen months.

At the same time, industry fundamentals deteriorated. "Memory chip prices are in free fall," *Forbes* reported early in 1997. "Spot price for the commodity 16-megabyte DRAM is currently around $6, down from $50 last year." Meanwhile, 20 new chip plants were planned or under construction in Taiwan. Hyundai and LG Semicon in Korea were putting some 80 percent of their semiconductor sales into capital spending. "This fresh supply could drive chip prices down to $3 or $4. Bad news for Micron Technology, Texas Instruments, Atmel and others."

PC makers benefited from falling chip prices and were still reporting impressive profits. But as competition heated up, the PC price wars began, with some computers marked down by as much as 40 percent in the weeks before Christmas of '96.

Even with prices slashed, computers sat on the shelves. At the end of 1996, Wal-Mart announced that it would no longer sell PCs in 700 of its 1,600 stores.[11]

THE ASIAN CRISIS

By the summer of 1997, excess capacity was rearing its ugly head, not just at Wal-Mart but in Asia. Go-go growth in Southeast Asia had spurred the building of countless factories, and the result was a glut in virtually every sector: cars, chips, ships, clothing, cement, plastic, petrochemicals, and steel. Meanwhile, China was flooding its neighbors in Southeast Asia with cheap, well-made goods—crimping their export-led economies.

In the first half of 1997, China exported 25 percent more goods than it had a year earlier. In Malaysia, Thailand, the Philippines, and Indonesia, export prices sank, real estate prices sagged, and trade deficits grew. Countries throughout the region faced pressure to devalue their currencies in order to make their exports cheaper, the better to compete with each other, and with China.[12]

And, ultimately, that is exactly what happened. In July, the Thai baht fell 12 percent against the dollar. Devaluations in the Philippines, Malaysia, and Indonesia followed, creating a domino effect that triggered stock market declines across the region.

Hong Kong held the line—but at a price. In October, the Hang Seng index plunged more than 16 percent in just two days. Within hours, what the media called "the Asian flu" spread to the United States. Fearing that the earnings of large U.S. companies exposed to Asia would suffer, investors headed for the exits.

On Monday, October 27, the Dow dropped 554 points—the largest one-day plunge in the market's history. Still, in percentage terms, the Dow's 12 percent drop from its August 6 peak paled in comparison with the 22.6 percent one-day plunge in 1987. And within days, the index bounced back, leading to the largest one-day gain in the market's history.

Seasoned market watchers found the one-day gain almost as spooky as the one-day loss: such volatility confirmed Gail Dudack's intuition that this was a market that had lost its rudder—a market driven by blind emotion.

Nevertheless, within a week many on Wall Street were shrugging off fears that the U.S. market would be affected by the "Asian contagion."

"Wall Street: Too Healthy Right Now to Succumb to a Case of 'Asian Flu,'" declared the headline in *The International Herald Tribune,* noting that "even the usually cautious Alan Greenspan last week characterized economic growth as 'robust' and inflation as 'low.'"[13]

The Fed chairman was right. Inflation was not a problem. The greater threat was deflation—falling prices that could, in turn, squeeze profit margins. A fundamental imbalance between supply and demand was keeping prices low. Desperate to boost earnings and bring in dollars, Asia's Newly Industrialized Countries slashed prices even further, and global competition intensified.

The U.S. economy avoided deflation, but in many areas prices remained flat. Overinvestment had created excess capacity at home and abroad, and as a result, U.S. corporations had lost "pricing power"—consumers would not accept price increases. Meanwhile, export opportunities for U.S. companies shrank as the dollar soared against most major currencies, making U.S. products more expensive abroad.

No wonder corporate earnings stalled in '97.

NO MIRACLE FOR THE CHICKENS

The ultimate consequence of "Greenspan's productivity bubble" would be unemployment. In a piece published on David Tice's Prudentbear.com, Donald Perry used a parable to make the point. Dr. Perry was not an economist, nor was he a Wall Street strategist. He was, in fact, an ecologist—an outside observer with common sense—and he compared the New Economy to a chicken farm:

"Basically, productivity in the coop increases when chickens lay more eggs per day," Perry wrote. "Early on farmers noted that hens could produce more eggs when confined to a cage, instead of running around searching for food, being chased by cocks, or having to evade predators. To understand productivity as it relates to the economy substitute the word 'chicken' for 'worker.' "

If chickens are laying more eggs—but the price of eggs is falling—the egg business is at best "treading water," Perry explained. Too many eggs, like too many cell phones or too many computers, leaves the chicken farmer with little power to raise prices. "What Greenspan fails to acknowledge," Perry observed, "is that while American business may be producing more eggs, the bottom is dropping out from under the price of eggs." The solution, for the egg farmer, is "to send some of the chickens to Campbell's [where they would wind up, quite literally, in the soup]. The farmer then has fewer chickens to feed, gets the highest average output per chicken, and makes a little extra money in the process.

"But human chickens aren't sent to Campbell's," he pointed out, "they get unemployment and buy fewer goods." And, "since there are fewer buyers the glut of eggs becomes even greater.

"Another complication is that while it is plain to see that putting chickens in sweat shops all over the planet produces huge numbers of eggs, who will buy these eggs? Obviously, the market must correct itself by 'wringing out the excesses.' Ultimately many egg producers are going to go out of business. So when you hear Greenspan touting productivity gains you should be thinking 'Who will be going out of business next?' Hint: Asian chickens produce more eggs on less food."

Before deciding that rising productivity is a boon, one needs to ask why it is rising, Perry suggested. Rising productivity "makes economic sense when production rises faster than 'hours worked,' but it makes little or no

sense when—as in recent years—hours worked fall faster than rising production." [14]

Or, as Gail Dudack put it: "When productivity gains are linked to jobs
vanishing, we see no miracle." [15]

1997: A TURNING POINT FOR THE MARKET

Gail Dudack had been a bull since she first appeared on *Wall $treet Week
with Louis Rukeyser* at the tender age of 25. But by the beginning of 1997,
she was convinced that share prices no longer reflected fundamental values.
At the time, Dudack was chief market strategist at UBS Warburg, and she
warned her clients: "By our measure, the equity market was fairly valued
until October 1996." After that, in Dudack's view, stocks were overvalued.

"Back then, you had to be careful about using the word 'bubble,'" she
recalled six years later. "But in October of 1997, on the 10-year anniversary
of the '87 crash, I saw an opportunity to sound a warning, and I published
a report that was, essentially, a review of Charles Kindleberger's *Manias,
Panics and Crashes: A History of Financial Crisis.* Those who believe that the
'90s are unique," Dudack told her clients, "should read this book." [16]

An economics professor at MIT writing in the late seventies, Kindleberger had outlined both the ingredients necessary to produce market
manias and the role that central bankers like Alan Greenspan can play in
fueling financial euphoria.

The first stage of a mania, according to Kindleberger, is usually an
exogenous shock to the financial system: "This could be the beginning or
end of a war, a bumper harvest or a new investment. Whatever the source
it is sufficiently large and pervasive that it alters the economic outlook
by changing profit opportunities in at least one important sector of the
economy."

In this case, Dudack told her clients, "We believe that the end of the
Cold War and the birth of the Internet both qualify."

"Easy money" (what Kindleberger called mismanagement of credit) is
a second prerequisite for euphoria. Here, Dudack pointed out that the
lending environment in the mid-nineties fit the scenario: "Credit cards are
ubiquitous, sub-prime lending (to borrowers who ordinarily do not qualify
for a loan) has been phenomenal and mortgages are available for 105% of
the value of a home."

A third ingredient: the con men. "Chapter titles such as 'Fraud and the Cycle,' 'Bubbles and Swindlers,' 'Noble Gamblers,' 'Venal Journalism,' 'Dubious Practices,' 'The Temptation of Bankers' and 'The Wages of Sin' tell it all," Dudack noted. "But," she warned, "many times these signs do not appear until after the crash. Japan would be a perfect example of this, where fraud in the brokerage industry and ties to the Mafia were identified after the Nikkei fell from 39,000 to 14,300."

Finally, Kindleberger argued that during a financial mania "faith in the central banker" (in this case the Fed chairman) feeds complacency. Investors believe that if things fall apart, he will rescue them, and as a result, "the mania is likely to go on much longer and much further since there is little perception of risk by investors."

Kindleberger made it clear that he did not believe central bankers have the power to eliminate financial manias. But he suggested that "the weight of the historical evidence strongly favors the case" that monetary policy (in this case, Fed policy) might "moderate" a boom that leads to a bust.

Greenspan's critics would charge that, as the bubble grew, he did not even try. "When the Fed sends a signal, it speaks to the world," said Morgan Stanley's Roach. "Greenspan condoned the bubble—and then concocted a theory as to why it was rational." [17]

RETIREMENT ROULETTE

As belief in "Alan Greenspan's Brave New World" blanketed the nation, wise-heads in Washington began to suggest that the government should begin gambling the Social Security Trust Fund's assets on stocks. Early in 1997, the Advisory Council on Social Security issued a 752-page report that outlined three plans for "rescuing" Social Security.

As usual, *Newsweek*'s Allan Sloan pulled no punches. "What all three proposals have in common," he observed, is that they "would throw us willy-nilly into a high-stakes game of retirement roulette, betting the nation's financial future (or the futures of millions of individual retirees) on the stock market."

"The council didn't start out to do this," Sloan pointed out. "Initially its members tried to agree on a cuts-and-taxes fix." [18] But some members feared that sharp tax increases and benefit cutbacks represented a politically unpalatable solution.

This is when they came up with the idea of betting 40 percent of the fund on stocks. (By law, the Social Security fund is required to invest only in Treasury bonds.) "How did the council's biggest faction—six of 13 members—decide to put 40 percent of the fund in stocks?" Sloan asked. "'That's the amount that makes things come out,' says panel member Robert Ball, the former Social Security commissioner who's pushing this plan hard."

Once again, Washington was working backward from high concept to empirical evidence. In what could be called the wish-fulfillment method of budgeting, the Advisory Council started with the amount that they guessed the Security Trust Fund would need, then determined that if 40 percent of Social Security savings were invested in equities, the fund would meet their goal—assuming, of course, that stocks returned an average of 11.28 percent a year.

An extraordinary assumption, as everyone on the Advisory Council knew—or at least had been told. The number was based, in part, on a report by Joel Dickson, a financial analyst at the Vanguard mutual fund group. The Council had charged Dickson with figuring out how much stocks had averaged, after inflation, for the longest period he could measure. Going back to 1900, he came up with 7 percent. A reasonable fellow, Dickson provided no guarantees: in his report to the Council he noted clearly that that there was at least a 50 percent chance his numbers wouldn't be right.[19]

Nevertheless, the Council took the 7 percent before-inflation figure, guessed that, in the future, inflation would average roughly 4 percent a year, and came up with 11.28 percent as the likely total return from stocks in the years ahead. (On that basis, the policy makers reckoned, if 40 percent of the money was invested in stocks, everything would work out just fine.)

Trouble is, what was generally considered the most reliable benchmark at the time showed equities had averaged just 10.71 percent a year over the 71-year period from 1926 through 1996. "In a triumph of statistics over common sense, the Council's plans all assume that stock prices from here on will rise more quickly than they have in the past," Sloan noted. "Stocks have risen about 1,000 percent since the bull market started in August of 1982. But no tree grows to the sky. Except, of course, for simulated trees in computer models."

The difference between 11.28 percent and 10.71 percent might not sound enormous, but while a dollar invested in 1926 at 11.28 percent would have become $1,975 by the end of '96, if that same dollar earned just 10.71 percent it would have grown to only $1,372.

But the real point here is not that the Council should have used 10.71 percent instead of 11.28 percent—but rather that *absolutely no one knows how much the stock market will return over the next 10, 25, 50, or 75 years.*

"Betting that stock prices will keep rising rapidly because they have been rising rapidly 'is like the guys on Noah's ark projecting six more weeks of rain on the 39th day,' said Joseph Rosenberg, chief investment strategist at Loews Corp. and one of Wall Street's most respected investors: 'You can't believe how dumb a government can be.' "[20]

Yes you can. At the beginning of 2003, despite the market's dismal decline, the Bush administration continued to favor diverting some portion of Social Security savings into private accounts, giving individuals the opportunity to gamble the money on stocks. No surprise, the mutual fund industry stood foursquare in favor of the proposal.[21]

What the plan's proponents seem to have forgotten is that the Social Security Trust Fund is not an investment club, it is a safety net—and not just for the elderly but for the nation. If that safety net is rent, and retirees have trouble making ends meet, inevitably, taxpayers will wind up bailing them out—either directly, by supplementing their income, or indirectly, by footing the bill for the extra medical care that a larger population of indigent elderly will need.

This is why they call it a Trust Fund.

THE FINAL RUN-UP
(1998–2000)

"Fully Deluded Earnings"

[There has been] much loose talk about "value creation." We readily acknowledge that there has been a huge amount of true value created in the past decade by new or young businesses and that there is much more to come. But value is destroyed, not created, by any business that loses money over its lifetime, no matter how high its interim valuation may get. What actually occurs in these cases is wealth transfer, often on a massive scale.

—Warren Buffett, 2000 letter to
Berkshire Hathaway's shareholders

In July of 1998, Jim Chanos happened upon an intriguing item tucked away in the most recent issue of *Business Week*. As a short seller, Chanos made his living by paying attention to detail. On this particular day, he was reading a *Business Week* advertising supplement. There, he found the results of a poll the magazine had taken at its seventh annual forum for chief financial officers three months earlier.

The magazine asked the 160 chief financial officers who attended the forum to respond to the following proposition:

"As CFO, I have fought off other executives' requests that I mispresent corporate results." Using "audience response electronic keypads," they chose from the following three answers:

1. Yes, I fought them off.
2. I yielded to the requests.
3. Have never received such a request.

What was refreshing was the honesty of the answers. One might think that a prudent CFO would be tempted to claim that no one at his company had ever suggested such malfeasance. In fact, only 33 percent responded: "Have never received such a request."

The majority—55 percent—acknowledged that their colleagues had at least suggested cooking the books: "Yes, I fought them off."

Incredibly, fully 12 percent went a step further, admitting, "I yielded to the requests." [1]

Why *Business Week* chose to publish the results in its advertising supplement was not entirely clear. What was certain was that by 1998, financial chicanery had become commonplace throughout corporate America. That two-thirds of these CFOs freely admitted that they had been asked to goose the numbers suggested that the type of person who might blanch at such a suggestion had probably fallen off the corporate ladder early on in the bull market.

Creative bookkeeping was not confined to the late nineties—and it was not limited to technology companies. Well-known names such as Oxford Health, Green Tree Financial, Boston Chicken, Sunbeam, and Cendant fell under the weight of their own bad numbers. Abuse was widespread. From 1997 to 2002, roughly 1,000 companies would be forced to admit that the earnings that they had reported were not quite correct. [2]

The market's spiral not only pushed share prices to unsustainable heights, it also fostered a corrupt corporate culture hooked on high growth. "Delivering double-digit earnings growth year after year is no longer simply what corporate re-engineers call a 'stretch goal' for an organization, or a rare achievement to be celebrated. It's become a mandate, a benchmark, a test of corporate manhood, an expectation hard-wired into the culture," wrote *The Washington Post*'s Steven Pearlstein as he looked back on the bull market. "The addiction to double-digit growth has spread across the corporate landscape to firms in older, mature industries desperate for the 'growth company' moniker that qualifies them for Wall Street's highest reward: a stock price equal to 20, 30, even 40 times earnings." [3]

The newspapers reported on the Sunbeams and the Cendants. Nevertheless, the media tended to embrace the theory that these were what *The*

Wall Street Journal called "notable exceptions." Just a few days before Chanos read the *Business Week* poll, *The Wall Street Journal*'s "Abreast of the Market" column reassured readers: "With accounting questions playing a big part in some spectacular recent stock blowups, investors might wonder just how believable are the earnings now fueling record stock prices. Rest easy: They are more believable than in previous decades.

"Some high profile disasters aside, U.S. corporate accounting has been getting steadily more conservative in recent years, not less so, many experts believe—a view backed up by new research. . . ." The column cited research by several accounting professors and wound up quoting Abby Cohen's assistant.[4]

But while the accounting professors provided theory, *Business Week* had, however inadvertently, done field research. Time would prove its poll correct.

THE WHOLE BUSHEL

Ultimately, the Jerome Levy Forecasting Center, a highly respected, non-partisan, independently funded consulting firm, would expose just how far and how deep the rot had spread in a seminal study of corporate accounting during the bull market: "Two Decades of Overstated Corporate Earnings."

"Over the past ten years, the financial media have spotlighted case after case of earnings misrepresentations . . . [but] the focus of public concern remained on finding the bad apples; *little attention was paid to the quality of the entire bushel,*" the study's authors wrote.

"Just how widespread and serious was the overstatement of aggregate corporate profits?" they asked. "The answer is startling. The evidence indicates that *corporate operating earnings for the Standard & Poor's 500 have been significantly exaggerated for nearly two decades*—by about 10 percent or more early in this period and by over 20 percent in recent years [emphasis mine]. These figures are conservative—the magnitude of the overstatement may be considerably larger."[5]

Both the press and the public were reluctant to face the fact that the problem was systemic. It was easier to acknowledge that a few corrupt CEOs were puffing up earnings statements. To admit that the entire system had been gamed—and not just in the late nineties but throughout much of the bull market—meant questioning the underpinnings of an "efficient" market. If that market was operating on tainted information, just how efficient could it be?

SEC Commissioner Arthur Levitt knew the answer, and by 1998 he was more outspoken than he had been when he first came to Washington. That September, in a speech that he delivered at the NYU Center for Law and Business, Levitt was blunt: "Too many corporate managers, auditors, and analysts are participants in a game of nods and winks. In the zeal to satisfy consensus earnings estimates and project a smooth earnings path, wishful thinking may be winning the day over faithful representation. As a result, I fear that we are witnessing an erosion in the quality of earnings, and therefore, the quality of financial reporting. Managing may be giving way to manipulation. Integrity may be losing out to illusion."[6]

Companies like GE boasted of "managing" their earnings so that they rose, consistently and smoothly, quarter after quarter, year in and year out. In this way, GE was able to always meet, if not beat, analysts' estimates. Of course, in the real world of business some years are better than others; profits do not rise in a straight line. This is why Jim Grant called managed earnings "fully deluded earnings." Grant quoted Jim Chanos: "The trouble with smoothing a naturally jagged pattern of earnings is that the underlying problems of the business itself are likely to be obscured—until the day when they can't be any longer."[7]

To mask problems, some companies created virtual revenues. One of the simplest ways to do this is to pay customers to buy your goods. And by the late nineties this is precisely what Cisco was doing. George Noble, a Boston-based portfolio manager best known for a successful stint running Fidelity's Overseas Fund, recalled stumbling onto one of Cisco's virtual customers. At the time, Noble was attending a road show for B2, a small broadband company that was trying to drum up interest in an IPO:

"To lend credibility to the whole thing, they were pointing out all the big investors they had, like Morgan Stanley—who by the way was also their underwriter. Then they said, 'We buy all of our equipment from Cisco. We gave Cisco an order for $330 million of equipment and we got 135% vendor financing.'"

Noble perked up. He decided to play dumb. "How does that work? What is vendor financing?"

"Well, the order was for $330 million of equipment and they gave us $450 million of financing at 9% interest and with no payment and principal for the first year," the company spokesperson explained.

"Is that good?" Noble asked, still playing the innocent.

"The Morgan Stanley banker shot up out of his chair because he wanted to dazzle us with how great the deal was for B2," Noble recalled. "Everyone knew where I was going with that question except the banker who went on to explain what a great deal it was."[8]

At least for B2. The company received $330 million of free equipment plus $80 million in cash. In return, Cisco received $330 million of revenues—on paper. Maybe B2 would be able to repay the loan. Maybe not.

Cisco was hardly alone. Telecom-equipment suppliers were particularly generous with their loans: by the end of 2000, they were collectively owed as much as $15 billion by customers, a 25 percent increase in a single year.[9]

"EXTRAORDINARY" ITEMS BECOME ORDINARY

All of this was, of course, perfectly legal. Contrary to the conventional wisdom, outright fraud was not the most pervasive accounting problem of the nineties. Most creative accountants played by—and with—the rules.

In the Levy Center report, Walter M. Cadette, David A. Levy, and Srinivas Thiruvadanthai outlined the two major ways that corporations used the rules to inflate their earnings:

1. by focusing investor attention on operating earnings rather than net income; and
2. by paying executives in stock options rather than cash, and so masking the expense.

In theory, what Standard & Poor's calls "operating earnings" is a fairly clean concept. These are the profits that a company makes in the ordinary course of doing business: the revenues it takes in by selling its product or service, minus taxes and expenses. Operating income does not include extraordinary one-time gains or expenses. For instance, if a company sells a division, this is a nonrecurring gain that will not appear the next year, and so should not be included under operating income. Similarly, if it lays off 1,000 employees and gives them generous severance packages, this is a one-time expense, outside of the ordinary cost of doing business, and so it's not supposed to be deducted from operating income. By comparing operating income year over year, an investor can see how the core business is faring.

That is the theory. But, as the Levy Center's report explained, over the course of the bull market companies found various ways to goose operating income. Sometimes, a company would mislabel one-time (and nonrecurring) revenue as operating revenue—as if it had sold products. This is precisely what IBM did in 1999 when it used a one-time $4 billion gain from its sale of its global network business to offset that year's normal expenses.

On other occasions, a company would sweep true operating expenses into the "one-time expense column." Once tucked into that column, the expense did not have to be subtracted from operating income.

In 1999, Warren Buffett elaborated on how this bit of legerdemain works: "A large chunk of costs that should properly be attributed to a number of years is dumped into a single quarter, typically one already fated to disappoint investors. In some cases, the purpose of the charge is to clean up earnings misrepresentations of the past, and in others it is to prepare the ground for future misrepresentations. In either case, the size and timing of these charges is dictated by the cynical proposition that Wall Street will not mind if earnings fall short by $5 per share in a given quarter, just as long as this deficiency insures that quarterly earnings in the future will consistently exceed expectations by five cents per share." [10]

Because investors were so focused on the notion of quarterly earnings growth, the ruse worked. "If you take something as a [one-time] restructuring charge, investors will forgive you immediately," explained Robert S. Miller, an executive brought in to clean up Waste Management. "We've almost lost the notion of what are earnings and what are one-time charges." [11]

Operating earnings have a place. The only way an investor can see whether a company's profits are growing, year by year, is if he has a clean snapshot of annual revenues minus annual expenses. Occasional one-time restructuring charges should not blur the picture too much. Trouble is, over the course of the bull market one-time extraordinary charges became "all-the-time" extraordinary charges.

Kodak took the trend to an extreme. From 1991 to 1998, Kodak took six extraordinary write-offs for restructuring costs that totaled $4.5 billion—more than all of its net profits for the preceding nine years. Granted, over that time Kodak had been in a major transition period, exiting five major business lines while sales dropped 25 percent. [12] Nevertheless, over a period of years, these "extraordinary" expenses had become a regular part of its business. Yet they were not subtracted from operating income. "Just how 'one-time' are restructuring costs if they occur every year?" asked Jim Chanos. "If opening and closing factories and hiring and firing employees are integral to a manufacturer's business, shouldn't they be treated that way in its earnings reports?"

Others agreed. In 2003, Gail Dudack, SunGard's chief market strategist, pointed out just how ordinary "extraordinary items" had become (see chart "Extraordinary Items as a % of Reported S&P EPS," Appendix, page 465). Up until the mid-eighties, "extraordinary charges were minuscule," she pointed out. "But then they began to grow. This year, Standard & Poor's forecasts that these one-time items will equal 38% of earnings per share on the S&P 500. Accounting gimmicks are making it almost impossible to analyze or compare income statements." [13]

Meanwhile, the media helped Wall Street keep all eyes focused on the numbers that corporations wanted investors to see. "Perhaps nowhere is the symbiosis between the media and the market more evident than in the reporting of operating results," the authors of the Levy Center report observed. "When a company announces its earnings, it typically issues a press release including operating earnings and management's comments on its results. The media pick up and broadcast these figures even though, unbeknownst to most consumers of the information, the company may file quite different results later with the SEC in its 10Q financial statements. The casual definition of operating results a company employs when issuing a splashy announcement for the public may not pass muster with the SEC. Yet firms do not publicize nor do the media cover the more regulated results filed with the authorities.

"A society of organizations and people profiting from the boom will exhibit resistance to any interference with it," the report concluded. "Every source of political power—business managements, the investors themselves, the public officials taking credit for the good times—will favor rules and policies that appear to protect, not threaten the goose laying the golden eggs."

OPTIONS AND PROFITS

One of the rules that protected the golden goose laying the virtual profits was the rule Senator Carl Levin had fought to change in the early nineties—the accounting wrinkle that let corporations hide the cost of the stock options that they awarded to their top executives. According to the Levy Center report, this was the second major way that companies artificially inflated their earnings.[14]

During the final run-up, stock options became an ever more popular way of padding executive pay without counting the cost: By 2000, the value of options granted by the nation's 2,000 largest corporations had climbed to $162 billion—up from $50 billion in 1997.[15] The lion's share of those options was still flowing straight to the very top of the corporate pyramid. "In 2000, the Bureau of Labor Statistics looked at who actually received options in 1999, and found that, nationwide, only 1.7 percent of non-executive private sector employees received any stock options—and only 4.6 percent of executives received them," reported a member of Senator Levin's staff. "In other words, in 1999—which was a banner year for stock options—98 percent of U.S. workers did not receive a single stock option as part of their pay."[16] Meanwhile, at the end of '99, the CEOs running the 800 largest public companies in the United States were sitting on options worth $18 billion—up 46 percent from a year earlier. These were "fully vested" options—which means that the waiting period had expired. If the market began to falter, they could cash them in at any time. Which is exactly what they would do.[17]

As for the effect of those options on corporate profits, a 1999 Federal Reserve study of 138 large firms estimated that by failing to account for the value of options, those companies had boosted their earnings by 10.5 percent.[18]

But this was just one way that companies used options to burnish their balance sheets. Options programs also created a tax shelter that could make a company look far more profitable than it really was.[19] As the use of options grew, the tax deduction turned into a windfall. At the end of the decade, when Jack Ciesielski, a CPA at R.G. Associates, totted up the tax benefit associated with options, he discovered that for some S&P 500 companies the amount of money saved in 1999 and 2000, thanks to the options deduction, was actually *equal to or greater than the cash the business generated.* The list included Sprint, PCS GP, Morgan Stanley, J.P. Morgan,

Lehman Brothers, Motorola, Bank of New York, and Countrywide Credit. In other words, "These leading lights of tech and finance actually *consumed* cash through their operations instead of coining it," observed Kathryn Welling, who published the list on *welling@weeden.*[20]

Meanwhile, as executives exercised their options to buy stock, the number of shares outstanding mounted. In 1990, just two U.S. companies had more than a billion shares outstanding—Wal-Mart and AT&T. By 1995, GE, Coca-Cola, Exxon, Merck, and Ford had joined the group, bringing the total to seven. Then things got out of hand. Seven years later, 65 companies had joined what Steve Leuthold called "The Billion Share Club." Near the top of the list: GE (9.9 billion), Cisco (7.3), Intel (6.7), Pfizer (6.3), Oracle (5.5), Microsoft (5.4), Citigroup (5.2), and AOL Time Warner (4.3). "Of course stock splits and stock based acquisitions explained part of this quantum leap," Leuthold acknowledged, "but stock options have also been a major factor."[21]

The potentially disastrous effect on earnings per share was obvious: when billions of new shares are issued, the earnings pie has to be sliced into smaller pieces. If earnings per share dropped too much, companies would never be able to meet Wall Street's quarterly estimates no matter how diligently they padded their earnings reports. There was only one solution: companies had to begin buying back their own shares.

And this is exactly what they did. At the height of the bull market, companies began paying a premium for their own overvalued shares, squandering money that could have been used either for research and development or to distribute dividends to shareholders. Some even borrowed to finance the buybacks. And so, in what was supposedly the most prosperous decade in U.S. history, corporate debt mounted. But unless executives wanted to cut back on their own lavish options programs, buybacks were necessary, whatever the price.

The total cost was breathtaking. In 1999, the Federal Reserve Board estimated that their sample of 138 large firms spent some 40 percent of their earnings buying back their own shares.[22]

Taking Shares with One Hand, Buying Them Back with the Other

Dell Computer provided a case study in just how costly options programs could become. In 1998, Michael Dell took home 12,800,000 options—in addition to nearly $3.5 million in salary and bonuses. That year Dell himself received 21 percent of all the stock options granted by the company to its employees. A year earlier, Dell had announced that it was expanding its share buyback program—even though its shares were trading at almost 40 times projected 1997 profits. The next year, the company paid $1.5 billion to buy back 149 million shares.[23]

In theory, companies gave out stock options in order to ensure employee loyalty and retain top talent. But who was going to steal Michael Dell—Gateway? Other founder-entrepreneurs—CEOs like Microsoft's Bill Gates or Amazon.com's Jeff Bezos—did not take options, though they did give them to their employees. Moreover, while receiving options, Dell was also selling his Dell stock—some 8 million shares in 1998 alone. No one quarreled with Dell's right to diversify: "It's unwise to keep all your eggs in one basket, even if that basket is Dell Computer," acknowledged *Fortune*'s Thomas Stewart in a story titled "Does Michael Dell Need Stock Options?" "But why is Michael Dell, wearing his founder's hat, selling stock, while in his managerial garb he sucks up so many options?"[24]

In fact, 1998 was a good year for Michael Dell to begin giving serious thought to diversification. A year earlier, Dell's shares had led the S&P 500, gaining 216 percent, and in '98, Dell once again ran at the head of the pack, climbing 248 percent. But this would be the stock's last golden year. From the end of '98 through the spring of 2000, Dell's shares would rise by only 58 percent—then plunge. By year-end, they had lost 70 percent of their value. In the summer of 2003, Dell still traded below its December '98 high.

By September of '98, Jim Chanos was shorting the stock. Worldwide computer sales continued to climb, but prices were falling. Chanos knew that the market was approaching saturation. Nevertheless, Dell's shares were changing hands at 67 times the previous year's net income and 49 times book value.

Meanwhile, in order to try to offset the cost of buying back its shares, Dell Computer decided to gamble on its own stock. In an effort to make buybacks less expensive, the company began buying call options that gave it the right to purchase Dell shares at a preset price for a defined period of time. If the stock continued to soar, that preset price would wind up being lower than the actual market price.

Dell's foray into the options market did not stop there. To pay for the call options, the company began selling "put" options on its stock. The "puts" gave the buyer the right to sell the stock back to Dell at a preset price over a specific period of time. If the share price fell during that time, the investor who bought the put would win the bet, but if the shares continued to climb, the revenues the company raised by selling the puts would become pure profit. For a while, the strategy paid off. In one quarter, Dell made more by selling options than by peddling computers.

But once Dell's share price began to plummet, the gamble backfired. In the fiscal year ending February 1, 2001, Dell paid an average of more than $43 a share for the roughly 68 million shares that it bought back that year. Meanwhile, Dell's shares were trading on the open market at an average price of $25. Dell's problems did not end there: "The company eventually must buy 51 million more shares at around $45—again, well above Dell's current price—through 2004," *Barron's* reported in 2002. Moreover, a built-in "trigger" provision requires that if Dell drops to $8, the box maker has to settle up on all the puts. Dell would have to spend $2.3 billion to cover this; it had $3.6 billion in cash at fiscal 2002's end.[25]

Investors who bought Dell stock thought they were investing in a computer company, not a hedge fund. But unbeknownst to most shareholders, Dell had temporarily turned itself into a company that specialized in high finance—and high risk. Because Dell had gotten involved in the derivatives game, the shares it bought that year cost an extra $1.25 billion—a number that slightly exceeded Dell's net income for the entire year. Under accounting rules, Dell was not required to show the cost in its financial statements.[26]

FINANCIAL "INNOVATIONS"

Dell was not the only company to sell puts on its own stock. Microsoft and Intel had adopted the same practice. "In the New Economy, everyone wanted to be in our business," recalled Senator Jon Corzine, chairman and chief executive of Goldman Sachs until 1999.[27] In other words, everyone wanted to be a financial engineer. And this worried Maureen Allyn, chief economist at Scudder, Stevens & Clark.

A tall brunette with a wide smile, Allyn watched this final phase of the bull market with a terrible sense of foreboding. "You had no idea what earnings really were," she remembered a few years later. "The government gave you one set of figures; the New Economists had another. Until finally, in the summer of 2001, the Department of Commerce's Bureau of Economic Analysis quietly announced that both the New Economists and the government's national profits data had been wrong. After reexamining the data, and adjusting earnings for the cost of stock options and other hidden expenses, they realized that there had been NO profits growth since 1995." [28]

Allyn, who had formed her idea of a reasonable price to pay for a stock back in 1974 when she bought Rite Aid for $3.50, had been an outspoken member of the bull market's Greek Chorus. "But, it was worse than I thought," she said in 2002. "Prior to the revision, the same government statisticians had reported profit growth of roughly 8% a year between the end of 1994 and 2000. Now, they said it was zero," said Allyn, "and they were using the IRS data, which is the best data you can get.

"At that point, I felt like Gilda Radner when she said, 'No matter how cynical I get, I can't keep up.' I was cynical—but I couldn't keep up."

Allyn had come to Scudder, a white-shoe money management firm with a Park Avenue address, in 1989, just in time to see Japan's financial bubble in full bloom. "I came in, looked at it, and said 'Run, don't walk,'" she remembered. "People were surprised by how adamant I was."

Nine years later, she was just as worried about the U.S. market—though she could not be quite as adamant. "Our chairman really got annoyed with me—my profit forecasts were so much lower than Wall Street's," Allyn recalled. "But," she added cheerfully, "I always found you can get away with a lot if you say it with a smile."

So, with a smile, she tried to warn her colleagues. Allyn was alarmed by the way the technological revolution was feeding—and being fed by—a revolution in the financial world. "The interaction between an incredible outpouring of financial innovation and a once-in-a-couple-of-generations technological revolution created a dangerous situation. Both of these are good things in themselves," added Allyn, "but together they created an upward spiral. What you had was the interaction of two complementary events that do not reach equilibrium. Instead, they continually reinforce each other until conditions become maximally unstable." In other words, the spiral could become a tornado.

Allyn ticked off a few of the examples of financial "innovation" that worried her. One was the way that companies like Dell were selling puts on their own stock: "Economists know that there is no more chance of getting a free lunch than there is of finding the fountain of youth. It doesn't stop people from looking for both of them," Allyn wrote in a memo to her colleagues. "Corporate treasurers of technology companies probably believe they did find a free lunch—they could sell puts on the shares of their own companies and pocket the premium. Since their stocks only went up, the puts always expired worthless. Free money! But we're talking about derivatives," Allyn warned. "These things can turn on you if the market changes!"

"Crossholding, American-Style" also made her list of dubious innovations: "Taking a page out of the Japanese play book American tech companies have become just about indistinguishable from *keiretsu*, the Japanese industrial groups that financed each other and held interlocking shares for strategic purposes," Allyn remarked. Cisco was not the only company financing its customers. "There are lots of examples. Microsoft has a massive portfolio of investments in alliance partners and new technologies. Oracle is another great example. They have $500 million in an Oracle Venture Fund to invest in promising startups. One condition: They've got to buy Oracle software."

But *keiretsu* did not top Allyn's list of potentially dangerous innovations. That space she reserved for one of the greatest sources of financial ingenuity: hedge funds. Combining computerized models with high finance, hedge funds served as the perfect example of how the revolution in technology was reinforcing the financial revolution. "At some point in the middle of 1999," Allyn recalled, "a few of them—the Soros/Druckenmiller Quantum Fund, in particular—began investing in technology. They couldn't resist getting involved. And they got badly, badly burned.

"A hedge fund is a particularly ill-suited vehicle for technology investing," she added. "The problem with hedge funds is that their investors wanted to see some distributions when the calendar turned over. Their friendly bankers knew their positions and lay in wait. As Soros noted, 'Quantum is far too big and its activities too closely watched by the market to be able to operate successfully in this environment.'[29] There was no way they could raise cash from these illiquid investments without having their heads handed to them."

But it was not only hedge funds that *invested* in technology that mixed high tech with high finance. In the fall of '98, Long Term Capital Management (LTCM) used high technology to create a new way to play financial markets—and in the process, it demonstrated just how volatile a combination high tech and high finance could be.

DRESS REHEARSAL FOR A BEAR MARKET: THE SUMMER OF '98

For the market as a whole, it had been a sorry summer. This, after all, was the August when Ralph Acampora returned from an African safari only to realize, as he put it at the time, "I'm going to have to shoot my best friend— the bull." Reluctantly, Acampora stepped up to Prudential's global in-house PA system: "Ladies and gentlemen," he announced, "I have something very important to say." Then he uttered the dread words: "bear market." Over the next two months, the Dow lost 1900 points.[30]

But that August, Acampora turned out to be far from Wall Street's biggest worry. On the 19th, Russia defaulted on payments on its bonds— an event that would send a shiver of uncertainty around the globe.

In Greenwich, Connecticut, Long Term Capital Management thought it had little to worry about. Led by the famed bond arbitrageur John Meriwether, LTCM's partnership included two Nobel Prize–winning economists. Under their guidance, an elite circle of traders played the options market, identifying tiny inefficiencies in the prices of the calls and puts that large institutions use to hedge against risk.

By 1998, LTCM had amassed $100 billion in assets. Only four years old, it had racked up annual returns of more than 40 percent, "with very little volatility . . . seemingly no risk at all," Lowenstein reported in *When Genius Failed,* the story of LTCM's rise and fall.[31] The partnership's investment strategy was founded on a firm faith in efficient-market theory, the theory, popular in academic circles, that said that at any given time, stock and bond market prices reflect all available information. Like other efficient-market theorists, LTCM's stars acknowledged that inevitably, tiny cracks appear in the system and a security is temporarily mispriced, but they contended that market forces quickly restore order.

LTCM's arbitrageurs aimed to take advantage of those cracks, secure in the knowledge that a rational market would always correct its errors. This is how they made their money. Using mathematical models, they also had devised ways to offset the risks of one bet against another. It seemed a perfect system, at least on paper.

"But what LTCM failed to take into account is the role of psychology in markets, a factor that hung over all its misunderstandings of the nature of markets," observed Leon Levy, who had recently closed his own highly respected hedge fund, Odyssey Partners. Even with the best technology, mathematical models just cannot predict the vagaries of human behavior.

When Russia defaulted on its bonds, it set off a domino effect. Floating anxiety prompted many hedge funds to want to raise capital, and a cascade of selling began. "With dozens of hedge funds trying to flee the markets, the selling pressure sent prices haywire around the world. Erratic prices served only to increase volatility," Levy explained.

Suddenly, LTCM found itself in an irrational market. That August, the fund lost roughly 45 percent of its capital—an event that, "according to LTCM's mathematical model, should happen no more than once in the history of Western civilization," Levy reported in his memoir, *The Mind of Wall Street.*[32]

LTCM had been undone by what Nassim Nicholas Taleb would call "a black swan."

CONFUSING PROBABILITY WITH CERTAINTY

Taleb, who was also an options trader, made his living by betting on unlikely events. Like a racetrack fan who gambles on long shots, he might place 1,000 wagers and lose 999 times. But he would only lose small amounts. And when he won that one time out of 1,000, the odds were so long that his return was huge. In the cases where he won, he was betting on the unthinkable—the option that no one thought could materialize (say, an option that depended on GE falling below $10).

Taleb recognized that while men resist randomness, markets resist prophecy. The fact that something has happened many times in the past does not mean that it *will* happen in the future. The fact that it has *never* happened does not mean that it *cannot* happen. "In 1992, who would have believed that the Nasdaq would cross 5000?" asked Taleb. "But it did. And in March of 2000, how many people believed that it could lose more than 3000 points over the next 13 months?" Yet it did. "All we can learn from history," Taleb added in a 2002 interview, "is that the unpredictable will happen—and does—time and again. The most dangerous error that an investor can make is to mistake probability for certainty."[33]

In 2001, Taleb wrote a book that rolled down Wall Street like a small hand grenade, *Fooled by Randomness: The Hidden Role of Chance in the Markets and in Life*.[34] There, he described the "the black swan," or "the rare event." This is the event that lies outside of our experience: we have never seen a black swan, just as, until the nineties, we had never seen the Dow climb 1000 points in less than four years. Based on past experience, the run-up that followed seemed to many highly improbable—some would have said unimaginable. But, Taleb observed, the fact that an investor has not seen a black swan does not mean that he can rule it out.

Financial history is studded with surprises that defy our efforts to find formulas. In a 2002 interview, Peter Bernstein pointed to that period in the 1950s when suddenly, low-risk, high-grade bonds offered a higher yield than stocks. In the past, stocks always paid higher dividends than AA bonds. After all, if an investor holds an AA 10-year bond for 10 years, he is all but guaranteed to get his money back, plus interest when it matures. If he buys a stock, on the other hand, he cannot be at all certain how much it will be worth in 10 years. This is why, in order to attract investors, companies that issued stock instead of bonds traditionally had to pay a higher dividend. The cause and effect seemed rational and perfectly clear. Until the 1950s, when "for the first time in history," Bernstein noted, the old rules were turned on their heads: bonds paid the higher yield. "A relationship sanctified by over 80 years of experience suddenly came apart."[35]

In *Against the Gods,* Bernstein quoted the essayist G. K. Chesterton, on how the unexpected "lies in wait" for us: "The real trouble with this world of ours . . . is that it is nearly reasonable, but not quite. Life is not an illogicality; yet it is a trap for logicians. It looks just a little more mathematical and regular than it is; its exactitude is obvious, but its inexactitude is hidden; its wildness lies in wait."[36]

Long Term Capital Management thought that it could calculate the market's risks and then balance them to create a risk-free system. But the black swan was lying in wait. In this case, the black swan was not just that Russia defaulted on its debt—though this certainly was unexpected. The real wild card was this: How would that default affect a chain of intricately linked derivatives contracts that circled the globe? How would so many traders react to so much ambiguity? Would they freeze? Would they sell? How would LTCM's own responses affect the efficient market that it thought it had modeled?

Financial markets defy such calculations. In the physical world, it is much easier to calculate probabilities, because the possibilities are more likely to be finite. "If you roll dice, you know that the odds are one in six that the dice will come up on a particular side," said Taleb, "because you know the dice have six sides. So, you can calculate the risk. But, in the stock market such computations are bull—you don't even know how many sides the dice have!"

Because the physical world offers a limited range of possibilities, events tend to arrange themselves on a symmetrical bell curve. Again, Taleb offered a practical example: "Let's say you graph the weights of all the babies born in the U.S. over 10 years. Birth weights might range from under a pound to, perhaps, 15 pounds. If you took a large enough sample, and you plotted it on a graph, you would wind up with a smooth bell curve; there would be no babies weighing 500 pounds to skew it. In physical reality, it would be impossible for a woman to give birth to a 500-pound baby. There are limits to what can happen."

But if you graphed price/earnings ratios of all the stocks on the S&P over 10 years, you would have to include the black swans—the unpredictable, unthinkable "outliers," instances of companies with a P/E of 300, or companies with no earnings and an infinite P/E. They would skew your curve. "This is why Long Term Capital Management blew up," said Taleb. "They thought that they could scientifically measure their risks."[37]

THE FED TO THE RESCUE

By late September, LTCM was on the verge of going under. Virtually all of the $100 billion in assets that it had amassed had been borrowed from Wall Street's top bankers. Once again the Fed rode to the rescue. On the afternoon of September 23, William J. McDonough, president of the New York Fed, summoned the chief executives of Bankers Trust, Bear Stearns, Chase Manhattan, Goldman Sachs, J.P. Morgan, Lehman Brothers, Merrill Lynch, Morgan Stanley Dean Witter, and Salomon Smith Barney to the Fed's 10th-floor boardroom—"not to bail out a Latin American nation," Lowenstein reported, "but to consider a rescue of one of their own."[38] Some were personally involved: David Komansky, the boss at Merrill Lynch, had $1 million of his own money in LTCM.

How could some of the shrewdest CEOs on Wall Street have allowed LTCM to play fast and loose with nearly $100 billion of their institutions' money? Presumably, they were not nearly as shrewd as their positions suggested. This, perhaps as much as greed, explains what went wrong in corporate America in the nineties.

Ultimately the Fed managed to jawbone a consortium of banks and investment houses into taking over LTCM. Some observers suggested that they had little choice: the lenders had to save face: "The belief here is that the reason why the Federal Reserve Bank of New York engineered the rescue of the Long Term Capital Management hedge fund in September 1998 was fear that the collapse of the fund would have exposed to public view the sloppy performance of the world's greatest financial institutions—and the careless, trusting supervision that had permitted this overconfident crowd of Ph.D. economists, mathematicians and gamblers to carry positions in excess of $100 billion . . . ," Martin Mayer explained in *The Fed.*

Only a few days before McDonough invited the bankers to the Fed's boardroom, "Alan Greenspan had testified to the House Banking Committee that 'hedge funds were strongly regulated by those who lend the money,'" Mayer reported. With the LTCM debacle, "the belief that Alan Greenspan knew whereof he spoke, a central tenet of the Fed's status, had been put in hazard." No one wanted to lift the curtain on the wizard—least of all the CEOs who ran Oz.

A month later, with the average stock down by one-third from its summer highs, the Fed chairman suddenly, and unexpectedly, cut rates by one-fourth of 1 percent. "In a private conversation a couple of weeks earlier, Greenspan had noted with weary regret that the whole world seemed to believe that the Fed was in control of what happened to the economy. Greenspan knew this was not true, but he also knew that if everyone believed it to be true, he must do something," Mayer reported.

Not two years earlier, the Fed chairman had been talking about irrational exuberance. Now it seemed that he felt responsible for keeping the bubble afloat. So, in October of 1998, "he went center stage with his top hat" and pulled a rabbit "out of the hat," Mayer wrote. "It wasn't Bugs Bunny or Roger Rabbit, it was a pretty scrawny little rabbit to which nobody really *had* to pay attention, and there wasn't anything else left in the hat. But the magician concentrated the attention of the world on his rabbit. . . ."[39]

The market jumped.

By the end of '98, the S&P would be up 26.7 percent for the year. In the final quarter, however, just five stocks accounted for a little more than half of the surge according to Merrill Lynch: Dell, Lucent, Microsoft, Pfizer, and Wal-Mart.[40] Far too much was riding on too few stocks.

As for Maureen Allyn, throughout '98, she had watched the market with growing dismay. "That year, Scudder sold itself to Zurich and, because I was a partner, I received a nice slug of cash," Allyn confided. "I put it all in Treasuries and munis. People at Scudder said, 'You're doing what?!'

"Most people thought I was insane. 'You really need to have equities,' they said. 'This is an equity culture.'

"Though privately, a few of the older portfolio managers said to me, 'I don't have any equities in my personal portfolio either.' They had been around—they knew everything was overvalued."

But younger colleagues, in particular, viewed Allyn with that mixture of pity and annoyance reserved for those who fail to appreciate a New Paradigm. One tried to be tactful: "I guess, being older, you're just not that hopeful about the future," she said.

Allyn's portfolio of bonds would allow her the luxury of early retirement. In 2002, Allyn, 57, retired to her home in New Jersey, where she kept two horses. "If you want to reach me call me before 10," she told friends. "After that, I'll be out riding."[41]

FOLLOWING THE HERD: DOW 10,000

If you are a zebra and live in a herd, the key decision you have to make is where to stand in relation to the rest of the herd. The grass is greener at the edge of the herd.

—Ralph Wanger, founder,
Liberty Wanger Asset Management

As 1999 began, Act III of the Great Bull Market approached a climax. Morgan Stanley began building a new tower in midtown Manhattan. In May, *Forbes* placed Priceline.com CEO Jay Walker on its cover and anointed him the "New Age Edison."

In October, streaming-media company Pixelon celebrated its initial public offering with a $16 million Las Vegas shindig (eating up 80 percent of the company's latest round of financing), featuring the Who, Tony Bennett, and the Dixie Chicks. Unfortunately, the company's CEO, Michael Fenne, was actually a fugitive con artist named David Kim Stanley. Three years later, he would be serving an eight-year sentence in Virginia.[1]

Individual investors were setting the direction for the market—and the pros were learning to ride their coattails. "Indeed, one of the great stories . . . has been the humbling of the vast majority of institutional portfolio managers by individuals, who increasingly are taking investment decisions into their own hands," wrote *Barron's* stock market editor at the end of 1998. "[Individuals], adhering to the Peter Lynch philosophy of buying stocks in companies whose products they like, have scored big in such is-sues as Gap, Home Depot, Microsoft, Intel and America Online."[2] Laszlo Birinyi, a research consultant and money manager in Greenwich, Con-necticut, put it another way: "It's the people standing in Charles Schwab who are running the show."[3]

Everyone, it seemed, was chasing stocks, and everyone was chasing the same stocks. In San Jose, Kathy Rubino discovered just how ubiquitous the marquee names had become when her phone rang early one morning in November. Barely awake, Rubino had just flipped on CNBC for the open-ing stock report when she answered the call—only to find an obscene caller on the other end of the line.

An anonymous caller in one ear spewing lurid comments, Joe Kernen in the other ear reporting on falling stock prices—Rubino's day was off to a bad start. Suddenly, the obscene caller interrupted himself: "Is that Kernen on CNBC?" he asked.

Rubino, stunned, off balance—and still groggy—found herself an-swering him: "The market has taken a plunge this morning," she replied.

"Jesus," the anonymous caller said, "any word on Cisco or AOL?"[4]

At the end of 1999, Yahoo! boasted a market cap of $120 billion. By contrast, Warren Buffett's company, Berkshire Hathaway, carried a mar-ket value of only $83 billion. Berkshire Hathaway's class A shares were now changing hands at around $54,000 a share, down by some 23 per-cent for the year. (For investors, this was a rare window: by June of 2003, Berkshire would be trading at roughly $74,000 a share, up 33 percent from the end of 1999. Over the same period, the S&P 500 lost roughly 32 per-cent.)[5]

But in 1999 Buffett was passé. This, after all, was the year that opened with the news that Henry Blodget expected Amazon.com to fetch $400 a share—which it promptly did—and ended, fittingly, with *Time* magazine naming Jeff Bezos, Amazon.com's CEO, "Person of the Year."

HENRY BLODGET AND AMAZON.COM

On a night flight from Houston to New York, Henry Blodget called in to check his voice mail. It was December of 1998, and Blodget, who was then CIBC Oppenheimer's senior Internet analyst, listened to yet another mes-sage from the Oppenheimer sales force.[6]

It was the question they had been asking for days: "How high could Amazon.com go?" Blodget didn't know. No one did.

Just two months earlier, Blodget had published his first report recommending the online bookseller's shares. At the time, Amazon.com was trading at over $80, and he had set a one-year target of $150, adding that he thought the stock was worth somewhere between $150 and $500. But, he cautioned in his report, "Amazon is one of the most controversial stocks in our universe. . . . We are recommending the stock for strong-stomached, long-term investors." Within weeks, the stock breezed past his one-year target.

Now his firm's sales team wanted a new target. Blodget had done some calculations. The stock was trading around $240. In another year it could go to . . . $300? Maybe as high as $500? The company had no earnings, so there was no way to estimate earnings growth. In any event, the share price had less to do with demand for the product than demand for the shares.

Blodget was new to the game: he had been an analyst for less than three years. But to some degree, he understood that in a market driven by a combination of momentum and emotion he was trying to forecast investor psychology: What would someone else be willing to pay for the stock?

$300? $500? Split the difference, he thought, *and make it $400.*

In truth, Blodget's research was not that cavalier. But when it came to setting a price, he was at a loss. How high? Who knew?

His research reports, on the other hand, made an honest attempt to analyze the company. While Mary Meeker was known for what *Barron's* called her "trademark breezy [writing] style," Blodget tried to write old-fashioned analytical reports.[7] The Amazon report that he had produced two months earlier was filled with charts and tables that attempted to compare Amazon both to barnesandnoble.com and to Dell—the model for a profitable New Economy company. Blodget made it clear that the comparison to Dell was a stretch: Dell sold computers; Amazon sold books. And Dell added value by carrying no inventory, getting the best price possible on the parts, then assembling the computers. But Blodget had to find some way to model Amazon.com's business.

At this point in his career, Blodget was trying hard simply to hold on to his job. A greenhorn on Wall Street, he was in over his head—though in that way he was like every other Internet analyst trying to predict what was going to happen in a completely unknown sector. The Internet was not a new industry. Was it a new medium like radio or television? Or was it merely a pipeline, in search of a business plan? Certainly it needed content. But no one yet knew what content would turn a profit over the long term, or how.

Meanwhile, Blodget had landed his job at Oppenheimer only after a six-year search for a career. In 1988, Blodget had graduated from Yale (where he majored in history and wrote a solid senior thesis about a 17th-century cleric). He then spent a year in Japan, teaching English. When he returned to the States he wrote a book about his experiences. It was never published—"nor should it have been," Blodget said wryly. It was, after all, a book written by a 22-year-old about the life experience of a 21-year-old.

Back in New York, Blodget began, in his words, "casting about for something to do" and became a freelance journalist. But it was not easy for a 22-year-old to break into journalism in Manhattan. And Blodget could not take the freelance lifestyle—"the job insecurity, never knowing when I would get a paycheck . . . I was 27 years old and earning just $11,000 a year," he recalled in a 2002 interview.

By 1994, Blodget remembered, "I began to notice that everything I was reading had to do with the market." He had been doing some work for CNN Business News; his father was a banker; Wall Street seemed a logical route to pursue. That year, Blodget enrolled in a training program at Prudential Securities. Two years later, he landed a position as an analyst at CIBC Oppenheimer.

On Wall Street, Oppenheimer was a bit of a backwater, but still, it was a good job. Blodget was now earning a real salary—less than six figures, but far more than $11,000. He began receiving phone calls from headhunters looking for someone to cover Internet stocks. "At that time, Wall Street didn't have anyone to cover the Internet," Blodget recalled. "They had PC analysts trying to follow the Internet—but very few people on Wall Street knew much about it. And no one had any experience. The headhunters started calling me because of my 'background' in journalism"—Blodget smiled sardonically—"and because I was following some of the early electronic data companies." Within months, Blodget became one of a handful of "experienced" Internet analysts on Wall Street. His main concern: "not being blown out of the water—keeping the job."

So in December of 1998 Henry Blodget found himself sitting on an airplane somewhere between Houston and New York, wishing for sleep. He had been working 60- and 70-hour weeks for months. But first he had to try to figure out a new number for Amazon. The sales team needed something to say—a line, a rap, a number. That is how they sold a stock. Amazon had already blown through his last target; Blodget decided that a 70 percent rise over the course of a year seemed reasonable for a company that had been growing so fast. He told himself, "It's no different from saying that a $24 stock will go to $40." But, of course, it was.

The next morning, Blodget arrived at his office at 6 A.M. and submitted his notes on Amazon. The response was muted. "One of my bosses stopped by my office and sort of raised his eyebrows—'$400 a share?' That was it," Blodget recalled. Meanwhile, he learned that AOL had announced a deal in Latin America. "I thought it was a bigger deal than it was—that seemed to me the news of the day." So, in his morning conference call on the Oppenheimer PA system, Blodget led with AOL. Then he announced his new target for Amazon—$400.

THE RESPONSE

Blodget had not anticipated the reaction. While at Oppenheimer, he was still a relatively obscure analyst; he had made other forecasts that did not receive that much attention. But Amazon.com was an extremely controversial stock. For one, its CEO, Jeff Bezos, served as a lightning rod for strong opinions. "He's the type of guy—either you love him or you hate him," explained one analyst. "Extremely charismatic, but tons of arrogance."[8]

Then there were the fundamentals. Three months earlier, Jonathan Cohen, Merrill's Internet analyst, had downgraded Amazon. Now Blodget was predicting that it would climb by more than $150.

Within minutes, the news of Blodget's forecast was traveling around the globe. A Bloomberg reporter got a tip and put the story online. CNBC picked it up. Then it hit the chatboards.

"My phone lit up like a Christmas tree," Blodget recalled four years later. "I thought, 'Oh, no, I blew it.'

"I hadn't made it into *Institutional Investor*'s rankings of analysts yet, and I was trying to build credibility," he explained. "And I just wasn't at all certain about Amazon. I always felt uncomfortable that Amazon was the call that launched my career. I would have felt better if it had been Yahoo!. I was much more certain about Yahoo!."

The irony, of course, is that he was much more wrong about Yahoo!.

"That was the one that really skewered me," Blodget confessed, with a rueful smile.

Henry Blodget made his much ballyhooed prediction that Amazon would hit $400 on December 16. That day the stock closed at $289—up 20 percent. By January 6, Amazon.com had blazed past Blodget's $400 target.[9]

Lise Buyer, Credit Suisse First Boston's Internet analyst, recalled her reaction when she heard of Blodget's prediction.

"I thought he was crazy. But Henry spotted the momentum and he rode it—hats off to him.

"I didn't agree with him then, and I don't now," added Buyer, who had been working in the financial world for some 14 years, both as a money manager and as an analyst, and so had a little more perspective on the market than most.[10]

Buyer was more inclined to agree with Merrill's Jonathan Cohen, who had downgraded Amazon with a "reduce" rating in September, calling it simply "too expensive" and declaring the analysis of his more bullish Wall Street colleagues "logically corrupt." The day after Blodget's announcement, Cohen reiterated his downgrade, saying that he thought that the stock was worth just $50.

By February, Jonathan Cohen had left Merrill Lynch, and Blodget had won his chair—a big move up from Oppenheimer. The media would suggest that Blodget took Cohen's job. In fact, headhunters did not call Blodget until more than a month after Cohen announced that he was leaving. Moreover, Cohen and Blodget were on friendly terms; before interviewing with Merrill, Blodget called Cohen for advice. "They'll love you," Cohen assured him.

"I discussed the idea of Henry coming on board with people at Merrill while I was still there—after I'd given notice," Cohen said in a 2003 interview. "I was friendly with him then, and continue to be. The notion that he took my job or that there were bad feelings between us is an urban myth."[11] But the story played well, an example of how the media used analysts to lend color and drama to financial news.

Certainly, the press loved Blodget. Over the course of the year, his name would pop up in print some 1,072 times. By March of 2001, *The Washington Post* reported, Blodget had been mentioned 95 times in *The Wall Street Journal*, 66 times in *The New York Times*, 53 times in the *Post* itself, and 27 times in *Business Week*.[12]

Yet he was not always a bull. In October of 1999, a full five months be-fore the technology bubble popped, Blodget called Internet stocks "fantasti-cally expensive" in an interview with *The Los Angeles Times*, and warned that a shakeout was likely: "We are probably nearing the end of a cycle. We are moving out of the period of low-hanging fruit." He reiterated an earlier pre-diction that 75 percent of Internet companies would fail or be purchased, and he added that many stocks could fall 75 percent from current levels and "still be expensive. . . . Investors are far too aggressive," he added.[13]

As for Amazon.com, 1999 would prove to be a roller-coaster year for the online bookseller. Nevertheless, the shares ended the year up by more than 40 percent. At that point the stock began its long good-bye, hitting a low in the fall of 2001. On March 30, 2003, shares of Amazon.com were worth roughly 64 percent less than they had been at the end of 1999. In hindsight it would seem that Jonathan Cohen had been right.

Lise Buyer did not agree. "At the end of 1998, who made money—in-vestors who listened to Jonathan and sold the stock? Or investors who lis-tened to Henry?" she asked. "Investors didn't care who was right on the numbers. They cared about how much the stock would be worth in six months."

She had a point: everything turned on your time frame. Certainly, a mutual fund manager interested in making a boffo showing in '99 would have been happy that he had followed Blodget's advice. At this point, the average mutual fund manager turned over 90 percent of the stocks in his portfolio each year. Chances are, by the time Amazon.com began to sink, he would no longer own it.

By contrast, individual investors were more likely to be caught. While individuals were trading more actively than ever before—in '99 they were selling 40 percent of their equity fund holdings each year—this was still a far cry from 90 percent.[14] As for those who still did what they were told, "buy and hold," they would be shorn. These were the investors who would have been better off listening to Jonathan Cohen.

CONFLICT OF AUDIENCE

In truth, Blodget and Cohen, like every other analyst on Wall Street who ever talked to the press, had two very separate audiences, with very different goals. In two years, the pundits would be fuming over the analysts' "conflict of interest." Few ever talked about their conflict of audience.

On the one hand, an analyst was writing for an audience of professionals: mutual fund managers and other institutional investors. As noted, these were the customers who voted in *Institutional Investor*'s annual rankings; these were the customers who brought large orders to a firm's brokerage business; and these were the customers who bought into the deals that a Wall Street firm like Merrill underwrote. Brokerage fees had been deregulated in 1975, and now competition from online brokers was fierce. By 1999, even at a firm like Merrill Lynch, commissions paid by individual investors for stock and bond trades came to less than $2 billion of Merrill's revenue of about $17.5 billion.[15] Individual investors were not paying enough to support the research effort, and on Wall Street, as elsewhere in a capitalist society, profit provides the motive. No surprise, research was rarely written with the small investor in mind.

Meanwhile, the institutional clients needed all the help they could get: they were still running hard, trying to keep up with the benchmark indices. (1999 would be the fifth year in a row that the total return on the S&P 500 topped 20 percent while the Nasdaq climbed more than 85 percent.) This is why so many felt they had to buy stocks like Amazon.com—whatever the price. If a growth fund manager blanched at paying $400 for a profitless bookseller, and as a result his fund returned "only" 15 percent, he could expect to lose investors, at least part of his bonus, and possibly his job. On the other hand, if he took the gamble on Amazon, along with everyone else, he would be safe. Even if the entire Internet sector blew up, and he lost, say, 15 percent of his clients' money, he would not be blamed as long as his benchmark lost 15 percent—or more.

If you were a professional portfolio manager, the best way to keep your head down was to invest with the herd. In 1999, more than ever before, money managers were judged, and rewarded, based on their "relative performance"—how well they did when compared to a benchmark index and/or to their peers. For them, the greatest risk was not losing money; the greatest risk was missing the upside if the market continued to go up.

Of course, a prudent individual investor had other concerns. He could not eat relative performance when he retired. What mattered to him was absolute performance—the dollar value of his portfolio in 5 or 10 or 15 years.

Blodget understood the pressures his institutional clients faced. "From '97 to '99, when I talked to them, they sounded more and more panicked," Blodget recalled. "They'd say 'What do I do? This stock is trading at 100 times earnings, and I don't understand it.'" Yet professional fund managers could not afford to ignore the Internet. As Blodget told *Forbes* in 2000, "It's important to remember [that] stocks like Yahoo! and AOL have been recently added to the S&P 500—the benchmark for a lot of professional money managers. [And these stocks] have the potential to go up 100% to 200% in a given period. AOL was up 300% two years ago—100% last year—and Yahoo! had pretty much the same performance. You have extraordinary risk if you do not buy them and are benchmarked [to the S&P 500]." [16]

The risk Blodget was talking about was not investment risk but career risk. And he was right—for most of his institutional clients, this was the major concern.

HENRY BLODGET AND THE INDIVIDUAL INVESTOR

But Blodget also understood that individual investors *could* afford to sidestep the high risk of the pure Internet plays. In an interview with *The New York Times,* he made that point clear.

It was August of '99 and Internet stocks were in a slump. The interviewer asked, "Given the sell-off, is now a good time to buy some of these stocks?"

"The first decision to make in investing in the Internet is whether to invest directly or indirectly," Blodget replied. "For most investors, the best strategy is to do it indirectly through companies like Cisco Systems, Microsoft and AT&T, companies that are taking advantage of the Net, but are not involved directly. For those who are aggressive and have a tolerance for the volatility of direct investing in the Internet, we recommend they hold a portfolio of the best companies and limit the exposure in those to somewhere between 5 percent and 10 percent of their overall portfolio." [17]

Not every Internet analyst agreed that the average individual investor might want to steer clear of the pure dot.com plays. When *Barron's* named Mary Meeker "Queen of the Net" at the end of '98, the magazine noted that individual investors "have been so quick to see the value in Internet stocks, while big institutional investors have done so only grudgingly," and asked Meeker why this was so.

" 'It's partly the Peter Lynch thing,' " Meeker responded, referring to the famed Fidelity manager's advice to buy stocks in companies whose products you like. " 'If you're getting your news on Yahoo, watching the Clinton testimony on Broadcast.com, just bought a mirrorball, as a friend of mine did, on eBay, and are doing your Christmas shopping on Amazon, you're more inclined to buy the stocks.' " [18]

Blodget, by contrast, continued to sound cautious when speaking directly to individual investors. On one occasion, a CNBC anchor asked, "If you had $50,000 to invest, which Internet stocks would you buy?"

"Well first, I would invest $50,000 in the Internet only if I had $1 million—I wouldn't put more than 5% of a portfolio into high-risk stocks," Blodget replied.

The interviewer brushed right past the point, Blodget recalled, saying something like, "Oh, ho! Sure, we know that—but if you were investing $50,000, what would you buy?"

Perhaps Blodget gave the clearest answer to what an individual investor should do when *Forbes* asked where he invested his own money.

At the tail end of the bull market, many money managers dodged the question. But Blodget was candid, revealing that he had "less than 40 percent" of his portfolio invested in stocks. "The other 60 percent is in stuff I hope will survive a nuclear war—cash, cash equivalents, or Treasuries," he later explained. And, he confided, "only 20 percent is in aggressive technology-related" equities, with just "5 percent to 10 percent in the Internet sector." [19]

It might seem that this piece of information would have turned heads. Yet Blodget's revelation passed without remark. No one asked the obvious question: "Just what does this mean about the risks you see in the market for high-flying stocks?" Blodget would have told them. He had already done so in January of 1999 when he told *The New York Times* that he thought valuations in the Internet market were "totally frightening." [20]

Incredibly, no one else in the media picked up on Blodget's disclosure. Here, after all, was a 30-something stock market guru telling the world that he was putting only 40 percent of his own savings into stocks—at a time when most of the pundits quoted in the press seemed to be suggesting that investors plunge as much as 60 to 70 percent of their portfolio into the market, even if they were much older than Blodget.

ABBY COHEN—ADVICE FOR THE MASSES?

The gurus that the media quoted were addressing that other audience. When Abby Cohen said that Goldman's model portfolio allocated 70 percent to equities and 30 percent to bonds, she was not talking to small investors. These were not her clients. Yet she was quoted as if she were the Ann Landers of Wall Street.

At one point, *The New York Times*' Peter Truell commented on the anomaly: "[Goldman] is an odd place to sprout a mass-market seer," he mused. "One of the few big partnerships left on Wall Street, Goldman is a fabulously successful investment bank that advises America's biggest corporations—and the world's biggest governments—on their financial plans. What it does not do is cater to small investors; it employs few stockbrokers, and those it does have, do business only with the very rich."[21]

Steve Einhorn, the partner who headed up research at Goldman until 1998, emphasized that Cohen was not directing her comments to small investors. "Abby said it a number of times—these were institutional portfolios that she was talking about. They weren't ratios that she was applying to individuals.

"There is no one-size-fits-all advice for individuals," he added. "Even when I spoke to our 'high net worth' individual investors, I would tell them that if we were raising our model portfolio allocation from 60 percent equities to 70 percent, that didn't mean that they should do the same. Everything depended on their age, income, how much savings they had, how much debt. I would tell them, 'If normally you hold 20 percent of your portfolio in equities, and we raise our allocation from 60 percent to 70 percent, you might want to raise yours proportionately, to, say 23 percent.' But this was never the message that the financial press wanted to transmit," said Einhorn. "I can remember being interviewed by reporters. I tried to tell them this, and their eyes glazed over. The press wanted something simple— they wanted a single number: 60 percent, 70 percent . . ."[22]

At Merrill, Blodget found himself in a somewhat different situation. In contrast to Morgan Stanley and Goldman Sachs, Merrill Lynch did run a large retail business peddling stocks to individual investors. These individuals were not Blodget's main audience—his firm had hired him to bring in investment banking business, not brokerage business.[23] Nevertheless, in June of 1999, Blodget addressed the issue in an interview with *USA Today*. He acknowledged that now that he was at Merrill, he realized that "individuals might buy on his recommendations," and "he wanted to 'remind individual investors what the downside is here.'" When the last biotech boom went bust, Blodget pointed out, shares of the leading companies "went sideways for several years." The best Internet shares could suffer a similar fate, he warned. *USA Today* quoted from a report that Blodget had written a week earlier: "The [Internet] leaders could easily pull back another 50% or more from current levels. (We don't think they will, but it is clearly possible.)" [24]

Meanwhile, the press continued to quote Wall Street's top analysts and market strategists without drawing any distinction between the two audiences—as if a professional running $1 billion and an individual with a $250,000 401(k) shared the same risks and priorities. As if an Internet analyst saying "You can't afford *not* to own Internet stocks" was talking to a 55-year-old with a $200,000 401(k) and little room for error. But in a democratic market it would have seemed elitist to draw such distinctions, so the press rarely did.

THE "BARTON BIGGS BIND"

Once in a while, a guru made it abundantly clear he or she was addressing a different audience—as Morgan Stanley's Barton Biggs did in April of 1999, when *The New York Post* ran a story expressing the complaint that the firm's chief global strategist used "Just Too Darn Many Long Words."

The bookers who scheduled guests for the all-business television channels were in a "Barton Biggs bind," the *Post* explained. "On the one hand, Biggs, chief global strategist for Morgan Stanley Dean Witter, is too important to ignore. On the other hand, bookers complain that Biggs is too intellectual and talks over the heads of their audiences and, sometimes, their on-air personalities. On one recent television appearance, for example, Biggs expressed frustration about the stupidity of one question and then gave a highly technical answer to another question."

"He just comes across as a grump," complained one booker, who preferred not to be identified.

Biggs was unperturbed. It was not his job to advise the small investor: "The clients at Morgan Stanley that I am working for are sophisticated investors and they will understand my references," he explained. "The average man on the street wouldn't understand, but that's not my audience." [25]

Einhorn agreed. "Analysts weren't writing for the typical individual investor. These reports were supposed to be filtered through a sales rep or a financial advisor." [26]

Of course, the average investor did not have a financial advisor. He might have a broker at Merrill—who might or might not point to the line in Blodget's September 1999 Internet report where he wrote, "The real risk is not losing money, but missing a big upside," and explain to his client, "You know, I don't think what Henry is saying here really applies to you. If you miss the upside no one is going to fire you. For you the real risk *is* losing money." [27] The broker's job, after all, was to sell stocks.

Meanwhile, the majority of investors got most of their financial advice through the media, and they preferred to believe that Abby Cohen, Mary Meeker, Henry Blodget, and even Barton Biggs, grump though he might be, were speaking directly to them. By and large, the financial press did little to dispel that illusion. The media needed the gurus—they brought color and authority to financial news. They made it exciting. They made it immediate. They made it *news*.

Dow 10,000

In March, when the Dow finally broke 10,000, and *The New York Times* quoted Ralph Acampora—"It's exciting. It's America. We all should get up and sing 'God Bless America.' "—hundreds of thousands of individual investors hummed along. 10,000 was such a nice round number. It seemed to put a floor under the market—as if now that the Dow had crossed that line, it could never go back.

There was even a sense of Manifest Destiny: "Though 10,000 is little more than a psychological hurdle for investors, the market's move is significant in what it reflects: the unparalleled strength of the economy and the dominance of the world economic stage by American corporations," the *Times* declared.

The *Times* also stressed that, amid all the exultation, there was "a lurking concern" over just "how narrow the market's advance has been: A growing portion of Americans' investment money is devoted to the 30 well-known companies in the Dow and the components of the Standard & Poor's 500-stock index, which rose near its record yesterday. But many portfolios have not matched the performance of the Dow and the S&P.

That is because a relatively small number of stocks have pulled the indexes higher."

Microsoft, IBM, Cisco, Lucent, AOL, Dell, GE, Wal-Mart . . . these were the stocks that individual investors were buying. In the first quarter of 1999, the indices continued to ride on the backs of a few high-flying brand names. But, the *Times* pointed out, Acampora was not concerned: "These are our big stocks that are leading. It's anything but irrational," he said.

Still, 76 percent of all stocks were trailing the S&P by 15 percent or more. The average stock trading on the NYSE was now 33.4 percent below its peak. This was the skeleton at the feast. The broad market lacked support. "Regardless," the *Times* concluded, "United States stocks are for now very much the place to be. Eight years of rising share prices are a powerful draw." [28] It was a superbly balanced story.

MUTUAL FUND MANAGERS—IN THE CLOSET

By the spring of 1999, portfolio managers were finding the lure of the big, market-leading companies irresistible. By the end of 1998, nearly one-fifth of all diversified U.S. stock mutual funds already owned AOL, and when the S&P added the Internet service provider to its index in 1999, other funds rushed in to buy it. [29]

A year earlier, the average actively managed fund had gained just 7 percent. Small wonder that by 1999, instead of trying to beat the indices, many money managers were joining them. Rather than trying to pick stocks, they simply bought the stocks in the index, concentrating on the brand names. This meant buying technology's blue chips—by early 2000, technology and telecom stocks would account for nearly 45 percent of the overall market value of the S&P 500. [30]

And so fund managers who were measured against the S&P gritted their teeth and shelled out 50 times earnings, 100 times earnings—whatever the rest of the herd was willing to pay. In the weightless economy, price/concept ratios trumped price/earnings ratios.

These portfolio managers were not running an index fund—a fund designed to shadow the S&P 500—but they behaved as if they were. Critics called it "closet indexing," pointing out that individual investors were paying steep fees for active management when they could do just as well—or better—by putting their money in a low-fee index fund.

Meanwhile, investors who thought that they had diversified by buying a range of mutual funds were badly mistaken. When David Tice, editor of *Behind the Numbers,* testified before Congress in June 2001, he pointed to the incredible overlap among the most popular growth-oriented mutual funds. Analyzing stocks held by Janus, American Century Ultra, Fidelity Growth, Fidelity Blue Chip, Janus Twenty, Putnam Voyager, Vanguard U.S. Growth, AIM Constellation, Fidelity Aggressive Growth, and Putnam New Opportunities, Tice revealed that Cisco was held by 10 out of 10 of the funds, followed by Sun Microsystems, (9 out of 10), GE (8 of 10), Pfizer (8 of 10), EMC (9 of 10), Microsoft (8 of 10), AIG (7 of 10), AOL (7 of 10), BEA (8 of 10), and Veritas (9 of 10). In fact, their portfolios were so similar that an analysis of how these 10 funds had performed over time showed a correlation coefficient of 80 to 95 percent. So much for the notion that by owning a variety of growth funds, individual investors could reduce risk.[31]

When he looked at the portfolio manager's favorites in the spring of '99, Steve Leuthold was again reminded of the Nifty Fifty of the early seventies. "People clung to the belief that if you bought the premier growth companies, they would hold up well, even in a market decline," the Minnesota money manager recalled. "These were the One-Decision stocks of the time—just buy them and hold them." Xerox, Polaroid, Digital Equipment—these were some of the names. "Today, portfolio managers are again staking their hopes on the future performance of the crème-de-la-crème of growth stocks," Leuthold added. "But anyone who has been in the business knows that no one has ever been able to estimate earnings 10 years out—and these stocks are priced as if you can."

Often, bears are prickly, but Leuthold was mellow. He did not insist that history would repeat itself. But, he suggested, history is, at the least "a vast early-warning system." It may not provide clear signposts, but it offers "some guide to the future."[32]

With that in mind, he took a look at his firm's list of the 99 stocks with the greatest institutional ownership as of March 30, 1999, then selected the 25 with the highest price/earnings ratios and dubbed them the "Religion Stocks." The stratospheric P/Es suggested blind faith; these were the "must-have" stocks, irresistible at any price. That spring the roster included the usual suspects: Dell, Microsoft, Yahoo!, Lucent, Wal-Mart, MCI WorldCom—and it bore a striking resemblance to the Religion Stocks of 1972.

Once again, technology stocks dominated. Once again, median P/Es were double those on the S&P 500. Once again, dividends were measly. And now, just as in 1972, nearly all of the companies on the list flaunted a 10-year record of double-digit earnings growth—at least that is what they reported.

The lists differed in just one important way: in 1999, the stampede had pushed the price/earnings ratios of the market's favorites even higher than in 1972. True believers insisted that the Religion Stocks of the nineties could support the higher valuation—this time it was different.[33]

— 18 —

THE LAST BEAR IS GORED

"Wall Street is moving from fact to fiction," Gail Dudack told her husband in the summer of 1999. "The sleaze factor is growing—people are doing things that may or may not be illegal, but the gray area is expanding." [1]

Chief market strategist at Warburg, the U.S. unit of global investment banking giant UBS A.G., Dudack had known that the boom was turning into a bubble ever since she sent a review of Kindleberger's *Manias, Panics, and Crashes* to her clients in October of 1997. And she said so, not only to the money managers who paid Warburg handsomely for her advice, but publicly, on television.

Bears can be abrasive, but Dudack's tone was far from contentious. Indeed, her style could best be described as ladylike as she laid out the unwelcome numbers, clearly and meticulously, without a trace of self-congratulatory glee. With her professional manner and melodious voice, the blonde baby-boomer became a favorite on shows like CNN's *Moneyline,* CNBC's *Squawk Box,* and the nation's most-watched financial news program, the Public Broadcasting System's *Wall $treet Week with Louis Rukeyser.*

Ironically, as the bull market approached a summit, Dudack's popularity as a television guest soared. "Financial programs wanted to 'present both sides,'" Dudack recalled. "So they would have me on and let me present my bearish views. Then they would say, 'Now, what stocks do you like?' They really didn't get it."

For by the late nineties, Dudack liked few stocks. Unlike many Wall Street professionals, she knew that this was not just an Internet bubble: stocks that investors thought of as "safe havens" were in fact overpriced. To her credit, even Abby Cohen was beginning to pull in her horns: at the end of '99, Cohen declared the market "fairly valued" and predicted that, in 2000, the S&P would rise less than 5 percent. But, she still insisted that the technology stocks on the S&P 500 were not overvalued.[2]

When *Money* magazine asked three gurus for their 2000 forecast, Dudack was the only one to suggest that a "stealth bear market" was already under way. Lehman Brothers' Jeffrey Applegate, by contrast, was "as gung-ho as ever," *Money* reported: Applegate expected a 15 percent gain for the year. PaineWebber's Ed Kerschner was only somewhat more cautious, predicting that earnings on the S&P would climb 7 percent, and that the Dow would hit 12,500. As 2000 began, Kerschner was still recommending high-fliers such as IBM, Lucent, MCI WorldCom, Gateway, and Cisco.[3]

Meanwhile, the media continued to beat the drum with headlines such as: "The Next Big Thing: Need a Few Hot Stocks to Jump-Start Your Retirement Portfolio? Then Get Up to Speed on Tomorrow's Technology—Today" (*Smart Money*, August 1999). An article that accompanied the main feature suggested that to "reduce risk," investors over 70 should have 25 percent of their savings invested in large-cap stocks, 5 percent in small caps, and 10 percent in foreign stocks. For those who had 10 years before they retired, the story advised allocating 65 percent to equities.[4]

The "media marriage of the century" also generated considerable excitement in the press. When AOL and Time Warner announced their plans to merge at the beginning of 2000, *Business Week* brought out the trumpets: "Welcome to the 21st Century: With One Stunning Stroke, AOL and Time Warner Create a Colossus and Redefine the Future."[5]

Predictably, *The Washington Post*'s Allan Sloan cast a jaundiced eye on the nuptial announcement. "Until recently," he observed, "AOL buying Time Warner was as likely as a flea buying an elephant. But the stock market made this takeover possible by valuing 15-year-old AOL at twice the value it accorded 76-year-old Time Warner. This despite the fact that Time Warner's businesses produce from four to six times (depending on who's counting) the operating profits of AOL's businesses. Thus, Wall Street says a dollar of AOL operating profits is worth eight to 12 times a dollar of Time Warner profit. New math?" [6]

Dudack saw the merger as a metaphor for what was happening. "In the twilight zone that we've entered, things of substance—bricks and mortar— are trash," she told friends. "What people value is paper—AOL's stock." So AOL, an Internet arriviste with a powerful brand name, and not much else, was able to capture Time Warner, a company with real assets, nearly five times AOL's revenues, and verifiable earnings—earnings that the SEC did not constantly question.[7] In January of 2000, AOL's stock was sizzling, changing hands at 217 times the company's earnings, and Steve Case, the company's founder, seized the moment, offering to trade 1.5 shares of AOL for each share of Time Warner. The marriage would not be consummated for another year, and by that time, AOL's shares had lost more than a third of their value. Nevertheless, AOL still paid just 1.5 shares for every share of Time Warner. Steve Case had cut it close, but his timing was superb.

"Come On, Gail, Get with It"

Dudack recognized that many on Wall Street were just too young, or too naïve, to understand what was going on.

Others, however, knowingly played the game. One of the Street's best-known gurus appeared with Dudack on CNN's *Moneyline* in 1999 and insisted that investors were pouring more and more money into equity funds. Dudack knew this wasn't true; at that moment skittish investors were beginning to park their savings in money market funds. After the show had ended, as they waited outside for a limousine to take them back to their offices, Dudack turned to her colleague: "Have you looked carefully at those fund flow numbers? You know what you said isn't right."

"Don't worry—if the money isn't there now, it'll be coming in. Come on, Gail, get with it," he added in a friendly tone. Startled, Dudack realized that he was trying to be helpful. He was attempting to give her career advice. As she had told *Money* magazine a few months earlier, being a bear "is not good for your career and it's not good for making friends." [8] Not long after, she went to a meeting with a client and was accused of being "unpatriotic" because she suggested that U.S. technology stocks were overpriced.

The numbers no longer matter, Dudack thought. People want to buy stocks and they want them to go up. They want to make a million dollars—and they want people to tell them things that will make it happen.

Dudack knew that she risked being labeled a Cassandra, one of those perverse seers who insist upon forecasting doom, even though no one is interested in hearing her bad news. In the summer of 1998, when Prudential's Ralph Acampora predicted that the Dow would crash, and Prudential wound up hiring a bodyguard to protect him, Dudack understood the public's reaction: *They believe that if you say that the market will go down, you make it happen.*

She could only imagine the dampening effect that the publicity would have on any professional's future forecasts. "Consciously or unconsciously, after something like this, anyone would think long and hard before saying something negative about the market again," she told her husband. "I don't want that to happen to me—I don't want to be at the center of controversy. I keep thinking about John Kenneth Galbraith's description of what happens to a bear during an investment mania. You'll be scorned, you'll be terrorized, and when the bubble begins to collapse, the public will be very angry. It will need a scapegoat."

The problem was that Dudack, like a growing number of Wall Street insiders, realized that the fin de siècle bull market had become a paper market. Companies reported earnings, on paper; share prices rose, on paper; investors accumulated profits, on paper. No one knew how much of it was real. Dudack did not want to be the messenger who was shot, yet she continued to speak out. "The outlook is worse than ever," she told *The Financial Times* in April of 1999.[9] "At least I can sleep at night," Dudack said privately. "I know that what I'm doing is unpopular, but I am prepared."

WALL $TREET WEEK—NOVEMBER 5, 1999

Still, she wasn't quite prepared for Louis Rukeyser to fire the first shot. The morning of Saturday, November 6, 1999, Dudack was making breakfast for her nine-year-old son when the phone rang at her Westchester home. First, a call came from a neighbor down the street. "Gail, why did they do this to you? What happened?"

Dudack had no idea what her neighbor was talking about. She did not know that the night before, she had been humiliated, on nationwide television, in front of the millions of viewers who watched the PBS hit *Wall $treet Week with Louis Rukeyser.*

Although she had been a regular on the show for more than 20 years, Dudack did not appear every week. She was part of a rotating group of technicians and market strategists that Rukeyser dubbed his "elves." Each week, they contributed to the show's "elves' index," predicting where the Dow would be in three months, but in any given week, only two or three appeared on air. So that Saturday morning, when the phone began to ring, Dudack did not know what had happened on *Wall $treet Week* the night before.

The show had opened with a special segment. Abandoning his usual, jocular manner, *Wall $treet Week's* harlequin-faced host took on the role of schoolmaster, metaphorical ruler in hand, ready to rap the knuckles of unruly elves. "Tonight," he announced, "we will be making one of our periodic checks on who the winners and sinners are among our market-forecasting elves." He paused, just a second, for dramatic effect. "And, based on that checkup, we're going to make one substitution tonight." One of the elves was about to be banished.

Rukeyser proceeded to excoriate the "one elf, and one elf only [who] has been stuck in the same position for the past 156 weeks running." Dudack, the show's sole bear, had been cautious since the fall of 1997.

Like Fidelity Magellan's Jeff Vinik, Dudack had been unpardonably early. In November of 1999, the bull was still on steroids—or so it seemed. Six months later, the Nasdaq would implode, losing 25 percent of its value in one week. But at that moment, in November of 1999, Dudack appeared terribly wrong.

It was one of the paradoxes of *Wall $treet Week* that, although Rukeyser preached long-term investing, his show featured a three-month forecast. To be fair, throughout the nineties, short-term predictions dominated most financial journalism. After all, who would remember if you gave advice that panned out 18 months later?

Dudack's three-month forecasts had missed their target for two years, and that was too long—even if, over the long haul, she was proved right. "Lou lacked the intellectual integrity to tolerate a different opinion, and to wait and see if Gail would be correct," Hank Herrmann, president and chief investment officer of Waddell & Reed Financial, and another frequent guest on the show, later observed.[10]

After pointing out that Dudack had earned the show's "dunce cap" for much of the past two and a half years, Rukeyser wound up the segment by sacking her on nationwide TV. Dudack, he explained, would no longer be part of the elves' index. He even announced her replacement on the air: "Coming in from the sidelines is that old Dartmouth basketball player, Alan Bond, who is ready and eager to try to run up a better record."[11]

Blindsided, Dudack fielded calls all weekend from friends, relatives, and colleagues. Monday morning, Dow Jones phoned to ask: "What do you have to say about what happened on *Wall $treet Week?*" Dudack still wasn't sure exactly what had happened, though she had begun to piece together the story. Later she would learn that Rukeyser had instructed his producer to e-mail her late Friday, shortly before the show aired. But Dudack did not get the message, dated Friday, 5:58 P.M., until she came into her office on Monday morning.

In the week that followed, letters began streaming in from Dudack's fans. Mainly, they were appalled that Rukeyser had fired her on the air. But many also were upset because it seemed that Rukeyser was manipulating the index. Some believed that he had removed Dudack from his index because he wanted it to be unanimously bullish.

As for Dudack, she saw the episode as "one of those markers that come at the top of a bull market: the last bear is gored."

AN ASIDE ON BEING "EARLY"

Dudack had recognized that for much of 1998 and 1999, her short-term forecasts had been wrong, but she had not been particularly perturbed. She knew that, at any time, the Dow could crack. She was basing her recommendations on the degree of risk versus reward that the market as a whole offered, and by now, the risk had become far too high. She did not know when that risk would become visible, but she told clients: "Valuations make no sense. This quarter, next quarter, the quarter after that—no one knows when, but the market will plunge."

In other words, Dudack was like an insurance salesman advising customers who lived too close to the river to buy flood insurance. She didn't know when the river would overflow, but she realized it was dangerously high—and once the deluge came, it would be too late to get out. Those who were able to follow Dudack's advice, and got out sometime in 1998, would be grateful. A buy-and-hold investor who stuck with the S&P 500 from June of 1998 through June of 2003 would make nothing. In fact, he would lose a little over 8 percent of his savings during those five years.

But in the fall of 1999, financial euphoria still reigned on Main Street, and Dudack sensed that Rukeyser did not want a bear casting a shadow over his purposefully upbeat show. From its beginnings in 1970, *Wall $treet Week* had been dedicated to making viewers feel that Wall Street was still a safe place for the "little guy" to invest his life's savings, that, despite the bear market of the seventies, and the insider trading scandals of the eighties, the rules of capitalism had never changed. "Buy and hold" was his creed, "Keep the faith" one of his taglines. Perhaps that was why the show was so self-consciously anachronistic.

RUKEYSER—"RAKISH RACONTEUR"?

Rukeyser himself, with his snowy Edwardian hairdo and elegantly tailored suits, seemed to have stepped out of another time and place. The set, which appeared to be a living room decorated by an Anglophile living somewhere in Darien, Connecticut, bespoke Old Money. (The set was such a perfect backdrop for its host that viewers wrote in to ask if it was, indeed, his living room.) Even in the nineties, the guests who gathered around the show's mahogany table seemed to represent what one observer called "the Town & Country Set—men in pinstripes, women wearing silk scarves the size of baby quilts around their shoulders." [12]

But while some might call the show stodgy—or even smug—*Wall $treet Week* was one of the most popular programs on the Public Broadcasting System's lineup, and it enjoyed an enormously loyal following. When the 67-year-old Rukeyser celebrated the program's 30-year anniversary in November of 2000, he still drew an audience four times the size of that watching either CNN's *Moneyline* or CNBC's *News Center* on an average day. [13] If CNBC's *Squawk Box* team offered the frat-house version of financial news, Rukeyser was the dean, and even as the bull market peaked, *Wall $treet Week* remained the nation's most popular financial news program.

The show's popularity was based, in large part, on its host's personality. Depending on who you were, you saw Rukeyser as a "rakish raconteur" (*Playboy*) or "relentlessly insouciant" (*The New Yorker*). [14] But most viewers found the tall, patrician-looking Rukeyser charismatic. *Modern Maturity* named him one of world's "50 sexiest men over 50." Critics might find the show's level of self-satisfaction grating, but millions of viewers looked forward to the arch, pun-filled opening monologue in which Rukeyser baited bears, politicians, and other "fat cats." His tone, which one reviewer described as equal parts "irreverence and self-satisfaction," assured viewers that he had an inside line on how the world worked.[15] And he was sharing it with them.

Eschewing financial jargon, Rukeyser was both credible and clear: he managed to explain the market in language that almost anyone could understand. For it was a tenet of the show that if an investor just paid attention to the fundamentals of investing, every right-thinking, hardworking American stood just as much of a chance as the pros.

Yet, for all of Rukeyser's successes in the late nineties, *Wall $treet Week* would fail its viewers. As the bear moved in on the market, Rukeyser had reason to regret losing Dudack, his only reliable skeptic. By the end of 1999, *Wall $treet Week*'s elves were beginning to disappear into the bear's many traps. In 2000, the show's bullish elves were wrong most of the time. By the beginning of September 2001, their track record was so abysmal that Rukeyser turned on them, calling his very own elves "comatose." In September of 2001, following the World Trade Center attacks, Rukeyser announced, "We're going to give the elves a rest for a little while."[16]

DUDACK'S REPLACEMENT

Rukeyser had a second, even greater reason to wish he hadn't fired Dudack from the elves' panel. Her replacement, Alan Bond, proved a singularly embarrassing choice. A month after Rukeyser tapped Bond to fill Dudack's spot, Alan Bond was indicted by the Manhattan DA, charged with taking more than $6 million in kickbacks.

Throughout the decade, Bond had managed an impressive list of retirement plans that included the NBA's retirement fund, a pension plan for the City University of New York, and the Ohio Police and Firemen's Disability Pension. By 1999, Bond, 38, ran more than $600 million and had become a frequent guest on Rukeyser's show. But in December of 1999, the U.S. Attorney's office in Manhattan unsealed an indictment charging that when Bond placed trades, he received kickbacks from the brokers who took his orders. The brokers had siphoned the paybacks from his clients' accounts. Allegedly, Bond told the brokerage firms to mark up the cost of each buy order; the firms, in turn, kicked back 57 to 80 percent of the markup to Bond, who instructed them not to report it on the statements that his clients received.

According to a separate complaint filed by the SEC, Bond spent the cash building an opulent lifestyle that included 75 luxury and antique automobiles, a large home, and a beachfront condominium in Florida—not to mention frequent shopping sprees to stores such as Saks Fifth Avenue and Tiffany & Co. His American Express bills ranged from $200,000 to $470,000 a month.

Unbowed by the indictment, Bond redoubled his efforts to profit at his clients' expense. In 2001, while out on bail, he continued to manage pension funds, and during this time, a second indictment would allege, he began directing virtually all of his profitable stock trades to his personal brokerage account. Unprofitable trades were posted to his clients' accounts. According to prosecutors and court documents, Bond managed the scheme by waiting until the end of the day before notifying Neuberger & Berman, the firm that posted his trades, which should be directed to his personal account and which to his clients' accounts. Sometimes he waited until after the markets closed.

From March 2000 to July 31, 2001, Bond reallocated trades about 50 times, the prosecutor's complaint alleged, canceling winning trades previously booked to clients' accounts and moving the trades—and the gains— to his personal account. Federal prosecutors said the "cherry picking" scheme netted Mr. Bond $6.3 million and cost three clients—two pension funds and an investment advisory group—more than $56 million. In August of 2001, the complaint did not attempt to explain why Neuberger & Berman accepted more than 50 eleventh-hour changes.[17]

WHY NEITHER GAIL DUDACK NOR JIM GRANT WILL EVER BECOME LOUIS RUKEYSER

In the meantime, in the months after she left *Wall $treet Week,* Gail Dudack watched the bear take control of the market. But as she predicted, the fact that she had been right did not make her more popular. Instead, in the fall of 2000, six months after her firm announced that it was merging with PaineWebber, she was fired.

"They called me in, thanked me for all that I had done for the firm over the years, and then explained that they had only one job—and they were giving it to Ed Kerschner, PaineWebber's chief stategist," Dudack told her husband that night.

Bears are rarely appreciated—even when they are right, as Michael Lewis noted in a 2003 Bloomberg column titled "Why James Grant Will Never Become Louis Rukeyser": "For anyone who sets out on a career of financial punditry, there is a very clear incentive to become a bull," Lewis observed. "Louis Rukeyser, for instance. The host of 'Louis Rukeyser's Wall $treet' has made a fantastically good living for going on 30 years by ridiculing bearishness in all its forms, and celebrating bullishness in most of its forms. . . .

"Even with the Dow falling fast, it is impossible to imagine a bearish version of Louis Rukeyser's gaudy worldly success," Lewis continued. "Just as we grossly exaggerate the importance of people who argue that the market is going up, even when those people are dimwits, we grossly diminish the importance of those who say the stock market is going down—even when those people are first-rate thinkers. James Grant, for instance. The editor of 'Grant's Interest Rate Observer,' is one of the most interesting market analysts alive. Even in a bull market his views are far more stimulating and original than those of most bullish pundits. For going on 15 years he has argued, with wit and clarity, that the U.S. stock market is a house of cards. If there was any justice in the world right now, James Grant would be a household name, feted for his prescience, offered huge sums for his public speeches, perhaps even recognized on occasion by New York taxi drivers." [18]

ACCUMULATING ASSETS— LAUNCHING A NEW FUND

But Jim Grant would never receive mass adulation on the streets of Manhattan, and when her firm merged with PaineWebber, Gail Dudack would not even be allowed to keep her job. It was unclear why UBS PaineWebber could not use two market strategists, one bullish and one bearish—especially since the S&P 500 already had begun to buckle. But Dudack understood why they wanted Kerschner: he had just completed a "dog and pony" show, raising over $1 billion, mainly from admiring individual investors, for PaineWebber's new Strategic Fund.

Kerschner launched the fund in November of 1999 and promptly poured his investors' savings into growth stocks such as Lucent, World-Com, and Citrix Systems. All three were clocked. By the end of 2000, the fund had shed nearly one-third of its value, placing it in the bottom 2 percent of all large-cap growth funds according to Morningstar.

The fund then took an alias, Brinson Strategy (the name borrowed from Brinson Partners, a money-management operation owned by UBS). In the fall of 2001, *The New York Times* would suggest that the fund's name may have been changed "to shield UBS PaineWebber's reputation."[19] Early in 2001, Kerschner added names such as Intel and Juniper Networks to his portfolio, and throughout the year, technology and telecommunications remained his favorite themes. The losses mounted. By the end of 2001, the fund had lost another 21 percent.

Like Bond, Kerschner was undeterred by experience. In 2001, he continued to urge investors to plunge their savings into stocks. In the summer of that year, UBS PaineWebber launched an advertising campaign featuring Kerschner, who appeared in full-page newspaper ads, assuring investors that, by year-end, the Dow would gain 50 percent.

In 2002, UBS changed the fund's name, once again to UBS Strategy, and revamped the portfolio's scope, making it a global fund. Casting a wider net did not help: that year, the fund lost another 22 percent. Finally, at the end of 2002, UBS decided to quietly give its Strategy Fund a proper burial, merging it with its $58 million UBS Global Equity Fund.[20]

THE GREEK CHORUS

In 1999, Dudack, of course, was not the only vocal bear in the financial world—though she was one of very few who had managed to hold on to a top position at a major Wall Street firm.

By and large, market watchers who became the bull market's Greek Chorus worked outside of the financial establishment that runs up and down the East Coast—from Fidelity's headquarters in Boston, through the intersection of Wall and Broad in downtown Manhattan, to the seat of power politics in Washington, D.C.—with outposts, of course, on the West Coast, in Silicon Valley, and in San Francisco, home of Charles Schwab.

Those who raised their voices in doubt tended to live outside the bureaucracy: they were money managers who ran their own shop (like Jean-Marie Eveillard, Marty Whitman, and Jeremy Grantham, to name just three); newsletter writers with a sense of history (like Richard Russell, Jim Grant, Marc Faber, Kate Welling, Fred Hickey, and Mark Hulbert), maverick columnists (like Allan Sloan, Alan Abelson, and Herb Greenberg), or independent researchers (like Steve Leuthold and David Tice) who knew how to look "behind the numbers"—and, again, answered to no one except themselves.

To most investors, 1999 seemed an apex. Even with the benefit of hindsight, they would view '99 as the last grand year of a spectacular bull market. With the benefit of foresight, the Greek Chorus recognized that if this was a climax, it was also an ending—and the beginning of a new cycle. In fact, the end of a bull market and the beginning of a bear market often overlap.

Most investors did not realize a bear market had begun, Richard Russell later suggested, because the bull market topped out so gradually—over a period of two years: "The advance-decline ratio on the NYSE topped out on April 3, 1998 at 13. Both the Morgan Stanley Cyclical Index (an index of cyclical stocks) and the Dow Jones Transportation Average topped out in May of 1999—the cyclicals on the 10th at 619.09; the transports on the 12th at 3783.50." The Dow Jones Industrial Average would not peak until January of 2000, followed by the Nasdaq and the S&P 500, three months later. "If they all topped out within say, a month or so, the effect would have been much more pronounced and dramatic," Russell commented. Instead, this was, as Dudack had suggested, a "stealth bear market." [21]

Marc Faber, an international investor based in Hong Kong, was accustomed to tracking the bear. Faber had watched financial manias come to an unhappy end in Japan, in Latin America, and in Southeast Asia. In August of 1999, he titled his monthly newsletter *U.S. Bear Market—Phase One.*

By November, Faber was certain "the first phase of the bear market is in full force. But it is well hidden," he acknowledged, "by the continued strength of just a few stocks like GE and Microsoft. The mood is extremely optimistic. Such is the case in the first phase of a bear market: negative news is dismissed as irrelevant and immaterial."

This first phase could stretch on for years, Faber added: "I have experienced many bubbles and investment manias, and I can confidently say that none of them came to an end with the first lot of bad news. In early 1972, inflation began to accelerate and interest rates rose in the U.S., but the

stock market continued to rise until January of 1973. . . . In fact, a bear
market rally in September/October 1973 led to a new high for the Dow
Jones." Most remarkably, Faber continued, "the market didn't fall immediately after OPEC announced, on October 16, a 70% increase in oil prices,
but continued to rally until October 29. Only then did reality set in." [22]

Like Faber, Richard Russell realized that the bear was now in charge. In
September 1999, Russell told his readers that the *Dow Theory* had sent a
"sell signal." He also warned that given the strength of the bull market, he
feared this bear market might be a drawn-out, grinding affair: *"The bear is
in no hurry,"* Russell wrote (his emphasis). "The bear is intent on wearing us
out. The reason I feel this way is because it's clear that the authorities won't
allow the markets to express themselves, or I should say the authorities will
do all they can to thwart the markets' expressing themselves. . . . The Fed
and the politicians are committed to fighting the bear tooth and nail." As a
result, Russell cautioned, "their fighting will serve to extend the bear market far beyond what might ordinarily be expected." [23]

INSIDERS SELL;
THE WATER RISES

TEXAS SENATOR PHIL GRAMM: *"If this is the bust, the boom was*
                            sure as hell worth it.
                            "You agree with that, right?"
FED CHAIRMAN ALAN GREENSPAN: *"Certainly."*

—Exchange between Senator Gramm and the
Fed chairman at a 2001 congressional hearing[1]

While both mutual fund managers and small investors followed the herd, insiders began running in the opposite direction. The rush for the exits began in the fall of 1999. From September of 1999 through July of 2000, insider selling of big blocks of stock (at least $1 million worth or 100,000 shares or more) rose to $43.1 billion—twice as much as insiders sold over the same span in '97 and '98. Indeed, the $39 billion worth of shares that insiders unloaded in just the first six months of 2000 topped the record $39 billion sold in all of '99.[2]

Six months after the selling began, the Nasdaq cracked—the most visible sign yet that a bear market had begun. That same month, the S&P 500 crested. After that, the long slide began.

Later, CEOs who sold shortly before the peak would claim that they just got lucky. "Who knew?" one asked *The Wall Street Journal*.[3] But it seemed that many knew. This was not what corporate PR departments dismissed as "part of a regular pattern of selling." This was a sudden bulge in insiders' sales: by February of 2000—just weeks before the Nasdaq would peak—insiders were selling 23 times as much stock as they bought, compared with the typical ratio of 10 to 1. In July, they were not fooled by a summer rally; that month the ratio remained at 22 to 1.[4]

How did they know? Some high-ranking executives knew that their own companies' earnings were fictitious. They also realized that they were running out of road: one can only restate earnings so many times. Others were in a position to know that many of the companies that they did business with were not nearly as profitable as they appeared: orders were down, and inventories were building, along with corporate debt.

Of course, insiders had every right to sell, and certainly it made sense for a multimillionaire to diversify. Some were, in fact, following pre-arranged selling plans—though in many cases those "plans" were set up in '99, when insiders began to realize that the bull was on his last legs. An orderly exit would attract less attention.

In the end, a 2003 *Chicago Tribune* study of sales by top executives at the 30 corporations listed on the Dow suggested that either these insiders were uncommonly lucky or they were using what they knew about their companies to time their sales.

Looking at sales by chief executive officers and chief financial officers from 1995 through the end of 2002, the *Tribune*'s analysis showed that in 25 percent of all cases, the share price of the company in question tumbled by at least 20 percent—and sometimes as much as 50 percent—in the six months following the sale. Insiders were equally fortunate in picking their spots when buying their own companies' stock: more than half of all purchases preceded gains of more than 20 percent, with several well above 50 percent.

None of the executives in the analysis had been accused of illegal insider trading, but the *Tribune* noted that its findings "raise questions about the advantages that executives enjoy in trading their shares because they have access to detailed, private information about their companies."[5]

Insider selling became so pervasive—and so lucrative—that by 2001, *The Wall Street Journal* was able to name 50 top executives to "the $100 million club." Those who qualified had sold more than $100 million worth of shares in their own companies sometime between October of 1999 (when insider selling began to double) through the end of 2000 (when the last train was leaving the station). In many cases, they sold at a point when their companies' shares were worth more than they ever had been before—and ever would be again.

Scient chairman Eric Greenberg, for instance, managed to reap more from selling his shares in the Internet consulting company during these 15 months than the entire company would be worth in 2001. But some insiders held on, notably Edward "Toby" Lenk, CEO of online retailer eToys, who watched a paper fortune of $600 million vaporize as the company slid into bankruptcy. Nevertheless, Lenk never bailed out. "There were lots of people at eToys and other Internet companies who wanted to build something meaningful, not just make a quick buck," he said.[6]

GLOBAL CROSSING

Some insider sales stood out by virtue of their sheer size. From 1999 through November of 2001, top executives at a soon-to-be-bankrupt fiber optic darling, Global Crossing, disposed of shares worth $1.3 billion—an amount that exceeded even the insider sales at Enron, the Texas energy trader that fabricated much of its business before going belly-up in 2001.

Global Crossing founder Gary Winnick had learned finance at the knee of Mike Milken, the junk bond king of the eighties. Formerly a bond salesman at Drexel Burnham Lambert, Winnick had served as one of Milken's lieutenants. It is perhaps no accident that Enron CEO Kenneth Lay also turned out to be a Milken admirer. (Milken had provided the financing when two old-line pipelines, InterNorth and Houston Natural Gas, merged to spawn Enron in 1985.)[7]

The story of Global Crossing's rise and fall turned out to be a classic tale of too much money chasing too few ideas, leading to the inevitable ending: overinvestment creating too much supply. Winnick's somewhat grandiose scheme involved building an undersea phone network linking 27 countries and 200 cities. Trouble was, the expected demand for 100,000 miles of fiber optic never materialized. When the company finally went under early in 2002, it carried $12 billion in debt. By 2003, a congressional committee was investigating charges that Global Crossing and another fallen telecom, Qwest, had inflated earnings by fabricating transactions between the two companies.[8]

In his heyday, Winnick spent lavishly, whether buying a $65 million,

15-bedroom home in Bel-Air, or hiring and firing five pricey CEOs in as many years. When Robert Annunziata came on board, for instance, his contract reportedly included first-class airline tickets for his mother, a pledge to buy him a new Mercedes—specifically a 1999 SL500—and a signing bonus of $10 million, plus options on another 2 million shares. Salomon telecom analyst Jack Grubman, who played an active role in advising both Winnick and WorldCom's Bernie Ebbers, had recommended Annunziata for the job, illustrating, once again, that the bull market of the nineties depended on a web of relationships.[9]

When it was all over, Winnick wound up a winner. Thanks to a combination of hype and accounting legerdemain, Global Crossing's shares rose fivefold. With the stock still in orbit, Winnick managed to unload shares worth nearly $734 million, making a neat profit of $715 million on an initial investment of $20 million.

Winnick was not alone. Cofounder Barry Porter reaped $95.9 million; directors Lodwrick Cook and Joseph Clayton cashed in $31.9 million and $16.7 million worth of shares, respectively, while former CEO John Scanlon sold stock worth $23.1 million.[10]

By contrast, the company's 8,000 employees were not able to sell the Global Crossing shares in their 401(k) plans in the month before the bankruptcy was announced. Their assets were frozen, Global Crossing explained, because the company was in the process of changing 401(k) administrators, shifting the plan's assets from Putnam and Merrill Lynch to Fidelity. Critics questioned the timing of the shift at a point when the company's finances were obviously precarious. When the so-called lockdown began, Global Crossing's shares had already plunged from a high of $67 to $12. When it ended, the telecom start-up was trading at $9.[11]

Arguably, the drop from $67 to $12 should have been enough to tip off employees that the stock was a lemon, but loyalty to company stock proved the undoing of many. They bet both their job security and their retirement savings on one company—and lost everything.

Executives were not the only insiders who managed to cash out before Global Crossing became a penny stock. Former President George H. W. Bush became an insider even before the company went public, simply by agreeing to give a speech.

In 1998, Lod Cook, an old oil-patch buddy, asked Bush to come to Tokyo to address potential customers of Gary Winnick's fledgling telecom operation. At the time, Cook, the former chairman of Atlantic Richfield, was serving as cochair of Global Crossing. The former president agreed, and in a gesture of friendship, he offered a 20 percent discount on his usual $100,000 speaking fee.

The speech went smoothly, and the next morning, over breakfast with Cook and Winnick at the Hotel Okura, Bush began asking questions about their venture, prompting Winnick to suggest that he take his fee in the form of stock rather than cash. Bush agreed.

Global Crossing went public later that year, and before long, the alchemy of financial euphoria had turned Bush's $80,000 honorarium into a $14 million windfall. Fifteen months later, in November of 1999, just as corporate insiders began to bail out en masse, a trust in Bush's name registered to sell a portion of his holdings for an estimated $4.5 million. According to *The Wall Street Journal*, rumor had it that proceeds would go toward maintaining the Bush family retreat in Kennebunkport, Maine.

The enormous sell-off by Global Crossing insiders turned out to be just one example of industry-wide sales by telecom executives. In the end, their gains dwarfed the profits made on Internet shares, *The Wall Street Journal* reported in 2002, referring to the profit taking as "one of the largest transfers of wealth from investors—big and small—in history. Hundreds of telecom executives, almost uniformly bullish, sold at least some portion of their stock and made hundreds of millions of dollars, while . . . outside shareholders took a bath." But few executives were publicly apologetic about timing their sales so well, the *Journal* noted, quoting Randall Kruep, former senior vice president at Redback Networks, a six-year-old company that went public in May 1999. "I would have gotten out faster if I could have," said Kruep, lamenting the fact that he was able to sell only $100 million worth of stock during 1999 and 2000. Rules that limited how soon insiders can sell stood in his way. In March of 2000, when Kruep was in the process of liquidating his shares, Redback stock changed hands at $191.03. By August of 2002, Redback traded at $1.07—and Kruep had a new job as chief executive of Procket Networks.[12]

Virtually all of these sales were perfectly legal. To prove insider trading in court, a mind reader would need to show exactly what an insider knew, when he knew it, and how he interpreted it before selling his stock.

THE FED TO THE RESCUE

While insiders fled, it should be said that Fed Chairman Alan Greenspan stayed with the ship, making every effort to provide the liquidity needed to keep Abby Cohen's tanker afloat.

The Fed chairman seemed to be of two minds on what action was needed. On the one hand, he was worried about inflation. Concerned that the economy was overheating, the Fed hiked interest rates six times between June 1999 and May 2000. Nevertheless, smack in the middle of that period, at the very end of 1999, he pumped $100 billion in new credit into the economy.

Greenspan fretted over inflation because he feared that soaring stock prices were generating a "wealth effect" that, in turn, was fueling consumer spending at a rate that could create an inflationary spiral. But in that case, "the great mystery," remarked *Newsweek* and *Washington Post* columnist Allan Sloan, "is why Greenspan hasn't attacked speculation directly by raising initial margin requirements"—the amount of stock an investor must have as collateral when borrowing from his broker to buy additional shares.

As noted, in 1996, Greenspan himself had acknowledged that if he wanted to prick the bubble, boosting margin requirements would do the trick.[13] Why, then, hadn't he tried it? "Greenspan has said repeatedly that raising margin rates would hurt only small investors, because big investors have plenty of ways to get around margin requirements, such as dealing in stock options or futures rather than owning stocks directly," Sloan reported.

But in Sloan's view, this was not the major reason why the Fed avoided stiffening requirements. "My feeling . . . is that Greenspan is also looking out for the well-being of brokerage houses, which make huge profits on margin loans."[14]

This Fed chairman was not about to cut off the liquidity that keeps a bull market party going. Lower rates made it easier to raise money for projects like Gary Winnick's 100,000 miles of fiber optic cable. The fact that the world had no need for so much cable did not concern either Winnick or his promoters on Wall Street.

Meanwhile, Alan Greenspan caught millennial fever. Responding to apocalyptic fears that as the world's clocks changed from 1999 to 2000, computers worldwide would crash, the Fed chairman once again rode to the rescue, cushioning the expected crash with cash. "In the run-up to the millennial-liquidity-crisis-that-did-not-happen, the Fed created more than $100 billion of new credit, thereby stimulating a stock market that hardly seemed to need any additional encouragement," Jim Grant noted in an op-ed piece that he wrote for *The Financial Times*.[15]

Washington, by contrast, was impressed. On January 4, 2000, President Clinton nominated Alan Greenspan to a fourth term as Fed chairman, and "Greenspan's Senate confirmation hearing—a tense scene on previous occasions—was more like a coronation this time around," noted Justin Martin, author of *Greenspan: The Man Behind Money*. Indeed, Martin reported, at about the same time, "Americans were treated to the spectacle of the leading presidential candidates for the 2000 election falling all over one another to see who could heap the highest praise on Greenspan. The prize went to John McCain. During a primary debate, [McCain] gushed: 'And by the way, I would not only reappoint Alan Greenspan—if he would happen to die, God forbid—I would do like they did in the movie *Weekend at Bernie's*. I would prop him up and put a pair of dark glasses on him.'"[16]

Not everyone was bowled over. Some, like Acorn Funds founder Ralph Wanger, believed that by keeping the bubble afloat, the Fed chairman was only postponing disaster. "In the end, what the market is valuing is the economy—and if the economy grows 6 percent and the market is going up 12 to 18 percent, after 10 years you've got an unstable situation. It reminds me of the conditions that lead to an avalanche," he continued. "Once enough snow has accumulated, it's hard to know what will trigger the avalanche. It can be almost anything—a tree branch, a deer, a skier—what really causes it is that you have an unstable snow buildup and any damn thing is going to trigger it. It doesn't matter what the final trigger is—unless it happens to be *you*. In which case it becomes an overriding concern, for a short period of time.

"When the avalanche comes crashing down, it takes everything in front of it."

In Wanger's view, Greenspan committed his final, fatal mistake by bringing a snow-making machine to an avalanche. At the time, a blizzard of buying had already created the instability that inevitably would lead to disaster: "What Greenspan should have done," said Wanger, "was to act like he was head of the ski patrol. You handle an unstable situation like that by setting off the avalanche under controlled conditions. You take care of the situation by having the avalanche earlier rather than later.

"That last slug of liquidity in the last quarter of the year" helped send stocks to the moon, Wanger observed. "Biotech stocks went up eightfold. There was money all over the place, money flowing into sector funds—and sector funds set up the potential for disaster." [17]

MARCH 2000

Many of those sector funds were technology funds. In the 12 months that ended March 1, 2000, the Nasdaq skyrocketed a stunning 108.4 percent— making both the Dow's 8.7 percent rise and the S&P 500's 11.5 percent advance over the same span seem puny. Individual investors were still following the momentum. During the first three months of 2000, roughly two-thirds of the cash that individual investors shoveled into mutual funds was tagged for tech funds, helping to drive the benchmark technology index past yet another much ballyhooed barrier: on March 10, the Nasdaq crossed 5000.

Then, on Monday, March 13, the trouble began. *The New York Times* called it "a small speed bump." [18] And so it seemed. Granted, the Nasdaq had lost 9 percent of its value in the first three days of the week, but then the tech index rebounded nicely. The next week, the Nasdaq took another hit, and once again bounced back. Investors took the swerve in stride. "Bull's Retreat Doesn't Cause a Stampede," the *Journal* declared in the final days of March.[19]

By year-end, *The Wall Street Journal* would take a very different view of the events of March 2000. Looking back on the "tech wreck" that began that month, Wall Street's paper of record compared it to "one-third of the houses in America sliding into the ocean." For by then, the index had fallen 54 percent, peak to trough, and investors had lost $3.3 trillion in paper wealth—the equivalent of the loss of said houses, "in dollars if not in effect," the *Journal* added, allowing for the fact that people might well have a sentimental attachment to their homes—not to mention a fondness for family members who could be trapped inside.[20] Then, too, these were only paper losses. But most 401(k) investors thought of the money as theirs even though they had not yet sold their shares, and had planned their retirements accordingly.

In retrospect, many observers would believe that the bear market began in March of 2000. That, after all, also was the month when the S&P 500 peaked. But market historians who stepped back to take a broader view realized that the Greek Chorus was right: the bear came on stage sometime in 1999.

You only had to do the math. By March 1, 2000, stocks trading on the Nasdaq had climbed $3.1 trillion in 12 months, Jim Bianco of Bianco Research pointed out. Over the same 12 months the total value of all U.S. stocks—including Nasdaq shares—rose by only $2.1 trillion. Anyone who subtracted the Nasdaq's gain from the total realized that by March of 2000, the overall market had fallen by $600 billion.[21]

"Bears," Peter Bernstein later observed, "are people who do their arithmetic."[22]

In other words, the bull did not suddenly roll over and die in the spring of 2000. What seemed a sudden shocking drop on the Nasdaq was part of a larger process that embraced not just the technology index but the whole market. The broad market had lacked support since the end of 1998, when just six stocks carried the S&P 500 over the finish line into positive territory. Gail Dudack was right: it was a "stealth bear market." And the bear would continue to take his time. "The dollar did not break down until May 2002," Dudack added three years later. "The unwinding of this bubble is like watching a movie in slow motion. The trough may be similar."[23]

Nevertheless, individual investors continued to trust stocks for the long run. Over the course of 2000, they would pour $260 billion into U.S. equity funds—up from $150 billion in 1998 and $176 billion in 1999. Of the $259 billion invested in 2000, $130 billion, or roughly half, went into what the Investment Company Institute characterized as "Aggressive Growth" equity funds. This was three times more than they had invested in 1999. Nearly $120 billion went into the somewhat less aggressive "Growth" equity funds—about twice the amount invested in these funds in 1998, and up roughly 20 percent from 1999.[24]

That "final slug" of liquidity that the Fed had provided in 1999 also helped keep the IPO market humming. Despite falling equity markets, 440 companies came public in 2000, almost all of them in the first nine months of the year, raising $100 billion—and breaking 1999's record of $68 billion, according to IPO.com, a web site that tracked IPOs.[25]

Meanwhile, Frank Quattrone, Mary Meeker's original mentor, had become the most visible investment banker in America. From his post in Silicon Valley, Quattrone had become the dealmaker sine qua non. There are hints that Quattrone, unlike Meeker, realized that the bear was on the premises: on December 4, 2000, he sent e-mails to staff, instructing them to clean out files related to initial public offerings.[26]

BEAR MARKET? THE 20 PERCENT RULE

But, unless they were insiders, most investors would not realize that the tide had turned until sometime in 2001. By and large, the media shared their faith. In 2000 the press rarely used the phrase "bear market" except in the past tense.

To its credit, as 2001 dawned, *The Wall Street Journal* seriously considered the possibility: "The new year begins with investors wondering if Nasdaq's bloodletting is the vanguard of a broad-based bear market," the paper observed, noting that the answer "depends mostly on whether the economy's downshift in recent months is a pause in the longest expansion in a century or the first stage of a recession." No surprise, Wall Street's paper of record was able to report that "much of Wall Street opts for the former view." The basis for Wall Street's faith, once again, was the central banker Boston money manager Jeremy Grantham liked to call "Archangel Alan." "Economists expect [the Fed] to lower rates soon, and propel stocks and the economy forward," the *Journal* reported.[27]

In reality, a bear market already had begun, not because the economy was heading into a recession (though it was), but because stocks were wildly overpriced. As Ralph Wanger had warned, the proximate cause of the first avalanche can be anything, and, in the end, the trigger is unimportant. The snow had been building up for a long, long time. Now much of that paper wealth was melting away.

But even though the Dow had declined 16 percent, peak to trough, over the course of 2000, that 16 percent loss "failed to meet the 20% bear market rule," *The Wall Street Journal* explained, echoing the received wisdom that a bear market has begun only when share prices have fallen 20 percent. In other words, if the market is down 21 percent in the morning, a bear market has begun—gain a couple of points in the afternoon, and you are back in a bull market. No wonder investors were confused. It was a statistic that nicely illustrated the difference between information and knowledge.

To back up their assertion that this was not, after all, the beginning of a lasting downturn, financial pundits compared the 2000 crash to the disastrous plunge of 1973–74. In '74, the bear devoured everything in sight. This time, by contrast, high-priced stocks such as Cisco Systems were still standing. At the end of 2000, Cisco ranked as the fourth most valuable company in the country, right behind General Electric, Exxon Mobil, and Pfizer. Wal-Mart ranked fifth, Microsoft sixth, followed by Citigroup, American International Group, Merck, and Intel. "Stocks like Cisco and EMC, both now at about 100 times trailing earnings, can remain high-priced for years," Lehman Brothers' Jeffrey Applegate asserted.

Apparently it did not occur to most market strategists to compare the losses of 2000 to the mauling of 1970—in what turned out to be only the first leg down of the bear market of 1966–82. Following that crash, the Nifty Fifty of the seventies also stood tall. Those blue chips would not be decimated for another three years.

But at the beginning of 2001, the majority of Wall Street's best and brightest seemed unencumbered by any too-detailed knowledge of market history. "As a group, market strategists are the most bullish they have been in the 16 years Merrill Lynch has surveyed them," the *Journal* reported.

Only Merrill's own head of quantitative research, Richard Bernstein, remained unenthusiastic, finding his colleagues' high spirits "both ironic, given that cash and bonds both trounced stocks last year, and sobering, since markets usually bottom at the point of maximum pessimism, not optimism." Bob Farrell, Merrill's veteran market timer, agreed: "Knowing the market's tendency to return to the mean, value investors will be the ones who make the most money in the next few years," Farrell predicted. "Technology stocks won't make a long-term recovery until their current owners give up on them."

But Merrill's bears were in a distinct minority. At the beginning of 2001, with the Dow at 10,786, most saw a buying opportunity. Indeed, Ed Kerschner, Gail Dudack's replacement at UBS Warburg, fairly salivated at the prospects for the year ahead, calling the moment "one of the five most-attractive opportunities to own stocks in 20 years." In 2001, he predicted, the S&P would jump 30 percent.

PUMPING WATER *INTO* THE BOAT

As for the Fed chairman, by the end of 2000, Greenspan had abandoned his quixotic fight against inflation. After all, he had, in fact, been tilting at windmills: the problem was not that the economy was too hot—it was too cold. When the Fed met on December 19, economic growth had slipped to 2 percent—down from 5 percent early in the year. The Fed hinted that it was likely to ease once again. And on January 3, 2001, even before the FOMC's next scheduled meeting, it announced that it was slashing the funds rate by a full half point, bringing it down to 6 percent. For Greenspan, to slice rates by so much in one fell swoop was unusual. The timing seemed, to many, political. The day that Greenspan called an emergency meeting to cut rates "just happened to be the day" that President Bush "held a confab with business leaders in Austin, Texas," Justin Martin noted in his biography of the Fed chairman. "Some big-name CEOs were present: GE's Jack Welch, Boeing's Phil Condit and Craig Barrett of Intel. These were the heads of businesses that were starting to feel pain from a slowing economy. . . . When the rate-cut announcement came down, Jack Welch raised a glass of water to toast Greenspan."[28]

Martin Mayer, a leading expert on the Fed, agreed about the timing of the cut. "The one thing certain to come from that meeting was a call for lower interest rates. To wait until after the call was uttered would have made the Fed seem subservient."[29] By anticipating the command, the Fed was, instead, a good servant.

When the Fed trimmed rates in January of 2001, the market rallied—briefly. Before the month ended, the Fed took another whack at the Fed funds rate, bringing it down to 5.5 percent, the first time in Greenspan's tenure that rates had dropped a full point in one month.

At about the same time, the Fed chairman did a surprising about-face on the question of President Bush's proposed tax cut. Long known as a fiscal hawk who put cutting the deficit well ahead of lowering taxes, Greenspan stunned Democrats by telling the Senate Budget Committee that "the sequence of upward revisions to the budget surplus projections for several years now has reshaped the choices and opportunities for us," giving Congress the green light to back the tax cuts.[30] Of course, surplus "projections" were just that—guesses about the future—and surpluses are meant to serve as a buffer against uncertainty. Over the next two years, the surplus, like so much of the phantom wealth of the nineties, would simply vanish.

Meanwhile, from 2001 to 2002, a string of rate cuts would have only a transient effect on the stock market. Because what ailed the market was not that rates were too high, but that earnings were too low. Cutting interest rates helps businesses flourish only if they have a reason to borrow, build, and expand. With profits anemic, businesses had no motive to borrow—thus rate cuts would not motivate them to spend. Easy money would fuel a boom in the housing industry, making it easier for individuals to refinance their mortgages and buy new homes, but it would not boost capital spending by business. And in the end, that is what would matter.[31]

By February of 2001, when Greenspan delivered his semiannual report before Congress, he was forced to acknowledge a "temporary glut" in high-tech manufacturing. Too much money meant too much supply—too many cell phones, too many chips, too many PCs. But, Jim Grant observed, Greenspan "missed the point that the glut was the product of the bubble—and of the systematic undervaluing of capital and credit—and therefore risk." Thanks to the euphoric effects of a nonstop bull market, anyone could raise money. Capital was cheap because risk seemed, to so many investors, nonexistent.

Failing to recognize the root of the problem, in 2001, Greenspan continued to be optimistic about corporate profitability, noting that "corporate managers 'rightly or wrongly' appear to remain remarkably sanguine about the potential for [technological] innovations continuing to enhance productivity and profits. At least," he went on, "this is what is to be gleaned from the projections of equity analysts who, one must presume, obtain most of their insights from corporate managers."[32]

DENOUEMENT AND DEBT

Over the next two years, the Federal Reserve would continue to cut rates systematically—the Fed's critics would say frantically—all the way down to 1 percent in June of 2003. After adjusting for inflation, "real" interest rates were now below zero. But while a central banker can open the spigot, he cannot control where the money will go. The Fed could not force businesses to spend.

"For those who believe that markets solve their own problems—and they are clearly dominant in the present Bush administration," Martin Mayer had written in the summer of 2001, "the disconnect between the Fed and the desired effects of its actions is of little concern. All they wanted from Alan Greenspan was his endorsement of a large tax cut, and he gave it to them."[33]

By 2003, many in the administration would be less confident that the stock market could solve its own problems. But it was not at all clear that Alan Greenspan possessed the needed magic either.

In May of 2003, Pimco chairman Bill Gross summed up the problem: "Sure, policy makers [can] keep on applying the kindling . . . to the fire" as they try reignite the economy—"low interest rates, increasing fiscal deficits, and perhaps even a Bernanke blowtorch if need be," added Gross, referring to Federal Reserve Governor Ben S. Bernanke's suggestion that the Fed stood ready to cut the funds rate to zero. (If necessary, Bernanke declared the Fed would use "nontraditional measures" to support the economy.)[34] "But that's not a self-sustaining fire," Gross observed. "If anything it leads to more bubbles and new instabilities. For a fire to keep on burning late into the night you need the logs to catch, and the world's economic fire-wood has long since been soaked by oversupply and feeble demand."

Meanwhile corporate, consumer, and government debt mounted. By 2003, the heap had grown to $32 trillion—up from about $4 trillion at the beginning of 1980, according to the Federal Reserve. In the private sector, corporate America was staggering under that burden of debt—another reason, Gross noted, why the government's efforts to stimulate capital spending were meeting with little success: "In order to get out from under the 16-ton sledgehammer of debt, companies use cash flow to build reserves or retire bonds—they don't invest."[35]

There was still some hope that the debt would prove manageable. "There's no question that we have a debt bomb, but I'm not sure how long the fuse will turn out to be," Morgan Stanley's Steve Roach observed in January of 2003. "It won't detonate if the economy remains strong enough to continue to generate enough real consumer-income growth and corporate cash flow to support the debt. Otherwise, we'll experience the darkest scenario of debt deflation, as a result of the worst set of policy mistakes committed by the Fed since the Great Depression."[36]

For the near future, one thing was all but certain: the nation would be able to pay off its debt only if interest rates remained low. Fed Chairman Alan Greenspan had no choice but to keep on whittling, even while the New Economy burned.

A FINAL ACCOUNTING

WINNERS, LOSERS, AND SCAPEGOATS (2000–03)

By February of 2002, 100 million individual investors had lost $5 trillion, or 30 percent of the wealth they had accumulated in the stock market—just since the spring of 2000. There was nowhere to hide. At year-end, $10,000 invested in an S&P 500 index fund three years earlier was worth less than $6,300; $10,000 stashed in a large-cap growth fund had shriveled to $4,900. Just 43 of 5,500 diversified U.S. stock funds wound up in the black.[1]

The bear had taken no prisoners. After three consecutive years of losses, the Dow now stood at just over 8341—down from a bull market peak of 11,722. Meanwhile, the Nasdaq had plunged from roughly 5048 to 1335.

Individual investors had been mauled. Who were they? Sixty percent lived in the suburbs; most had college, graduate, or professional degrees; a disproportionate number were baby boomers between the ages of 35 and 49 living on the East or West Coast (southerners were less likely to invest). Active traders tended to be Republicans. Nearly half earned more than $75,000 a year.

But many were less well educated, earned lower incomes, and would have less time to make up for their losses before facing retirement. A majority of Americans earning $30,000 to $50,000 were now in the market, as were 40 percent of all senior citizens.[2]

Jim Tucci was typical of the older investor. In just two years, the 60-year-old Boston sales manager had seen half of his $600,000 nest egg disappear. Tucci had lost part of his savings gambling on Internet stocks—but those were not his only losses. In 2001, he sought safety in reputable names such as IBM, Merrill Lynch, General Motors, and Delta Airlines. By early 2002, half of that money was gone.[3]

Those who could afford it least lost the most. In 2003, a Vanguard survey revealed that 401(k) investors with balances of $50,000 to $100,000 saw their savings shrink by 5.3 percent a year over the three years ending December 31, 2002. Over the same span, investors with more than $250,000 lost less than 1 percent a year.

Part of the difference could be explained by age. Older investors who had been saving longer were more likely to have accumulated more than $250,000. By and large, they also proved less susceptible to the "cult of equities," and so had done a better job of diversifying, entrusting a larger share of their savings to bonds. Nevertheless, the average investor in his late 50s saw his 401(k) grow by only 1.2 percent a year over the five years ending in December 2002—far less than the 4.9 percent earned by investors with accounts of $250,000 or more.[4]

Age alone, then, did not explain the enormous gap. Once again, much would hinge on how soon any investor joined the party, and how much he invested during the final blow-off. Here wealthier investors enjoyed a distinct edge. As the Securities Industry Association's surveys had demonstrated, they were more likely to have carved out a position in the bull market in the eighties or early nineties. Middle-income investors, by contrast, came to the party later; many did not buy their first stock or stock fund until sometime *after* 1995.[5] By then, 401(k)s had multiplied. More middle-income investors were running their own retirement funds, and they had become more confident of their investing prowess. Many who bought their first stock in 1996 would not really begin shoveling money into the market until 1999 or 2000, buying on dips all the way down.

These investors were not as likely to have financial advisors. They turned to the media for their investment advice, and so were drawn, like moths to the flame, to the white-hot stocks that made headlines.

SHIRLEY SAUERWEIN

Some were luckier than others. In the late nineties, Shirley Sauerwein's story took an unexpected twist. Sauerwein was the social worker from Redondo Beach, California, who made her first foray into the market in 1991, buying a company that she heard about while listening to the news on her car radio. The good news/bad news was that the company would turn out to be MCI WorldCom—a highflier that would go under, costing shareholders some $180 billion.[6]

By 1999 the $1,200 she had bet on a fledgling telecom company was worth $15,000—part of a mid-six-figure portfolio that included Red Hat, Yahoo!, General Electric, and America Online. At that point, Sauerwein had cut back her social work to weekends and was spending weekdays trading full-time from home. She also managed her husband James's retirement account.

That year, *The Wall Street Journal* had singled out Sauerwein as an example of the individual investor's new power: "Along with Wall Street's heavy hitters, Main Street investors like Ms. Sauerwein have emerged as a powerful financial force in the 1990s, simultaneously boosting their net worths beyond their wildest dreams and helping to propel the market to records." To a skeptical reader, Sauerwein sounded like a lamb waiting to be fleeced.

"I'm not a smart cookie," Sauerwein declared at the time. Yet she seemed to have avoided falling prey to the widespread belief that stocks always go up. "I never thought this would last," she said in '99. "I just thought, 'I'll get in and buy some tulips.'" She also made it clear that her sense of self-worth was not at stake: "If a stock goes up, it's not because I'm a whiz." Like many of the most successful professional traders, she realized that, at bottom, this was only a game. That would make it far easier to sell.

In fact, even when she was winning, Sauerwein took profits off the table. In the late nineties, she began trimming some of her holdings—including WorldCom. "I'd read something about management—and how they were spending their own money. It sounded extravagant," she recalled. "How people run their own lives tells you something, and I thought to myself, 'They're not keeping an eye on business.'" She also sold Nokia: "I saw that people were giving cell phones away, and I thought, 'There can't be much profit in that . . .'" Finally, in 2000, Sauerwein made a brilliant move. That year, she cashed in all of the stocks in her husband's 401(k),

sweeping the money into a money market account: "At that point the account had gone down less than 5 percent, but I just had a strong feeling that
there had to be a significant downturn," she recalled.

In 2002, Sauerwein was back to social work full-time. Like virtually
everyone else, she had taken losses in the crash. "In the last year, I delayed
too long in selling some of those positions in my own account because I
didn't want to be stuck with taxes," she confessed. "Big mistake. And I held
on to GE. But I can't complain, I did okay. At least I moved the money in
James's 401(k). We calculated that if I hadn't, we would have lost $150,000.
And I sold anything in my own account that was on margin long ago. I've
had so many friends who have had margin calls."[7]

Because Sauerwein had gotten so much of her money out before the
market unraveled, she managed to hold on to the bulk of her gains. At that
point, she had no intention of gambling with her profits. "Sometimes when
my husband watches *Wall $treet Week with Louis Rukeyser* on TV he says,
'We should get back in,'" Shirley reported in 2002. "But I say no. I'm
pretty firm," she added pleasantly. "Guys like to talk about stocks, but I
think a lot of what they say is just false knowledge."

After a moment's thought, she chuckled softly, "James's best position is
being married to me."

The 401(k)—A "Tattered Promise"

Unfortunately, most 401(k) investors were not married to Shirley Sauerwein. Instead, Vanguard's study revealed that if you pooled the experiences
of all 401(k) investors—young and old, rich and poor—it turned out that
more than 70 percent lost at least one-fifth of their savings during the three
years ending December 31, 2002, with 45 percent of those surveyed losing
more than one-fifth.[8]

An astounding number of media pundits seemed to think that this was
good news. "401(k) plan participants are not suffering too much," *Business
Week* concluded after perusing Vanguard's numbers. CBS trotted out an expert who offered some head-in-the-sand advice: "Don't focus on the dollar
amount you've lost . . . investors need to look at their losses relative to the
whole market," he said.[9] In 2002, for instance, while the market lost a grisly
22 percent, the average portfolio in the Vanguard's survey fell by just 13
percent. This was the good news. Forget the fact that 13 percent of

$200,000 is $26,000. Just think of it in the abstract—13 percent versus 22 percent. Once again, "relative returns" were being used to mask real losses. But investors would not be able to retire on relative returns.

CBS was not alone in trying to take an upbeat view. Even in a brutal bear market, the media continued to tell investors what they wanted to hear: "Don't worry—you're doing just fine." Some pointed out that if you counted the fresh money that employers and employees were continuing to contribute to 401(k) accounts, things were not as bad as they seemed. In fact, the Vanguard study showed that the average account's balance actually grew by 1 percent in 2002, with the new money making up for the 13.3 percent loss.

In other words, investors were pouring fresh money into a large sieve. But this is not how the media pitched the story. And no doubt, many investors felt better. "After hearing dreary news about the stock market throughout 2002, investors may have been relieved to see 401(k) year-end balances higher than 2001's," noted Gail Marks Jarvis, a columnist at the St. Paul, Minnesota, *Pioneer Press*. "But," she pointed out, "investors weren't truly insulated from the stock market's treachery. The regular pay-check contributions simply masked the losses."

The fact that new money camouflaged losses might be one reason why, in contrast to corporate insiders, most investors did not bail out. "Account balances are a common way participants monitor investment results," said Stephen Utkus, principal of the Vanguard Center for Retirement Research. "They are, in effect, the partially rose-colored glasses through which participants have viewed the recent dismal results of the U.S. equity market." [10]

So, in February of 2003, Vanguard's report showed that, on average, 401(k) investors still had 64 percent of their savings committed to stocks. Granted, portfolios were more balanced than they had been in 1999, when investors had 73 percent of their savings riding on equities. But this did not mean that investors had made a conscious decision to diversify. Over three years, the bear had rebalanced their portfolios for them. Meanwhile, the Vanguard study revealed that investors seemed frozen, neither buying nor selling stocks or stock funds.

Jennifer Postlewaithe was an exception. By the summer of 2003, she was back in the market. Postlewaithe was the investor who had turned a $90,000 nest egg into $500,000 in the six years following her 1994 divorce. Her husband, a history professor, had never been interested in the market.

But Postlewaithe had watched a neighbor build a fat portfolio, and she had always been eager to try her hand.

"I was so proud of myself. Here I was, independent for the first time in my life, investing my own money," Postlewaithe recalled. At the beginning, she researched companies like Dell by reading Value Line, but as she became more confident, she became bolder. By 2000, she was investing online and buying companies that she heard about on CNBC. All of her money was in stocks, and most of it was in technology. At that point, she also began buying "on margin"—borrowing money from her online broker so that she could purchase more shares.

When the Nasdaq meltdown began in the spring of 2000, Postlewaithe was visiting relatives in England. She read about the Nasdaq's plunge, but she assumed it was a temporary correction. Meanwhile, her portfolio served as the collateral for her margin debt, and as its value fell, so did the amount that she was allowed to borrow. Within a very short time, she was over her limit. While she was still traveling, her broker began selling her positions in order to pay off the excess debt. This was perfectly legal, and Postlewaithe was quick to admit that it was her own fault that she hadn't kept track of her margin balance while she was traveling. Nevertheless, the results were disastrous.

Within a very short time, Postlewaithe had lost roughly 60 percent of her savings. "The one good thing is that I had sold some of my Dell shares six months earlier to purchase a small house in New Zealand," she recalled. "I sent the money to my brother, who lives there, and after he purchased the house for me, I asked him to take the money that was left over and put it into New Zealand stocks and bonds. The bonds were paying 8.5 percent, and the stocks have gone up by about 35 percent since I bought them," she reported in 2003. "It's the old story—I was lucky to have eggs in more than one basket."

As for her U.S. accounts, "Like many others, I don't like to look at my statements," Postlewaithe admitted. "Fortunately, some of my money was in an IRA—and with a retirement account, they don't let you buy on margin. So my losses in the IRA weren't as steep." But in 2003, she was still carrying margin debt in her taxable account. "Because I have so little left I've decided to ride it out and not pay off my margin debt," she explained in July. "I'm praying that the market will continue to go up. As you know, the profit is greater when you're on margin because you're leveraged."

And, although she preferred not to open her statements, she did continue to trade. "I must admit, I still love it," she said. "So many companies are wriggling along in a fairly flat line that I have found I can buy on the dips and sell on the rises—sometimes in the same day. I find that on days when earnings are reported, if the company beats the analysts' estimates, and I buy at, say, 9:35 A.M., I can make $1 or so a share."

"I do it because I need to build my accounts up and also because I really enjoy it," she added. "Is it gambling? I suppose it is a somewhat educated guess. I do a little more research than I was doing at the market's high, but I confess I just take a look at a chart of the company's share price, do a quick reading of what they produce, and that's it."[11]

Jim Tucci, by contrast, washed his hands of the market. In March of 2002, he sold a portfolio of equities that had once been worth $600,000, clearing just $121,000. "At one point if you included the stocks and an investment property that I owned, I had been a millionaire—with a high school education," said Tucci. "When I was raising a family, I worked two jobs for 13 years—finally I became national sales manager of my company."

Now, all he had to show for his efforts was $121,000. But Tucci did not dwell on the past. Instead, in 2003, he decided to put his financial house in order. He sold the investment property—a condo on Boston's Beacon Hill—and used the proceeds to pay off the mortgage on his home. His nest egg had shrunk, but at least he was debt free. Then the New Economy struck again. In April of 2003, at age 61, he was laid off. Jim Tucci was now part of the "jobless recovery" that all but inevitably follows a long period of overinvestment.

In the first half of 2003, a rally offered hope that the market might give back what the bear had taken way. But Jim Tucci would not get back into the market. "I'm sure as heck not going to buy anything," he said, "And even if I were, who would I listen to for advice? No one seems to even give off a whiff of honesty about any of this stuff."[12]

Even buy-and-hold investors who had stuck with the program were realizing that it could take a long time to dig out of the hole. In June of 2003, Bloomberg's usually optimistic mutual fund columnist, Chet Currier, acknowledged that, by his reckoning, since October of 2002, investors had regained only about $2.21 trillion of the $7.41 trillion erased from their net worth between March 2000 and October 2002. (Somehow, no one ever talked about the savings lost before March of 2000.)[13]

While investors waited to recoup lost paper gains, they squandered the opportunity to make money by putting their cash to work elsewhere. For example, if an investor sold stock worth $100,000 in June of 2000 and shifted into a diversified portfolio of municipal bonds, Treasuries, foreign bonds, gold, and real estate investment trusts, he stood a decent chance of averaging at least 7 percent a year over those three years. At that rate, his $100,000 would have grown to nearly $125,000. By contrast, the Vanguard study suggested that the typical investor who sat on a $100,000 portfolio of stock from 2000 to 2002 had wound up with $80,000—or less.[14]

In fact, by 2002, roughly 40 percent of all investors age 40 to 59 showed balances of less than $50,000 in their 401(k), an Employee Benefit Research Institute survey revealed. Less than one-fourth reported having more than $100,000 in their retirement accounts. The grand illusion of the nineties—that hordes of small investors were on their way to becoming millionaires—was much like the "reality TV" born of the same decade. It was make-believe.

By 2003, observers had begun questioning the basic premise behind 401(k)s: the notion that employees could be their own pension managers. *The Wall Street Journal* noted that the Zeitgeist was shifting: while a 401(k) might work well "for the 15% to 20% of the population that has the know-how and desire" to take control of their retirement savings, many investors wanted more help. "Time to Turn Over the Reins?" the *Journal* asked. Spotting an opportunity, in the spring of 2003, Fidelity introduced a new service that let workers turn over management of their account to professionals—in return, of course, for an extra fee.

By now, it was becoming clear that, for many investors, 401(k) accounts would never match the nest eggs they would have had under a traditional pension system. In 2002, Edward N. Wolff, a New York University economist, did the math: to produce the equivalent of a $20,000 annual company pension at the age of 65, a 401(k) investor would need to have accumulated $200,000 in savings by age 50. At the time, the 401(k) accounts of households in the 47-to-64 age group averaged only $69,000. The most desirable solution to the problem, Wolff suggested, "may be to re-establish the [old-fashioned] pension system."[15]

But in 2003, it did not appear likely that employers were going to agree to switch back to what was, for them, a more costly alternative. Moving in precisely the opposite direction, they were cutting back funding of their 401(k)s. Companies like Goodrich, Textron, Goodyear, Ford Motors, and Charles Schwab had already announced that they were temporarily reducing or suspending their matching contributions.

All in all, the *Journal* reported, "the 401(k) is looking increasingly like a tattered promise." [16]

ON WALL STREET

In Lower Manhattan, the big losers were the brokers, bankers, traders, money managers, and analysts who lost their jobs as the financial world downsized. Some were laid off, others left under a cloud. By the spring of 2003, Frank Quattrone, the Credit Suisse First Boston banker who had taught Mary Meeker how to spot an IPO, was being investigated for possible criminal obstruction of justice. In March he resigned from CSFB.

In contrast to the average individual investor, many of Wall Street's pros still had the nest egg they had accumulated during the boom. Their bonuses were not paper gains; they could not be restated. Some used the money to bet on the market and lost much of it. But many pros agreed with Paul Scharfer, the venture capitalist who, in 1997, had confided: "I have a favorite saying, 'Make money on Wall Street, bury it on Main Street. Take it out of harm's way.' " [17] If you lived behind the scenes on Wall Street, it was harder to suspend disbelief.

A few prescient money managers, such as Fidelity Magellan's former manager Jeff Vinik, and the Acorn Funds' skeptical founder, Ralph Wanger, made a graceful exit. As noted, Vinik dissolved his hedge fund while he was still on a roll, in the fall of 2000. Wanger sold his fund company in February of the same year—a month before the Nasdaq's meltdown began—and put all of the money in bonds. Asked if he had timed the market, Wanger replied:

"Well, I guess we did. Eventually," he added, "the grown-ups win." [18]

THE GURUS AND THE GREEK CHORUS

Gail Dudack also landed on her feet, setting up her own shop as managing director of research at SunGard Institutional Brokerage. Meanwhile, as fate would have it, in March of 2002, Lou Rukeyser was summarily sacked from his own show in much the same way that he had disposed of Dudack.

Rukeyser was blindsided when the *Baltimore Sun* broke the news that

Maryland Public Television and AOL Time Warner's *Fortune* magazine were poised to create a new *Wall $treet Week*—without Rukeyser: "I was unaware of any of this until yesterday," he later told Dow Jones newswires. "Most people who have heard that MPT [Maryland Public Television] is going to try do *Wall $treet Week with Louis Rukeyser* without Louis Rukeyser think it must be somebody's idea of a bad April Fool's joke," he added.

It turned out that Rukeyser and Maryland Public Television had, in fact, been negotiating over Rukeyser's role on the program. "The reality is this," Rukeyser ultimately acknowledged, reading from a prepared statement, "MPT is my partner, and I decided we had to make changes and we were going to work together on what those changes should be when they decided unilaterally not to proceed with me as the host of the show I created, wrote and maintained for 32 years.

"They then tried to get me to remain with the program in a senior-commentator capacity, but I decided I didn't want to have anything further to do with them. Since then, my phone has been off the hook with alternative offers, and I will certainly consider all of them."

Rukeyser did just that and quickly found a new home—at CNBC.[19] Many saw it as a perfect match.

In the meantime, Alan Bond, "that old Dartmouth basketball player" Rukeyser had chosen to replace Dudack on *Wall $treet Week*'s elves' panel, wound up in jail. In 2003, Bond was sentenced to 12½ years for cheating clients and taking kickbacks from brokers.[20] As for Ed Kerschner, the market strategist who had slid into Dudack's chair at UBS Warburg, he remained ebullient: in June of 2003, he predicted that corporate earnings would grow 6.3 percent by the end of the year.[21] A month later, UBS Warburg announced that Kerschner, 50, would be retiring at the end of the year "to pursue other interests."

Though never Kerschner's equal as a cheerleader, in the summer of 2003 Abby Cohen remained optimistic, forecasting 10,800 on the Dow and 1150 on the S&P 500. Yet she sounded cautious: her prediction for corporate earnings came in below the Wall Street consensus.[22]

In June of 2003, newsletter writers such as Richard Russell, Jim Grant, David Tice, Kathryn Welling, and Marc Faber still expected a long bear winter. Steve Leuthold, by contrast, was bullish over the short term. "We're invested balls-to-the-wall, right now," Leuthold reported cheerfully. But he made it clear that he viewed the upturn as a trading opportunity. He did not think that it was the beginning of a long-term bull market.[23]

THE CEOs

Inevitably, many investors wanted someone to blame. Most were willing to acknowledge that in the end, the decision to buy had been theirs: "I read everything—I thought I knew what I was doing," a 34-year-old well-educated New Yorker who booked guests for a television network later confided. "But I didn't," she confessed, coloring slightly, still surprised at how everything could have gone so wrong.[24]

Still, they were angry—at the CEOs who absconded with their savings, at the analysts who slapped a "buy" recommendation on virtually every stock in sight, at the talking heads who had assured them if the Fed just cut rates one more time, all problems would be solved.

Congressmen, in particular, enjoyed berating CEOs, especially when the cameras were rolling. Some, like Senator Carl Levin, a longtime advocate of subtracting the cost of options from profits, pushed for genuine reform. Many senators and congressmen now stood with him, including Senator Shelby, now chairman of the Senate Banking Committee, and Senator John McCain, an influential Republican who had run for his party's presidential nomination. The Council of Institutional Investors—the leading organization representing large investors like pension funds—had opposed reform in 1994 but now supported it.

No matter. In 2002, Senators Levin and McCain proposed two different amendments to the Sarbane Oxley bill, legislation passed after the Enron debacle requiring stricter corporate disclosure. Their proposal called for options reform. But in each case, corporate lobbyists were able to block the amendments, preventing them from ever coming to an actual vote. In 2003, FASB, the independent board charged with overseeing accounting standards, issued its own proposal for reform and sent it out for public comment. The board hoped to finalize a new options accounting standard early in 2004.

In the spring of 2002, in the wake of revelations that executives at companies such as Enron, Tyco, and WorldCom had been looting their firms while frosting their books, President Bush made a special trip to Wall Street to express his outrage. But, as *The New York Times'* Floyd Norris pointed out, while "his words were harsh . . . his proposals were generally not. . . . Bush challenged companies to stop lending money to their executives, but made no proposals to restrict such loans by law or to increase what companies must now disclose about the loans." He called on chief executives to explain their own pay packages, "'prominently and in plain English,'" Norris noted, "but he called for no new disclosures, let alone limits on executive compensation."[25]

Cynics could not help but enjoy all of the political posturing: "When George W. Bush went to Wall Street and delivered his speech about corporate reform in front of a banner that read 'Corporate Responsibility,' I thought: it doesn't get any better than this," Michael Lewis confided to his readers. "It was as if Bill Clinton had flown to Las Vegas to deliver a speech in front of a banner that read 'Sexual Abstinence.'

"But I was wrong. It did get better," he continued. "Tipped off by a friend, I went to the C-Span Web site and watched the tape of Monday's hearings of the House Financial Services Committee. The committee, previously known mainly as a good place to attract campaign funds from Wall Street, dragged before it for a public whipping the cast of WorldCom Inc. There, as [Salomon telecom analyst] Jack Grubman and [WorldCom CEO] Bernie Ebbers stared stoically into the middle distance, California's Maxine Waters referred to the corrupt research reports of a Street investment bank she called 'Salomon Barney Frank!' [confusing the name of the Wall Street firm with the name of Congressman Barney Frank]. And she was reading from a prepared statement," Lewis noted.[26]

It is not that Lewis felt particular sympathy for Ebbers or Grubman— just that he realized the finger-pointing was Washington's way of ignoring the larger, structural problems. The CEOs brought before Congress had not caused the market to crash. In fact, by exaggerating their earnings, they helped keep a wildly overpriced market afloat. And they were not the only ones. Everyone was part of the dance, as Ralph Wanger had pointed out. But now, Washington, Wall Street, and Main Street wanted someone to blame.

This, too, was part of the cleansing ritual that follows any financial frenzy, as John Kenneth Galbraith had noted in *A Short History of Financial Euphoria*. Galbraith explained that there are two reasons why the public focuses on a few individuals when assessing blame: "In the first place, many people and institutions have been involved, and whereas it is acceptable to attribute error, gullibility and excess to a single individual or even to a particular corporation, it is not deemed fitting to attribute them to a whole community, and certainly not to the whole financial community. Widespread naivete, even stupidity, is manifest; mention of this however, runs drastically counter to the . . . presumption that intelligence is intimately associated with money. The financial community must be assumed to be intellectually above such extravagance of error."

The second reason, Galbraith explained, is that investors are reluctant to admit that the market itself could have been wrong, allowing stocks to trade at ridiculous prices for a significant period of time. Those who believe in an efficient market insist that the market itself must be "a neutral and accurate reflection of external influences: it is not supposed to be subject to an inherent and internal dynamic of error," Galbraith observed. "This is the classical faith. So there is a need to find some cause for the crash, however far fetched, that is external to the market itself. Or some abuse of the market that has inhibited its normal performance."[27]

In other words, while individuals can be fingered, few wish to recognize the systemic problem in corporate accounting that, in the Levy Center's words, had infected not just a few apples, but "the whole bushel."[28]

Similarly, while individual money managers might be roundly criticized for taking too many chances, the mutual fund industry as a whole escaped widespread blame. Few questioned why so many fund managers were forced to stay fully invested—even when it became clear that the market was tanking. "We have a special relationship with corporate America," one industry executive explained privately.[29] If his firm's funds began withdrawing capital from overpriced stocks, the firm would be violating that special tie. He said nothing about a special relationship with the customers who invested in his firm's products.

THE ANALYSTS

As the market fell apart, Wall Street's analysts became the most logical targets. "Where was the research?" the media asked. In fact, the financial press had been aware, for many years, that Wall Street research was tainted by the Street's interest in selling stocks, drumming up investment banking business, and remaining in the good graces of large institutional clients who owned those stocks. This was not a problem that popped up at the end of the bull market. Even in the eighties, sell recommendations had become rare.

As the bull market spun out of control, some journalists threw a spotlight on Wall Street's hidden agenda. In 1998, for example, in a story headlined "Who Can You Trust? Wall Street's Spin Game," *Business Week*'s Jeffrey Laderman told the story of Thomas K. Brown, a top-ranked regional banking analyst at Donaldson, Lufkin & Jenrette with 15 years' experience. Recently Brown had been fired. "His sin? He was an outspoken critic of banks that had paid heavily to amass huge empires without much to show for their money," Laderman reported. "I believed many of the acquisitions are destroying shareholder value," said Brown.

DLJ had been trying to break into the top ranks of investment banking, and Brown was not seen as an asset, Laderman explained. DLJ offered Brown a $450,000 exit package in exchange for an agreement that he not talk about the firm for five years. He turned it down.

And this was but one of a number of stories that ran in widely read newspapers and magazines in the late nineties, exposing the limits of Wall Street research.[30] But while the market was going up, these stories barely created a ripple. It was not until after the indices tanked, at the very end of 2000, that a series of scathing articles by *New York Times* columnist Gretchen Morgenson finally caught the public's attention.[31] Now, suddenly, the media was horrified. CNBC's anchors began to needle their guests. Closing the barn door, it seemed that the press could not write enough stories about the Wall Street analysts who had led investors astray.

Allan Sloan would have none of it. Sloan did not hold Wall Street analysts in particularly high regard; he did his own research. But he was struck by the hypocrisy of the media's attack:

"WE wrote about these people," Allan Sloan exclaimed, while accepting the Loeb Prize, the Pulitzer of financial journalism, in June of 2001. "And now we say they're guilty; it's their fault. I mean, come on, we're responsible.

"Instead, it's 'let's-find-a-villain.' And now, supposedly, people like Mary Meeker and Henry Blodget are the villains; they're the people who sowed the madness in America; they're the ones who cost people billions of dollars.

"Now, forgive me," Sloan continued, "I don't remember reading about Mary Meeker invading a newsroom with a gun and saying, 'Write about me or die.' I don't remember Henry Blodget saying, 'I've got your children hostage and unless you write about my idiotic prediction that Amazon is going to $400 a share, you'll be getting pieces of the kids back in envelopes.' Nobody did any of that."[32]

HENRY BLODGET

Somehow, as the lynch mob gathered, Henry Blodget became the designated scapegoat for the entire analytic community. Of the thousands of analysts who recommended lemons, Blodget was singled out to wear the scarlet *A*. By 2002, it became virtually impossible to read a story about any analyst without seeing his name mentioned.

Finally, in April of 2003, the mob handed down its sentence. Blodget would pay $4 million and be barred from the securities industry for life. The judgment capped an investigation launched by the National Association of Securities Dealers. The crime, as *The Wall Street Journal* described it, was that Blodget "privately harbored doubts" about companies that he recommended.[33] In other words, he was convicted of having impure thoughts. In the settlement, Blodget neither admitted nor denied wrongdoing. At 37, he was still a very young man; the ban from the brokerage business left him without a career.

This is not to say that Blodget did not make some fatal mistakes. The first was to take the position as Merrill Lynch's Internet "ax"—a job plainly described in the press at the time, with conflict of interest built in. He had explicitly been hired to recommend stocks while bringing in the IPO business that Merrill badly needed.[34]

But of the constellation of star analysts who recommended overpriced stocks, why was Henry Blodget punished? Some would say because his e-mails proved that he did not believe his own recommendations. But unless one assumes that the rest of Wall Street's analytic community was consuming large quantities of mood elevators that they did not share with Henry, the same could be said of almost anyone who was recommending stocks trading at 40 or 50 or 300 times earnings. All but the most deluded knew that a clock was ticking. But, as one analyst explained, "you knew the stock was overvalued—and you also knew it was going to go up." No one could predict precisely when investors would stop answering the chain letter. And if an analyst was "early" in predicting a stock's demise, small investors would be no more forgiving than larger clients.

Why, then, Henry Blodget? Harvey Eisen, who ran money for Sandy Weill at Traveler's before forming his own firm, Bedford Oak Partners, offered the simplest, and probably the most accurate, answer: "Wall Street needed a tar baby."[35]

Granted, Salomon telecom analyst Jack Grubman was tarred and feathered, too. In a separate settlement, Grubman agreed to pay $15 million, without admitting or denying wrongdoing, and, like Blodget, he was barred from the securities industry for life. But Grubman had already enjoyed a full career—and in his case, the choice seemed less arbitrary. Grubman was not just an analyst; he had helped to run corporations such as Global Crossing and WorldCom, companies engaged in world-class fraud.[36] Like Frank Quattrone, the investment banker who became the emperor of Silicon Valley, Grubman wielded an enormous amount of power. And he understood precisely what was going on.

Far from being an innocent, Grubman possessed a competitive killer instinct that Andy Kessler—who counted himself as one of Grubman's friends—described in *Wall Street Meat*. At one point, the firm where both worked decided to turn a corporate retreat into a costume party. Before becoming an analyst, Grubman had enjoyed a brief career as a boxer, and "came dressed in bright red shorts and a yellow cape, wearing boxing shoes and gloves," Kessler recalled. "About halfway through the party I borrowed padded gloves from someone dressed as a lacrosse player and started boxing with Jack. It started playfully enough, but then I landed a left jab on his face and he decided to teach me a lesson. I covered up like Ali playing rope-a-dope with Foreman, but Jack just beat the crap out of me, with a sick grin on his face."[37] And at the time, Kessler was a colleague, a drinking buddy, and a friend.

Blodget, by contrast, was a far less aggressive player. He also possessed a nice sense of self-irony. Blodget realized, even at the time, that he was a five-minute celebrity. "He wore his fame so easily," said a Wall Street veteran who had seen many a guru come and go. Moreover, Blodget's overly optimistic projections did much less damage than Grubman's equally rosy estimates, in part because his reign proved so brief. Blodget stumbled into the spotlight with his Amazon.com forecast in November of 1998 and left Merrill Lynch three years later in November of 2001. To be sure, at the height of his career, Blodget began to rival Morgan Stanley's Mary Meeker as the Street's top Internet seer. But why was he barred from the industry, while Meeker—who served openly both as Morgan Stanley's top Internet investment banker and its top Internet analyst—escaped punishment? Meeker's reign lasted longer, and she was a much more successful rainmaker, bringing in far more IPO business than Blodget ever did.

Indeed, in 2000, Meeker reportedly helped raise close to $425 million

in investment-banking revenue—more than any other Morgan Stanley analyst, and more than twice what she had attracted in 1999. As a stock
picker, she did not do quite as well. That year, according to *The Wall Street
Journal*, Meeker ranked 70th out of 111 analysts. Nevertheless, in 2003,
when Morgan Stanley reorganized its research department, it named
Meeker "co-head" of technology sector research, not just in the U.S., but
globally.[38]

By the summer of 2003, a number of Wall Street analysts had been
charged with securities law violations, but Meeker escaped legal censure.

Some said Meeker was not hunted down because she was a woman.
Others claimed that Morgan Stanley circled its wagons around her while
Merrill Lynch hung Blodget out to dry. When the IPO business faded,
Merrill realized that it no longer needed an Internet star. The firm offered
Blodget a buyout and cut him loose. By contrast, Morgan Stanley kept
Meeker warm and safe, inside the herd.

But some observers believed that the real reason that Mary Meeker escaped both persecution and prosecution is that Eliot Spitzer did not need
her. He already had Blodget.

ELIOT SPITZER

An ambitious politician, New York State Attorney General Eliot Spitzer
had his eyes on the governor's mansion in Albany. To get there, he needed
publicity. In other words, he needed a crusade. In a 2003 interview, Spitzer
cast himself as the individual investor's savior: "I was the only person who
tried to protect the small investor," he declared.[39]

Why, then, did he wait until after the small investor had lost his savings? "According to Spitzer, his interest in Wall Street research dates back
many years, to conversations with his old friend Jim Cramer," Michael
Lewis noted in his Bloomberg column. "Many years ago, Cramer showed
his law school classmate the shocking truth that big Wall Street firms were
simply giant machines for peddling securities, irrespective of their value,
and not disinterested research institutes devoted to the pursuit of the
truth."

So when Spitzer became attorney general in November of 1998, he
knew how Wall Street worked. At that point, "it would have taken some
guts, and might even have done some good, to call attention to the conflicts

of interest and intellectual dishonesty in Wall Street research," Lewis observed. "Now it has no effect on anything important. The time for regulatory courage has long since passed."[40] The money already had been lost, and investors no longer were inclined to confuse hype with hope. The most bullish analysts already had been widely discredited.

But from a politically opportunistic point of view, 2002 was the perfect time for an attorney general to stand up and take an interest in skullduggery on Wall Street. While the market was rising, no one wanted him to rain on his or her parade. Now, investors and voters were fully prepared to be indignant.

Moreover, from Spitzer's point of view, Blodget offered an easy target. The e-mail trail showed that he was skeptical about many of the stocks he recommended and was becoming resentful of the pressure to push them. In truth, the e-mails revealed his honesty: Blodget was not comfortable in his role. But that was not how Spitzer interpreted them, and not how he used them. Somehow, Blodget's e-mails were leaked to *The Wall Street Journal.* In a 2003 interview, Spitzer denied that his office was responsible.[41] In any case, the e-mails put Eliot Spitzer, champion of the small investor, on the front page.

While protecting the little guy, Spitzer also avoided tangling with the big boys. Who had hired Blodget and given him his marching orders? Someone higher up at Merrill had decided that the firm needed an Internet analyst who could bring in banking business. Where were their e-mails—hadn't they ever put the idea in writing? What about Merrill's CEO, David Komansky?

Blodget's role, after all, was well known around the firm. "At some point during the many conferences Merrill Lynch held for its investors and brokers, the bosses invariably wheeled Blodget in to speak rapidly and with total certainty about the wisdom of sinking money into Internet stocks," Lewis pointed out. "And the bosses did well by Blodget. By [compensation expert] Graef Crystal's calculations, Merrill Chief Executive David Komansky was able to pay himself $32.6 million in 1999 (up from $12 million in 1998) and $34.5 million in 2000, in large part because of the huge sums of money Merrill's Internet group brought in.

"If you must lynch somebody," Lewis wrote, "why not Komansky?"

The answer was all too obvious. "If Spitzer went after Komansky himself—if he didn't permit Komansky the pleasant fiction that he is shocked by Blodget's behavior—Spitzer would be far less likely to get a quick and politically useful settlement. What he would get is a war. He might win that war but not without doing a great deal of damage to himself. And damaging himself is the one thing Eliot Spitzer will not do."[42]

If Eliot Spitzer were interested in serious reform on Wall Street, he might have brought a criminal indictment against Merrill Lynch. That would be war. That was precisely what former New York Mayor Rudolph Giuliani had done in the late eighties when, as a young federal prosecutor, he was laying the groundwork for his political career. Giuliani indicted Drexel Burnham Lambert on racketeering charges. The firm went bankrupt.

But Spitzer was far less feisty than Giuliani. "We didn't want to bring the firm down," he said in 2003. Yet in an earlier interview with *The New Yorker*'s John Cassidy, Spitzer admitted, "The problems were structural. Everybody [on Wall Street] had permitted analysts to become appendages to the investment-banking system." This was why, Spitzer explained, "it didn't seem reasonable to drop the criminal ax on Merrill Lynch because of this."[43]

Yet it did seem reasonable to drop the ax on Henry Blodget.

Meanwhile, Rudy Giuliani, the man known for cleaning up Wall Street in the eighties, demonstrated his talents as a switch-side debater. By 2002, Giuliani had set up a consulting firm and was now representing Merrill Lynch, informally pleading its case with Spitzer. On Monday, April 8, the very day that two members of Spitzer's staff went to the state supreme court to get an order requiring Merrill Lynch to hand over documents, Giuliani spoke to Spitzer on Merrill's behalf.

In 2003, Spitzer said that he "wouldn't go into the details of the conversation," but Giuliani, it seems, was pitching the notion that Merrill had been a "good corporate citizen" because it stayed in New York City after the September 11, 2001, attack on the World Trade Center. What that had to do with the case at hand was totally unclear.

Spitzer agreed and claimed that he was not persuaded.[44] But, that afternoon, when the SEC told him that his court order could disrupt large parts of Merrill's business, Spitzer immediately sent his lieutenants back to the judge, to ask the court to stay the order.[45] Spitzer and Merrill would try to reach a settlement. After all, Eliot Spitzer simply wanted to make a point.

"Henry Blodget was one very small cog in a corrupt system," he acknowledged in 2003.[46] But Spitzer's mission was to get the cog, not to upset the system.

In the end, Spitzer's investigation of Wall Street research was settled, over dinner, at Tiro a Segno, an Italian club on MacDougal Street in Manhattan's Little Italy.

There, Spitzer, Harvey Pitt, the SEC commissioner who followed Arthur Levitt (before resigning amidst a scandal over his own possible conflict of interest), Robert Glauber, chairman of the National Association of Securities Dealers, and Dick Grasso, the chairman of the NYSE, broke bread. In addition to his duties at the NYSE, Grasso served on Merrill Lynch's board.

A few weeks later, the group met again, in Washington, D.C., at the Georgetown Club, where, Cassidy reported, "they reached an outline agreement on the sort of settlement they wanted to arrive at." Asked if he didn't feel that he was sitting down with the foxes to decide how to redesign the henhouse, Spitzer expressed outrage, while simultaneously insisting that he did not understand the question.[47]

In a blaze of publicity, Spitzer and Merrill eventually reached an agreement. Merrill Lynch would pay a fine of $100 million—"less than one third of what the firm paid for office supplies and postage last year," Bill Moyers noted on *NOW,* his current affairs series on PBS. "And the IRS told us yesterday that both the company's penalty and legal fees may be tax-deductible. A business expense for deceiving the public," Moyers remarked.[48]

LOOKING AHEAD: WHAT FINANCIAL CYCLES MEAN FOR THE 21ST-CENTURY INVESTOR

Despite three years of falling prices, which have significantly improved the attractiveness of common stocks, we still find very few that even mildly interest us. This dismal fact is testimony to the insanity of valuations reached during the Great Bubble. Unfortunately, the hangover may prove to be proportional to the binge.

The aversion to equities that Charlie and I exhibit today is far from congenital. We love owning common stocks—if they can be purchased at attractive prices. . . . But occasionally successful investing requires inactivity.

> —Warren Buffett explaining why he and his partner, Charlie Munger, remained unenthusiastic about stocks (with the S&P 500 trading at 848.17, the Dow at 8181), February 21, 2003[1]

"Over the long haul, U.S. stocks always outperform other investments."

"You can't time the market."

"Buy and hold."

These were the truisms of investing during the Great Bull Market of 1982–99—the conventional wisdom that stood investors in good stead for nearly two decades. Unfortunately, the rules that work superbly in one cycle can prove disastrous in the next.

Conventional wisdom, after all, is grounded in the experience of a particular time and place. As fickle as fashion, conventional wisdom masquerades as eternal truth. And we accept it as such. The consensus provides confidence, conviction, and a sense of community. (In that, it is much like CNBC.) In an era of sound bites, bromides easily become slogans, and the more often we repeat them, the less we think about them.

Conventional wisdom rarely stands the test of time. When tested against empirical data over decades, the popular wisdom of any era tends to fall apart. This is especially true in financial markets. There are no rules that work in all cycles. "Long-term investment success just isn't that simple," remarked a 63-year-old Steve Leuthold in 2000. If it were, there would be many more 60-year-olds on Wall Street.[2]

The most successful long-term investors are those who avoid becoming mesmerized by the week-to-week or month-to-month action of the markets, step back, and take a longer look at the larger cycles that drive a multi-faceted global economy. While one bull market cycle is ending, another is beginning somewhere else—in another sector, in another class of assets, or in another country. There is always someplace in the world to make money.

Even in the seventies, when both Treasuries and the S&P 500 disappointed, shrewd investors put their money to work by investing in real assets. From 1970 through 1980, oil returned an average of 34.7 percent, gold 31.6 percent, U.S. coins 27.7 percent, silver 23.7 percent, stamps 21.8 percent, Chinese ceramics 21.6 percent, U.S. farmland 14 percent, and housing 10.2 percent, staying nicely ahead of inflation in a decade when the consumer price index rose by an average of 7.7 percent a year.[3] Some of these investments could even be found in the U.S. stock market: energy stocks, for example, soared.

But in 1970, few investors were interested in oil and gas. Most were still obsessed with the Nifty Fifty—the market darlings that were about to betray them—and failed to notice just how cheap commodities had become. The pattern is an old one. "When a major theme ends, tremendous undervaluation exists in other sectors, because all the money was flowing during the final, manic stage of the boom into just one major investment theme," Marc Faber, author of *Tomorrow's Gold*, observed in 2002. "While everyone's eyes are fixed on the cycle that is peaking, enormous opportunities arise elsewhere." Over the course of a 30-year career, Faber had watched the tide turn many times: "gold, oil and gas, and foreign currencies—these were the major investment themes of the 1970s; Japanese stocks in the 1980s; emerging markets between 1985 and 1997; and US equities in the nineties."[4]

A Swiss-born, multilingual investment advisor, Faber arrived in Hong Kong in 1973 at the age of 27, armed with a Ph.D. in economics from the University of Zurich and a passion for economic history. There, he worked for White, Weld & Co. until 1978, when the investment bank merged with Merrill Lynch. Faber then became managing director of Drexel Burnham Lambert's Hong Kong operation, a position he held until 1990, when he opened his own shop, Marc Faber Ltd. Throughout the nineties, he continued doing what he had been doing all along: managing money for some of Asia's wealthiest Chinese families while also writing *The Gloom, Boom and Doom Report,* a monthly financial newsletter read on four continents. By 2003, Faber had moved his business to Thailand, where he was learning a sixth language.

Over the years, Faber demonstrated a certain knack for spotting bubbles: In August of 1987, for example, he predicted that the Dow was headed for a nasty spill. That same year, he warned that Japan's market was poised for a crash. In 1994, he cautioned that markets in Southeast Asia were "grossly overvalued." And in October 1998, Faber called the top of the longest-running bull market in U.S. history. "From here on," he told readers, "we believe that volatility in Western financial markets will increasingly be on the downside—interrupted by huge bear market rallies—and lead to widespread losses. . . . It is our view that a major and long-term top in the Western stock markets is already behind us."

In each case, Faber was right. In October of 1987, the Dow took a drubbing—just three months after he sounded the alarm. In 1988, the Nikkei's plunge began, and from 1997 to 1998, Asia's tigers tanked, wiping out the gains of the preceding four years. Finally, in October of 1998, just as Faber surmised, the majority of U.S. stocks already had begun to slide from the heights achieved in '98, '97, or, in some cases, '96.

As a career path, being a prophet of doom has its limits. Luckily, Faber's fascination with history's financial cycles also helped him sight booms (which is why his wealthy Chinese clients entrusted him with their money). In the seventies, for instance, he began investing in South Korea and Taiwan; in the mid-eighties he put his clients' cash to work in the Philippines and Thailand; in the late eighties he moved into Latin America, and in

STOCKS FOR THE LONG RUN?

"The ratio of equity returns to returns on 30-year Treasuries is now back to the level of September 1980. In other words, a buy-and-hold investor would have done just as well holding Treasuries as investing in the S&P 500 over the past 22 years." —Martin Barnes, *The Bank Credit Analyst*, March 2003

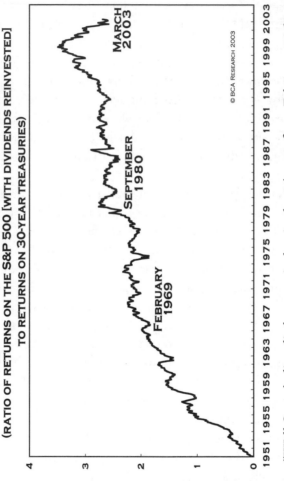

U.S. STOCK–TO –BOND TOTAL RETURN RATIO
(RATIO OF RETURNS ON THE S&P 500 [WITH DIVIDENDS REINVESTED]
TO RETURNS ON 30-YEAR TREASURIES)

© BCA RESEARCH 2003

"Wall Street's dirty little secret is that in the 34 years from February 1969 to March 2003 stocks outperformed long-term Treasuries by a paltry 1% a year, on average. This is a dismally small gap, given the extra volatility in stocks." —Martin Barnes, *The Bank Credit Analyst*, March 2003

1993 he bravely began buying Russian stocks. In other words, Faber rode Asia in the boom years, got out when those markets reached perilous heights, and began investing in Latin America and Russia—just when everyone else was piling into Asia's overvalued shares. In each case, his strategy was the same: move into a region when things look gloomy, wait for the boom, and get out before it turns into a bubble.

But by the late nineties, Faber believed stocks were overpriced in virtually every corner of the world. And in 1998, when he warned that the bull market in the United States had ended, Faber urged his readers to stash their savings in Treasuries. At the time, bonds held little appeal for most investors, but those who followed his advice flourished.[5]

Of course, Faber was not always right. By the end of 2000, he had cooled on the long bond: "The dollar has been so strong for so long that, inevitably, it will fall," he predicted. "And when it docs, foreigners, who own 37 percent of all Treasuries and 23 percent of all corporate bonds, will pull their money out." As it turned out, the dollar's decline would not begin for another two years, and as of June 2003, central banks abroad continued to support Treasuries—though a weaker dollar had begun to make U.S. stocks less attractive to some foreign investors. But while Faber's advice to move out of the long bond was premature, the alternatives he suggested, "gold mining stocks, natural resource stocks, and highly rated municipal bonds," proved profitable for the next three years.[6]

And Faber would always rather be early than late. "The greater damage is always done during the final phase of a bull market," he observed. Instead of trying to ride a market to the very top, he would rather bail out before the final blow-off and concentrate his energies on finding the next investment theme. For the "greater the mania in one sector of a market, or in one stock market, the more likely that neglected asset classes elsewhere offer huge appreciation potential. This," said Faber, "is one of the cardinal rules of investing, and will always work for the patient long-term investor."[7] But first, an investor must shrug off the conventional wisdom of the previous era.

STOCKS FOR THE LONG RUN?

One of the most oversold "truths" of the eighties and nineties was that, over the long run, equities *always* outperform bonds. An entire generation of baby boomers was trained to believe that "bonds are boring." Real Men bought stocks. In the summer of 1998, when the bear staged a dress rehearsal for the crash of 1999–2000, more than one commentator advised that investors should shift part of their portfolio into bonds only if they couldn't take the stress of the stock market's volatility. In other words, if they were mildly unstable.

Ironically, during the very period when the cult of equities flourished, bonds were quietly enjoying their own magnificent bull market. Indeed, if an investor stashed half of his savings in long-term Treasuries in September of 1980, and half in the S&P 500, he would discover, in March of 2003, that the two portfolios had done equally well.

Even looking back over 34 years, from February 1969 through March of 2003, "stocks outperformed long-term Treasuries by a paltry 1% a year," noted Martin Barnes, editor of *The Bank Credit Analyst.* In other words, for 34 years an investor could have been sleeping soundly—or lying awake, making that extra 1 percent. Granted, when compounded over 34 years, 1 percent adds up, but the 1 percent was not guaranteed, making it "a dismally small gap, given the extra volatility in stocks," Barnes observed. This Barnes called "Wall Street's dirty little secret."[8] (See chart "Stocks for the Long Run?" on page 356.)

Wall Street preferred to keep investors' attention focused on equities. Selling stocks is, after all, a far more lucrative business than peddling plain-vanilla Treasuries, in part because transaction fees on equities are higher (especially now that investors can buy government bonds, commission-free, through www.treasurydirect.gov), in part because investors were willing to pay a premium to buy equities at a time when the potential gains seemed open-ended—in others words, in a raging bull market. Just as gamblers will pay more for a lottery ticket if the pot is very large, so in the nineties, equity investors accepted whatever fees Wall Street or the mutual fund industry cared to impose.

Finally, Barnes pointed out, the fact that the long bond kept pace with the stock market from 1980 to 2003 is not as unusual as the popular wisdom of the nineties might suggest. Looking back over 80 years or so of stock market history, he reported, "The only true golden periods for stock were the 1950s and 1960s. That was when stocks persistently outperformed bonds, with only occasional short-lived reversals."

"The key thing to note about this 'golden era' of equity outperformance," Barnes added, "is that it began when equities were very cheap: the

LONG-RUN RETURNS: STOCKS AND TREASURIES

	Stocks		Treasuries	
	Real Return	Starting Valuation	Real Return	Starting Valuation
1950–1969	11.7	Cheap	–2.1	Expensive
1969–1979	–2.5	Expensive	–2.5	Neutral
1980–2003	8.3	Cheap	8.3	Cheap

(SOURCE: MARTIN BARNES, THE BANK CREDIT ANALYST)

S&P 500 was trading at 7 times [the previous year's] reported earnings in 1950. Meanwhile, bonds were expensive because the long-term Treasury yield was pegged at around 2%, far below the underlying rate of inflation."

Treasuries, in turn, enjoyed their own golden period from 1980 to 2003—a cycle that began when they, too, sold for a song.

To be sure, 10- or 20-year returns can be deceiving: "If an investor had bought the S&P 500 in, say, January of 1982, and had the foresight to sell in January of 2000, his equity portfolio would have beaten his bond portfolio hands down," Barnes was quick to acknowledge.[9]

But he or she would have had to time the market. "Buy and hold" would not be enough.

"BUY AND HOLD"

Inevitably the question arises: What if an investor bought stocks in, say, 1995, held until 2010, and continued to invest in the S&P each month? Would "buy and hold" work?

No one knows. The real question comes down to this: Is the likely reward worth the risk? The danger is that, like a gambler in a casino, an investor who lost money after the bubble burst would think, "If I just stay a little longer, maybe I can make up for my losses . . ."

" 'Stocks for the long run' is an idea that has been drilled into the public—and the public has found it comforting," Peter Bernstein, author of *Against the Gods,* observed in the spring of 2003. "People say, 'I don't care if my stocks are down. In the long run, I'll be fine. But that's a leap of faith. It's not necessarily wrong—but it is a leap of faith."[10]

What made Bernstein's comment so notable is that in the early nineties he had written the foreword to a book that soon became the gospel for buy-and-hold investors, Jeremy Siegel's *Stocks for the Long Run: The Definitive Guide to Financial Market Returns and Long-Term Investment Strategies.*

By the spring of 2003, however, Bernstein believed that the old rules no longer applied. "For now, equities aren't the best place to be for the long run," he told Kathryn Welling in an interview published in *welling@ weeden.* "The long run here is not necessarily going to bail you out," Bernstein warned. "Or, even if it does, the margin by which equities will outperform could be too small to compensate for the volatility."[11]

But what of Siegel's argument that for more than 200 years, U.S. stocks have returned an average of 7 percent a year, after inflation? "The average dividend yield during all those 20-year periods that Jeremy [Siegel] looked at was over 4 percent," Bernstein replied. Capital gains contributed only 2.1 percent to that long-run 7 percent annual return. The rest was dividends. But in the spring of 2003, equities offered an average dividend yield of roughly 2 percent. "Which means that in order to achieve 7 percent real growth over the next 20 years, we'd need 5 percent real growth in earnings and dividends," said Bernstein, "and that's not exactly a reasonable expectation over the long run. Impossible, in fact."

The hard truth is that the market cannot grow that much faster than gross domestic product. In March of 2000, stocks were valued at 181 percent of GDP—up from 60 percent at the beginning of the decade.[12] Yet "over time," Bernstein noted, "real growth in earnings and dividends consistently lags long-run growth rates in real GDP—not just in the United States but in all other developed countries. Between 1900 and 2001, for instance, U.S. GDP growth averaged 3.3 percent in real terms, versus 1.5 percent earnings growth and just 1.1 percent dividend growth. And the U.S. economy was the most successful on the planet!" Bernstein added.

Of course, an investor could gamble that dividends would climb higher—or that investors would push price/earnings ratios back to stratospheric heights, boosting capital gains. "But that's *not* a risk I would want to take under current circumstances," said Bernstein in February of 2003, making it clear that whatever might happen over the short term, he was assessing prospects for the the long term (emphasis his).

Yet, Bernstein acknowledged, it would be extremely difficult for most

investors to realize that "the world has changed"—that they had entered a
new era of investing: "Boom and bust. That's a familiar pattern. So what is
expected is that after the bust, you pick up the pieces and go forward. That
this is different I think is hard to recognize. And people are reluctant to recognize it. In particular, the difference pulls them away from traditional
ways of managing their affairs. I mean, it doesn't occur to people to say,
'Now I have to do things differently.'

" 'Yes,' they think, 'I won't get caught in the next bubble, I'll get out
sooner.' But that's different from saying, 'The basic investment structure
that I've been using, which served me pretty well, is no longer appropriate.'
That's a big step.' "

"THE REAL HUMDINGERS"

Yet by failing to take that step, an investor could be walking into the bear's
den. The history of the stock market shows that magnificent bull markets
beget brutal bear markets. (See chart "The Market's Cycles 1882–2003" on
page 2.)

This is why, in the summer of 2003, *The Bank Credit Analyst's* Martin
Barnes was "not optimistic about stocks on a long-run basis. After a bubble
has burst, the classic pattern is for the market to trade sideways for years,"
he explained, pointing to a chart of past financial manias. (See chart "The
Profile of a Bubble," Appendix, page 460.)

History does not guarantee that bull and bear markets will be symmetrical. But both economics and investor psychology suggest that Warren
Buffett may well have been right when he predicted that "the hangover is
likely to be proportional to the binge." Bubbles, after all, are caused by too
much cash chasing one investment theme, leading to overinvestment followed by excess supply.[13] "By 1999 the cost of capital for technology stocks
was zero. When the cost of capital is zero—how many businesses do you
start? You're only limited by the waiting line to get lawyers and bankers to
do the paperwork," remarked Acorn Funds founder Ralph Wanger in
2003. "Whatever the idea is, it becomes a lousy idea if you dump enough
money into it. Now that all has to get unwound."[14]

That takes time. In the meantime capital spending dries up. When
supply exceeds demand, prudent businessmen see no reason to expand.
"Business spent $4.7 trillion on equipment and software from 1995 to

2000, 37 percent more than the prior six-year period. Now, utilization rates of this beefed up capacity are the lowest in 20 years," Martin Feldstein, the president and chief executive of the private National Bureau of Economic Research, warned in 2003.[15]

The Fed could pump liquidity into the economy, but it could not direct how it was used. In 2003, Kurt Richebächer, editor of *The Richebächer Letter*, measured just how much capital investment had slowed: "From the beginning of the U.S. economy's slowdown in the third quarter of 2000 until the fourth quarter of 2002, fixed investment by businesses in the nonfinancial sector fell $165.9 billion, or 12.9%." Over the same span, "consumer spending rose by 7.8% to $681.7 billion," he reported.

Trouble was, consumer spending could not build the base needed for a new bull market (though it could add to the mountain of consumer debt). The long-term growth and profits that an economy needs to create the foundation for a healthy stock market can come only from productive capital investments. This is what adds to the wealth of nations. An economy cannot *consume* its way out of a slump, Richebächer stressed—it needs to *produce.* Capital spending for the sake of spending (to create more profitless Internet sites, for example, or to produce more SUVs that then have to be sold with 0 percent financing and a rebate) will not help.

And until profits revive, there will be no reason for profitable businesses to boost their investments. In 2003, Richebächer reported, "profits are down 28.6% from their 2000 peak—and 36.4% from their 1997 peak." [16] This, in a nutshell, is the economic explanation of why it can be so difficult to pull out of a major bear market: until share prices reflect the underlying economic reality, there is no basis for a new bull market to begin.

Investor psychology also plays a role. As Charles Dow had observed: "There is always a disposition in people's minds to think the existing conditions will be permanent. When the market is down and dull, it is hard to make people believe that this is the prelude to a period of activity and advance. When prices are up and the country is prosperous," investors are even more loath to believe that the years of plenty will end.[17]

So, in the spring of 2003, "the interesting thing is that people haven't given up," noted Acorn's Ralph Wanger. "That's the real news. People haven't given up because the party was too good. How long will it take them? Before that happens, the stock market normally must revert to the mean—the historic average for stock prices. And, to do that, you have to spend some time below the mean—otherwise it's not a mean. We haven't even started doing that." [18]

The mean serves as the magnetic center of all cycles. Over the years, the S&P 500 has traded at an average of 14 to 15 times earnings. During booms, financial markets trade far above their mean; during busts, far below. "We've looked at the price history of every asset class—stocks, bonds, currencies, commodities—and we have not found any that didn't revert to its mean," reported GMO's Jeremy Grantham. "Whatever Greenspan does, whatever happens out there in the world, however strong the economy is, there is going to be a lot of pain. And then it will overrun its course.

"The really bad news is that all bubbles over-correct, and that the timing and extent of the over-corrections appear to be largely unknowable but they usually take several years," he added in June of 2003. [19]

Granted, the mean can move. Just because the S&P 500 has traded at 14–15 times earnings in the past doesn't mean that it always will. Changes in global economics and politics, could, over time, take the mean P/E on U.S. equities higher or lower. At the beginning of the 21st century, Jeremy Grantham believed that, with interest rates low, the mean might have migrated to 17½. But no one believed that the mean had risen to 31—or even 21.

Yet in June of 2003, the S&P fetched about 31 times earnings for the preceding 12 months, and roughly 19 times forecast earnings for the coming 12 months—if you believed the analysts' earnings estimates. [20] Stocks still were not cheap. This was the major reason why value investors such as Richard Russell or Warren Buffett feared that the bear market was far from over.

Price/earnings ratios offer one rough guide to the long-term returns that investors can reasonably expect. "History tells us that when you buy stocks with average P/Es on the S&P 500 under 10, then over the coming 10 years you'll receive a median return of 16.9%," Russell told his readers in June of 2003. By contrast, "when you buy stocks when P/Es are 16 to 17, over the coming 10 years your median return will be 10.7%. When you buy stocks when P/Es are 18 to 20 then over the coming 10 years your median return will be 7.5%. When you buy stocks when P/Es are 22, then over the coming 10 years your median return will be 5.0%.

"What about today? What can you expect if you buy stock here?" Russell asked early in the summer of 2003. With the S&P fetching more than

30 times trailing earnings, Russell's answer was: "Over the coming 10 years you'll probably show a loss."

P/E ratios are not the only signpost, Russell added. "Using a different method based on a 10-year average of previous earnings, Peter Bernstein has shown that if you buy stocks now the odds are that over the coming 10 years, your stocks will be down one-third on average from where they are today." [21]

Dividend yields also hinted that future returns were likely to prove paltry—especially since historically, dividends have made up such a large part of the stock market's total return. "When you look at past secular market bottoms, the P/E on stocks was 10 and the dividend yield was 5 percent. You can talk about stocks at 15 times earnings being good value, but if you go back to 1942, 1949, 1974, 1980, and 1982, you will find P/Es of 10 and 5 percent dividend yields. We are not even close to that," Ned Davis, founder of Ned Davis Research, an independent research firm, observed in June of 2003. "My guess is that, down the road, we'll be facing another leg down—a crash more like 1973–74." [22]

Davis was not alone. In the summer of 2003, old hands on Wall Street feared that the market had not yet touched bottom. After peaking, the average bear market in the last century has given back over five years of gains. If one assumed that the millennial boom peaked at the beginning of 2000, history suggested that the market could decline to 1995 levels. When 1995 began, the S&P stood at 459 and the Nasdaq at 751. As for the Dow, it began the year at 3834.

Five years is only a guess: history's averages cover a broad range, and no two bear markets are alike. Each is unhappy in its own way. Nevertheless, those who believed big booms beget big busts worried that before the bear was done, the market would plunge below '95 levels. When the bear market of 1966–82 found its low watermark in 1974, it gave back eight years of gains.

At that point, investor psychology all but guaranteed that it would take many years to build a base for a new bull market. In a classic bear market, investors go through three stages, according to Russell: "The earliest stage is characterized by denial, increased anxiety, and fear. The second stage is panic. People suddenly say, 'I've got to sell.' The third phase is despair." [23] In the bear market that ran from '68 to '82, investors did not reach that third phase until after the second crash, the sickening plunge that ended in 1974. By then, the average stock purchased in '68 had lost 70 percent of its value. A few years earlier, investors were eager to buy into the go-go market—at any price. Now investors no longer wanted to hear about stocks—at any price. This is why, in January of 1975, when Richard Russell tried to tell his readers that the market had finally scraped bottom (as indeed it had), they sent him hate mail.[24] It would take another seven years for the scars to begin to heal. And it would require a new, innocent, and unscarred generation of investors to launch a full-scale bull market.

But despite the most ominous forecasts, within even the strongest boom and bust cycles, there are always intermissions. In 1990, for example, the bull paused, and the S&P 500 fell 6.6 percent. Similarly, during the lean years that stretched from 1966 to 1982, there were bright moments: in 1975 the S&P jumped 38.3 percent. At such moments, the bull stumbles or the bear pauses to digest—these are the boomlets and corrections that economists call "cyclical" bull and bear markets. They can last a year or more. But it is the longer waves, the "secular" bull and bear markets that determine the market's primary trend for 10 or 15 or 20 years.

"My great belief is that the only things that really matter in the stock market are the great bull cycles and bear cycles—not the interim bull markets, [but] the real humdingers, the ones ending in 1929, 1965 and 2000," Jeremy Grantham declared in 2002. "They're the ones that really count. And the bear markets that follow . . . tend to be very long. The first one in the 20th century lasted for 10 years, 1910 to 1920. The second one lasted from 1929 to 1944. And the third one lasted from 1965 to 1982, 17 years. In between you had mega-bull markets where you made 10 times your money as we did from 1982 to 2000. So this bear cycle won't play itself out overnight," Grantham added.[25]

Bernstein agreed. "Over, say, the next ten years, the risk of being out of the market—because it might go up—is much lower. Any upswing that you might miss is far more likely to be a short-term one, than a long-term structural opportunity," he cautioned in February of 2003.

THE BEAR PUTS OUT HONEY: BEAR MARKET RALLIES

Bernstein did not rule out the possibility of "monster" bear market rallies. "Rallies of 30% and even more are common in secular bear markets. Japan has had 9 rallies greater than 25% since 1990, and 3 that were greater than 40%," he observed. "The U.S. experienced 13 bull markets of greater than

30% during its secular bears of 1902–1921, 1929–1949, and 1966–1982." [26] The media often does not distinguish between secular (long) and cyclical (short) bull and bear markets. So, during a bear market rally, a prophet will declare that a new bull market has begun—and it has— but this is not what Grantham would call one of "the real humdingers." It is not a bull market that will reward a buy-and-hold strategy.

In June of 2003, the market was turning up, and investors began to ask: Could the Dow once again cross 10,000? The answer was yes. The Dow might well break 10,000—or even 11,000—but the important question was this: Could it stay there, and if so, for how long? Since Japan's grueling bear market began in 1989, Japanese stocks had rallied four times, rising 48 percent, 34 percent, 56 percent, 62 percent—and these upturns lasted for months. But the majority of investors who got back in during the rallies had their heads handed to them. The bear is sadistic in that way: he likes to lure investors back in. This is why bear market rallies also are called "sucker rallies."

Should an individual investor view bear market rallies as trading op- portunities—a chance to get in, make a profit, and get out? In the summer of 2003, Richard Russell said no. It is too difficult to time a saw-toothed market. At the time, Russell himself was sticking to short-term treasuries, while hedging his portfolio with gold and gold mining shares. [27]

The problem is that bear markets often create the impression that something is happening, without quite delivering on the promise. "In the aftermath of a bubble, the stock market can become extremely volatile— without getting anywhere," Ned Davis noted in the summer of 2003. "We did a study of 17 cyclical bull markets within secular bear markets," he added. "In those markets the S&P 500 went up an average of 50% and the rally lasted an average of 371 days. But, they didn't last as long as other cyclical bull markets—and didn't go quite as high. . . . The rally was just a phase of a long-term bear market." [28]

Bull markets reward risk taking, but when the bear puts out honey, he is usually laying a trap: "In recent years, U.S. investors have felt that they must be playing the market—even when the risks are high," Marc Faber observed. "They learned to think that they should invest like George Soros—but the average investor is not George Soros. When I play tennis, I don't try to play like Agassi," Faber added. "I have to play a different game. Agassi can play to win. I have to play a game where I don't make any mistakes." [29]

In a bear market, this is what is most important: *not making mistakes.* The goal is to conserve capital. When a long bear market finally ends, those with cash will find bargains galore.

But as investors learned in the late nineties, making a mistake, even on one stock, can be costly: lose 40 percent on one $50,000 investment and you need to make more than 60 percent on the remaining $30,000 investment—just to get back to square one. In the meantime, the investor has lost the opportunity to make money elsewhere—even if it was only an opportunity to make 5 percent. Over three years, 5 percent compounded, adds up to more than 15 percent.

Investors who buy when too much money is chasing too few stocks often find that it takes a very long time to make up for what they have lost. Even the fleeting crash of 1987 could have a lasting effect on a portfolio, Steve Leuthold's research revealed. Comparing an investor who put $1,000 into the S&P at its peak in August of '87 to one who stashed his savings in risk-free T-bills, Leuthold showed that it would take the equity investor 3 years and 10 months to catch up with the timid T-bill investor—assuming that he constantly reinvested his dividends. If not, the "catch-up" time would be 7 years and 10 months. And this was following the briefest of cyclical bear markets: stocks snapped back from the October crash in a matter of months. High returns in the years that followed would airlift investors back to their master plan.

By contrast, an investor who had the misfortune to invest $10,000 in the S&P 500 in January of 1973, at the peak of a bear market rally, would have to wait 12 years and 11 months to catch up with a neighbor who kept his money in T-bills—if the equity investor reinvested dividends. If he did not, the "catch-up" period would be 23 years and 1 month.[30] The hypothetical example assumes that he bought at the zenith of the rally, but unfortunately, that is about when individual investors are inclined to join a bear market rally—after prices have been rising for many months and they feel secure. This is what many did during the bear market rally that followed the crash of '29, and again in 1990, when Japanese stocks rallied following that market's first leg down.

In each case, investors were following the rule that they learned in a bull market: "The trend is your friend." But in a bear market, "you have a whole different rule book," Ralph Wanger observed. "In a straight-up growth market, your rule is to be 100 percent in equities all the time. Buy strength. Disregard risk. Only look at the income statement. And all stories are true, because we want them to be true. It's like the nice guy you met in the bar telling you he loves you truly—and he does.

"In the volatile bear market that tends to follow an exponential growth market, many of these rules invert," said Wanger, speaking from experience. "You don't buy strength; you sell strength. You don't look at the income statement, you look at the balance sheet [which shows a company's debts]. All stories are false. It turns out that the guy in the bar is a married orthodontist from Connecticut." [31]

And "selling strength" means viewing a bear market rally, not as a buying opportunity, but as a selling opportunity—a chance to realize losses and put the money to work someplace else.

MANAGING RISK IN A BEAR MARKET

Ultimately, secular bear markets teach investors to learn to manage risk in a different way, focusing, *not on the odds, but on the size of the risk.* Just how steep is the downside?

A practical example explains the difference. "Let's say you're offered a wager where you're told that the chances are 999 out of 1,000 that you'll make $1, but if you accept the wager, there's a 1 in 1,000 chance that you'll lose $10,000," said Nassim Nicholas Taleb, author of *Fooled by Randomness.* "Would you take the wager? Of course not. The frequency or probability of the loss is only 1 in 1,000, but that, in and by itself, is totally irrelevant. That probability needs to be considered within the context of the magnitude of the risk—the danger of losing $10,000."

Yet when investing their life savings, those who have been trained by a long bull market tend to focus on the frequency rather than the size of the risk. "Investors pay too much attention to what happens 'on average,'" said Taleb. "Investing in equities is often a successful strategy, *but it does not matter how frequently a strategy succeeds if failure is too costly to bear.*" In other words, an investor must always ask himself: What is the worst thing that can happen—and can I stand it? [32]

This is why a 55-year-old investor with a nest egg of $250,000 "would be crazy to put 80 percent of his money into the stock market," Peter Bernstein declared in 2002. Even if the odds are high that over the next 10 years he will make money, "if he's wrong, he is dead." There is always the possibility, however slim, "that bears like Bob Prechter could be right," said Bernstein, referring to Robert Prechter's 2002 prediction that the Dow could fall below 1000. "No one knows." [33]

The most dangerous error investors make, Bernstein and Taleb agreed, is "to mistake probability for certainty." By concentrating on what is most probable, or what happens "on average," investors often ignore the worst-case scenarios. For precisely this reason, said Taleb, investing can be more treacherous than a game of Russian roulette. "Reality is far more vicious. . . . First, it delivers the fatal bullet rather infrequently, like a revolver that would have hundreds, even thousands of chambers instead of six. After a few dozen tries, one forgets about the existence of a bullet, under a numbing false sense of security.

"Second, unlike a well-defined precise game like Russian roulette where the risks are visible to anyone capable of multiplying and dividing by six, one does not observe the barrel of reality. One is thus capable of unwittingly playing Russian roulette—and calling it by some alternative 'low risk' name. We see the survivors and never the losers. . . . The game seems terribly easy and we play along blithely." [34] So, in the late nineties, investors buying stocks at 100 times earnings did not recognize the size of the risks they were taking. They called the game of picking stocks by an alternative, low-risk name: "investing in an efficient market."

In fact, Taleb's black swan could appear tomorrow. The stock that everyone said was a safe haven could blow up. Following a bear market rally, the Dow could suddenly drop 1000 points. "People tend to think of low-probability events as being distant in time," said Bernstein. "In other words, we say, 'Well, yes, gold went to $800 an ounce, but that was more than 20 years ago.' Or, 'Well, yes, in 1980 we had double-digit inflation—that couldn't happen now.'" But he was emphatic: "Probability has nothing to do with time." The surprise that would upset the best-laid forecasts could be waiting just around the corner. "When I explain this to people, they nod their heads," he added, "but it is very difficult to get them to believe it, to act on it." [35]

STRATEGIC MARKET TIMING

The trick, then, is not to try to time the bear market's treacherous peaks and valleys (even though they might last a year, or longer), but to recognize the primary long-term trend—to recognize, in Richard Russell's words, "whether the tide is coming in or going out."

The Dow Theory that Russell used for nearly 50 years does not attempt to forecast the market's short-term gyrations. As noted, it focuses on the underlying cycles. The strategy stood Russell in good stead. During the final two decades of the 20th century, readers who followed the advice in *Richard Russell's Dow Theory Letter* earned, on average 11.9 percent a year, beating a buy-and-hold strategy, on a risk-adjusted basis, from June of 1980 to the end of 2001, according to Marc Hulbert, the editor of a newsletter that tracks financial newsletters. Russell's record was particularly impressive given the fact that those two decades included a 17-year bull market—a time when a buy-and-hold strategy normally trumps market timing.[36]

Does Russell's market timing work even better in a bear market? "The value of the strategy is more apparent in a bear market," Hulbert allowed—then smiled. "But that's like saying fire insurance works better when there is a fire."[37]

Hulbert was right. Long-term market timing is designed to function like insurance—to protect an investor from the worst losses of a secular bear market. "In a bear market, everyone loses, but it is the people who lose the LEAST who are the winners," Russell warned his readers in 2002.[38]

What Russell's success suggests is that timing the long term can be far more fruitful than trying to predict the short term: "People ask what is going to happen next year, and I say I haven't the faintest idea," Jeremy Grantham admitted. "In general, the short term is unknowable and in an uncertain world, it should be unknowable."

By 1997, Grantham, like Gail Dudack, knew that the financial frenzy would not end pleasantly, though he did not know when. "These things are predictable, but at uncertain horizons," said Grantham, a perspicacious, if occasionally prickly, Englishman. In other words, he could predict the ending, but not the way there.

Some clients were unsatisfied. "How," they asked, "is it possible to forecast the long run if you cannot predict the short run? After all, the long run is made up of a series of short runs." This is a question that Grantham heard often, indeed more often than he wished to remember. ("Who knew you'd be giving the bear market speech for four years?" he grumped, referring to the amount of time it took for clients to admit that the bull market had indeed peaked and ended.) Still, he recognized, it was a very good question.

After two years of "constantly fighting with audiences and clients over this paradox," he finally arrived at a satisfactory answer: feathers.

"Think of yourself standing on the corner of a high building in a hurricane with a bag of feathers," said Grantham. "Throw the feathers in the air. You don't know much about those feathers. You don't know how high they will go. You don't know how far they will go. Above all, you don't know how long they will stay up. You know canaries in Jamaica end up in Maine once in a blue moon. They just get swept along for a week in a hurricane. Yet you know one thing with absolute certainty: eventually on some unknown flight path, at an unknown time, at an unknown location, the feathers will hit the ground, absolutely, guaranteed. There are situations where you absolutely know the outcome of a long-term interval, though you absolutely cannot know the short-term time periods in between. That is almost perfectly analogous to the stock market."

Grantham recalled his clients' response. "They would just say, 'Oh,' then grin, and shut up. It was such a revelation to me. If you can find the right analogy, suddenly people understand." [39]

New Themes

By 2003, market veterans such as Grantham, Peter Bernstein, Gail Dudack, Marc Faber, Richard Russell, Jim Grant, *The Bank Credit Analyst*'s Martin Barnes, Pimco's Bill Gross, and Bob Farrell, Merrill's longtime star market timer, all had begun to suggest that investors needed to rearrange their priorities. Those investing for the long term should look beyond the S&P 500, the Nasdaq, and the Dow. Over the first decade of the new century, specialized sectors might shine, but by and large, the risk implicit in investing in common stocks outweighed the likely reward. The game was no longer worth the candle.

In 2003, Treasuries were not an appealing alternative. They, too, had just enjoyed a long bull run. This meant that investors would need to jettison yet another piece of conventional wisdom: that the only alternative to stocks is bonds. Just as at the beginning of the seventies, new themes were emerging.

In each era, you have to ask, "Who are the richest people in the world?" Bob Farrell noted. "In the fifties, it was the Duponts, the industrialists. In the sixties it was Sam Walton—the growth was in consumer stocks. By the end of the seventies, it was the Arabs and their oil—in the eighties, the real estate tycoons, especially in the Far East. Then, in the nineties, you had the technology entrepreneurs. Now, something else is going to generate wealth. My theory is that the next wealth generator is going to come from China or Russia—and natural resources. Emerging markets peaked in the early nineties," Farrell added. "You had real wealth destruction in '97—from that you can build another platform for wealth."[40]

"Getting the right asset class is so much more critical as a protector or a driver of your returns than focusing on individual stocks," added Jeremy Grantham. "Individuals make a big error by spending too much of their time worrying about the names, and too little thinking about how their portfolio is structured and whether they are diversified enough."[41]

COMMODITIES

As a new century began, investors who wanted to diversify began looking at natural resources. They seemed ready for a long-term move. In the eighties and nineties, while U.S. stocks and bonds soared, what the financial world calls "commodities" (which includes precious metals such as gold and industrial metals such as platinum, as well as crude oil and lumber, food, and fiber) languished, reaching a nadir at the end of the 20th century. Most made their lows between 1998 and 2002, and by June of 2003 many observers believed that a new cycle was beginning. "Commodities are up 77 percent from the lows they made in 1998," Marc Faber observed, "a remarkable rise considering that investors had been saying that commodities would never rise again!" And because they were rising from such depths, plenty of upside remained. (See chart "Commodities Near All-Time Low," Appendix, page 466.)

The bear market in commodities that began in 1980 had started the way many bear markets do: overinvestment had led to excess capacity. "A decade of high real prices (and fat profit margins) during the 1970s encouraged a massive expansion in the supply of commodities on a global scale," explained John Di Tomasso, founder of the Di Tomasso Group, a commodity trading advisor based in Victoria, British Columbia. "Then, from 1980 until 1993, prices came under constant pressure. A price recovery began in 1993 but it was snuffed out by the 1998 Asian financial crisis. As

COMMODITY MARKET CYCLES 1937–99

Begins	Ends	Duration (years)	Change (%)
1939	1954	15	99
1954	1970	16	–41
1970	1981	11	106
1981	1999	18	–68

SOURCE: DI TOMASSO GROUP

a result, commodity prices tumbled from what were still relatively low levels. For producers this turn of events was a catastrophe.

"By the end of the nineties, many commodity prices stood near 100-year lows in real terms, and well below cost of production. Commodity producers had a serious problem. The combination of low selling prices and a high cost structure caused by rising energy prices put pressure on producers to take action, especially the inefficient or poorly financed producers."

When prices fall, "producers tend to respond in predictable ways," Di Tomasso continued. "Mines are closed; exploration budgets are slashed; husbandry is neglected; herds are reduced; and crops are substituted. New production is discouraged. In a free market economy, production without profit cannot continue indefinitely. At some stage, prices must rise at least to the point where producers can earn a living. Otherwise, overall production of these raw materials will shrink, causing prices to ultimately rise, anyway—Adam Smith's 'invisible hand' restoring equilibrium in the marketplace."

By 2000, Di Tomasso believed that the tide must turn: "Viewed within a long-term perspective, if reversion to historical 'norms' is a reasonable expectation, then commodity prices, in aggregate, could double," he predicted. It has happened before—from the 1932 low to the 1934 high, in the midst of deflation and the Great Depression, commodity prices, on average, rose by 100 percent. "The point is this—commodity prices can increase if the decline in demand is met with a proportionately larger decline in supply (for example, OPEC's modest crude oil production cutbacks in 1999 were followed by a tripling of energy prices)."[42]

He was right: as a new century began, the commodity index began to climb. Meanwhile, as emerging markets matured, demand for energy, food, and the raw materials of an industrial society grew. "If the world grows as much as people expect, demand will continue to rise," said Faber in the summer of 2003. "In Asia, I can imagine oil consumption doubling over the next 10 years. Already, scooters are beginning to replace bicycles. China is importing more copper and iron ore. And each year, Asians are eating better—wheat, corn, soybeans, coffee, cocoa, they should all benefit. Prices won't go down, and the volume of food sold will go up." [43]

"Meanwhile," Faber argued, "the easy-money policies of the world's central bankers will, in the long run, reinforce inflation in commodity prices. They keep on lowering rates, hoping to revive the economy. But they forget that you can have inflation and recession at the same time, as was the case in Latin America in the eighties." Gail Dudack agreed. "You could have the worst of all worlds: inflation in necessities—food, energy, housing, medical care—and deflation in other areas, with global competition keeping the price of manufactured goods [and profit margins] low."

Some investors favored spreading their risk by betting on a basket of commodities. In 2002, Pimco launched a fund that tracked an index of commodity futures contracts and was backed by Treasuries that protect against inflation (TIPS). This meant that an investor would benefit from any gains in commodity prices while also earning a T-bill rate on his underlying collateral. The fund was designed to "provide a hedge against inflation, particularly unexpected inflation," Robert Greer, Pimco's real return manager, explained. Equally important, the index fund allowed an individual to invest in energy, grains, metals, livestock, food, and fiber without trying to trade commodities futures himself. Finally, Greer suggested, "commodities could provide some protection from many geopolitical surprises that could adversely impact stocks and/or bonds." [44]

In the nineties, many "natural resource" funds focused primarily on oil and natural gas. In the 21st century, both the supply/demand equation and global uncertainty made energy an attractive long-term investment theme. But to many who followed the financial world's cycles, the entire spectrum of commodities offered an even better hedge. Four years before Pimco opened its commodities fund, Jim Rogers, who had co-founded the Quantum fund with George Soros, launched his own commodity index and a private fund based on it. By the spring of 2003, Rogers's fund boasted a compound annual return of 14 percent. "I would much rather be in commodities than shares in the next few years," said Rogers.[45] At that point, it seemed likely that more funds might begin to follow the broad-based model, offering individual investors the opportunity to stake out a claim in the commodities market without betting all of their chips on oil and gas.

GOLD AND THE DOLLAR

Gold's allure may be irrational, but for centuries the metal that John Maynard Keynes called "this barbarous relic" has had a nearly mystical hold on the human imagination. Perhaps it has something to do with the fact that gold's value seems eternal. "Gold is the child of Zeus; neither moth nor rust devoureth it," Pindar wrote in the fourth century B.C. Fittingly, gold dissolves only in cyanide.

Traditionally, gold has been viewed as a borderless currency. As recently as 1989, "the Soviet Union, on the brink of collapse, sold off or swapped virtually its entire gold reserve in an effort to sustain its credit," Timothy Green observed in *The World of Gold*, a valuable study of the metal. "The unique advantage of gold is that it is no one else's liability; the dollar, sterling, the deutschmark, and the yen are . . . Go to China, and see the crowds packing the gold shops that have sprung up in Beijing, Shanghai, and Guanghzou, turning their paper yuan, which has depreciated almost daily in the last year or two, into ornaments of pure gold," he wrote in 1993.[46]

A decade later, Richard Russell, Marc Faber, Jim Grant, Jean-Marie Eveillard, *The Bank Credit Analyst*'s Martin Barnes, and David Tice, editor of *Behind the Numbers,* favored real assets—especially gold—as a hedge against the dollar. By 2003, gold already had begun its ascent: Jean-Marie Eveillard's First Eagle Gold fund, for instance, rose 37.31 percent in 2001 before jumping 106.97 percent in 2002. (In 2003, as stocks rallied, gold lost ground, but in July, Eveillard's fund remained up by more than 6 percent.)

Despite enormous gains, investors like Richard Russell believed that gold's turn in the sun had just begun. If they were right, the upside remained steep. In the middle of 2003, gold traded at around $350 an ounce; in the metal's last secular bull market, which ended in 1980, it peaked over $800. Investors bullish on "gold for the long run" focused not on the question of deflation or inflation but on the central bankers' global print-a-thon. As long as central bankers like the Fed flooded the world with paper currency, the danger was that it would become less valuable.[47]

Throughout the Great Bull Market of 1982–99, the dollar had served as the world's safe haven, with the greenback rising along with U.S. stocks and bonds. This is why foreign investors were so eager to load up on Treasuries. Meanwhile, Treasury Secretary Robert Rubin had concentrated his considerable intelligence and energies on keeping the dollar strong. At the beginning of the 21st century, however, Washington appeared content to see the dollar slide. Unemployment had risen; corporate profits were anemic. The administration's hope was that a weaker dollar would help U.S. exporters by making their products cheaper abroad.

The danger was that the dollar's decline would accelerate. By June of 2003, the dollar had already tumbled to a point where one euro purchased $1.13; a year earlier, one euro equaled $.92. If the dollar continued to lose value, it was not at all clear what other currency could serve as the world's safe haven. Economic problems in Japan ruled out the yen, and despite the euro's recent rise, the new currency seemed neither old enough nor stable enough to serve as a magnet for the world's wealth.

Investors were beginning to move their money into real assets. "The recent rally in commodities, in gold, and possibly in real estate, are the shots across the bow for a long-term investor to shift back to hard assets in particular and commodities in general," said Faber.[48]

But not all hard assets are created equal. U.S. real estate made Faber (and many others) uneasy because it sat on a mountain of mortgage debt.[49] Granted, real estate is always a local story: in cities like Manhattan, the prices of luxury condominiums had reached such frantic heights that apartments might better have been priced by the square inch rather than the square foot. Granted, in other markets, reasonable values still could be found, but much depended on interest rates. If rates rose, real estate prices would, all but inevitably, fall. In the end, for an individual investor, everything turned on the particular property, its location, how long he intended to hold it, and its "use value," not just as an investment but as a home.

For an investor looking for a home for his money, however, gold seemed to many the safe harbor of choice. Historically, when investors have lost faith that paper assets will hold their value (whether stock certificates or paper currencies), gold has provided shelter. For example, "during the Great Depression, Homestake Mining rose from $65 in 1929, to a high of $544 in 1936. Homestake also paid $171 in dividends—which was more than twice the price of its stock in 1929," Marc Faber pointed out. During the seventies, gold once again soared.[50]

Still, even those who were most bullish about the long term did not pretend to forecast the short term. Faber feared that speculators might push gold into a Nasdaq-like bubble, which would then blow off. Richard Russell remained convinced that a long-term secular bull market in gold had begun, but over the short term, he anticipated a series of cyclical bear markets.

EMERGING MARKETS

In 2003, price/earnings ratios suggested that U.S. stocks were not cheap. By contrast, P/Es in Asia had not yet recovered from the '97 crash. "Here, in Thailand, many companies trade between 5 and 10 times earnings and pay a dividend of 7%," Faber reported. "You can buy companies at or below book value in Thailand, Indonesia, and the Philippines." [51]

Gail Dudack agreed, suggesting that the prospects for growth looked better in the emerging markets than in the United States. "China, Thailand, Indonesia, Malaysia, Singapore, the Philippines, Australia, maybe some Middle Eastern countries—investors would be wise to find exposure to these parts of the world," she said in the summer of 2003. "But an investor should be aware that bubbles could form there over the next five years, as well." [52]

An investor who wanted to place a bet on both commodities and emerging markets might do well to look at some of China's neighbors, Marc Faber suggested. "For most Asian countries, exports to China are more important than exports to the U.S.," he explained. As China's industrial base expands, so does its demand not only for oil but for raw materials such as copper and iron ore. Meanwhile, as China's middle class grows, so does the market for food, fiber, energy, and precious metals. "Neighbors in Southeast Asia are likely to profit from China's expanding economy," said Faber, "along with resource-rich countries like Australia, New Zealand and Russia." [53]

Lee R. Thomas III, Pimco's global bond strategist, suggested that investors step back and consider global demographic trends. On the one hand, aging populations in the United States and Europe need to save more, Lee observed in June of 2003. The long bull market in stocks had only masked "a looming pension crisis." By 2003, the need for increased saving was apparent, but *the key economic problem of the next decade will be how to recycle increasing saving into profitable capital spending projects,"* Thomas declared (emphasis mine).

In a post-bubble world "low growth, low inflation, and low interest rates" are all but inevitable, he argued, leading to low real returns for both stocks and bonds. "What is the solution if Japan, the U.S., and Europe all need to save more, but it is getting hard to find places to invest all this savings?" he asked. "The answer is to invest elsewhere, in the parts of the world where capital is still scarce, and where populations are still young. During the 18th century, the advice to anyone seeking to grow his wealth was, 'Go west, young man.' Today the advice a western investor should heed is, 'Go east, young man (or woman).' Or, perhaps, 'Go south.' Go anywhere capital still is scarce and prospective real returns remain high. Invest in the emerging markets." [54]

INCOME: "THE ROYAL ROAD TO RICHES"

Finally, if there was one new investment theme that stood out at the beginning of the 21st century, it was a desire for dividends.

"What is rare is always most valuable," Maureen Allyn, Scudder's former chief economist, remarked in 2003, "and what is rare now is income." [55]

During the Great Bull Market of 1982–99, dividends fell out of fashion. Indeed, they began to look decidedly dowdy. Who cared about a 5 percent dividend when capital gains of 15 to 20 percent were all but guaranteed? In the past, investors cherished their dividends; after all, they accounted for half of the stock market's returns from 1926 through 1981. Without them an equity investor would have lost money in more than a third of those 56 years.

But as Act III of the bull market began in 1995, all eyes were focused on capital gains. From the fall of 1996 through the fall of 2001, only 1.5 percent of the S&P 500's 10.1 percent average annual return came from dividends.

Companies were not paying dividends for a simple reason: they didn't have to. "There was no pressure from shareholders," observed Jim Floyd, a senior analyst at Leuthold's firm. Even when bonds were paying 6 percent, stocks were able to compete on capital gains alone. Investors new to the market knew little about the history of dividends—or how important they were to supporting the mythology that surrounded "stocks for the long run."

In the late nineties, investors did not just ignore dividends, they shunned companies that paid them. If a corporation lifed its dividend, its share price might well fall. In a corporate culture hooked on growth, sharing earnings with investors was seen as a sign of weakness. The conventional wisdom had it that if a company's managers were on the ball, they could earn far more by retaining profits and plowing them back into the business.

By 2003, however, the times were changing. In February, when Goodyear announced that it was dropping its dividend, the company's share price plunged by 17 percent. The loss of the dividend was not the only reason shareholders dropped the stock (sales of the tires also had something to do with it), but the sharp reaction indicated that they were not pleased.[56] "Dividends are going to come back," said Ralph Wanger. "Shareholders are going to say, 'You know you talked us into keeping the money in the company—you said you had great investment opportunities and we'd all be better off. And you deceived us. Half of the money you wasted making acquisitions at ridiculous prices and building factories for products that never got made, the other half you stole—awarding yourself stock options and writing yourself checks.'

"Earnings are an accounting theory," Wanger declared, "and dividends are cash flow."

Certainly, Wanger was right about earnings being theoretical: in the aftermath of the bubble, there were so many theories about how to count them that no one was entirely certain just how profitable some of the nation's largest corporations were. This is the problem with capital gains—they are gains only on paper, unless and until an investor sells his shares. "Today's [low] dividend yield puts investors totally at the mercy of one another—what John von Neumann characterized as 'combat and competition,'" Peter Bernstein observed at the end of 2001. "When cash flow is a trickle, the investor cannot obtain cash, for any purpose, without finding a buyer [for his stocks]. The buyer may or may not be there when needed. The price the buyer is willing to pay may or may not provide the total return the investor originally expected. Investments without cash flows are risky, uncertain."[57]

Unlike earnings, dividends are forever; they can never be restated. "Dividends also demonstrate that management has enough confidence in the firm's future to part with some cash," Haywood Kelly, Morningstar's editor in chief, observed. "This is why, historically, even though dividends per se do not increase the value of a firm, stocks have tended to rise when companies boost their dividends. The market senses that insiders—those who know the company best—are bullish on its prospects. Moreover, a high yield relative to other stocks suggests that shares are cheap." [58]

BEWARE OF COMMON STOCKS BEARING GIFTS

But in the early years of the 21st century, common stocks did not appear to be the best place to search for dividends. First, few companies paid a decent dividend. Secondly, as noted, in 2003 share prices remained relatively rich; another leg down in the bear market and capital losses could cancel several years of dividends. Finally, by 2003, corporate accounting had been so confused and so corrupted that it was not clear how many companies could afford to pay a dividend—or raise it—even if they wanted to.

By 2002, corporate debt stood at "six times earnings for U.S. stocks— the highest level in more than 40 years," GMO's Jeremy Grantham observed. [59] If interest rates remained low, most would be able to handle the debt service. But that remained an uneasy "if."

This was just one reason why investors hungry for dividends would do well to take a close look at a corporation's balance sheet before buying shares in a company that promised income, warned Kurt Richebächer, editor of *The Richebächer Letter*. By this reckoning, "in 1997, non-financial corporations paid $218.1 billion in dividends from $337.7 billion in after-tax profits." All well and fine. "But five years later, they were paying dividends of $258.8 billion compared to profits of only $197 billion."

"This meant that U.S. companies have been financing their dividends by either drawing down their cash reserves or borrowing," observed Marc Faber, citing Richebächer's numbers. In many cases, "soaring depreciation charges are creating the cash flow for dividends," Faber explained. "But when you depreciate $100 million worth of assets that are becoming obsolete and need replacement, you are supposed to be making a $100 million investment in new equipment." In 2002, however, capital spending was declining. "A company might depreciate something by $100 million and spend $40 million, using the rest for dividends"—creating the impression that the corporation was far wealthier than, in fact, it was.[60]

Of course, some companies paid a reliable and decent dividend. But for some investors, preferred stock might be a better choice. Not only do preferred shares pay a dividend, they also tend to be less volatile than common shares—an appealing advantage if an investor is dipping one toe into a new class of assets.

Pros like Gail Dudack, Richard Russell, and Martin Barnes also favored AA corporate bonds, highly rated municipal bonds, real estate investment trusts (REITs), and foreign government bonds—but only if an investor was able to buy them at a reasonable price. By the summer of 2003, high-yield emerging market bonds, for instance, had just completed a giddy run. In many cases, highly rated bonds of U.S. corporations also looked pricey—though a tax law passed in 2003 cut taxes on those dividends, adding to their allure. (The tax break also applied to some, but not all, preferred stocks.)

THE MIRACLE OF COMPOUNDING

To an investor accustomed to the returns of a bull market, the idea of collecting 4 or 5 percent a year might well sound boring—and so it is, Richard Russell acknowledged, "until (after seven or eight years) when the money starts to pour in. Then, believe me, compounding becomes very interesting. In fact, it becomes downright fascinating!"

Most investors have seen compounding tables that show how, over time, interest or dividends build wealth. (Boiling those tables down to a rule of thumb, "the rule of 72" says that 72, divided by an investor's total return, tells him how long it will take for compounding to double his savings. For instance, if an investor earns capital gains of 3 percent and dividends of 5 percent for a total return of 8 percent, his money will double in nine years.)

In 50-odd years of investing Richard Russell had never bought a stock that did *not* pay a dividend. Russell called compounding "The Royal Road to Riches," in part because this is the route that "Old Money" has always taken. "In the investment world, the wealthy investor has one major advantage over the little guy, the stock market amateur and the neophyte trader," he declared. "The advantage that the wealthy investor enjoys is that HE DOESN'T NEED THE MARKETS, because he already has all the income he needs. He has money coming in via bonds, T-bills, money market funds, stocks and real estate. In other words, the wealthy investor never feels pressured to 'make money' in the market."

If an investor is paid while he waits for a new secular bull market to begin, he is less likely to make costly mistakes. He can afford to be patient: "When bonds are cheap and bond yields are irresistibly high, the wealthy man buys bonds," Russell explained. "When stocks are on the bargain table and stock yields are attractive, he buys stocks. When real estate is a great value, he buys real estate. When great art or fine jewelry or gold is on the 'give away' table, he buys art or diamonds or gold."

And, if no outstanding values are available, the rich man sits on his hands. "Periods of inactivity" can be painful, as Warren Buffett acknowledged in the spring of 2003, but not nearly as painful as watching savings evaporate.

Ultimately, Russell's point was this: the poor man can become the wealthy man *if he behaves as if he is already wealthy,* scorning investments that do not provide income. The only exception is a situation that offers "safety, an attractive return, and a good chance of appreciating in price," said Russell, setting a high bar. "At all other times," he counseled his readers, "the compounding route is safer and probably a lot more profitable, at least in the long run."[61]

TIPS

Unfortunately, even the "miracle" of compounding is another one of those pieces of conventional wisdom that work only in certain seasons. In a period when inflation averages 7.7 percent a year (as it did in the seventies), an investor who holds on to an investment paying 5 percent loses 2.7 percent a year.

By contrast, in an era when inflation hovers between 1 and 2 percent (as it did in 2003), a decent dividend makes all the difference. If an investor is saving for retirement, all that matters is the "real return" on his savings, after inflation. His only concern is not *how much* money he will have but how much that money will be *worth.* If an investor could stay, say, 2 to 3 percent ahead of inflation on every penny he saved over a lifetime, he would do very well.

Unfortunately, in 2003 virtually every pundit acknowledged that infla tion was not dead, merely hibernating. (The idea that we had come to the End of History came and went sometime in the nineties.) No one knew when it might return. Both reasonable and unreasonable men offered co-gent and not so cogent arguments as to why inflation or deflation was more likely. Some, like Gail Dudack and Marc Faber, recognized that it would be quite possible to have both at the same time.

Whenever inflation appears—whether in 10 months or in 10 years—it turns the "miracle" of compounding on its head. If an investor buys a secu-rity that promises to pay 5 percent a year over 10 years, and inflation rises to 6 percent, he has nothing to compound, except losses.

There is, however, a final "alternative investment" that provides an un-paralleled hedge against inflation for long-term investors. In 1997, the U.S. government created TIPS (Treasury Inflation-Protected Securities), Trea-sury bonds that come with insurance against rising prices.[62]

Like plain-vanilla Treasuries, TIPS are backed by the federal govern-ment. When they mature, an investor can be certain of getting his principal back, plus a guaranteed fixed dividend. The difference is that TIPS also offer a buffer against inflation: each year that the dividend falls short of in-flation (as measured by the consumer price index), the government pays a bonus to bridge the gap. In other words, the investor knows that his savings will always outpace inflation. His total return floats, but it cannot fall below the guaranteed yield. The fixed yield on TIPS can seem small, but with the inflation booster built in, TIPS compare favorably to other Treasuries. By 2003, TIPS had become so popular that funds investing in TIPS were soaring. For example, the Vanguard Inflation-Protected Securities Fund boasted a total return of 16.6 percent in 2002, and 7.1 percent in the first five months of 2003.

Because mutual funds trade TIPS, they offer the possibility of fatter re-turns in the form of capital gains as well as dividends. Of course, this also means the investor is exposed to capital losses—red ink that could expunge not only the dividend and the inflation bonus, but part of an investor's principal.

By contrast, if an investor buys TIPS directly from the government and holds until the bonds mature, he pays no fees and is certain of getting his original investment back, plus income that stays ahead of inflation. There is no credit risk and no interest-rate risk—making TIPS the only risk-free long-term investment on Wall Street.

In an uncertain world, a risk-averse investor could hardly do better.

A history of financial cycles cannot pretend to protect investors against losses. As everyone knows, history is a poor teacher, and human beings poor students in her classroom. Nevertheless, if one truly thought that men and women were doomed simply to repeat their mistakes, only misanthropes would write history—and only masochists would read it.

In truth, a knowledge of history is an investor's best defense against error. Despite all the financial engineering that attempts to eliminate risk, cycles appear to be as inevitable as the seasons. Investors who understand these cycles are more likely to survive the winter of a bear market and to avoid its final phase—despair. They know that eventually, summer always returns, and more than that, they know that somewhere on the planet it is always summer.

NOTES

PROLOGUE

1. The story that follows is based on interviews with the author. All interviews with Blodget were completed early in 2002, and all quotations are from the interviews unless otherwise noted.

2. David Rynecki, "Internet Stock Analyst Takes Unorthodox Approach," *USA Today,* 10 May 1999, 4B; Brenda L. Moore, "Some Savvy Pros Had an Early Line on This Year's Biggest Winners," *The Wall Street Journal,* 23 December 1998, CA2.

3. Goldman's stock had risen 53 percent since the firm went public in May, Morgan's was up 85 percent for the year. The *Times* made it clear that the reason for hiring Blodget was to try to boost Merrill's investment banking business: "As much as one-quarter of the revenue generated by investment banking departments these days comes from advising technology companies on mergers and public stock offerings," the *Times* observed. "So why has Merrill largely missed out on technology bankers' big bull market? . . . Merrill's total of $2.2 billion in technology underwriting this year, as calculated by Thomson, gave the firm . . . only about half the market share of more influential rivals like Morgan Stanley, Credit Suisse First Boston and Goldman Sachs. . . . Investors in Goldman and Morgan have been handsomely rewarded this year, in part, because of their prowess in the technology sector.

" 'It is not clear to me that they are going to make strides quickly enough,'

Steven Galbraith, an analyst at Sanford C. Bernstein & Company, said of Merrill. . . . 'What is more, Merrill has not been a believer in the star system,' Mr. Galbraith said. Having a name-brand stock picker, like Mary Meeker, the celebrated Morgan Stanley analyst who helped put that Internet practice on the map, is essential, he argues. On that count, though, Merrill may now be trying to cultivate a rising star. In February, it hired a 33-year-old CIBC Oppenheimer analyst, Henry Blodget, who went way out on a limb last year by predicting that Amazon.com would hit $400 a share. . . . Hiring Mr. Blodget, . . . is simply one indication of the way Merrill Lynch has expanded its technology research effort, said Steve Milunovich, the firm's global team coordinator for technology research." Laura M. Holson, "Market Place; Technology Bankers Work to Give Merrill a Silicon Shine," *The New York Times,* 27 December 1999.

4. David Barboza, "Market Place; Anything.com Likely to Be Hottest Issue in Class of '99," *The New York Times,* 18 January 1999.

5. The original e-mail from the disgusted broker was sent by Martin C. Brown (Grand Rapids) on November 30, 2000, and was addressed to Andrew Melnick, one of the analysts' supervisors. It was headlined "Enough Already." Melnick passed it on to Blodget, urging analysts to use the next rally as an opportunity to downgrade technology stocks. Blodget then sent the e-mail to colleagues in research on December 1, 2000. Blodget sent the message regarding Infospace on October 20, 2000. Blodget received the query on GoTo.com from John D. Faig at Aexp.com.

6. In March of 1999, *Crain's New York Business* noted, "Blodget is not as unabashedly bullish as some might think. True, he is a big believer in the Internet's business potential, and at CIBC maintained 'buy' ratings on most of the firms he followed. However, his observations on the rise in Internet stocks are peppered with descriptives such as 'bubble,' 'euphoria' and 'tulip bulbs'— language usually associated with Internet skeptics." Jon Birger, "New Executive: Henry Blodget, Merrill Lynch's Top Pick: Internet Analyst Lured from CIBC, On-Target Research Should Attract IPO's," *Crain's New York Business,* 22 March 1999, 11.

7. Spitzer's remark to *USA Today* ("Merrill Analyst Pitched Stock He Called 'Junk,' Spitzer Says") on April 15, 2002, was quoted in the class action complaint of Jon M. Rosenbaum v. Merrill Lynch & Co., Henry Blodget.

8. See Chapter 20 ("Winners, Losers, and Scapegoats [2000–03]").

9. John Kenneth Galbraith, *A Short History of Financial Euphoria* (New York: Whittle Books, in association with Penguin Books, 1990), 17, 22–23.

CHAPTER 1

1. William G. Shepherd, "The Size of the Bear," *Business Week,* 3 August 1974; William Gordon, "Poppa Bear Market," *Barron's,* 26 August 1974.

2. Despite his reservations about valuations, Russell acknowledged that the bull dominated the market throughout much of the late nineties. But in August of 1998, he began to warn readers that they were in the first phase of a bear market. (See *Richard Russell's Dow Theory Letter,* 4 August 1998, and 26 August 1998). By October of 1999, his advice to readers was unequivocal: "Get OUT of stocks and get into T-bills or T-notes or the highest-rated munis bonds" (*Richard Russell's Dow Theory Letter,* 6 October 1999). See Chapter 18 ("The Last Bear Is Gored").

3. Russell quotes Dow in *Richard Russell's Dow Theory Letter,* 8 August 2001, 3.

4. Interview by the author. For Dudack's chart of the market's cycles, see page xix. Returns are calculated on a calendar year basis (January 1 through December 31) as of the beginning of 1882, the first full cycle for which total return data is available. Dudack cites Global Financial Data as the source for total returns on the S&P 500. Global Financial also provided data for inflation adjustment, which is based on the Bureau of Labor Statistics Consumer Price Index (CPI), dating back to 1913 (the first year for which the CPI is available), and an index used by the Federal Reserve to show changes in prices of consumer goods prior to 1913.

   As Dudack's table shows, in the past dividends have played a critical role, buffering investors' losses during the weak cycles and boosting their returns during the strong cycles.

5. James Grant, *The Trouble with Prosperity: The Loss of Fear, the Rise of Speculation, and the Risk to American Savings* (New York: Times Books, 1996), 216–17.

6. For an extended discussion of economic and psychological factors driving financial cycles, as well as cycle theories, see Marc Faber, *Tomorrow's Gold, Asia's Age of Discovery* (Hong Kong: CLSA Books, 2002), chapters 6 and 7. Also, see Chapter 21 ("Looking Ahead, What Financial Cycles Mean for the 21st-Century Investor") for information on the complementary economic and psychological factors that drove the bull market of the nineties to an unhappy end.

7. By the 1990s, "market timing" was out of fashion—most investors had forgotten about long-term cycles and thought that market timing meant trying to predict six-month moves. But Mark Hulbert, editor of the *Hulbert Financial Digest*—a financial newsletter that tracks the performance of other finan-

cial newsletters—points out that over long periods of time investors who have
followed Dow Theory have beaten a buy-and-hold strategy. A columnist for
Forbes and, later, for *The New York Times,* Hulbert has written about Russell's
success in his columns. (See, for example, "The Dow Theory Still Lives,"
Forbes, 6 April 1998, 153.)

In an interview with the author, Hulbert updated his report on Russell's
progress: "A reader who followed Russell's 'buy' and 'sell' signals from June
1980 to December 31, 2001, would have earned 11.9 percent a year. We measure Russell's returns by keeping his subscriber in an index fund throughout
those periods when Russell's theory signals buy or hold, then putting him into
T bills when Russell's Dow Theory sends a 'sell' signal," Hulbert explained,
"and that's how we arrive at an average return of 11.9 percent."

On paper, a theoretical investor who bought and held the S&P 500
throughout that period would have done even better—earning 14.1 percent
annually—though very, very few investors actually got into the market of June
1980 and held, without wavering, over the next 21 years. Moreover, the success of the buy-and-hold strategy depended on making a correct guess as to
how long the bull market would continue. "Russell's market timing lagged behind a buy-and-hold system over 18 years of those 21 years largely because, in
16 of those years, a bull market insured that a buy-and-hold philosophy would
trump any other strategy," Hulbert explained. "But at the time, no one could
be certain how long the bull market would continue. Making one big bet that
this would prove to be the longest-running bull market in U.S. history was 42
percent riskier than Russell's strategy of trying to buy when the market was
low, and sell when it was high. This is why," Hulbert explained, "after adjusting for the risk involved in betting on the market's long-term direction,
Russell's less risky advice actually beat a buy-and-hold strategy, on a risk-
adjusted basis."

8. Russell recalled the response in an interview with the author. All further quotations are from interviews unless otherwise noted.

9. Ken Smilen, interview with the author. See Maggie Mahar, "The Case of the
Vanishing Investor," *Barron's,* 10 October 1988.

10. Andrew Tobias, foreword to *Extraordinary Popular Delusions and the Madness
of Crowds* by Charles MacKay (New York: Three Rivers Press, 1980), xi.

11. Acampora as quoted in Lauren Rublin, "Yes, the Dow Had an Impressive Quarter, but What's This Talk of Dow 7000?" *Barron's,* 3 July 1995,
MW3.

12. Ralph Acampora, interview with author.

13. Bethany McLean, "A Vision of Dow 18,500: This Guru Gives New Meaning to the Word Bullish," *Fortune,* August 1997.

14. Acampora reported Bartiromo's remark to the author in a September 2001 interview. See also Mark Yos, "Ralph Acampora: The Reluctant Guru," Dow Jones News Service, 14 September 1998, for a reference to the media calling Acampora Wall Street's king, and Abby Cohen its queen.

15. Ralph Acampora, interview with the author.

16. Acampora recalled the conversation that follows as well as the events of August 4 and 5 in an interview with the author.

17. On Prudential's position in the investment banking business, see Brian O'Keefe, "How Do You Restore Integrity to Wall Street Research—and Make Money Too? Prudential Has an Answer," *Fortune,* 11 June 2001, 195: "For years, the Rock had tried to break into the upper tier of investment banking, with little to show for it. . . . With the new strategy Strangfield hoped to land more individual investors, and generate a larger share of trading commission from investors grateful for unbiased research."

18. Acampora reported that Prudential sent a bodyguard with him when he made his next public appearance. *The Post* headline ran on August 5, 1998. For the *Barron's* reference to Acampora's nickname, see Jonathan R. Laing, "High Anxiety: As Market Gurus Debate, Investors Watch Nervously after Last Week's Slide," *Barron's,* 10 August 1998, 17.

19. CNN, *Street Sweep,* 4 August 1998.

20. While many investors would believe that the bull market did not reach its climax until the spring of 2000, the summer of '98 marked a major turning point. Both the S&P 500 and the Dow continued to advance following the 1998 meltdown, but only a small group of stocks were carrying the market forward. When they cracked, the indices collapsed.

    There is an argument to be made that the summer of 1998 was not only a turning point but an optimal time for an investor to cut his losses by selling stocks and buying bonds. See Chapter 16 ("Fully Deluded Earnings").

21. Ralph Acampora, interview with author, fall of 2001.

22. John Kenneth Galbraith, *A Short History of Financial Euphoria* (New York: Whittle Books, in association with Penguin Books, 1990), 87.

23. Galbraith, *Financial Euphoria,* 7. In the same context, Galbraith told the story of Roger Babson, an economist who predicted the 1929 crash only to be roundly denounced by everyone from *Barron's* to the New York Stock Exchange.

24. Wein told the story that follows in an interview with the author.

25. James Grant, *The Trouble with Prosperity,* 250; James Grant, "The Downside of an Upturn," *The New York Times,* 9 October 1996.
26. James Grant, *The Trouble with Prosperity,* xi, 246.
27. Treasury Secretary O'Neill made the statement on Fox News. His remark was quoted in Jeanne Cummings et al., "Enron Lessons: Big Political Giving Wins Firms a Hearing," *The Wall Street Journal,* 15 January 2002.
28. Gail Dudack, interview with the author.
29. Tom Petruno, "Review & Outlook: Mutual Funds: After 3 Years of Losses, Stock Funds' Biggest Challenge May Lie Ahead," *The Los Angeles Times,* 6 January 2003, C-1.

CHAPTER 2

1. Investment Company Institute and Securities Industry Association, "Equity Ownership in America," fall 1999, 14.
2. Edward Wolff, "Reconciling Alternative Estimates of Wealth Inequality from the Survey of Consumer Finances," AEI Seminar on Economic Inequality, 9 February 2000. See also Louis Uchitelle, "Economic View: The Have-Nots, at Least, Have Shelter in a Storm," *The New York Times,* 20 September 1998; and William Wolman and Anne Colamosca, *The Great 401(k) Hoax: What You Need to Know to Protect Your Family and Your Future* (New York: Perseus, 2002).
3. A comment overheard by the author.
4. According to Daniel Kadlec, *Chicago Magazine* originally challenged their claim of earning compound annual average returns of 23.4 percent in the 10 years ending in 1993 ("Jail the Beardstown Ladies," *Time,* 30 March 1998). The error, Kadlec explained, was due to the fact that the ladies were making incorrect entries into their computer. When the returns were updated through 1997, Kadlec noted, the audit showed that "the ladies have picked up some slack, earning an average annual return of 15.3%."
5. In addition to paying $400 million to Orange County, Merrill returned $20 million in collateral it had kept after the bankruptcy. See Andrew Pollack, with Leslie Wayne, "Ending Suit, Merrill Lynch to pay California County $400 million," *The New York Times,* 3 June 1998, A1.

    See also Leslie Wayne and Andrew Pollack, "The Master of Orange County," *The New York Times,* 22 July 1998, 1.
6. James K. Glassman and Kevin A. Hassett, *Dow 36,000: The New Strategy for Profiting from the Coming Rise in the Stock Market* (New York: Times Business, 1999), 110–11, 116; Walter B. Wriston, *The Twilight of Sovereignty: How the*

Information Revolution Is Transforming Our World (New York: Scribner's, 1992), 9, 45, 170; Thomas Friedman, *The Lexus and the Olive Tree: Understanding Globalization* (New York: Farrar, Straus & Giroux, 1999), 95, 141. Here I follow Thomas Frank's excellent discussion of the democratization of the market in *One Market Under God* (New York: Doubleday, 2000), chapters 3 and 4.

7. Seidman had made the remark on CNBC and repeated it in an interview with the author.

8. Jane Bryant Quinn provided the original numbers in her column in *Newsweek,* 10 November 1997. In 2002, she updated the numbers using data provided by finance professors Charles Jones and Jack Wilson of North Carolina State University. ("You Bet Your Life," *Newsweek,* 1 April 2002, 63.)

9. Clyde McGregor, interview with the author.

10. Gail Dudack, chief investment strategist and director of research, SunGard Institutional Brokerage, 4 December 2002.

11. Edward Wyatt, "Pension Change Puts the Burden on the Worker," *The New York Times,* 5 April 2002, 1. On the growth of the 401(k), see also Maggie Mahar, "The Great Pension Raid," *Barron's,* 2 December 1991, 8.

12. According to the Employee Benefit Research Institute's 2000 report, "On average, employees in the EBRI/Investment Company Institute database have three-quarters of plan balances invested directly or indirectly in equities." The EBRI report also broke down 401(k) allocation by age, revealing that 401(k) participants in their 50s showed that in 2000 they had 49.2 percent of their savings invested in equity funds, another 19 percent in company stock." (EBRI, "Plan Year 2000 Activity," January 2002.)

13. Robert McGough, "Heard on the Street: For Some Stocks Price Doesn't Matter," *The Wall Street Journal,* 16 March 1999.

14. George Kelly, interview with the author.

15. David Tice, interview with the author. Tice testified before the Capital Markets, Insurance, and Government-Sponsored Enterprises Subcommittee of the House Financial Services Committee on June 14, 2001. The 57-page transcript is available on NEXIS, copyright by the Federal Document Clearing House.

16. Interview with the author.

17. David Tice, testimony before the Capital Markets, Insurance, and Government-Sponsored Enterprises Subcommittee of the House Financial Services Committee on June 14, 2001.

18. Byron Wein, interview with the author.

19. In 1999, Carol Loomis distilled remarks from several speeches that Buffett had given that year, including a talk that he had given to a group of friends and a speech given at Allen & Co.'s Sun Valley conference. ("Mr. Buffett on the Stock Market," *Fortune,* 22 November 1999, 218–20.)

20. Russ Mitchell and Jack Egan, "How Long Will They Fly?" *U.S. News & World Report,* 31 May 1999, 54–56.

21. In 1998, Dell rose 241 percent, followed by Apple (up 152 percent), EMC (up 190 percent) Lucent (up 175 percent), and Cisco (up 139 percent).

22. Over the four years from December 31, 1998, through January 2, 2003, Wal-Mart's returns totaled 29.2 percent, while UT returned 22.9 percent.

23. See Chapter 19 ("Insiders Sell; the Water Rises").

24. Richard Russell, *Richard Russell's Dow Theory Letter,* 6 October 1999.

25. Steve Leuthold, *In Focus,* February 2002.

26. Sharon Cassidy, interview with the author. (Cassidy's name has been changed to protect her identity.)

27. Bridget O'Brian, Ianthe Jeanne Dugan, and Randall Smith, "Nasdaq, Falling Again, Is Now 50% Below High: Novice Investors Get a Tough Initiation into the Bear's Ways," *The Wall Street Journal,* 20 December 2000, C1 (updated by author in 2002).

28. Ed Wasserman, interview with the author. (Wasserman originally told part of his story in the *Yale Alumni Magazine*'s 1970 class notes, February 2002, 68.)

29. Frederick Lewis Allen, *Lords of Creation* (Chicago: Quadrangle Books, 1935), 352.

30. Mark Haines, "Bursting the Bubble," interview by Alex Jones, *Media Matters,* September 2001.

31. In an interview with the author, Ralph Acampora recalled the conversation. In a separate interview with the author, Levitt explained that he believed that many of CNBC's typical viewers understood that stocks were overpriced: "They knew it was a pump-and-dump scheme—they wanted to get in on the pump, and thought they could avoid the dump."

32. Peter Bernstein, interview with the author. See also interview with Peter Bernstein, "Betting on the Market," *Frontline,* 14 January 1997.

33. The remark was made by Paul Scharfer, who specialized in financing biotechnology companies at Sunrise Securities Corp. In 1996, he had sunk $1.4 million into a 4,800-square-foot house on three acres in Sagaponack, Long Island—a part of the Hamptons that saw a boom in development in the nineties. There, his neighbors included Richard Grasso, chairman of the

New York Stock Exchange (Patrick McGeehan, "Now Suddenly Rich, Wall Streeters Spark a Very Fancy Boom," *The Wall Street Journal,* 10 April 1997.)

34. See Chapter 14 ("Abby Cohen Goes to Washington; Allan Greenspan Gives a Speech").

35. Charles MacKay, *Extraordinary Popular Delusions and the Madness of Crowds* (1841; reprint, with a foreword by Andrew Tobias [New York: Three Rivers Press, 1980]), xviii, 369.

CHAPTER 3

1. From January 1948 through January 1968 the S&P rose by some 641 percent.

2. Edwin Levy, interview with the author. James Grant originally recounted Levy's experience in *Grant's Interest Rate Observer,* 27 September 2002.

3. Jim Awad, interview with the author.

4. John Brooks, *The Go-Go Years: The Drama and Crashing Finale of Wall Street's Bullish 60's,* foreword by Michael Lewis (New York: John Wiley & Sons, 1973, 1999), 11.

5. Brooks, 113.

6. Brooks, 212, 279.

7. Roger Lowenstein, *Buffett: The Making of an American Capitalist* (New York: Doubleday, 1996), 110.

8. Warren Buffett, Letter to Partners, 11 July 1968, as quoted in Lowenstein, 110.

9. Lowenstein, 119–20.

10. Bob Farrell, interview with the author.

11. Bob Farrell, interview with the author.

12. Brooks, 262–63.

13. Brooks, 353.

14. Steve Leuthold, interview with the author. See also Maggie Mahar, "Three Wall Street Truths You Can't Trust," *Bloomberg Personal Finance,* November 2000.

15. Steve Leuthold, *In Focus,* April 1999, 20, 121. (*In Focus* is private research done by the The Leuthold Group for its clients, primarily institutional investors.)

16. Jim Awad, interview with the author.

17. Steve Leuthold, *In Focus,* April 1999, 11. Here Leuthold was focusing on the 25 most expensive stocks in the Nifty Fifty—those with the highest price/earnings ratio. Implicitly, these were the most popular, since investors were willing to pay a higher multiple for this group of 25. Leuthold called them the "Religion Stocks."

18. Jeremy Siegel, *Stocks for the Long Run,* 3rd ed. (New York: McGraw Hill, 2002), 153–55. The difference between Siegel and Leuthold was not so much a matter of numbers as a question of how you applied those numbers to investor behavior in the real world. Leuthold agreed that if an investor had both the psychological and financial wherewithal to hold on to his losers for the very long haul, he would reap double-digit returns. Indeed, if an investor held from the end of 1972 through March of 1999, Leuthold acknowledged that the bull market would have lifted his average annual return on the Nifty Fifty to 12.6 percent a year. According to his calculations, this still made the Nifty Fifty a relatively poor investment when compared to the S&P 500: $50,000 invested in the Nifty Fifty at the end of 1972 would be worth $295,000 less than $50,000 invested in the S&P 500.

But Leuthold's more important point is that, in the real world, it is extremely unlikely that the average investor would hold on to his losers for 20 to 25 years.

Some stocks that were popular in 1972 flourished—McDonald's, Johnson & Johnson, and Merck, to name a few. But even growth stocks with the best fundamentals were overpriced in 1972. McDonald's, for example, was a solid company: its earnings would grow 253 percent over the next five years. But despite the earnings growth, over the same span, its share price fell by 19 percent—only then did the market find the stock fairly priced.

In 1999, Leuthold noted that in his new and expanded edition of *Stocks for the Long Run,* Siegel had come to recognize the importance of high price-earnings ratios, observing that "the 25 stocks with the highest P/E ratios yielded about half the subsequent return as the 25 with the lowest P/E ratios." Siegel also emphasized the importance of the price an investor pays when he gets in, acknowledging that Nifty Fifty–type stocks "should not be considered buys at any price." Nevertheless, as the bull market came to an end, most investors still clung to the thesis of *Stocks for the Long Run,* stated in the first chapter: "Accumulations in stocks have always outperformed other financial assets for the patient investor" (5).

See Chapter 2 ("The People's Market") on exactly what it means to say that U.S. stocks "always" outperform other investments.

19. Warren Buffett, as quoted in Lowenstein, 161.

20. Lowenstein, 149.

21. The NYSE survey showed that, as of 1970, one third of investors had bought their first stock sometime after 1965. Others came in after 1970, when it seemed that the market had bottomed.

Because Buffett had the cash to buy when stocks were cheap and re
frained from buying when they were expensive—his returns rose consistently
from 1973 to 1982 (see table below).

BERKSHIRE HATHAWAY'S RETURNS

Year	in per-share book value of Berkshire	Annual Percentage Change in S&P 500 with dividends	in S&P 500 without dividends
1973	4.7%	14.8%	−17.4%
1974	5.5%	−26.4%	−29.7%
1975	21.9%	37.2%	31.5%
1976	59.3%	23.6%	19.1%
1977	31.9%	−7.4%	11.5%
1978	24.0%	6.4%	1.1%
1979	35.7%	18.2%	12.3%
1980	19.3%	32.3%	25.8%
1981	31.4%	−5.0%	−9.7%
1982	40.0%	21.4%	14.8%

(See Chairman's Letter, Berkshire Hathaway Annual Report, 2002, dated
March 6, 2003, page 3, for a comparison of gains in Berkshire Hathaway's per-
share book value versus the S&P 500 with dividends reinvested; see also Gail
Dudack, SunGard Institutional Brokerage, "Weekly Update" July 3, 2002, for
gains on S&P 500 without dividends reinvested.)

22. The story that follows is based on an interview with the author. For the story of
how Allyn fared in the late nineties, see Chapter 16, "Fully Deluded Earnings."

23. It could be argued that since the seventies was a period when inflation was unusually high, "real returns" distort the market's performance. But the fact is, in
the real world, only "real returns" (after inflation) measure the concrete value
of money: its purchasing power. Moreover, just as inflation was much higher
in the seventies than it would be at the end of the century, dividends were also
much higher than they would be in 2000. When the bull market of 1982–99
ended, investors did not have to worry about inflation eating their savings, but
they also had little in the way of dividends to reinvest.

What the stretch from 1966 to 1986 illustrates is that success in the market is not simply about being patient—everything turns on when you got in. 1954 was a good beginning point; 1968 was not. 1974, on the other hand, presented the buying opportunity of a lifetime. But for most investors, the bottom came too late. By then, they had no money left.

24. Bob Farrell, interview with the author.

25. "The Death of Equities: How Inflation Is Destroying the Stock Market," *Business Week,* 13 August 1979, 54. Note these numbers are all before inflation. Returns on the EAFE are from October 1970 through October 1980. See also Marc Faber, *Tomorrow's Gold* (Hong Kong: CLSA Books, 2002), 33, for a table showing how real assets trumped both U.S. stocks and bonds from June 1970 to June 1980.

On the whole, the only investors who made money in the stock market in the seventies were those who traded small caps. But a trader had to be nimble enough to move in and out of the small-cap market, buying in the valleys, selling at the peaks, tripping from peak to peak.

26. "The Death of Equities," 54. Not everyone agreed with *Business Week.* A month later *Forbes* ran a cover story that challenged Wall Street's obituary. "Back from the Dead?" asked the cover. The article that followed reminded readers that the great bull market of 1954–1969 "was born in an atmosphere of gloom and doom differing from today's only in its rationalizations, not its intensity." When *Forbes* published its story, the Dow was hovering in a more promising range, vacillating between 850 and the high 880s.

27. "The Death of Equities," 54.

28. These numbers are after adjusting for splits. Marc Faber makes the point in his newsletter, *The Gloom, Boom and Doom Report,* June 2001.

29. "Up & Down Wall Street," *Barron's,* 23 August 1982; "Barron's Mailbag," *Barron's,* 6 September 1982, 45.

30. Warren Buffett, Chairman's 1981 letter to Berkshire Hathaway shareholders, 26 February 1982. As 1982 began, Buffett remained pessimistic: "We applaud the efforts of Federal Reserve Chairman Volcker and note the currently more moderate increases in various price indices," Buffett wrote in his 1981 letter to investors, dated February 26, 1982. "Nevertheless, our views regarding long-term inflationary trends are as negative as ever. Like virginity, a stable price level seems capable of maintenance, but not of restoration."

CHAPTER 4

1. As always when dividing history up into neat periods, beginning and ending points are subjective. One could easily argue that the first phase of the bull market ended in 1987, and that the second phase did not begin until 1992. But the recession of 1990–91, coupled with the Gulf War, marks a clear economic and political turning point. In retrospect, one could say that those two events inspired political and economic policy for the next 13 years. Meanwhile, the fact that the market bounced sharply in 1991 confirms that the underlying trend was positive. The bull was still in charge of the market.

2. "The Rebirth of Equities," *Business Week,* 9 May 1983, 120.

3. Dennis Slocum, "Stock Markets Update: Rally Indicates Portfolio Managers Switching from Defence to Offence," *The Globe and Mail,* 21 August 1982, B5.

4. Dow Jones News Service, "*Barron's* Four Technical Analysts See Start of Big Bull Market," 11 October 1982.

5. Bob Farrell, interview with the author.

6. Most of the new IPOs traded "over the counter" rather than on one of the major exchanges, and by the fall of 1983 Farrell reported that at least 20 percent of the 5,254 over-the-counter stocks that he watched had tumbled more than 50 percent from their peaks earlier that year. See Dow Jones Newswires, "Many Unlisted Stocks Suffer Big Decline from Earlier Highs," 10 November 1983.

7. Bob Farrell, interview with the author. Over the course of 1983, the S&P gained more than 19 percent, but by the end of the year it was stalling out.

8. Herb Greenberg, "Individual Investors Taking Little Stock," *The Chicago Tribune,* 19 May 1985.

9. "The Rebirth of Equities."

10. Gail Dudack made this point in Jack Egan, "The Bull Turns 5 and Roars On," *U.S. News & World Report,* 10 August 1987, 54.

11. Linda Sandler, "Heard on the Street: Liquidity Is Stoking Stock Prices, Some Say, But Others Warn It Could Dry Up Suddenly," *The Wall Street Journal,* 3 August 1987. Over the six years ending in '89, "merger and acquisition activity has risen by more than 50% on an annual basis," *Barron's* reported. "The number of deals $100 million and over has risen by 150% since 1983." Benjamin Stein, "End of an Era? Why the Great Takeover Frenzy of the Eighties May Have Peaked," *Barron's,* 28 August 1989, 14. In a June 1989 PaineWebber report, "Beyond the Debt Deluge," analysts Thomas Doerflinger and Edward Kerschner reported that from 1984 to 1988, 121 firms had disappeared

from the S&P 500, representing 14.1 percent of the market capitalization of the index.

12. Even though inflation was falling, real interest rates (interest rates minus infla-tion) remained steep enough that from a businessman's point of view, the real cost of borrowing money to build his factory and buy his own real estate was unreasonably high. It made much more sense to scoop up an existing company.

13. For an extended, insightful analysis of how inflation and high real interest rates drove a takeover frenzy that was fueled by junk bonds, see Benjamin Stein, "End of an Era?"

14. *Business Week* described the reversal of debt/equity ratios in Sarah Bartlett, "Power Investors: Now All Street Firms Want to Hold the Company—Not Its Shares," 20 June 1988. PaineWebber's report "Beyond the Debt Deluge" de-scribes how, with the advent of the LBO, managers had a "radically different goal."

15. Ellyn Spragins, "When Power Investors Call the Shots," *Business Week,* 20 June 1988, 126.

16. Bryan Burrough and John Helyar, *Barbarians at the Gate: The Fall of RJR Nabisco* (New York: HarperPerennial, 1991), 514.

17. James Grant, "Michael Milken, Meet Sewell Avery," *Forbes,* 23 October 1989.

18. Byron Wein, interview with the author. See Chapter 16 ("Fully Deluded Earnings") on Cisco's earnings.

19. James Grant, "Michael Milken, Meet Sewell Avery."

20. Jeffrey M. Laderman, "The Bulls Breathe Fire," *Business Week,* 25 November 1985, 34.

21. Dean Rotbart, "Market Hardball: Aggressive Methods of Some Short Sellers Stir Critics to Cry Foul: Loosely Allied Traders Pick a Stock, Then Sow Doubt in an Effort to Depress It—Gray Area of Securities Law," *The Wall Street Jour-nal,* 5 September 1985.

22. Dean Rotbart, "Market Hardball."

23. Jim Chanos, interview with the author.

24. Dow Jones News, "Young Analyst Foresaw Baldwin-United's Ills." (Dow Jones News Service edited *Wall Street Journal* stories), 28 September 1983.

25. Dow Jones News, "Young Analyst Foresaw Baldwin United's Ills."

26. Jim Chanos, interview with the author.

27. Jim Chanos, interview with the author.

28. Kate Welling, "Wounded Bear," *Barron's,* 3 June 1991, 16.

29. In 1987, *The Wall Street Journal* reported that, according to the NYSE's best estimate, the number of individual investors had risen from 30.6 million at

the end of 1981 to 36 million at the end of 1985. Tim Metz, "Bull's Run: Stocks Five-Year Rise Has Showered Benefits Unevenly in Economy: Institutions, Brokers, Some of Rich Gained the Most While Millions Lost Jobs," *The Wall Street Journal,* 10 August 1987.

30. *The Wall Street Journal* reported on a Labor Department study showing that 10.8 million Americans lost their jobs in plant closings and layoffs in the five years to January 1986. Meanwhile, the Conference Board's researchers estimated that from 1984 through 1986, corporate restructurings and mergers eliminated 600,000 management jobs. (Tim Metz, "Bull's Run: Stocks Five-Year Rise.") While unemployment stood at "only" 5.9 percent in '87—down from 9.7 percent in '81—many relatively well paid middle-class and upper-middle-class workers had lost their jobs.

31. Tim Metz, "Bull's Run: Stocks Five-Year Rise."

32. See Robert Shiller, *Irrational Exuberance* (New York: Broadway Books, 2000), 218.

33. On Fidelity Magellan, see Joseph Nocera, *A Piece of the Action: How the Middle Class Joined the Money Class* (New York: Simon & Schuster, 1994), 337; for net sales of stock funds versus bond and income funds, see Stan Hinden, "1986, a Year of Thrills and Chills for Mutual Fund Investors," *The Washington Post,* 12 January 1987, f28.

34. Maggie Mahar, "The Case of the Vanishing Investor," *Barron's,* 10 October 1998.

CHAPTER 5

1. "Business Digest," *The New York Times,* 14 August 1987.

2. James Grant, *Grant's Interest Rate Observer,* 14 December 1987, 11.

3. "American Survey: Mini-Money Management," *The Economist,* 6 June 1987 (no byline).

4. Tim Metz, "Bull's Run: Stocks Five-Year Rise Has Showered Benefits Unevenly in the Economy," *The Wall Street Journal,* 10 August 1987.

5. In May of 1987 *Forbes* reported, "According to Lynch, Jones & Ryan, there are more securities analysts raising 1988 earnings estimates for the companies they follow than there are analysts who are reducing their estimates. Skeptics say analysts must do this to justify the high prices they are advising their institutional investor clients to pay for stocks today." Gretchen Morgenson, "A Checklist for Stock Market Prognosticators," *Forbes,* 4 May 1987.

6. Buffett's letter to shareholders was quoted in "What Buffett Isn't Buying Now: Warren Buffett Says Stocks Are Too High," *Fortune,* 27 April 1987, 7.

7. Maggie Mahar, "The Case of the Vanishing Investor," *Barron's*, 10 October 1988.

8. John Kenneth Galbraith, *A Short History of Financial Euphoria* (New York: Whittle Books, in association with Penguin Books, 1990), 10.

   Galbraith points out, "*The Times* later relented and arranged with the *Atlantic* editors for publication of an interview that covered much of the same ground. However, until the crash of October 19 of that year, the response to the piece was both sparse and unfavorable. 'Galbraith doesn't like to see people making money,' was one of the more corroding observations. After October 19, however, almost everyone I met told me that he had read and admired the article; on the day of the crash itself, some 40 journalists and television commentators from Tokyo, across the United States and on to Paris and Milan called me for comment."

9. Mark Hulbert, "The Acid Test," *Forbes*, 16 November 1987. Russell was not the only market timer who saw Black Monday coming, he reported. Robert Prechter, editor of *The Elliott Wave Theorist*, advised his readers to sell stocks and got into cash on October 7. In early August, Martin Zweig, editor of the *Zweig Forecast*, recommended that 90 percent of an investor's portfolio be in stocks; by early October, he had cut his recommendation to 20 percent and advised readers to take a small position in puts—a bet that the market would fall.

10. Steve Leuthold, interview with the author.

11. Richard Broderick, "Avoiding the Herd on the Street," *Corporate Report Minnesota*, June 1988, 48.

12. Byron Wein, "Knowing When the End Is Near," *Investment Strategy Letter*, 24 March 1987.

13. Maggie Mahar, "In the Pits: Reports from the Battle Scene in 'Frisco, Chicago," *Barron's*, 15 October 1987.

14. Friday evening, Ackerman tracked the author down in a Boston hotel, where she was on assignment for a story. At that point he told her, "It's over."

15. Maggie Mahar, "In the Pits."

16. Hank Gilman, "Fidelity Runs into a Wall: Crown Prince of Financial Services Firms Faces Cuts, Rumors of Layoffs," *The Boston Globe*, 28 February 1988.

17. In an interview with the author, Havey Eisen, chairman of Bedford Oak Partners, recalled: "Peter Lynch told me how they handed the stock out, alphabetically, to the traders." In August of 1987, Lynch had told *Barron's* that, if forced to sell by mass redemptions, this would be his strategy: "You just sell 10,000 of everything or 2,000 of everything. You know, if you only have 50

stocks, you've got a problem. You've got to sell a million shares of everything."
Jaye Scholl, "Neff and Lynch: Contrasting Styles, Comparable Success," *Barron's,* 10 August 1987.

18. Joseph Nocera, *A Piece of the Action: How the Middle Class Joined the Moneyed Class* (New York: Simon & Schuster, 1994), 349. The question, of course, is whether Johnson—or anyone—could have predicted the crash. Nocera argued, "It's obvious now—and it should have been obvious at the time—that the first eight months of 1987 marked the final, frenzied run-up that always comes before an awful fall," and notes that "a surprisingly long list" of soothsayers saw the crash coming: "In January, and again in October, *The Atlantic Monthly* ran articles (one by Galbraith, the other by . . . investment banker Peter G. Peterson) . . . in *Harper's,* financial writer L. J. Davis weighed in as did Michael M. Thomas in *The Nation.* Elaine Garzarelli, a quantitative analyst for Shearson Lehman Brothers . . . was so sure that the end was near that when appeared on CNN a week before the crash, she said flatly that the stock market was on the verge of collapse. James Grant, of *Grant's Interest Rate Observer,* was similarly convinced . . . Jim Rogers, the well-known investor . . . was a bear . . ." (344, 345).

19. Anne Swardson, "Mutual Fund Withdrawals Slow Down; Some Funds Sell Stocks to Pay Off Customers," *The Washington Post,* 21 October 1987, F1.

20. Bill Powell with Peter McKillop, "Looking into the Abyss," *Newsweek,* 2 November 1987, 24.

21. Edward Wyatt, "Assessing the Legacy of the '87 Crash," *The New York Times,* 19 October 1997. "J. Gary Burkhead, a vice chairman of Fidelity Investments, said in an interview that Fidelity's stock sales on Oct. 19 totaled only about 10 percent of the early trading on the Big Board," *The New York Times* later reported. "In addition, he said, its trading on Black Monday accounted for just under 4.5 percent of total volume on the New York exchange, in line with the 2 percent to 4 percent of daily volume that Fidelity accounted for in all of 1987. But," the *Times* noted, "according to the report of the Securities and Exchange Commission on the crash, the magnitude of Fidelity's sell orders on Oct. 19 indicate that it did play a significant role for the day."

22. Maggie Mahar, "The Case of the Vanishing Investor."

23. Alan Murray, "A Silver Lining to the Crash?" *The Wall Street Journal,* 26 November 1987.

24. Grossman did not act on Welch's advice. "Reporters were never told of the chairman's problem," Grossman reported in "Regulate the Medium, Liberate the Message; Original Intent in the Electronic Age," *Columbia Journalism Re-*

view, November/December 1991, XXX, no. 4, 72. But when Grossman wrote
the article in 1991, he was concerned that GE, through NBC, had just been
"allowed to acquire 100 percent ownership of FNN, cable's number-one consumer news and business service. It then promptly closed down FNN," Grossman observed, "merging it into CNBC, GE's newer and smaller financial
cable program service, giving it a monopoly position in the field." In Grossman's view, "GE should certainly not be allowed to own [the major] financial
cable news service. Nor, following the ITT-ABC precedent, should GE—one
of the nation's largest defense contractors, financial service companies, consumer product producers, and advertisers—have ever been permitted to own
and control NBC, one of the nation's most powerful broadcasters."

25. Steve Leuthold, interview with the author.

26. Peter L. Bernstein, *Capital Ideas: The Improbable Origins of Modern Wall Street*
    (New York: The Free Press, 1991), 291. Bernstein takes his numbers from the
    Brady Report.

27. Benjamin Stein, "Whimpers from the West, or, Can I Still Have Dinner at
    Mortons?" *Barron's,* 2 November 1987.

28. Barbara Donnelly, "Efficient Market Theorists Are Puzzled by Recent Gyra-
    tions in Stock Market," *The Wall Street Journal,* 23 October 1987.

29. Barbara Donnelly, "Efficient Market Theorists Are Puzzled."

30. "1962 All Over Again? It May Be Happening Says Steve Leuthold" (Q&A in-
    terview with Kate Welling), *Barron's,* 26 October 1987.

31. Steve Leuthold, interview with the author.

32. Richard Broderick, "Avoiding the Herd on Wall Street," *Corporate Report
    Minnesota,* June 1988, 48.

33. Edward Wyatt, "Legacy of the '87 Crash: Assessing the Role of Mutual Fund
    Investors," *The New York Times,* 19 October 1997.

34. Charles Schwab, as quoted in Maggie Mahar, "The Case of the Vanishing In-
    vestor."

35. In *A Piece of the Action,* Joseph Nocera seems, at first, to support the myth:
    "After the crash of 1987, small investors did not turn and run, at least not in
    huge numbers . . ." But he then clarifies what happened, confirming Schwab's
    experience. The fund companies, Nocera explains, saw customers "move their
    money in ways that reflected a new caution, shifting assets from an aggressive
    fund to a less aggressive one, from an equity fund to a bond fund, from a bond
    fund to a money market fund. But they kept their assets in the company"
    (367–78). In other words, individual investors remained loyal to their mutual

fund companies—which was gratifying for the companies—but they did not stick with stocks. And for the stock market, that was all that mattered.

See Thomas Frank, *One Market Under God* (New York: Anchor Books, 2001), 1–88, for an extended, insightful discussion of populist myths and what Frank calls "the democracy bubble."

36. Hank Gillman, "Fidelity Runs into a Wall: 'Crown Prince' of Financial Service Firms Faces Cuts, Rumors of Layoffs," *The Boston Globe,* 28 February 1998, 81.

37. In 1968, close to 35 percent of household assets were invested in stocks, directly or indirectly, through mutual funds, defined contribution plans like 401(k)s, bank trusts, and estates, according to the Federal Reserve. In 1989, households had only about 13 percent of their assets in equities.

38. Maggie Mahar, "The Case of the Vanishing Investor."

39. Interview with the author.

40. Bryan Burrough and John Helyar, *Barbarians at the Gate: The Fall of RJR Nabisco* (New York: HarperPerennial, 1991), 186.

41. Thomas Doerflinger and Edward Kerschner, "Beyond the Debt Deluge," PaineWebber report, 1989; Burrough and Helyar, *Barbarians at the Gate,* 187.

42. Sarah Bartlett, "Power Investors: Now Wall Street Firms Want to Own the Company—Not Just Its Shares," *Business Week,* 20 June 1988, 123.

43. Doerflinger and Kerschner, "Beyond the Debt Deluge."

44. Burrough and Helyar, *Barbarians at the Gate,* 512.

45. James Stewart, *Den of Thieves* (New York: Simon & Schuster, 1991), 503.

46. James Stewart attributes these numbers on junk bond gains to Lipper Analytical Services in *Den of Thieves,* 503–4.

47. Burrough and Helyar, *Barbarians at the Gate,* 511, 512, 514.

48. Jim Chanos, interview with the author.

49. Bob Farrell, interview with the author.

CHAPTER 6

1. Goldman's 1990 profits were reported in *The Economist,* which noted that "for the first time in years, Goldman is making money at every turn [with] the firm's oil and foreign-exchange operations contributing almost one-third of the profit" ("Wall Street's Shining Maiden," 29 September 1990, 93). By 1991 Goldman officially would become Wall Street's most profitable firm, with pretax profit of roughly $1.1 billion (Michael Siconolfi, "Goldman Sachs Assumes the Crown," *The Wall Street Journal Europe,* 23 September 1992, 9).

2. Abby Joseph Cohen, interview with the author.

3. On attire and manners at Goldman in 1990, see William Power and Michael Siconolfi, "Who Will Be Rich? How Goldman Sachs Chooses New Partners: With a Lot of Angst," *The Wall Street Journal,* 19 October 1990, A1.

4. "Wall Street's Shining Maiden," 93.

5. Jack Willoughby, "Can Goldman Stay on Top?" *Forbes,* 18 September 1989, 150.

6. That year, Goldman would promote two more women to partnership, bringing the total to three by year-end.

7. Martin Mayer, *The Fed: The Inside Story of How the World's Most Powerful Financial Institution Drives the Markets* (New York: The Free Press, 2001), 317.

8. Abby Joseph Cohen, interview with the author.

9. Michael Ellison, "Abby Cohen: Mother of All Optimists Stands Firm. Wall Street Loves Her," *The Guardian,* 24 October 1998, 24.

10. Michael Ellison, "Abby Cohen."

11. Abby Joseph Cohen, interview with the author.

12. Roger Lowenstein, "Bottoming Out? A Bearish Strategist Says It Isn't Happening Yet," *The Wall Street Journal,* 6 September 1990, C1.

13. Kate Welling, "Bullish but Not Ranting: Investment Strategist Abby Cohen Tempers Her Optimism," *Barron's,* 12 June 1989.

14. Pat Widder, "Will 3000 be a launching pad or a roadblock for the Dow?" *The Chicago Tribune,* 16 July 1990.

15. Abby Joseph Cohen, interview with the author.

16. Alan Abelson, "Up & Down Wall Street," *Barron's,* 23 December 1991.

17. Jack Egan and Edward Baig, "Is the Bull Back?" *U.S. News & World Report,* 25 February 1991.

18. Roger Lowenstein and Craig Torres, "Market Milestone: At 3000, Dow Reflects a Very Different Rally from One Last July," *The Wall Street Journal,* 18 April 1991; Craig Torres and Douglas Sease, "Further to Go? Stocks Aren't Cheap but Market Could Keep Barreling Ahead," *The Wall Street Journal,* 15 April 1991.

19. Douglas Sease, "Dow's Drop Seen as Temporary Setback," *The Wall Street Journal,* 25 November 1991.

20. Terence P. Pare, "Investing for Hard Times," *Fortune,* 30 December 1991, 74. After all, Cohen pointed out, corporations buying back their own shares accounted for "as much as 3.2% of that return," and at the end of 1991 the buy-

backs were not likely to continue. By then, companies were far more interested in issuing shares than in buying them.

21. Abby Joseph Cohen, interview with the author.

22. Jonathan Laing, "Stay Relaxed: Abby Cohen Says There's No Bear in Sight," *Barron's,* 30 August 1999.

23. Antony Bianco, "The Prophet of Wall Street: How Abby Cohen came to be one of the most closely watched forecasters on the planet," *Business Week,* 1 June 1998.

24. Bill Seidman, interview with the author.

25. Bill Seidman, interview with the author. For an entertaining history of Seidman's career in Washington, see William Seidman, *Full Faith and Credit: The Great S&L Debacle and Other Washington Sagas* (New York: Beard Books, 1993).

26. Bill Seidman, interview with the author.

27. Justin Martin, *Greenspan: The Man Behind the Money* (Cambridge: Perseus Publishing, 2000) 2*ff.* "To help make ends meet," Martin explains, "Rose [Greenspan's mother] took a job in the domestic department at Ludwig-Bauman, a furniture store . . . in the Bronx. Following the divorce, Herbert [Greenspan's father] became very distant. Visits to his son were infrequent at best" (2).

28. Bob Woodward, *Maestro: Greenspan's Fed and the American Boom* (New York: Simon & Schuster, 2000), 55.

29. Interview with the author.

30. John Cassidy, "The Fountainhead," in *The New Gilded Age: The New Yorker Looks at the Culture of Affluence,* edited by David Remnick (New York: Random House, 2000), 37.

31. John Cassidy, "The Fountainhead," 31, 32.

32. Justin Martin, *Greenspan,* 128–29.

33. John Cassidy, "The Fountainhead," 31, 37.

34. Bob Woodward, *Maestro,* 16, 21, 24.

35. Bob Woodward, *Maestro,* 28.

36. Leon Levy with Eugene Linden, *The Mind of Wall Street* (New York: Public Affaris, 2002), 154.

37. Of Greenspan's 24 consecutive cuts, James Grant observed: "The Federal Reserve's . . . cuts in short-term interest rates from 1989 to 1992 brought to mind the 24 major printings of a runaway best-seller whose publisher had initially expected to sell only 2,000 copies. It did not burnish the publisher's rep-

utation for commercial judgments." *The Trouble with Prosperity: The Loss of Fear, the Rise of Speculation, and the Risk to American Savings* (New York: Times Books, 1996), 197.

38. Martin Mayer, *The Fed,* 220.

39. William Seidman, *Full Faith and Credit: The Great S&L Debacle and Other Washington Sagas* (New York: Beard Books, 1993).

40. Maggie Mahar, "Shooting the Messenger," *Barron's,* 7 May 1990.

41. Maggie Mahar, "Shooting the Messenger."

42. James Grant, *The Trouble with Prosperity,* 206.

43. James Grant, *The Trouble with Prosperity,* 206.

44. The survey, done by Sindlinger & Co, was published in *Investor's Business Daily.*

45. Greenspan would be the survivor. As Justin Martin notes in *Greenspan: The Man Behind the Money,* "Despite a deteriorating relationship with Clinton, Greenspan still wound up getting renominated in 1996. Clinton became another president in a long line who simply didn't have a choice. . . . Republicans made up the majority in Congress now. An election loomed in 1996, and they weren't about to let the president select a new Fed chairman without a fight" (211).

46. Charles Gasparino, "The Soaring '90s: Behind the Investing Giants and Stocks That Marked a Decade; Analyze This," *The Wall Street Journal,* 13 December 1999, C1.

47. Andrew Bary, " 'Net Queen: How Mary Meeker Came to Rule the Internet," *Barron's,* 21 December 1998, 23.

48. Heather Green, "The E Biz 25: Visionaries," *Business Week,* 27 September 1999.

49. Heather Green, "The E Biz 25: Visionaries."

50. Interview with the author.

51. Interview with the author.

52. Joe Nocera, *Frontline,* PBS, September 2001.

53. Interview with the author.

54. Interview with the author.

55. Both the report that Quattrone tried to steal Meeker from Morgan Stanley and that she claimed responsibility for having brought Netscape to his attention appeared in Peter Elkind's "Where Mary Meeker Went Wrong," *Fortune,* 14 May 2002, 68.

56. Dave Kansas and Molly Baker, "Did Netscape Mania Reflect Frothy Market? Maybe Not," *The Wall Street Journal,* 11 August 1995, C1: "Certainly in the

past the occasional red hot IPO hasn't tended to signal much about the overall market."

57. Heather Green, "The E Biz 25: Visionaries."

58. Byron Wein, interview with the author.

59. Janice Maloney and James Aley, "So You Want to Be a Software Superstar: Beyond the Valley of the Geeks," *Fortune,* 10 June 1996.

60. Interview with the author.

CHAPTER 7

1. Maggie Mahar, "The Great Pension Raid," *Barron's,* 2 December 1991, 8.

2. In 1991, when the insurance fund covered pensions up to $27,000, median household income was roughly $30,000. If an employee retired before age 65, the insurance fund guaranteed less.

    Private-sector employers funded the insurance pool; as of 1993, they paid $19 per worker per year if their pension was considered to be "fully funded"— more if it was underfunded. (See Mark Trumbull, "No Taxpayer Bailout Needed for Pensions: Federal Pension–Insurance Agency's Financial Problems Can Be Resolved, Experts Say," *Christian Science Monitor,* 11 February 1993.

    Nevertheless, there were times when retirees fell through the cracks of the federal insurance program. For example, if a company went bankrupt, an employee who had been offered a "supplemental" retirement package in exchange for retiring early might well find that the federal insurance did not cover the supplement. See Maggie Mahar, "The Great Pension Raid," 8.

3. William Wolman and Anne Colamasca, *The 401(k) Hoax* (New York: Perseus Publishing, 2002), 46.

4. Wyatt, "Pension Change Puts the Burden on the Worker," *The New York Times,* 5 April 2002, C2.

5. In *The 401(k) Hoax,* Wolman and Colamasca provide the numbers on the share of unionized workers covered by defined benefit plans in 1998, and argue that while "unions have always gotten more flak than companies for the way they administer pension plans . . . there is no serious evidence that their misdeeds are more flagrant than those of the bosses. Call it the 'Hoffa effect.'" (161).

6. In 2000, the Employee Benefits Research Institute estimated that 30 percent of all U.S. workers had no employer-sponsored retirement plan, 20 percent were covered by defined benefit plans, and 50 percent were covered by defined contribution plans.

7. 401(k) investors were now committing 56 percent of their savings to stocks. See Ellen Schultz, "Personal Finance (A Special Report): Identifying the Issue, for Your Benefit, All Those Corporate Extras Are Going to Get a Lot More Complicated," *The Wall Street Journal,* 9 December 1994, R25.

8. Ellen Schultz, "Tidal Wave of Retirement Cash Anchors Mutual Funds," *The Wall Street Journal,* 17 September 1995, C1.

9. Maggie Mahar, "You Must Buy Stocks," *Barron's,* 20 May 1996, A12 (quoting from Federal Reserve numbers).

10. Jennifer Postlewaithe, interview with the author. The investor's name has been changed to protect her privacy.

11. Shirley Sauerwein, interview with the author; and "Behind the Movers of the Soaring '90s: A *Wall Street Journal* Roundup," compiled by Mitchell Pacelle, Randall Smith, Rebecca Buckman, Greg Ip, and Susan Pulliam, *The Wall Street Journal Europe,* 14 December 1999, 17. The *Journal* reported on Sauerwein's investing in 1999; in 2002, the author followed up on her story.

12. *The Collected Writing of John Maynard Keynes,* vol. XII, *Economic Articles and Correspondence* (Cambridge: University Press, 1983), 108. Jeremy Grantham, chairman of Grantham, Mayo, Van Otterloo & Co., quoted Keynes on this point in a letter to his investors, August 12, 2002.

13. Earl C. Gottschalk Jr., "Personal Finance (A Special Report): Planning for Retirement: On Your Own, Companies Are Giving Employees Investment Control of Their Retirement Money; That Can Be Good—or Bad," *The Wall Street Journal,* 9 December 1994, R19.

14. Thomas Frank, *One Market Under God* (New York: Anchor Books, 2001), 41.

15. Fred Kelly, *Why You Win or Lose* (Burlington, Vermont: Fraser Publishing, reprint edition, 1995).

16. Malcolm Forbes Jr., as quoted in Dean LeBaron and Romesh Vaitilingam, with Marilyn Pitchford, *Ultimate Book of Investment Quotations* (Oxford: Capstone Publishing, 1999), 173.

17. For an excellent summary of inflation-adjusted returns from various investments from World War II through 1991, see Barton Biggs, "Are Stocks Everyone's Best Friend?" *Barron's,* 23 March 1992.

18. Maggie Mahar, "The Great Pension Raid."

19. Maggie Mahar, "The Great Pension Raid."

20. As a result of the Retirement Protection Act of 1994, passed in January of 1995, if a pension fund was 150 percent funded, it would lose its tax break if it continued to add to its pension.

21. In 2001 a Profit Sharing/401(k) Council of America survey reported that 18

percent of 401(k) plans had more than half of plan assets invested in company stock. Meanwhile, the average 401(k) had 39 percent of its assets invested in company stock, down from 41 percent the previous year, Steve Leuthold reported in his *Investment Insight,* December 2001, 52–53.

22. Mary Williams Walsh, "8 Billion Surplus Withers at Agency Insuring Pensions," *The New York Times,* 25 January 2003, 1. By 2003, the insurance pool's own surplus was shrinking, and there was talk of raising the premiums that corporations paid to keep the fund going. In the worst-case scenario, observers expected that the government (i.e., taxpayers) would bail the fund out.

23. Gary Wasserman's story is based on interviews with the author. (Note: Gary Wasserman is the older brother of Ed Wasserman, who appeared in Chapter 1.)

24. Bill Fleckenstein, interview with the author.

25. Wasserman took a loss on a small position in Internet stocks, but by then his portfolio had already paid for his son's college education.

26. According to "Equity Ownership in America 2002," a report done jointly by the Investment Company Institute and the Securities Industry Association, an estimated 14 percent of all shareholders made their first equity investment in "1999 or later": 16 percent from 1996 to 1998; 26 percent from 1990 to 1996, and 44 percent before 1990. The report is available on SIA.com.

27. Maggie Mahar, "The New Investors," *Barron's,* 30 August 1993, 8.

28. Maggie Mahar, "The New Investors," 8.

29. For a fuller discussion of the Fed's rate cutting, see Jim Grant, *The Trouble with Prosperity: The Loss of Fear, the Rise of Speculation, and the Risk to American Savings* (New York: Times Books, 1996) 197, 239.

30. Maggie Mahar, "You Must Buy Stocks," *Barron's,* 20 May 1995, 12; and Maggie Mahar, "Sitting Tight," *Barron's,* 29 July 1996.

31. Maggie Mahar, "You Must Buy Stocks."

32. The survey "Equity Ownership 2002," showing when various groups first began buying stocks, was published jointly by the Investment Company Institute and the Securities Industry Association. See table "Who Owns Stocks?" Appendix, pages 463–64.

33. Michael Malone, interview with the author. Portions of the interview were quoted in Maggie Mahar, "You Must Buy Stocks," and Maggie Mahar, "Sitting Tight."

34. Maggie Mahar, "The Case of the Vanishing Investor," *Barron's,* 10 October 1998, 8. The story quotes the Securities Industry Association on the percentage of trades by individual investors in 1985 and 1988.

35. Maggie Mahar, "The Case of the Vanishing Investor," 8.

36. "1991 had been a disaster for the real estate market in most areas," *Business Week* reported in the autumn of 1992, and in 1992, despite the fact that mortgage rates stood at 19-year lows, "residential real estate in California and much of the Northeast remains a picture of despair," the magazine noted, citing prices down "by as much as one-third" from their highs in the eighties. (Larry Light, with Nancy Peacock, Sandra D. Atchison, and Dori Jones Yang. "Real Estate Slump? What Real Estate Slump?" *Business Week,* 28 September 1992, 119.)

37. Maggie Mahar, "The New Investors."

38. Peter Bernstein, interview with the author.

39. David Craig, "Sunny Outlook for Recovery Encouraging," *USA Today,* 2 January 1992, 1.

40. Maggie Mahar, "The New Investors," 8.

41. *The Merrill Lynch Baby Boom Retirement Index,* prepared by Dr. Douglas Bernhaem, Stanford University, and sponsored by Merrill Lynch & Co., 1994.

42. A 1993 survey of upscale boomers with incomes of $50,000 or more showed that they were saving, on average, more than $6,000 a year. (Maggie Mahar, "The New Investor.")

43. Peter Bernstein, interview with the author.

44. Typically, 401(k) plans offered three stock funds for every bond fund. Investors who tried to spread their money evenly wound up putting three-quarters of their money into stocks. (Robert Shiller, *Irrational Exuberance,* New York: Broadway Books, 2001.) Meanwhile, many employers matched contributions with company stock—and in many cases, employees were not allowed to sell that stock for a fixed number of years. Finally, over the course of the nineties fixed income alternatives like GICs, Treasuries, or TIPS became rarer, as did opportunities to invest in "asset allocation funds" that allowed a value manager to go into cash or bonds when stocks became pricey. For a fuller discussion of how the most popular growth funds of the nineties tied a fund manager's hands, see Chapters 12 and 13.

45. William Gross, interview with the author. To be fair, it is worth noting that Pimco is a highly lucrative business: its "load" funds are not inexpensive. Nevertheless, the company's advertising is, by Wall Street standards, low-key, not to mention honest, and long-term returns on Pimco's bond funds suggest that investors were receiving value for their money.

46. Richard Teitelbaum, "Getting the Most from Your 401 k," *Fortune,* 25 December 1995, 183.

47. Jeffrey M. Laderman, *Business Week,* 17 December 1993.

48. *The Washington Post,* 24 June 1994, ho1.

49. In *Irrational Exuberance,* Robert Shiller debunks "the widely cited 'fact' that in the United States there have been no 30-year periods over which bonds have outperformed stocks. The supposed fact is not really true," Shiller writes, because as Jeremy Siegel pointed out in his book *Stocks for the Long Run,* stocks underperformed bonds in the period 1831 to 1861 (15). "That may seem a long time ago," Shiller notes, "until one realizes that there are not many non-overlapping 30-year periods in U.S. stock market history: only four complete periods since 1861. Given the relatively short history of 30-year periods of stock market returns, we must recognize that there is little evidence that stocks cannot underperform in the future."

There are, of course, hundreds of ways of slicing and dicing "long-term" stock market returns: before inflation, after inflation, with or without dividends, over 10 years, over 20 years, since 1926, since World War II. . . . Financial pundits have used all of them in their search for a rule of thumb that will predict the future. In fact, there is no rule. All that can be said with certainty is that the future is unpredictable. This is why, over any 10-year period, stocks are riskier than, say, a 10-year Treasury bond that promises to pay 4.5 percent a year for 10 years, as long as the investor is willing to hold the bond until it matures.

Shiller sums up the difference between stocks and bonds: "Stocks are residual claims on corporate cash flows, available to shareholders only after everyone else [including bond holders] has been paid. Stocks, therefore, are by their very definition, risky. Investors have also lost sight of another truth: that no one is guaranteeing that stocks will do well. There is no welfare plan for people who lose in the stock market" (*Irrational Exuberance,* 195).

50. "Equity Ownership in America, 2002" broke households down by total financial assets instead of income, the results again showed that less affluent investors came to the market later. See note 32 above, and see table "Who Owns Stocks?" Appendix, pages 463–64.

51. For more of Cassidy's story, see Chapter 1.

CHAPTER 8

1. Chanos, the short seller who exposed Enron's bad accounting at the beginning of 2001, made the remark in a 2002 interview with the author.

2. Shawn Tully, "What CEOs Really Make—Salaries and Compensations," *Fortune,* 15 June 1992, 94.

3. Under IRS rules, employees pay income taxes on the gain they receive when they exercise their options, while their company receives a tax deduction equal to the gain.

4. John Byrne, "Executive Pay: The Party Ain't Over Yet," *Business Week,* 15 April 1993, 56; James Kim, "CEOs Cash in Options for Record Pay," *USA Today,* 16 April 1993, 2B; Christi Harlan, "High Anxiety: Accounting Proposal Stirs Unusual Uproar in Executive Suites—FASB's Stock-Option Plan Threatens Pay Packages: Lobbying Gets Intense—A Risk to High-Tech Firms," *The Wall Street Journal,* 7 March 1994; Brian Dumaine, "A Knock-out Year for CEO Pay," *Fortune,* 25 July 1994, 94.

5. Amanda Bennett, "Executive Pay: A Little Pain and a Lot to Gain," *The Wall Street Journal,* 22 April 1992, R1.

6. Kathy M. Kristof, "Special Report: Executive Pay—The More Things Change," *The Los Angeles Times,* 23 May 1993, 1.

7. John Byrne, "The Party Ain't Over Yet. SEC filings showed that Hirsch paid $12.25 a share for the 163,835 shares he sold in July of '92 at $90.15 to $95.64 (for a total of $15.3 million). See Georgette Jasen, "Four Executives Display Good Timing on Stock Moves," *The Wall Street Journal,* 19 August 1992, C1.

8. See Chapter 19 on insider selling.

9. Andy Kessler, a partner in Velocity Capital Management, made the remark in an op-ed piece that he wrote for *The Wall Street Journal,* "Manager's Journal: The Upside-Down World of High-Tech," 19 July 1999.

10. Christi Harlan, "High Anxiety."

11. Christi Harlan, "High Anxiety."

12. Maggie Mahar, "Wall Street's New Top Cop: Levitt Relishes Ambassadorial Duties, but Is He Tough Enough?" *Barron's,* 22 November 1993, 10.

13. Levitt was president of Shearson's predecessor. See Scott McMurray, "At a Crossroads: Continued Survival of Amex Is Threatened as Its Listings Decline," *The Wall Street Journal,* 2 July 1985.

14. Arthur Levitt with Paula Dwyer, *Take on the Street: What Wall Street and Corporate America Don't Want You to Know* (New York: Pantheon, 2002) 7.

15. Maggie Mahar, "Wall Street's New Top Cop."

16. Maggie Mahar, "Wall Street's New Top Cop."

17. Arthur Levitt with Paula Dwyer, *Take on the Street,* 10.

18. Arthur Levitt with Paula Dwyer, *Take on the Street,* 9–10.

19. Arthur Levitt, interview with the author.

20. Levin drew this figure from the Executive Compensation Report's survey of

1,100 companies. The 1993 figures are included in "Broad-based Stock Op tions—1999 Update" (William M. Mercer, Inc., 1999).

21. Arthur Levitt, interview with the author.

22. At the time, Shelby was a Democrat. The following year, he would cross over to join the Republican Party.

23. Member of Levin's staff, interview with the author. All quotations from the hearing are drawn from a transcript of the meeting and written testimony submitted at the time of the hearing.

24. Unfortunately, most Wall Street analysts lacked the training to competently evaluate the effect of options packages on earnings—even if they had the time and inclination. And the effect was substantial: In 2002, Bloomberg News columnist David Wilson reported that Microsoft, IBM, and Intel were among 11 members of the Dow whose fiscal 2001 net income would have been at least 10 percent lower if they had accounted for options. That group included Alcoa—which, if it had expensed options, would have had to admit that earnings were 20 percent lower than reported; American Express, 18 percent; General Motors, 38 percent; J.P. Morgan, 37 percent; Minnesota Mining & Manufacturing and Procter & Gamble, 11 percent apiece. Finally, if they had expensed options, Kodak and Hewlett-Packard would have found themselves in the red: Kodak's option grants in 2001 would have reduced earnings by $79 million (Bloomberg News, 3 April 2002).

25. The study Bradley referred to, showing that technology companies might have to admit that earnings were only half of what they claimed, was done by the Wyatt Company, a consulting company that focuses on human capital and financial management.

26. Arthur Levitt with Paula Dwyer, *Take on the Street*, 108.

27. Arthur Levitt, interview with the author.

28. For examples of companies taking on debt to finance buybacks designed to offset the dilution caused by options programs, see Chapter 16 ("Fully De luded Earnings"), which discusses the enormous losses Dell suffered after issuing call options to finance its employee stock options.

29. As James Montier, a global strategist at Dresdner Kleinwort Wasserstein has pointed out, the fact that dividend payouts tend to cause a drop in share prices "gives management a clear incentive to reduce dividends." (For the outside shareholder, the drop in share price is offset by the dividend, but an insider sitting on a pile of options receives no dividend.) Montier made the remark in a Q&A published in *welling@weeden*, 19 April 2002.

Instead of paying dividends, many companies stepped up share buyback programs. For an executive holding options, buybacks offered two advantages: (1) the announcement of a buyback program tended to boost share prices (whether or not the company ever followed through on the repurchase schedule), boosting the short-term value of his option, and (2) buybacks masked the dilution caused by options grants.

Meanwhile, management assured shareholders that they were cutting back dividends so that they could "enhance shareholder value" by plowing capital back into their companies. Often, they pointed to share repurchase programs as a better way to enhance value.

But even later in the decade, the net effect of the much-touted share repurchase programs remained "minuscule," Montier noted. "All of 50 basis points [one-half of one percent] was added by buybacks in 2001, for example . . . There was this huge myth about stock repurchases—that they had been a benefit to investors." In fact, throughout the nineties, "In general, investors would have been substantially better off if managers had returned the cash to them, rather than investing it for them." (For charts and a fuller description of Montier's research, see *welling@weeden,* 19 April 2002, 6 [www.weedenco.com/welling/contents]).

For the full effect of options programs on earnings, see Chapter 16 ("Fully Deluded Earnings").

30. Bunt's transaction as reported in "Insider Trading," *Orlando Sentinel,* 2 November 1998, 23. From January of 1998 to October of 2000, Bunt exercised the right to buy some 124,000 shares. In addition to the 25,000 shares sold in October '98, he exercised the option to buy 15,000 shares in January of 1998 and immediately sold them at $76.69, netting a little over $50 a share. On January 23, 2002, he unloaded some 34,000 shares. By year-end, GE's share price had fallen more than 32 percent since the date of his sales on January 23.

31. "Over his lifetime, he [Senator Lieberman] ranked #13 among his Senate colleagues for contributions from the securities and investment industry, having collected $652,000; and has gotten more than $101,000 from the computer industry." See "Wall Street Winners and Losers," PublicCampaign.org, 23 July 2002.

32. Miriam Hill, "Federal Accounting Standards Board Relies on Large Firms for Research, Advice," *The Philadelphia Inquirer,* 24 February 2002.

33. Citing the National Center for Employee Ownership and the Bureau of Labor Statistics, David Leonhardt reported these numbers as "the best estimates available" in "Corporate Conduct: Compensation: Stock Options Said Not to Be as Widespread as Backers Say," *The New York Times,* 18 July 2002.

34. Thomas Donlan, "Optional Equity," *Barron's,* 22 July 2002. See also David Leonhardt, "Corporate Conduct."

35. See Jennifer Reingold, "Executive Pay: The Numbers Are Staggering, but So Is the Performance of American Business. So How Closely Are They Linked?" *Business Week,* 19 April 1999, 72.

36. "Internally, companies value options all the time," according to TIAA-CREF chairman and CEO John Bigg's testimony before the U.S. Senate Finance Committee on April 18, 2002. "I can assure you that company executives and compensation consultants routinely use the Black-Scholes model to value employee options."

Various economists have developed various formulas to price options; the most popular is the Black-Scholes model, developed by economists Fischer Black and Myron Scholes, who won a Nobel Prize in economics for his work on the model.

But in its proposal, FASB did not insist that companies use the Black-Scholes model when expensing options. It left the question open for public comment. Honest men might disagree on what formula to use, but no one could honestly argue that employee stock options had no value.

FASB did, however, insist that options be expensed when an employee receives them.

Some observers would object: Why should a company measure the expense of an option and subtract it from profits before it is exercised? Why not wait until the executive exercises his options—at that point, the value is clear: it is the difference between the price he pays and the market price the day he exercises his options.

But the cost to the company is the cost of the option as a substitute for other forms of employee compensation, based on its value when the employee accepts options in lieu of cash compensation. That means that the value must include the risks involved, including the risk that the option will expire before the stock rises to the strike price. For this reason, the value at the time the options are issued may be significantly less than the profit that the employee might make. Particularly in a bull market, if companies were forced to expense options based on the full profit that the executive made when he exercised the option, the expense would, in most cases, turn out to be much larger than the value of the option when it was issued—with all of the uncertainties attached to its value at that time.

Admittedly, in the case of employee stock options, "the difficulty [of valuing them] is increased," Buffett acknowledged, "by the fact that options given to executives are restricted in various ways." For example, the executive cannot trade the option on the open market, and often he must wait several years before he can use the options to buy shares. "These restrictions restrict value," Buffett noted. "But they do not eliminate it."

37. "A Knockout Year for CEO Pay," *Fortune,* 25 July 1994.

38. Merton Miller and Graef Crystal, "Big Bucks for Big Execs: Who Pays for the Golden Egg?" *The Washington Post,* 20 March 1994, cO5.

39. Arthur Levitt, interview with the author.

40. Arthur Levitt, interview with the author.

41. Arthur Levitt with Paula Dwyer, *Take on the Street.*

42. *Business Week* published a list (see below) of the CEOs' "treasure chests" based on the market price of the shares at the end of the year. (John Byrne, "Special Report: CEO Pay: Ready for Takeoff," *Business Week,* 24 April 1995, 88.)

Executive/ Company	Value of Nonexercised Stock Options*
Michael Eisner Walt Disney	$171,880,000
Wayne Calloway Pepsico	$64,618,786
Lawrence Ellison Oracle	$60,518,900
Eckhard Pfeiffer Compaq Computer	$54,364,449
Paul Fireman Reebok International	$54,055,000
Gordon Binder Amgen	$49,634,253
William McGuire United Healthcare	$49,301,612
Robert Goizueta Coca-Cola	$46,440,625
James Donald DSC Communications	$41,210,000
Charles Wang Computer Assoc. Intl.	$37,420,811

Executive/ Company	Value of Nonexercised Stock Options*
John Tolleson First USA	$35,827,449
Reuben Mark Colgate-Palmolive	$33,093,694
Daniel Tully Merrill Lynch	$30,991,969
Edward McCracken Silicon Graphics	$29,905,068
Carl Reichardt Wells Fargo	$28,257,380
Harry Merlo Louisiana-Pacific	$27,795,000
Albert Dunlap Scott Paper	$23,343,750
John Welch General Electric	$22,634,375
Roy Vagelos Merck	$21,603,418

*BASED ON STOCK PRICE AT THE END OF THE COMPANY'S FISCAL YEAR.

43. Jeffrey Taylor, "Bill Curbing Investors' Lawsuits Wins SEC Support of 'Safe Harbor' Provision," *The Wall Street Journal,* 17 November 1995, A2.

44. Prepared witness testimony given by James Chanos on February 6, 2002, to the House Committee on Energy and Commerce in March of 2001. *Business Week Online* reported on how the Safe Harbor Act had reduced litigation: "Cases frequently take a year longer to get before a jury, and the cost of simply filing a suit has risen to more than $500,000 in some instances, plaintiffs' attorneys say. The odds of winning have also decreased. Before the passage of the Reform Act, 12% of all cases were dismissed outright by judges. That number has increased to 28% since the law was passed." Mike France, "This Crash Won't Make Lawyers Rich," 26 March 2001.

45. Jim Chanos, interview with the author.

46. Jeffrey Taylor, "Bill Curbing Investors' Lawsuits Wins SEC Support of 'Safe-Harbor' Provision," *The Wall Street Journal,* 17 November 1995, A2.

47. Anne Kates Smith, "News You Can Use: Some Call It Securities Reform but

Most Consumer Groups Think a Pending Bill Will Severely Crimp Investors' Rights," *U.S. News & World Report,* 13 November 1995, 117–18.

48. According to LiteralPolitics.com on January 23, 2003, "Ruder made the statement to *The New York Times* in 1995."

49. Robert A. Rosenblatt and Gebe Martinez, "House Rejects Clinton Veto of Bill Restricting Fraud Lawsuits; Securities: Chamber Overrides President in 319–100 Vote," *The Los Angeles Times,* 21 December 1995, 1.

50. Robert A. Rosenblatt and Gebe Martinez, "House Rejects Clinton Veto of Bill Restricting Fraud Lawsuits."

51. Jeffrey Taylor, "Congress Sends Business a Christmas Gift—Veto Is Overridden on Bill Curbing Securities Lawsuits," *The Wall Street Journal,* 26 December 1995, A2.

CHAPTER 9

1. Charles MacKay, *Extraordinary Popular Delusions & the Madness of Crowds* (New York: Three Rivers Press, 1980), 394. Here, MacKay describes the role of the chivalric leaders during the second, more organized, stage of the Crusades.

2. *Richard Russell's Dow Theory Letter,* 18 January 1995; 19 July 1995.

3. To define the third phase of a bull market, Robert Rhea, the great Dow Theorist of the 1930s, wrote, "The final stage of a bull market is sometimes recognizable because people then buy stocks simply because they are going up, or because other people are buying. They consider it old-fashioned to regard earnings or prospects." *Richard Russell's Dow Theory Letter,* 18 December 1996.

4. The survey also revealed that many in the second-most affluent group (those with assets of $100,000 to $500,000, not including their homes) came into the market before 1990: 55 percent reported making their first purchase before the decade began, while another 25 percent bought their first stock sometime between 1990 and 1995. See "Equity Ownership: Characteristics by Household Financial Assets," Investment Company Institute, Securities Industry Association. Gail Dudack reported on this survey in her October 2, 2002, research report.

5. By the end of 1995, equities trumped real estate as the investment of choice, for the first time since the go-go market of the late sixties and early seventies. In 1995, Federal Reserve data showed that the value of household stockholdings outweighed the value of home equity, rising to $5.5 trillion, compared to $4.2 trillion in home equity. The data, which comes from a Federal Reserve

survey, was reported widely. See, for example, Suzanne Woolley, "Our Love Affair with Stocks," *Business Week*, 3 June 1996.

6. Edward Yardeni, "Portfolio Strategy," Deutsche Morgan Grenfell, 27 January 1997.

7. "News in the Age of Money," *Columbia Journalism Review*, November/December 2000, 19.

8. *Richard Russell Dow Theory Letter*, 20 December 1995.

9. Elizabeth Sanger, "The Money Channels/Financial News Is Hot," *Newsday*, 3 December 1995.

10. Charles Fishman, "The Revolution Will Be Televised (on CNBC): Don't Touch Your Dial! CNBC Has Become the Live Feed of the New Economy," *Fast Company*, 1 June 2000, 184.

11. Pablo Galarza, "Inside the Box: *Squawk Box* Has Brains, Beauty, Wit—and an Audience of Fanatics. This Is a Stock Market Show?" *Money*, 1 July 1998, 116.

12. Tim Jones, "Behind the Scenes at CNBC, Hard News—With a Dash of Sass," *The Chicago Tribune*, 18 October 1998, 1.

13. Charles Fishman quotes Haines saying that his job is "to figure out if they're lying" in the sidebar to "The Revolution Will Be Televised." Haines made the remark about "making them squirm" in "20 Most Wanted," *Entertainment Weekly*, 16 July 1999, 33.

14. When Haines interviewed Ariba CEO Keith Krach in October of 2000, Haines ended the interview saying, "Well, can't argue with the numbers. They look terrific. Thank you very much, sir." (Mark Haines and Eric Gustafson, CNBC/Dow Jones Business Video, 19 October 2000.)

15. For Haines's interviews of Lay and Skilling, see Mark Haines, "Enron—CEO—Interview," CNBC/Dow Jones Business Video, 27 October 2000; Mark Haines, Jerry Klauer, "Enron President and CEO Interview, CNBC/Dow Jones Business Video, 17 April 2001. Despite repeated requests, CNBC refused to comment on Haines's disclosure regarding his ownership of Enron shares.

16. Byron Wein, interview with the author.

17. Charles Fishman, "The Revolution Will Be Televised" (sidebar).

18. Jonathan Weil, interview with the author.

19. Steven Lipin, interview with the author. See also Anita Raghavan and Steven Lipin, "Going It Alone: More Companies Shun Investment Bankers, Do Their Own Deals," *The Wall Street Journal*, 6 March 1996, A1.

In January of 1996, Lipin probably annoyed other members of the financial community by coauthoring a *Journal* story that threw a spotlight on how "dozens" of companies—ranging from IBM and AT&T to General Signal Corp., McCormick & Co., and Borden Inc.—were using supposedly "one-time" write-offs to fudge their earnings. ("Are Companies Using Restructuring Costs to Fudge the Figures? A Repeated Strategic Move Makes Future Earnings Seem Unrealistically Rosy—The Role of Elsie the Cow," *The Wall Street Journal,* 30 January 1996, A1. See also Chapter 16 ["Fully Deluded Earnings"] on "one-time" write-offs.)

20. In June of 2002, Faber broke the news that WorldCom would be restating earnings on *Business Center,* CNBC, 25 June 2002.

21. Herb Greenberg, interview with the author.

22. "Asleep at the Switch? Media Correspondent Terence Smith Explores How Business Reporters Largely Missed the Impending Implosion of Enron, the Largest Corporate Bankruptcy in U.S. History," *The News Hour with Jim Lehrer,* 19 February 2002.

On *The News Hour,* Faber claimed, "Enron is a special case. It was not disclosed. It was not there for us to see." But in June of 2002, when asked whether he didn't wish that reporters had dug more deeply into WorldCom's finances, Faber once again blamed his audience: "You know, I'm not sure that we can really place that great a blame on journalists for somehow failing to find these things out. I think a lot of them were being brought to light to a certain extent, at least in terms of questions being asked, and investors at that time, they were just giddy. They didn't want to know—they didn't want to hear about it . . . don't think the attention span of the viewing and/or reading public was particularly long or large for those kinds of stories. It didn't seem to really hit with the public that was, at that point at least during this period in time very giddy." Howard Kurtz and Bernard Kalb, "Corporate Stars Lose Luster," *Reliable Sources,* CNN, 29 June 2002.

On *Squawk Box,* Faber attempted to find good news in the Enron story. As late as October of 2001 he suggested that Enron's problem was only one of credibility, or a "perception of weakness" that could be dispelled by a new bank agreement:

"And finally on Enron. We've been reporting it all morning, Joe and myself, talking about Enron. Haven't heard yet, but expectations were, from people familiar with and close to the situation, that Enron would announce this morning a new bank agreement for either $1.25 billion or as much as $2.5 billion. *And that certainly should go a long way to calming any fears of liquidity problems and the like at Enron. Really, what it is still is a credibility problem,* though we should point out that *the counter parties that trade with Enron in the key energy trading part of its business, continue to do business with it. Many of them have come out and said we have no problem with Enron,* but they would like to sort of create a fortress balance sheet, completely eliminate this *perception* of weakness and, as well, perhaps bring in a well-known equity investor to also sort of add another stamp of approval. That I have heard they have not yet been able to secure. But we'll see about the bank financing. [Emphasis mine.]" David Faber, reporting on *Squawk Box,* CNBC, 31 October 2001.

23. "Asleep at the Switch?"

24. Charles Fishman, "The Revolution Will Be Televised."

25. Charles Fishman, "The Revolution Will Be Televised."

26. This is how Kernen described his method of selecting the winners and losers. See Charles Fishman, "The Revolution Will Be Televised."

27. Rick Marin, "Wall Street Babylon," *The New York Times,* 27 February 2000.

28. Interview with the author. The study was done by an independent consulting firm.

29. Susan E. Kuhn, "How Crazy Is This Market?" *Fortune,* 15 April 1996. Meanwhile, "The boomer obsession with stocks and investing has made mutual funds as much a part of the prosperous American family's profile as sport-utility vehicles and golden retrievers," Kuhn reported, capturing the era in a sentence. According to the Investment Company Institute, about one-third of all Americans own mutual funds.

30. Dave Kansas, "New Economy: A Dot-Com Editor Sheds His Five-Year 'Cocoon,' and Looks at How Journalism Has Changed in the Age of the Internet," *The New York Times,* 16 July 2001.

31. Dave Kansas, interview with the author.

32. Bill Fleckenstein, interview with the author. Fleckenstein comments on CNBC's coverage of quarterly earnings reports, and CNBC producer Bruno Cohen's reply appeared in Jim Rutenberg, "CNBC Struggles Even as Financial News Abounds," *The New York Times,* 29 July 2002.

33. *Richard Russell's Dow Theory Letter,* 15 February 1995. See the introduction on the market's long-term trends.

34. See, for example, Ed Wyatt, "Will Fund Investors Prove to Be Faithful or Fickle," *The New York Times,* 6 October 1996, for a timeline showing flows into equity funds that goes back to 1965. The table was headlined: "Lest We Forget the 70's."

35. See Chapter 1 and the chart "The Market's Cycles." See also Barton Biggs,

"Are Stocks Everyone's Best Friend?: A Report on Returns from a Variety of Investments," *Barron's,* 23 March 1992.

36. Ed Wyatt, interview with the author.

37. Jonathan Clements, "Vanguard Founder Blasts Funds' Focus," *The Wall Street Journal,* 16 May 2000.

38. Ed Wyatt, interview with the author. There is some evidence that by buying last year's best fund, an investor can catch a tailwind, though the timing can be tricky—and the momentum may last only for a year. See Chapter 10 ("The Information Bomb"). Meanwhile, investors held funds for an average of 2½ years—losing the advantage of the momentum effect.

39. Bill Fleckenstein, interview with the author. Fleckenstein made his initial comments, and Cohen replied in a *New York Times* article: Jim Rutenberg, "CNBC Struggles Even as Financial News Abounds," 29 July 2002. Just 10 days later, CNBC announced that Cohen had been fired. Dan Cox, "CNBC You Later—Biz News Head Cohen Booted Amid Falling Ratings," *The New York Post,* 8 August 2002, 27.

40. Frederick J. Sheehan Jr., "Quarterly Market Review and Outlook," John Hancock's Asset Management Services, 2 January 2001.

41. Howard Kurtz put the number at $300 million in "Risky Business," *The Washington Post,* 27 August 2000, WO8.

42. Interview with the author.

43. James J. Cramer, *Confessions of a Street Addict* (New York: Simon & Schuster, 2002), 61.

44. James Cramer, "Investor Nirvana," *Worth,* May 1997.

45. Chris Gessel, "Investor's Business Daily."

46. William Powers, "Nothing to Tout About," *The National Journal,* 14 April 2001.

47. William Powers, interview with the author.

48. Powers made the remark in a column that asked "the question that floats over the Enron story like a big, silent blimp: Where were the journalists? We are talking, after all, about a huge public corporation, one that was required by law to release reams of data about itself on a regular basis. While top Enron executives appear to have worked hard to conceal the company's true financial condition, the public record has long contained hints of trouble. They were exactly the kinds of hints that journalists are supposed to be good at noticing: numbers that didn't quite add up, vague references to odd-sounding business arrangements.

"But in order to see them, you had to be looking hard. To get at their meaning, you had to be willing to dig." William Powers, "Late to the Party," *The National Journal,* 19 January 2002.

49. Jonathan Weil, interview with the author.

50. Susan E. Kuhn, "Market Mania? How Crazy Is This Market? Stocks Are Wild," *Fortune,* 15 April, 1996, 78; Gretchen Morgenson, "Reality Check: What Could End the Bull Market? A Crash in Tech Stocks. Don't Rule It Out," *Forbes,* 27 January 1997, 42.

51. Dave Kansas and Jonathan Weil, interviews with the author.

52. Mark Hulbert, interview with the author.

53. Dr. Richard Parker, a fellow at Harvard's Joan Shorenstein Center, noted just how the business of financial journalism had grown from 1992 to 1997, and how important advertising dollars from financial service companies had become in "The Revolution In America's Financial Industry: How Well Is the Press Covering the Story?"

"In striking ways, this growth of 'personal finance' journalism has transformed business reporting and newspaper business sections, with several important implications for financial institution coverage," Parker said. "For one, it has brought insignificant new advertising revenues to papers across the country. Along with computer-related advertising, financial services advertising has grown fastest among national business-section advertisers over the past 20 years—and now accounts for 30 percent of national newspaper ad revenues.

"Advertising spending by financial service companies offering non-FDIC-covered products alone has risen from $359 million in 1992 to $869 million in 1997," Parker noted, citing New York–based Competitrack, Inc. for his numbers. See "Money, Markets and the News: Press Coverage of the Modern Revolution in Financial Institutions," a symposium held at the Joan Shorenstein Center of Harvard's John F. Kennedy School of Government, March 1999.

54. Mark Hulbert, interview with the author.

55. A. J. Liebling, *The Press* (Pantheon, 1981), 6. See also Thomas Frank, who quotes Liebling in *One Market Under God* (Anchor Books, 2000), 310, in his discussion of "Triangulation Nation: Journalism in the Age of Markets."

56. *Richard Russell's Dow Theory Letter,* 20 December 1995.

57. In an interview with the author, Sloan shared his draft of the speech.

58. Allan Sloan, interview with the author.

59. Allan Sloan, "Baby Berkshire Frenzy May Reflect a Market Gone Mad," *The Washington Post,* 14 April 1996.

60. Warren Buffett, Chairman's Letter, Berkshire Hathaway 1995 Annual Report, 1 March 1996.

Of course, a rising tide lifts all *boats,* but Buffett changed "boats" to "yachts" in a reference to the title of the 1940s book *Where Are the Customers' Yachts? Or A Good Hard Look at Wall Street,* by Fred Schwed (John Wiley & Sons, 1995). The title was based on a question that came up when J.P. Morgan was showing a client the yachts in the marina of the New York Yacht Club. Many of the owners were investment bankers. "But where," asked the client, "are the customers' yachts?"

61. Warren Buffett, Chairman's Letter, Berkshire Hathaway 1995 Annual Report, 1 March 1996. In the annual report, Buffett also reported that Berkshire was using stock to make acquisitions.

62. Allan Sloan, "Is It Time to Face Up to the Bear Facts?" *The Washington Post,* 16 April 1996, D03.

63. Allan Sloan, "Is It Time to Face Up to the Bear Facts?"

CHAPTER 10

1. Peter Bernstein, interview with the author.

2. For an original, provocative discussion of how modern technology aims at destroying time, see Paul Virilo, *The Information Bomb,* trans. Chris Turner (London: Verso, 2000).

3. Martin Whitman, interview with the author, and Martin Whitman, *Value Investing* (New York: John Wiley & Sons, 1999), 82–96.

4. David Tice, interview with the author. See Bill Alpert, "Payback Time: After Taking a Licking, David Tice's Prudent Bear Fund Bounces Back," *Barron's,* 7 September 1998, 22.

5. David Tice, interview with the author. See also Chapter 2 ("The People's Market") and Tice's testimony before the Capital Markets Insurance and Government-Sponsored Enterprises Subcommittee of the House Financial Services Committee on June 14, 2001. The 57-page transcript is available on Nexis, copyright, the Federal Document Clearing House.

6. Jeff D. Opdyke, "Heard in Texas: Hot Texas Stocks? Here's a Cooler View," *Texas Journal* (WSJ), 8 June 1994, T2.

7. Jeff D. Opdyke, "Heard in Texas."

8. Sunbeam-Oster Report, Tice Associates, December 1996.

9. See Jonathan Laing, "High Noon at Sunbeam: Does Chainsaw Al Have a Truly Revived Operation—or Something Else—in His Sights?" *Barron's,* 16 June 1997, 29.

10. "Dunlap Makes Plans to Shine Up Subeam," *Chicago Tribune,* 24 November 1996; Michael Martin, "Sunbeam Plugs into Overseas Market," *International Herald Tribune,* 13 November 1996; "Sunbeam 3Q—Better Times Seen Ahead Under Dunlap," Dow Jones News Service, 13 November 1996; "Sunbeam Profit Seen on Slimmer Product Line," *National Post,* 30 December 1997.

11. "Goldman Ups '97 Net View," Dow Jones News Service, 13 November 1996.

12. Herb Greenberg, "Against the Grain Short-Order Request: Sunbeam Is Toast," *Fortune,* 28 April 1997, 398.

13. Jonathan Laing, "High Noon at Sunbeam: Does Chainsaw Al Have a Truly Revived Operation—or Something Else—in His Sights?"

14. In July 1997, Greenberg repeated his warnings in "Short Positions," *San Francisco Chronicle,* 24 July 1997; and in the spring of 1998, when Sunbeam was trading at $57, *Barron's* again raised a red flag. Jonathan Laing, "A Return Visit to Earlier Stories: Into the Maw: Sunbeam's 'Chainsaw Al' Goes on a Buying Binge," *Barron's,* 9 March 1998, 13.

15. Henry Goldblatt, "First: Viewers Are Bullish on CNBC When the Markets Go Nuts, Ratings Soar," *Fortune,* 29 December 1997, 52.

16. "Sunbeam's Al Dunlap Breaks News of Retaining Morgan Stanley to Explore Merger Sale or Acquisition of Company on CNBC," PR Newswire, 23 October 1997.

17. Herb Greenberg, interview with the author.

18. Greenberg's comments, made in a column written on June 1, 1998, are quoted by Gerard Monsen in "The Unofficial Herb Greenberg FAQ."

19. This is only a small sample of some of the first-rate research and commentary available from independent research boutiques and newsletter writers. Others are referenced throughout this book.

20. See Kate Welling's interview with Hickey in "High Tech Contrarian: Staying Ahead of the Curves Isn't Popular, Just Profitable," *Barron's,* 26 August 1996; and Alan Abelson, "Up & Down Wall Street: Bear Skinned," *Barron's,* 5 August 1996. For Grant's analysis of Cisco's accounting, see *Grant's Interest Rate Observer,* 15 September 2000.

21. Richard Stern and Allan Sloan, "The Day the Brokers Picked Their Own Pockets," *Forbes,* 16 November 1987.

22. Henry Blodget, interview with the author. See Prologue for the story of Henry Blodget's late-night caller.

23. Floyd Norris, "The Problem with Analysts: You Get What You Pay For," *The New York Times,* 7 September 2001.

24. Herb Greenberg, interview with the author.

25. Bethany McLean, "Retirement Guide Investing: How Your 401(k) Stacks Up," *Fortune,* 19 August 1996, 124.

26. Peter Bernstein, interview with the author.

27. Both mutual fund managers and pension fund managers found themselves constantly second-guessed, either by the marketing executives running the mutual fund company or the pension fund consultants hired by many corporations to look over the shoulder of the portfolio managers running their pension plans. See Chapter 13 ("The Mutual Fund Manager: Career Risk vs. Investment Risk").

28. Mark Hulbert, interview with the author. See also, Mark Hulbert, "Momentum Is Fleeting: So How to Capture It in Funds?" *The New York Times,* 7 July 2002. In the interview and his column, Hulbert cited research done by Mark M. Carhart, head of quantitative research at Goldman Sachs.

29. Mark Carhart, interview with the author.

30. To track the fund's performance, Hulbert assumes that an individual investor bought the top-rated funds, and then switched in and out of them as they rose and fell in the ratings, paying fees each time. In the real world, Morningstar director Don Phillips observes, it is unlikely that an investor would do this—and Morningstar does not intend the stars to be taken as buy and sell recommendations.

    " 'Louis Rukeyser's Mutual Funds,' a popular mutual fund letter that focuses exclusively on three-year returns did even worse," Hulbert pointed out. "For this period (1/1/96 to 3/31/03), we report that this category of growth funds produced a 3.3% annualized loss, vs. a 5.5% annualized gain for the Wilshire 5000, with 44% more volatility than the Wilshire.

    "A portfolio of growth funds on the Louis Rukeyser Honor Roll lagged the Wilshire from the beginning of 1996 through March 31 of 2003 by an average of 8.8 percentage points a year, with 44% more volatility than the Wilshire. These results underline the inadequacy of using three-year periods to separate fund managers with genuine ability from those who are just lucky."

31. A. Michael Lipper, interview with the author. The remarks that follow were made in a 2003 interview. "Morningstar would also say that they were not trying to cast a judgment," Lipper noted, but inevitably the stars implied a grade. See Chapters 12 and 13 on mutual funds. As for Lipper's rankings, it was left to the investor to decide how to use them. "The decision about time period is a critical factor," said Lipper, "and I always felt it should be made on the basis of the investor's time horizon. If you're a 401(k) investor, you may want to use

actuarial-type time periods and measures," he suggested, referring to the analytical tools used by insurance companies when assessing risk. "These are very long time periods," he added, "and you may want to exclude very good periods and very bad periods."

32. A. Michael Lipper, interview with the author. Peter Lynch was the manager of Fidelity Magellan in the eighties; John Templeton, who founded the Templeton Funds, sold the funds to the Franklin Group in 1992, while John Neff ran Vanguard's Windsor and Gemini Funds until his retirement in 1995.

33. Nassim Nicholas Taleb, *Fooled by Randomness: The Hidden Role of Chance in the Markets and in Life* (New York: Texere, 2001), 27.

34. Taleb, *Fooled by Randomness*, 27.

35. Nassim Nicholas Taleb, interview with the author. See also Maggie Mahar, "No Such Thing," *Bloomberg Wealth Manager*, June 2003.

36. Thomas Frank, *One Market Under God: Extreme Capitalism, Market Populism, and the End of Economic Democracy* (New York: Doubleday, 2000), 303, 307.

37. See Chapter 3 ("The Stage Is Set").

38. See Maggie Mahar, "Three Wall Street Truths You Can't Trust," *Bloomberg Personal Finance*, November 2000, 50.

39. Maggie Mahar, "Could the Trade Deficit Torpedo the Tanker?" *Bloomberg News*, 8 February 1999. In the column, the author quoted *Bloomberg News* on "the consensus among economists."

40. Kathryn Graven quotes this "popular Japanese saying" in "Charging Bulls: Japanese Stock Buyers Follow the Fads, Send Tokyo Prices Soaring," *The Wall Street Journal*, 29 May 1987.

41. *Richard Russell's Dow Theory Letter*, 4 December 1996.

CHAPTER 11

1. Allan Sloan, "Online's Bottom: How Creative Accounting Makes AOL Look Good," *Newsweek*, 30 October 1995, 66.

2. Robert Seidman, *In, Around and Online*, Issue 2.15—Week Ending 14 April 1995.

3. Kara Swisher, *aol.con* (New York: Times Business/Random House, 1998), 224–26.

4. Interview with the author.

5. See Maggie Mahar, "Caught in the 'Net," *Barron's*, 25 December 1995, 25.

6. Allan Sloan, "Online's Bottom: How Creative Accounting Makes AOL Look Good."

7. Maggie Mahar, "Caught in the 'Net."

8. Linda Sandler and Jared Sandberg, "Heard on the Street: America Online Lures Investors, Dismays Shorts," *The Asian Wall Street Journal,* 13 November 1995, 15.

9. Allan Sloan, "America Online's Numbers Could Add Up to Trouble in Internet Mania," *The Washington Post,* 21 May 1996, D03.

10. Allan Sloan, "America Online's Numbers Could Add Up to Trouble in Internet Mania."

11. Interview with the author.

12. Times Wire Services, "Technology, No. 2 AOL Exec Quits after 4 Months on the Job," *The Los Angeles Times,* 26 June 1996.

13. Kara Swisher, *aol.con,* 156–57.

14. David Henry, "AOL Faces Crippling Cash Shortage," *USA Today,* 15 August 1996.

15. Allan Sloan, "Profits? What Profits? (America Online)," *Newsweek,* 11 November 1996, 60.

16. Allan Sloan, interview with the author.

17. Allan Sloan, "Profits, What Profits?"

18. Amy P. Hutton, "Four Rules for Taking Your Message to Wall Street," *Harvard Business Review,* May 2001, 125.

19. Paul Keegan, "Can Bob Pittman, of MTV Fame, Make AOL Rock?" *Upside* magazine, 1 November 1998. Pittman seemed to be saying that customers were not too discriminating about quality, but he did give them credit for valuing consistency. "Put New Coke in this can of Coke, they'll be mad. They'll make Coke change it. Our members think they own AOL. And they do. When they speak up and say, 'I want something,' damn it, we better respond!" Keegan commented: "This argument doesn't exactly amount to a ringing endorsement of the product. Pittman seems to be saying that customers are too busy to comparison shop."

20. Amy P. Hutton, "Four Rules for Taking Your Message to Wall Street."

21. Allan Sloan, "Profits, What Profits?"

22. Allan Sloan, "Profits? What Profits?"

23. Joshua Cooper Ramo, "How AOL Lost the Battles but Won the War: America Online Defied the Techies, Catering to the Chatting Masses; Its Suprising Deal Could Make CEO Steve Case's Strategy Look Brilliant," *Time,* 22 September 1997, 46.

24. Allan Sloan, interview with the author.

25. Allan Sloan, "America Online's Numbers Could Add Up to Trouble in Internet Mania."

26. Lise Buyer, interview with the author. After working at T. Rowe Price, Buyer went to Wall Street, where she became an Internet analyst. At the end of 2000, she decided to leave Wall Street.

27. David S. Hilzenrath, "AOL Fined Over Old Accounting Practices: Company to Pay SEC $3.5 Million," *The Washington Post,* 16 May 2000, E01.

28. See Martin Peers and Julia Angwin, "AOL Time Warner to Restate Eight Quarters of Its Results," *The Wall Street Journal,* 24 October 2002.

29. David A. Vise, "AOL Probe Widened to 'Abetting' of Other Firms," *The Washington Post,* 12 March 2003, A01.

CHAPTER 12

1. James J. Cramer, "How the Mutual Funds Run America," *New York,* 2 October 1996, 34.

2. Ken Brown, "The Best and Worst Mutual Funds," *Smart Money,* 1 February 1999, 93; Suzanne Woolley, "Our Love Affair with Stocks," *Business Week,* 3 June 1996.

3. Investment Company Institute, *1996 Mutual Fund Factbook,* Chapter 10.

4. James J. Cramer, "How the Mutual Funds Run America," 35, 36.

5. By 2001, investors began to ask questions about some of Van Wagoner's holdings. It turned out that between 10 and 14 percent of Van Wagoner's portfolios consisted of "private placements"—shares in companies that were not publicly traded, giving Van Wagoner and his fund managers unusual leeway when totting up the value of the shares in their funds. The question was whether they overvalued these holdings in order to make their losses seem less catastrophic. See Tom Lauricella, "Some Van Wagoner Stakes Lost $0 in 2000—as Private Placements Their Value Was Set by Fund Firm Itself," *The Wall Street Journal,* 11 December 2001, C1; Jason Zweig, "Invest/Fund File/ Contrafund on Sale—Janus Managing Risk—Vanguard Guru Retires Momentum Mori," *Money,* 1 May 2003, 63.

6. Roger Lowenstein, "Common Market—The Public's Zeal to Invest," *The Wall Street Journal,* 9 September 1996.

7. John Wyatt, "A Simple Test for Growth Stocks," *Fortune,* 16 January 1995, 125; Reed Abelson, "A Fund Family's Credo: Growth, Growth, Growth," *The New York Times,* 23 June 1996. Over the next five and a half years (from July 1, 1996, through December 30, 2002), Bed Bath & Beyond would trump

both prison and greenway, rising some 400 percent. (An investor who bought BBBY in 1995, when Pilgrim first mentioned the stock, would have fared even better.) Meanwhile, Callaway Golf fell 60 percent, while Corrections Corp., which was taken over by PZN, fell 49 percent.

8. James J. Cramer, "How the Mutual Funds Run America."

9. On the effect of II's ratings, see prologue in Michael Santoli, "Stop It, Both of You: Fund Managers Deserve Their Share of Blame for the Stock-Ratings Debacle," *Barron's*, 1 January 2002.

10. Some observers praised CEOs, such as General Electric's Jack Welch, for being able to produce smooth earnings growth, quarter after quarter, with no surprises. But as early as 1994, *The Wall Street Journal* raised sharp questions about how GE engineered its results: Randall Smith, Steven Lipin, and Amal Kumar Naj, "Managing Profits: How General Electric Damps Fluctuations in Its Annual Earnings: It Offsets One-Time Gains with Write-Offs Times Asset Purchases and Sales," *The Wall Street Journal*, 2 November 1994, A1. At the end of the story, Howard Schilit, an accounting professor at American University in Washington, summed up the argument: "Earnings management can be very dangerous for the investor because you are creating something artificial. The numbers should reflect how the company is actually doing."

11. Michael Santoli, "Stop It, Both of You: Fund Managers Deserve Their Share of Blame for the Stock-Ratings Debacle."

12. George Kelly, interview with the author.

13. See Chapter 8 ("Behind the Scenes, in Washington"), on how the use of options allowed companies to avoid subtracting the cost of employee compensation from their profits. For a full analysis of Cisco's accounting, see *Grant's Interest Rate Observer*, 15 September 2000.

14. Robert Frank and Robin Sidel, "Firms That Lived by the Deal in the '90s Now Sink by the Dozens," *The Wall Street Journal*, 6 June 2002. See also Chapter 16 ("Fully Deluded Earnings").

15. Robert Frank and Robin Sidel, "Firms That Lived by the Deal." *The Wall Street Journal* did the study of the 50 biggest acquirers with Thompson Financial.

16. Roger Lowenstein, "Common Market—The Public's Zeal to Invest"; Louise Witt, "Small Circle of Pain" *Bloomberg Personal Finance*, January/February 1998, 80.

17. See Louise Witt, "Small Circle of Pain"; and Jeffrey Laderman, "The Stampede to Index Funds," *Business Week*, 1 April 1996.

18. Eric J. Savitz, "Dangerous Curves: In This Market the Tortoises Are Leaving the Hares in the Dust," *Barron's*, 10 March 1997.

19. See Sandra Ward, "After the Deluge," *Barron's,* 6 August 2001; Thomas Eason, "The Funds: 'It's Loony,' " *Forbes,* 17 May 1999, 340.

20. Leuthold isolated the 99 stocks where U.S. institutions (including mutual funds) have the most dollars invested, and then examined their price/earnings ratios. He published the list of institutional favorites as of August 1996 in *Perception for the Professional,* April 1997, vol. 17, no. 4.

21. Susan E. Kuhn, "Market Mania? How Crazy Is This Market?" *Fortune,* 15 April 1996, 78. See Chapter 3 ("The Stage Is Set") on the Nifty Fifty of the late sixties and early seventies; see Chapter 17 ("Following the Herd") on parallels to the Nifty Fifty of the nineties.

22. Susan E. Kuhn, "Market Mania?"

23. Kenneth Labich, "Gambling's Kings on a Roll and Raising Their Bets Last Year: Americans Visited Casinos More Often Than Theme Parks," *Business 2.0,* July 1996.

24. Sharon Cassidy, interview with the author. The market would crash before Cassidy retired—see Chapter 2. ("The People's Market"). Cassidy and Malone both appeared in a 1996 *Barron's* story focusing on how individual investors of the mid-nineties felt compelled to invest, ignoring all risks. See Maggie Mahar, "You Must Buy Stocks," *Barron's,* 20 May 1996, A12.

25. Interview with the author.

26. The poll of 10,114 mutual fund investors was conducted by Louis Harris Associates for the Liberty Financial Investor Reality Check, Business Wire, 16 October 1996.

27. Lipper Analytical Services' index of funds with the highest earnings growth rates and valuations was up some 40 percent for the year, while the index of portfolios with the lowest prices relative to book and earnings had gained just 22.4 percent. "With the Dow preparing to punch through 5000, opportunities to buy cheap stocks seem few and far between," noted Leslie P. Norton in "Fund of Information: Food for Thought—What's a Value Investor to Do? Catching Up with Tweedy Browne," *Barron's,* 20 November 1995, 31.

28. Mark Hulbert, interview with the author.

29. Jean-Marie Eveillard, interview with the author. Eveillard's SoGen funds were later renamed "First Eagle Funds."

30. See Maggie Mahar, "Is 'New Value' Value Added?"

31. Maggie Mahar, "Is Europe Ripe for Recovery? No, Says One Veteran," *Bloomberg News,* 12 November 1998. The risk adjustment was made using the formula devised by Franco & Leah Modigliani.

32. Jean-Marie Eveillard, interview with the author.

33. Earnings often lag not just GDP, but GDP per capita, Peter Bernstein has observed: "Between 1900 and 2001, for instance, U.S. GDP growth averaged 3.3% in real terms, vs. 1.9% growth in GDP per capita, while earnings grew by 1.5% and dividends by 1.1%. And, the U.S. economy was the most successful on the planet over that stretch," Kate Welling quoted Bernstein on this point in *welling@weeden,* 11 April 2003.

34. Jean-Marie Eveillard, interview with the author.

35. "Manager's Forum: Wall Street, California, Global Conqueror SoGen International's Helmsman Scans the World," *The Los Angeles Times,* 12 November 1996, D4. Eveillard explained why he had taken a 7 percent position in gold: "It's a matter of perceiving that the downside risk is modest on two counts: No. 1, the price has already been cut in half in nominal terms over 15 years, so presumably most of the damage has already been done. No. 2, there continues to be very strong jewelry demand coming from developing countries, particularly Asia. So it's the idea of owning a depressed asset where the downside risk is modest, but acknowledging that I have no insight whatsoever into the timing and the extent of a move upwards." Here Eveillard made it clear that he was not a market timer in the sense of being a short-term investor who tries to pick the top and bottom of a stock or a market, but that, like many value investors, he paid attention to longer cycles and refused to buy when prices became too high.

Investing in gold in '96, Eveillard was "early," but over time the bet would pay off. In August 1993 he opened a gold fund, SGGDX; as of May 31, 2003, the fund boasted a five-year average annual return (without adjusting for load) of 15.61 percent; since inception, the fund had returned 5.32 percent.

36. "Manager's Forum."

37. Jean-Marie Eveillard, interview with the author.

38. Clyde McGregor, interview with the author.

Of course, some investors did take their profits. But mutual fund investors did not begin selling in large numbers until September of 2001—and even then, net redemptions equaled only 1.65 percent of total assets in U.S. Focused Equity Funds. Even in July of 2002, net outflows stood at just 2.4 percent of total assets—still significantly less than in October of 1987, when mutual fund investors withdrew 3.6 percent of assets. See page 462 in Appendix (chart of equity flows).

39. Jean-Marie Eveillard, interview with the author.

40. "Manager's Forum."

41. Jean-Marie Eveillard, interview with the author.

CHAPTER 13

1. Clyde McGregor, interview with the author. See also Maggie Mahar, "Total Return," *Bloomberg Personal Finance*, January/February 2002.

2. A. Michael Lipper, interview with the author. For Lipper's 1987 remarks see Julie Rohrer, "So You Want to Start a Mutual Fund," *Institutional Investor*, March 1987.

3. Interview with the author.

4. Interview with the author.

5. Interview with the author.

6. Don Phillips, interview with the author.

7. A. Michael Lipper, interview with the author.

8. Don Phillips, interview with the author. See also Mark Hulbert, "Same Yardstick Different Races," *The New York Times*, 7 January 2001. Hulbert pointed out that under Morningstar's system, younger funds are more likely to receive five stars, and noted that Morningstar had commented publicly on the problem.

9. Interview with the author.

10. Mark Headley, interview with the author.

11. Interview with the author.

12. As *The Wall Street Journal* reported in 2002, a study of 742 fund mergers from October 1994 through December 1997 published in the *Journal of Finance* suggested that inheriting a floundering fund can be costly for the acquirer's shareholders in part because "tax laws dictate the inheritor hold onto a large chunk of the loser's positions. . . . This is because shareholders of the acquired fund wind up with an equal investment in the successful fund, and don't owe taxes on the transaction. To maintain that tax-free status the acquiring fund's manager usually has to hold at least a third of the securities acquired for a minimum of one year." Ian McDonald, "Less Is Less: The Dark Side of the Urge to Merge Funds," *The Wall Street Journal*, 10 July 2002.

    According to the study, the acquiring fund tended to suffer: "After topping its category average by more than two percentage points the year before the merger the average acquirer falls to just about even with its peers a year after the merger."

13. Ken Brown, "The Best and Worst Mutual Funds" (A Special Report), *Smart Money*, 1 February 1999, 93.

14. A. Michael Lipper, interview with the author.

15. See Rich Blake, "How High Can Costs Go? (Payments for Mutual Fund

Placements Are Getting Securities and Exchange Commission Scrutiny)," *Institutional Investor,* 1 May 2002, 56.

16. Robert McGough and Karen Damato, "Buying Pressure: Despite Rising Doubts, Mutual-Fund Officials Pour Cash into Stocks—Pushed by Their Investors, They Pay Steep Prices and Take On More Risk—Just a Drunken Frat Party?" *The Wall Street Journal,* 30 December 1996, A1.

17. George Kelly, interview with the author.

18. McGough and Damato note the low cash levels at the end of 1996. See Chapter 5 ("Black Monday") for a description of Fidelity Magellan's forced sales during the October 1987 crash.

   See chart, prepared by Gail Dudack, chief market strategist at SunGard Institutional Brokerage, in the Appendix (p. 461) showing how the cash level in equity mutual funds declined throughout the bull market cycle. "Portfolio managers believed that it was mandatory to stay fully invested," said Dudack. "The client was making the asset allocation decision. As a result there is no safety cushion if investors decide to liquidate equity funds."

19. Robert McGough and Karen Damato, "Buying Pressure."

20. Interview with the author.

21. *welling@weeden,* 4, no. 14 (28 June 2002).

22. Andrew Bary, "Fund of Information: Who Needs Peter Lynch? Upstart Magellan Manager Scores Big," *Barron's,* 21 June 1993, 3. In his story, Bary quoted Rekenthaler.

   At the end of the decade, William Green quoted Vinik on "growth at a reasonable price" in "Investing/Hall of Fame/Master Class: The Champ Retires Undefeated—Jeff Vinik Is Closing His Hedge Fund after Four Stellar Years," *Money,* 1 December 2000, 67.

23. James S. Hirsch, "Magellan's Cut in Stocks Held Hurts Results," *The Wall Street Journal,* 12 February 1996, C1; Edward Wyatt, "Mutual Funds: Who's Out to Topple Jeff Vinik? The Knives Are Out for Jeffrey N. Vinik," *The New York Times,* 5 May 1996.

24. Robert McGough, "Fund Track: Fidelity's Vinik Backs Bonds and Cyclicals," *The Wall Street Journal,* 15 May 1996, C25; Edward Wyatt, "Market Place: Magellan Shifted from Technology in November," *The New York Times,* 12 January 1996. See also James S. Hirsch, "Magellan's Cut in Stocks Held Hurts Results," *The Wall Street Journal,* 12 February 1996, C1.

25. David Whitford and Joseph Nocera, with additional reporting by Nelson D. Schwartz; and Reporter Associates Maria Atanasov, Amy R. Kover, and Jeanne C. Lee, "Has Fidelity Lost It?" *Fortune,* 9 June 1997.

26. Edward Wyatt, "Mutual Funds: Who's Out to Topple Jeff Vinik?"

27. Gail Dudack, interview with the author.

28. *Richard Russell's Dow Theory Letter,* 4 December 1996.

29. Gene Marcial, "Technicians Keep Predicting a Market Drop," *Business Week,* 30 May 1983; Jane Bryant Quinn, "Interest Rates Real Villain in Market Dive," *Pittsburgh Post Gazette,* 18 April 1994.

30. Steve Bailey and Steven Syre, "Fidelity's Balance Is Off on 1 Asset—Truth," *The Boston Globe,* 14 January 1996, 45. In a November 6 interview with *U.S. News & World Report,* Vinik had said that "Micron is a stock whose valuations are reasonable and the fundamentals are still outstanding." (Jack Egan, "News You Can Use, 1996 Investment Outlook" (addendum), *U.S. News & World Report,* 116.) In a September semiannual report that reached investors in November, Vinik said tech stocks were "relatively cheap."

31. Edward Wyatt, "Mutual Funds: Who's Out to Topple Jeff Vinik?"

32. Andrew Bary, "Trading Points," *Barron's,* 27 May 1996, MW11. (*Barron's* did not take a position as to whether Wall Street was right about both Vinik and bonds, but it noted that "for individuals, Magellan's lackluster performance this year only reinforces the notion that stocks are the sole solid investment for the long haul."

    While calling Vinik's portfolio a burnt-out case, Forbes did acknowledge his courage: "I give Jeff Vinik high marks for implementing his cogent strategy of capital conservation in a frothy market," wrote Martin Sosnoff. "The Last Days of Jeff Vinik," *Forbes,* 1 July 1996, 99.

33. James J. Cramer, "How the Mutual Funds Run America," *New York,* 2 October 1996, 34.

34. Gail Dudack, interview with the author.

35. Ned Davis, Ned Davis Research, May 1996.

36. Gail Dudack, interview with the author. It should be noted that Vinik's success in the late nineties was not due to a bet on bonds. In his hedge fund, Vinik made his money both by shorting stocks and taking long positions, with many of his long positions in the undervalued mid-cap and small-cap stocks that had lagged the big caps.

37. A. Michael Lipper, interview with the author.

38. Edward Wyatt, "Who's Out to Topple Jeff Vinik?"

39. Edward Wyatt, "Manager of Biggest Mutual Fund Quits After Recent Subpar Gains," *The New York Times,* 24 May 1996.

40. In 1996, Jeff Vinik was not the only star manager to walk away from Fidelity. A year later, more than 20 fund managers had left the firm in 16 months. At

the same time, Fidelity's relative performance was slipping—from 1994 through 1996 only 4 of Fidelity's 34 stock funds had beaten the S&P 500.

Fidelity now commanded 15 percent of the 401(k) market, almost double the share controlled by their chief rival, Vanguard. "It has immense resources at its disposal, with annual revenues of over $5 billion and reported earnings of $423 million," *Fortune* noted. "In addition, with those hundreds of billions in assets at its disposal, Fidelity has become the single most important player on Wall Street and a stockholder of immense power, with its tentacles in thousands of companies." David Whitford and Joseph Nocera, with additional reporting by Nelson D. Schwartz; and Reporter Associates Maria Atanasov, Amy R. Kover, and Jeanne C. Lee, "Has Fidelity Lost It?" *Fortune,* 9 June 1997.

Fortune also reported that when it tried to interview top Fidelity executives "to a man . . . [they] denied that the company was facing any problems or even that it was changing in any real way. And they made little effort to hide their annoyance at having to answer questions. As Ned Johnson put it upon first being introduced to a *Fortune* reporter: 'Are you people so f—ing bored that you have nothing better to write about than us?' *Fortune* described Johnson as wearing "his trademark aviator glasses" when he made the remark.

"Fidelity remains an extraordinarily arrogant institution," *Fortune* concluded, "seemingly oblivious to the idea that managing a half-trillion dollars of America's money carries with it any special need for candor."

Apparently *Fortune* hit a nerve. In an interview with the author, a *Fortune* reporter involved with the story revealed that after it was published, Fidelity withdrew its advertising from the magazine. Fidelity refused comment, saying, "We do not talk about our advertising."

41. For the details of Friess's story, see Charles Gasparino, "Instinct and Irony: A Top Fund Manager Is Humbled When He Makes Ill-Timed Moves—Brandywine's Foster Friess Left the Market Early, Returned Far Too Late—Haunted by the Human Toll," *The Wall Street Journal,* 15 October 1998, A1.

42. Charles Gasparino, "Instinct and Irony."

43. Ralph Wanger, interview with the author.

44. George Kelly, interview with the author.

45. Ralph Wanger, interview with the author.

CHAPTER 14

1. Abby Joseph Cohen, interview with the author. See also Anthony Bianco, "The Prophet of Wall Street," *Business Week,* 1 June 1998, 124.

2. Jeffrey M. Laderman, "Step Aside, Elaine. Now, the Big Name Is Abby Cohen Called the 6000 Dow and Currently Forecasts 6400," *Business Week*, 4 November 1996, 182.

3. Nelson D. Schwartz, "I have No Ego; I Just Want to Be Right," *Smart Money*, April 1997, 129.

4. See Chapter 6 ("The Gurus") and Antony Bianco, "The Prophet of Wall Street: How Abby Cohen Came to Be One of the Most Closely Watched Forecasters on the Planet," *Business Week*, 1 June 1998; and Heather Green, "The E Biz: 25 Visionaries," *Business Week*, 27 September 1999.

5. Abby Joseph Cohen, "It Was a Very Good Year, and Count Your Cash; Why Wall Street's Boom Is Still for Real," *The Washington Post*, 29 December 1996, C01.

6. Lewis made the statement, in a somewhat different context, in a column that he wrote for Bloomberg, but it perfectly describes Wall Street's relationship to Cohen—and why her male colleagues were able to accept her with barely a trace of envy.

7. Peter Truell, "The Wall Street Soothsayer Who Never Blinked," *The New York Times*, 27 July 1997.

8. John Brooks, *The Go-Go Years* (New York: John Wiley & Sons, 1994), 14, 108.

9. Randall Smith and James A. White, "Heard on the Street: Without a Dr. Doom to Prognosticate, Who Are the New Oracles on Wall Street?" *The Wall Street Journal*, 12 March 1992.

10. Lawrence A. Armour, "Can We Talk? What's Ahead for the Stock Market, the Economy and the Future of Investing: Market Guru Abby Cohen of Goldman Sachs, Perennial Bear Jim Grant and Mutual Fund Dean Shelby Davis Square Off," *Fortune*, 9 June 1997, 189.

11. Peter Truell, "The Wall Street Soothsayer Who Never Blinked," *The New York Times*, 27 July 1997.

12. Roach quoted Greenspan's words in a research report published in 2002 titled "Smoking Gun." In an interview with the author, Roach confirmed the chairman's statements. Alan Abelson originally reported on Roach's findings in "Up & Down Wall Street: Irrational Adulation," *Barron's*, 22 July 2002.

13. David Wessel, "Worried Fed Watches Stock Market's Climb," *The Wall Street Journal*, 25 November 1996, A1.

14. "Pundit Watch," SmartMoney.com, August 1998.

15. Peter Truell, "It's Getting Extremely Hard to Be a Bear on Wall Street," *The Journal Record*, 7 January 1997; Dave Kansas, "Lone Bear on Wall Street Joins the Herd," *The Wall Street Journal*, 5 December 1995, C1; Larry Bauman,

"Abreast of the Market: Stocks Stumble in Profit-Taking; DuPont Falls, J.P. Morgan Gains," *The Wall Street Journal*, 5 December 1996.

16. Maggie Mahar, "Proud Bear: If Salomon's David Shulman Is So Smart, Why Has He Been So Wrong?" *Barron's*, 9 October 1995, 21.

17. Interview with the author. Shulman left to become a general partner with Ulysses Management LLC, a private investment firm. Travelers and Smith Barney later became part of Citigroup.

18. David Wessel, "Sometimes, Stocks Go Nowhere for Years," *The Wall Street Journal*, 13 January 1997, A1.

19. Byron Wein. The story that follows is drawn from an interview with the author.

20. Bob Woodward, *Maestro: Greenspan's Fed and the American Boom* (New York: Simon & Schuster, 2000), 178–79.

21. Robert Rubin, interview with the author.

22. Bob Woodward, *Maestro*, 179.

23. Suzanne McGee, "Bulls Start Buying as Greenspan Spurs Big Drop," *The Wall Street Journal*, 9 December 1996, C1.

24. Deborah Lohse, "Investors, Defying Greenspan, Boost Nasdaq 2%," *The Wall Street Journal*, 10 December 1996.

25. "Review & Outlook [Editorial]: The Delphic Dollar," *The Wall Street Journal*, 10 December 1996, A22.

26. Tom Squitieri, "GOP Leader Hits Remarks by Fed Chief," *USA Today*, 9 December 1996, 01A.

27. E. S. Browning, "Heard on the Street: Bank Sticks' Rally Puzzles Some Investors," *The Wall Street Journal*, 10 December 1996.

28. Edward Yardeni, "Weekly Economic Analysis," Deutsche Morgan Grenfell, 27 January 1997.

   Over the next two years, Fed Chairman Alan Greenspan would use the word "bubble" again, but invariably in a context where he was only raising the question. For example, in congressional testimony on June 17, 1999, he said: "The 1990s have witnessed one of the great bull stock markets in American history. Whether that means an unstable bubble has developed in its wake is difficult to assess." In an August 27, 1999, speech in Jackson Hole, Wyoming, he fell back on the "investors know best" theory of rational markets: "To anticipate a bubble about to burst requires the forecast of a plunge in the prices of assets previously set by the judgments of millions of investors, many of whom are highly knowledgeable about the prospects for the specific companies that make up our broad stock price indexes."

29. Bob Woodward, *Maestro*, 184.

30. Steve Roach, interview with the author.

31. James Grant, "Irrational Exuberance Towards Mr. Greenspan," *The Financial Times*, 10 January 2000, 13.

32. Martin Mayer, *The Fed: The Inside Story of How the World's Most Powerful Financial Institution Drives the Markets* (New York: Plume, 2002).

CHAPTER 15

1. Dean Foust, "Alan Greenspan's Brave New World," *Business Week*, 14 July 1997, 44.

2. Michael J. Mandel, "Where to Invest in 1997: The Triumph of the New Economy," *Business Week*, 30 December 1996, 68.

3. Jeff Madrick, "Economic Scene: Tarnished New Economy Loses More Luster," *The New York Times*, 30 August 2001.

This is not to say that productivity did not grow at all in the late nineties, but while it climbed at a faster rate than it had from 1973 to 1995, it did not grow as quickly as it had in the fifties and sixties. "There is perhaps an increase of five-tenths of a percentage point a year in the long-term productivity growth trend," Madrick concluded, "and over time," he acknowledged, "this will be significant. But promises of a once-in-a-century transformation are not supported by the facts."

4. See James Grant, *Grant's Interest Rate Observer*, 26 May 2000; 16 February 2001.

5. Mark Veverka, "New Economy? What New Economy?" *Barron's*, 22 October 2001. "Granted, the convenience of online banking was not reflected in government productivity figures," Veverka noted, "but its impact was 'probably modest,' the study's authors surmise."

6. Leon Levy, with Eugene Linden, *The Mind of Wall Street: A Legendary Financier on the Perils of Greed and the Mysteries of the Market* (New York: PublicAffairs, 2002).

7. See Paul Krugman, "Enemies of Reform," *The New York Times*, 21 May 2002. See Chapter 16 ("Fully Deluded Earnings") for further discussion of corporate earnings.

8. Alan Abelson, "Up & Down Wall Street: Cereal Killer," *Barron's*, 3 September 2001. Abelson reported that Sanford Bernstein cleaned up the numbers by "adjusting for nonrecurring items and the effect of stock options and pension plans." For a discussion of how these items inflated earnings, see Chapter 8 ("Behind the Scenes, in Washington [1993–95]") and Chapter 16 (" 'Fully Deluded Earnings' ").

9. "Q & A With Jeremy Grantham," *Business Week,* 18 March 2002.

10. James Grant, "The Bulls Stand Corrected," *The New York Times,* 29 October 1997.

11. Gretchen Morgenson, "Reality Check," *Forbes,* 27 January 1997, 42.

12. Joseph Kahn, "China's Overcapacity Crimps Neighbors: Glut Swamps Southeast Asia's Exports, Roiling Currencies" *The Wall Street Journal,* 14 July 1997.

13. Mitchell Martin, "Wall Street: Too Healthy Right Now to Succumb to a Case of 'Asian Flu'—Asia's Financial Turmoil/The View from Wall Street," *International Herald Tribune,* 3 November 1997, 11.

14. Perry's piece was originally published on October 28, 2002, on Prudent-Bear.com.

15. Dudack made the remark in 2003.

16. Gail Dudack, "Happy Anniversary," UBS Global Research, 17 October 1997. The quotations from Kindleberger that follow are drawn from Dudack's report.

17. Steve Roach, interview wih the author.

18. Allan Sloan, "Retirement Roulette (Investing Social Security Funds in the Stock Market)," *Newsweek,* 20 January 1997.

19. In order to go back to 1900, Dickson had to make some educated guesses: "Since the Consumer Price Index, which is used to peg Social Security benefits to inflation, didn't exist until 1917, Dickson had to create his own pre-1917 measure of inflation and had to rely on studies by G. William Schwert of the University of Rochester for stock performance from 1900 to 1925," Sloan reported. "After thus piling assumption on assumption, Dickson decided that 7 percent above inflation for stocks . . . was a reasonable guess." As noted, he did not claim that it was anything more than a guess.

20. Allan Sloan, "Retirement Roulette."

21. Erin E. Arvedlund, "Wall Street Meets K Street: Washington Draws a Bead on Mutual Funds," *Barron's,* 3 March 2003, F2.

CHAPTER 16

1. Jim Chanos, interview with the author. Jim Grant originally reported on Jim Chanos's discovery in *Grant's Interest Rate Observer,* 17 July 1998.

2. Jeff Madrick, "Economic Scene; Bush Is Talking Tough on Corporate Ethics, but Where Is the Regulatory Bite?" *The New York Times,* 11 July 2002.

3. Steven Pearlstein, "Hooked on a Fast-Growth Habit," *The Washington Post,* 25 November 2001.

4. Greg Ip, "Abreast of the Market: Do Big Write-Offs Artificially Inflate Earnings?" *The Wall Street Journal*, 6 July 1998, C1.

5. Walter M. Cadette, David A. Levy, and Srinivas Thiruvadanthai, "Two Decades of Overstated Corporate Earnings: The Surprisingly Large Exaggeration of Aggregate Profits," The Jerome Levy Forecasting Center, 2001.

6. Arthur Levitt, "The Numbers Game," remarks delivered at the NYU Center for Law and Business, 22 September 1998.

7. *Grant's Interest Rate Observer*, 3 December 1999.

8. Noble originally recounted the story to Kate Welling who published it in *welling@weeden* (9 March 2001). Noble repeated it in an interview with the author.

9. David Henry, "The Numbers Game," *Business Week*, 14 May 2001.

10. The Levy report quotes Buffett on page 11.

11. Nanette Byrnes, Richard A. Melcher, and Debra Sparks, "Who Can You Trust: Earnings Hocus-Pocus: How Companies Come Up with the Numbers They Want," *Business Week*, 4 October 1998, 134.

12. Nanette Byrnes, Richard A. Melcher, and Debra Sparks, "Who Can You Trust."

13. Gail Dudack, SunGard Institutional Brokerage, Weekly Report, 5 March 2003.

14. For a full discussion of how accounting rules allowed companies to mask the cost of options, and Levin's battle to reform options accounting, see Chapter 8 ("Behind the Scenes, in Washington").

15. Gretchen Morgenson, "Scandal's Ripple Effect: Earnings Under Threat," *The New York Times*, 10 February 2002.

16. Interview with the author.

17. Michael K. Ozanian, "Upward Bias," *Forbes*, 15 May 2000. On insider selling as the market peaked, see Chapter 19 ("Insiders Sell; the Water Rises").

18. The Levy Institute report included the estimates from the Federal Reserve Study (Lian and Sharpe, 1999) as well as a 2000 estimate by Bear Stearns analysts that if the cost of options had been subtracted from profits, earnings for S&P 500 companies would have been as much as 8 percent lower. That same year, a study by Smithers & Co., an economic consulting group based in London, reckoned that if S&P companies had been forced to expense options, operating earnings would have fallen by a full 17 percent. See *Grant's Interest Rate Observer*, 15 February, 2002.

19. Even though corporations were not required to show the cost of options as an

expense of doing business, the IRS did let them take a deduction for options (implicitly acknowledging that they were an expense). Under the formula, companies were allowed to deduct the difference between the price that an executive paid for the stock when he exercised his option to buy shares at a fixed price, and the market price when he sold.

20. Ciesielski's *Analyst's Accounting Observer* can be found at www.aaopub.com. Welling published the results of his findings in *welling@weeden,* 3 August 2001.

21. *In Focus,* The Leuthold Group, June 2002.

22. The Levy Center report cites the Federal Reserve study.

23. Loren Steffy "Options Charade," *Bloomberg News,* April 2000.

24. Thomas A. Stewart, "The Leading Edge: Does Michael Dell Need Stock Options?" *Fortune,* 2 August 1999, 240.

25. Erin E. Arvedlund, "Dell-uded Put Sales Come Home to Roost: A Bottom in Tech?" *Barron's,* 6 May 2002.

26. Floyd Norris, "Dell's Share-Price Bet Cost It $1.25 Billion," *The New York Times,* 3 May 2002.

27. Jon Corzine, interview with the author.

28. Maureen Allyn, interview with the author. Unless otherwise noted, the quotations that follow are drawn from an interview with the author and an internal memo that Allyn wrote while at Scudder.

29. Allyn quoted Soros from Jaye Scholl, "Exit Shaken," *Barron's,* 1 May 2000.

30. For the story of Acampora's call, see Chapter 1 ("The Market's Cycles").

31. Roger Lowenstein, *When Genius Failed* (New York: Random House, 2000), xix.

32. Leon Levy with Eugene Linden, *The Mind of Wall Street* (New York: Public Affairs, 2002), 142, 143, 144.

33. Nassim Nicholas Taleb, interview with the author. See Maggie Mahar, "No Such Thing," *Bloomberg Wealth Manager,* June 2003.

34. Nicholas Nassim Taleb, *Fooled by Randomness* (New York: Texere, 2001).

35. Peter Bernstein, interview with the author. See Maggie Mahar, "No Such Thing."

36. Peter Bernstein, *Against the Gods: The Remarkable Story of Risk* (New York: John Wiley & Sons, 1996).

37. Nassim Nicholas Taleb, interview with the author. See also Maggie Mahar, "No Such Thing."

38. Roger Lowenstein, *When Genius Failed,* xviii.

39. Martin Mayer, *The Fed* (New York: The Free Press, 2001), 11–12; 266–67.

40. James Tyson, "Cruise Control Investing," *The Christian Science Monitor*, 1 January 1999.
41. Maureen Allyn, interview with the author.

CHAPTER 17

1. "Boo! And the 100 Other Dumbest Moments in e-Business History," *Business 2.0*, 28 April 2002.
2. Andrew Bary, "The Trader: Wow! '98 Had Enough Thrills for Several Years," *Barron's*, 28 December 1998, MW3.
3. Ianthe Jeanne Dugan, "Where No Investor Has Gone Before; Amateurs Steered the Ship Through a Spacey Year," *The Washington Post*, 3 January 1999, H01. As proof, Birinyi pointed to trading activity on the New York Stock Exchange. That year, $63 billion of net buying was in blocks of $10,000 or less. In comparison, $44.7 billion was in "big-block" trades.
4. Rubino's story originally appeared in Mike Cassidy's column in *The San Jose Mercury News* ("Market Actions Add to a Sicko's Heavy Breathing," 23 November 1999).
5. Andrew Bary, "What's Wrong, Warren? Berkshire's Down for the Year, but Don't Count It Out," *Barron's*, 27 December 1999, 16.
6. The story that follows and all quotations from Blodget are, unless otherwise noted, based on three interviews with the author. All interviews were completed early in 2002.
7. When *Barron's* crowned Meeker 'Net Queen, it quoted from some of her reports: "Of Yahoo, for example, she said last spring, 'Hmm, what's the value of leadership in the fastest-growing medium in the history of the planet?' In a recent year-end outlook piece, she wrote that stocks of the Internet leaders are 'yes, cheap. Why? It's simple; the market opportunities are really large.'" Andrew Bary, "'Net Queen: How Mary Meeker Came to Rule the Internet," *Barron's*, 21 December 1998, 23.
8. Interview with the author.
9. Amazon closed at $138; since the stock had split three for one since Blodget made his forecast, this was the equivalent of $414.
10. Lise Buyer, interview with the author. Unless otherwise noted, all further quotations are drawn from an interview with the author.
11. Jonathan Cohen, interview with the author.
12. The Eileen Buckley article "Holding Analysts Accountable" (*The Industry Standard*, 10 June 2000) counted how often Blodget was mentioned in '99. In "Who Blew the Dot.com Bubble? The Cautionary Tale of Henry Blodget"

(*The Washington Post,* 12 March 2001), Howard Kurtz, reported on the references to Blodget through 2001.

13. Joseph Menn, "Noted Analyst Sees Net Stock Shakeout," *The Los Angeles Times,* 2 October 1999, C-1.

14. Jonathan Clements, "Getting Going: Vanguard Founder Blasts Funds' Focus," *The Wall Street Journal,* 16 May 2000.

15. In "Internet Trades Put Merrill Lynch Bull on Horns of a Dilemma" (*The Wall Street Journal,* 12 February 1999), Charles Gasparino and Randall Smith quote Joan Solotar of Donaldson, Lufkin & Jenrette when estimating what share of Merrill's revenue comes from its retail brokerage business. See Chapter 10 ("The Information Bomb") on how deregulation turned the economics of Wall Street research upside down.

16. James M. Clash, "Henry Blodget Debates Jeremy Grantham," *Forbes Global,* 12 June 2000.

17. Kenneth N. Gilpin, "Market Insight: America Online Is No Longer Invincible," *The New York Times,* 9 August 1999.

18. Andrew Bary, " 'Net Queen: How Mary Meeker Came to Rule the Internet," *Barron's,* 21 December 1998, 23.

19. James M. Clash, "Henry Blodget Debates Jeremy Grantham." Blodget explained what he meant by "stuff I hope will survive a nuclear war" in an interview with the author.

20. See Prologue.

21. Peter Truell, "The Soothsayer Who Never Blinked," *The New York Times,* 27 July 1997.

22. Steve Einhorn, interview with the author.

23. The year that Blodget was hired, *The New York Times* was one of many publications that made it clear that Blodget was hired to bring in investment banking business. See Prologue.

24. David Henry, "Internet Stock Bull Dresses in Caveats," *USA Today,* 8 June 1999, 03B.

25. Kimberly Seals McDonald, "Just Too Darn Many Long Words," *The New York Post,* 11 April 1999, 61.

26. Steve Einhorn, interview with the author.

27. Henry Blodget, "Merrill Lynch Overview Internet e-Commerce—Investment Philosophy: Key Points," 14 September 1999, 16.

28. Gretchen Morgenson, "Dow Finishes Day Over 10,000 Mark for the First Time," *The New York Times,* 30 March 1999.

29. Robert McGough, "In New York: Heard on the Street—Some Stocks Just

Seem Irresistible, Whatever the Price," *The Wall Street Journal Europe,* 16 March 1999.

30. "Anatomy of a Bear Market," *McKinsey Quarterly,* 28 January 2003.

31. Tice testified before the Capital Markets, Insurance and Government-Sponsored Enterprises Subcommittee on June 14, 2001. See Chapter 2, note 15.

32. Andy Engel, Steve Leuthold, Mike Schurmann, "Religion Stocks and the Nifty Fifty," The Leuthold Group Leuthold/Weeden Research, 1972 and 1999. For a discussion of the implications of Leuthold's research for buy-and-hold investing, see Maggie Mahar, "Three Wall Street Truths You Can't Trust," *Bloomberg Personal Finance,* November 2000.

33. In "The Trader: Wow! '98 Had Enough Thrills for Several Years," Andrew Bary made out the argument that, in part because interest rates are so low, the Nifty Fifty of the nineties enjoy brighter prospects than the stars of the seventies. *Barron's,* December 1998.

CHAPTER 18

1. Gail Dudack, interview with the author. (All quotations and descriptions of Dudack's thoughts and feelings that follow are drawn from interviews with the author beginning in the fall of 2001.)

2. Jonathan Fuerbringer, "Still Bullish, but Pulling in the Horns," *The New York Times,* 26 December 1999.

3. Suzanne Woolley, "Wall Street's Take on 2000; Six Pros Make Their Predictions for the Year Ahead," *Money,* February 2000.

4. Jersey Gilbert and Tiernan Ray, "The Next Big Thing," *Smart Money,* August 1999; Jersey Gilbert, "Retire Ten Years Early—You Can Get There from Here: Surely You're Tempted by the Idea of an Early Retirement (Who Isn't?) But Can You Really Afford It? Here's How to Find Out; See Table, 'The Right Mix,'" *Smart Money,* 1 August 1999, 96.

5. Richard Siklos and Catherine Yang, "Welcome to the 21st Century: With One Stunning Stroke, AOL and Time Warner Create a Colossus and Redefine the Future," *Business Week,* 24 January 2000.

6. Allan Sloan, "Cable Carried Incentive for AOL Merger," *The Washington Post,* 18 January 2000, E01.

7. See Chapter 11 ("AOL: A Case Study") on AOL's accounting, and Sloan's efforts to warn his readers. In 1998, the SEC again disputed AOL's earnings, and in 2001, investors continued to question the company's bookkeeping. In the first quarter, AOL cited free cash flow of $651 million, but fund managers

such as David Tice, editor of *Behind the Numbers,* argued that cash flow was only $70 million after AOL paid to settle a lawsuit related to Time Warner's sale of Six Flag entertainment parks.

8. Suzanne Woolley, "Wall Street Sizes Up 1999," *Money,* December 1998, 58.

9. "Investor's Chronicle," *The Financial Times,* 23 April 1999, 29.

10. Hank Herrmann, interview with the author.

11. All of Rukeyser's on-air comments come from a transcript of *Wall $treet Week,* 5 November 1999. Technically, Dudack was not banished from the show; she was fired from her position on the elves' panel. But the way in which it was done virtually ensured that she would never again appear on *Wall $treet Week.*

12. Susan Douglas, a professor of cultural studies and communications at the University of Michigan, made this observation in "Wall Street Week," *The Progressive,* January 1997.

13. Gary Strauss, "TV's Financial Dean Celebrates 30 Years," *USA Today,* 3 November 2000.

14. John Brooks, "Onward and Upward with Wall Street," *The New Yorker,* 14 November 1983; Warren Kalbacker, "20 Questions," *Playboy,* 3 January 1982.

15. James Conaway, "Wall St. Wiz; How Louis Rukeyser gets 10 million viewers inside his tent each week," *The Washington Post Magazine,* 6 November 1983, 24.

16. At the end of 2000, Rukeyser himself acknowledged that "neutral" had been the correct forecast for most of the year. On September 7, 2001, Rukeyser called the elves "comatose," and on September 21, he announced that following the tragic events of September 11, he had decided to give the elves a rest.

17. The first set of allegations were reported in *The Wall Street Journal* (Michael Schroeder, "A Popular Fund Manager Allegedly Took Kickbacks," 17 December 1999, C1). The *Journal* reported the second set of charges in August of 2001 (Jerry Markon and Michael Schroeder, "U.S. Charges Bond Bilked His Clients . . . Fund Manager Faces '99 Kickback Case, Too," 10 August 2001, C1). For the end of Bond's story, see Chapter 20 ("Winners, Losers, and Scapegoats").

18. Michael Lewis, "Why James Grant Will Never Be Louis Rukeyser," *Bloomberg News,* 29 October 2002.

19. Patrick McGeehan, "Expert's Top Choices, Gone Awry," *The New York Times,* 7 October 2001.

20. For more on how mutual fund companies discreetly bury failing funds, see Chapter 13 ("The Mutual Fund Manager: Career Risk versus Investment Risk"). Christopher Davis reported on PWKAX's 2000 performance in

"Morningstar's Take," 9 February 2001. In October of 2002, Morningstar's Christopher Traulsen reported on the second name change (to UBS Strategy), with Kerschner still at the helm ("Morningstar's Take," 25 October 2002). Finally, in December, Morningstar reported the merger (Karen Wallace and Dan Culloton, "Fund Times: Janus Reshuffles Its Deck, and More," "Morningstar's Take," 13 December 2002).

21. *Richard Russell's Dow Theory Letter,* November 2000.

22. Marc Faber, *The Gloom, Boom & Doom Report,* November 1999, 2.

23. *Richard Russell's Dow Theory Letter,* 21 October 1998.

CHAPTER 19

1. Comments made at a congressional committee hearing and reported by Jackie Calmes, "Washington Wire: A Special Weekly Report from The Wall Street Journal's Capital Bureau," *The Wall Street Journal,* 27 July 2001.

2. Alan Abelson reported on insider sales, citing Steve Leuthold's research, in "Up & Down Wall Street," *Barron's,* 14 August 2000.

3. Mark Maremont and John Hechinger, "Fifty Corporate Insiders Bailed Out Before the Slump and Made a Mint," *The Wall Street Journal,* 22 March 2001.

4. David Henry, "More Insiders Sell Big Blocks of Stock: Surge May Foretell Market Weakness in 3 to 12 Months," *USA Today,* 18 September 2000, 01B.

5. Andrew Countryman, "Window of Opportunity: Talk About Good Timing: Execs Sell Before the Fall," *The Chicago Tribune,* 2 March 2003, 1. *The Tribune's* analysis was based on information regarding insider transactions provided by Thompson Financial, a research firm. More than half of all sales were followed by a drop of least 10 percent. Even in the period from 1995 to 1999, when the Dow posted consecutive double-digit gains, two-fifths of the insider sales were followed by a drop of at least 10 percent over the next six months.

6. Mark Maremont and John Hechinger, "Fifty Corporate Insiders Bailed Out Before the Slump and Made a Mint," *The Wall Street Journal,* 22 March 2001.

7. Even after Milken was tried, convicted, and jailed, Lay tipped his hat to Milken, calling him a "visionary." When the king of junk was released from prison, Lay invited him to speak at an Enron conference. "Drexel may have been accused of arrogance," Ken Lay told *The Economist,* "but they were just being very innovative and very aggressive." The remark underlined how the sleight-of-hand accounting of the nineties was, in many ways, simply an extension of the financial engineering of the eighties. See Marie Brenner, "The Enron Wars," *Vanity Fair,* April 2002, 195; and "Face Value: Enron's Energetic Inspiration: By Bending All the Rules of the Energy Business, Kenneth Lay

Has Turned Enron from a Stodgy Gas Concern into a Soaring New-Economy Company," *The Economist,* 3 June 2000.

8. Mark Bimein, "What Did Joe Know? Joe Nacchio's Qwest Booked Hundreds of Millions in Bogus Deals," *Fortune,* 12 May 2003.

9. Laurie P. Cohen and Dennis K. Berman, "How Analyst Grubman Helped Call Shots at Global Crossing," *The Wall Street Journal,* 1 June 2002.

10. Rebecca Blumenstein, Deborah Solomon, and Kathy Chen, "Global Crossing Cosseted Executives," *The Wall Street Journal,* 21 February 2002.

11. Allan Sloan, "Pride After the Fall: An Investing Parable," *The Washington Post,* 5 February 2002.

12. Dennis K. Berman, "Dialing for Dollars: Some Insiders Sold Out Stakes," *The Wall Street Journal,* 12 August 2002.

13. At a Fed policy meeting in 1996, Greenspan said, "I recognize there is a stock-market bubble problem," and added, "We do have the possibility of . . . increasing margin requirements . . . I guarantee that if you want to get rid of the bubble, whatever it is, that will do it." See Chapter 14 ("Abby Cohen Goes to Washington; Alan Greenspan Gives a Speech").

   In 2000, when Sloan raised the question, margin requirements allowed an investor to borrow $500 for each $1,000 of stock, although some brokerage houses had more stringent rules. "Increasing the margin rate to 100 percent, which would eliminate borrowing to finance new purchase [of stock] would send a powerful message. Not to mention trashing some ultra-speculative stocks whose price moves are influenced by day traders, who typically borrow heavily," Sloan observed (Allan Sloan, "Greenspan Misses the Mark in the War on Stock Prices," *The Washington Post,* 14 March 2000).

14. Allan Sloan, "Greenspan Misses the Mark in War on Stock Prices," *The Washington Post,* 14 March 2000.

15. Jim Grant, "Irrational Exuberance Toward Mr. Greenspan," *The Financial Times,* 10 February 2000.

16. Justin Martin, *Greenspan: The Man Behind the Money* (Cambridge, Mass.: Perseus Publishing, 2001), 226.

17. Ralph Wanger, interview with the author.

18. Gretchen Morgenson, "If You Think Last Week Was Wild," *The New York Times,* 19 March 2000.

19. Robert McGough, "Bull's Retreat Doesn't Cause a Stampede—Some Once Feared a Market Tailspin," *The Wall Street Journal,* 29 March 2000.

20. Greg Ip, "A Year of Living Dangerously," *The Wall Street Journal,* 2 January 2001, R1.

21. Bianco Research, L.L.C. (www.arborresearch.com/biancoresearch), / March 2000.

22. Peter Bernstein, interview with the author.

23. Gail Dudack, interview with the author.

24. "2001 Mutual Fund Factbook," Investment Company Institute.

25. Terence O'Hara, "2000; It Was the Best of Times and the Worst of Times, and the Difference Was All in the Numbers," *The Washington Post*, 31 December 2000, H1.

26. Tom Cahill, "CSFB Suspends Banker Quattrone Pending Investigation," *Bloomberg News*, 3 February 2003.

27. Greg Ip, "A Year of Living Dangerously." Quotations that follow from Bernstein, Farrell, and Kershner are drawn from the same article.

28. Justin Martin, *Greenspan: The Man Behind the Money*, 243–45.

29. Martin Mayer, "Averting a Meltdown," *Worth*, July/August 2001.

30. Justin Martin, *Greenspan*, 244–45.

31. In the first half of 2003, it seemed, to many, that the Fed's cuts were finally having a salutary effect—but capital spending was not rising. For a discussion of the difference between fueling consumption and boosting capital investment, see Chapter 21 ("Looking Ahead: What Financial Cycles Mean for the 21st-Century Investor").

32. Jim Grant, "Blame Greenspan," *Forbes*, 3 September 2001.

33. Martin Mayer, "Averting a Meltdown."

34. In a speech that he gave at the University of California, San Diego, on July 23, 2003, Bernanke reiterated an earlier suggestion that the Fed would be willing to cut the Fed funds rate to zero—even though such "an action imposes costs on savers and some financial institutions." In the July speech, he also talked about the Fed going a step further, to try to lower long-term rates by using "non-traditional measures."

     "Such measures might include, among others, increased purchases of longer-term government bonds by the Fed, an announced program of over-supplying bank reserves, term lending through the discount window at very low rates, and the issuance of options to borrow from the Fed at low rates." "Text of Bernanke's Comments at the University of California," *The Wall Street Journal*, 23 July 2003.

35. Bill Gross, "Investment Outlook—Is That All There Is—To a Fire?," www.pimco.com, May/June 2003.

36. Jonathan R. Laing, "The Debt Bomb: Only Housing Is Keeping the Fuse on America's Borrowing Habit from Burning Down," *Barron's*, 20 January 2003.

When *Barron's* reported on debt, it cited Federal Reserve figures as of the third quarter of 2002, showing a total of 31 trillion. By 2003, the number had risen to 32 trillion. *Barron's* acknowledged that some questioned the $31 trillion number: "Some contend that today's debt level of $31 trillion, or 295% of current GDP of $10.5 trillion, is somewhat artificial. About $10 trillion of the debt consists of the borrowings of financial players—banks, savings institutions, finance companies, issuers of asset-backed securities and government-sponsored enterprises such as Fannie Mae and Freddie Mac. These entities mostly use their borrowings to fund corporate loans, mortgages, auto loans and credit-card balances. So, in a sense, about a third of today's aggregate debt total is being double-counted. That wasn't true in the early thirties, when the ratio of U.S. debt to GDP hit its previous high of 264%, because the financial sector was far less developed at the time."

But *Barron's* also noted that defaults on corporate debt had climbed while revenues slowed, "particularly in the wholesale electric-power, telecom and high-tech sectors. According to Moody's [the credit-rating agency], a staggering 18.4% of all speculative-grade debt, on a dollar-weighted basis, went into default in the 12 months ending Aug. 31 2002." Default rates were shrinking, but Moody's noted that corporate revenues—which provide the cash needed to pay off debts—had fallen to just 113 percent of corporate debt levels. This was the second-worst ratio of debt to revenue since the Great Depression. "That revenue-to-debt ratio should be a lot higher—it ran 130% to 145% in the mid-nineties . . . ," warned John Lonski, Moody's chief economist.

CHAPTER 20

1. "The Betrayed Investor," *Business Week,* 25 February 2002; Ian McDonald, "Mutual Fund Investors 2002: A Dreary Fund Odyssey; There May Be Hope Ahead," *The Wall Street Journal,* 31 December 2002 (updated).
2. "The Betrayed Investor." *Business Week* cited the Pew Research Center for People and the Press as its source.
3. Jim Tucci, interview with the author. Tucci originally told his story to *Business Week* (see "The Betrayed Investor"). In 2003, he updated the story, expanding on and correcting some details.
4. "Participants Report Card for 2002: The Impact of the Bear Market on Retirement Savings Plans," The Vanguard Group Retirement Research, February 2003. Over five years the Vanguard survey showed an even more striking difference between more affluent and less affluent 401(k) investors: From January 1998 through December 2002, the average investor with less than

$250,000 earned less than 1 percent a year, while those with larger accounts gained an average of 4.9 percent annually.

5. See Chapter 9 ("The Media: CNBC Lays Down the Rhythm"). Also see table "Who Owns Stocks?" Appendix, pages 463–64.

6. Rebecca Blumenstein and Susan Pullam, "WorldCom Report Finds Ebbers Played Role in Inflating Revenue," *The Wall Street Journal,* 6 June 2003, A1.

7. Shirley Sauerwein, interview with the author. For a reference to the original 1999 *Wall Street Journal* story, see Chapter 7 ("The Individual Investor").

8. These losses do not include new money that came into the account during the three years surveyed. In the financial press, Vanguard's sample was widely accepted as a fair proxy for small investors' losses nationwide. (It would be some time before multiple surveys could give a composite picture of just how much individual investors of all stripes lost, not just in 401(k)s but in taxable accounts.)

9. Ray Martin (the *Saturday Early Morning Show's* financial advisor), "Tweaking Your 401(k)," 19 October 2002; Toddi Gutner, "How Hard a Hit?" *Business Week,* 17 March 2003.

10. Gail Marks Jarvis, "Despite Declines, Investors Hang Tough," *Pioneer Press,* 3 March 2003.

11. Jennifer Postlewaithe, interview with the author.

12. "The Betrayed Investor."

13. Chet Currier, "The Bear Market Is Dead—Long Live the New Bull," *Bloomberg News,* 13 June 2003.

14. Neither example includes the profits either might have made on new contributions to the fund during those three years. But that calculation would only widen the gap between the passive buy-and-hold investor and the investor who sold his losers and spread his risk.

15. Louis Uchitelle, "Do 401(k)'s Give Workers an Illusion of Wealth?" *The New York Times,* 26 May 2002.

16. Ruth Simon, "Why Even a Rally Won't Save You—Host of Deep Problems Raises Doubts About Role of 401(k)s; Time to Turn Over the Reins?" *The Wall Street Journal,* 1 May 2003.

17. See Chapter 2 ("The People's Market").

18. Ralph Wanger, interview with the author.

19. Brian Steinberg, "Louis Rukeyser's Last 'Wall Street Week' Will Be June 28," Dow Jones News Service, 21 March 2002; Jay Hancock, "Minus Rukeyser, It'll be 'Wall Street Weak,'" *The Baltimore Sun,* 27 March 2002.

20. "Former Money Manager Going to Prison," *Bloomberg News,* 12 February 2003. For Bond's story, see Chapter 18 ("The Last Bear Is Gored").

21. Stacey L. Bradford, "Pundit Watch: Has a New Bull Market Begun?" SmartMoney.com, 2 June 2003.

22. "Happy Daze," *Barron's,* 23 June 2003.

23. Steve Leuthold, interview with the author. For Russell's and Faber's views on long-term investments, see Chapter 21 ("Looking Ahead: What Financial Cycles Mean for the 21st-Century Investor").

24. Interview with the author.

25. Floyd Norris, "Bush, on Wall Street, Offers Tough Talk and Softer Plans," *The New York Times,* 10 July 2002.

26. Michael Lewis, "In Praise of Corporate Corruption Boom," *Bloomberg News,* 12 July 2002.

27. John Kenneth Galbraith, *A Short History of Financial Euphoria* (New York: Whittle Books in association with Penguin Books, 1993), 23.

28. See Chapter 16 ("Fully Deluded Earnings").

29. The remark was made in a conversation between a mutual fund company executive and one of the firm's portfolio managers, and was reported in an interview with the author.

30. Regarding the $450,000 offer if the analysts would remain silent, Laderman reported that a DLJ spokeswoman said ex-employees who ask for or get more than the typical two weeks' severance package are always asked to sign a "nondisparagement" agreement. Jeffrey Laderman, "Who Can You Trust? Wall Street's Spin Game: Stock Analysts Often Have a Hidden Agenda," *Business Week,* 5 October 1998. See also Erick Schonfeld, "The High Price of Research; Caveat Investor: Stock and Research Analysts Covering Dot-Coms Aren't as Independent as You Think," *Fortune,* March 2000; "Bad Advice, Faith," *Bloomberg News,* July 2000; and James Grant, "Talking Up the Market," *The Financial Times,* 19 July 1999.

31. Gretchen Morgenson, "How Did So Many Get It So Wrong?" *The New York Times,* 31 December 2000.

32. In an interview with the author, Sloan shared a draft of his speech.

33. Charles Gasparino, "Ex-Analyst Blodget Is Barred by NASD, Will Pay $4 Million," *The Wall Street Journal,* 28 April 2003.

34. See Prologue.

35. Harvey Eisen, interview with the author.

36. See, for example, Laurie P. Cohen and Dennis K. Berman, "How Analyst Grubman Helped Call Shots at Global Crossing," *The Wall Street Journal,* 1 June 2002.

37. Andy Kessler, *Wall Street Meat* (Escape Velocity Press, 2003), 69.
38. Ann Davis, "Morgan Stanley's Meeker Given Role in Broker's New Reporting," *The Wall Street Journal*, 29 July 2003.
39. Eliot Spitzer, interview with the author.
40. Michael Lewis, "The Dishonesty of Eliot Spitzer's Inquisition," *Bloomberg News*, 22 May 2002.
41. Eliot Spitzer, interview with the author.
42. Michael Lewis, "The Dishonesty of Eliot Spitzer's Inquisition."
43. Eliot Spitzer, interview with the author; John Cassidy, "The Investigation," *The New Yorker*, 7 April 2003.
44. Eliot Spitzer, interview with the author.
45. John Cassidy, "The Investigation."
46. Eliot Spitzer, interview with the author.
47. Eliot Spitzer, interview with the author.
48. Bill Moyers, commentary, "NOW with Bill Moyers," 31 May 2002.

CHAPTER 21

1. Warren Buffett, 2002 Annual Report to Shareholders, Berkshire Hathaway, 21 February 2003.
2. See Maggie Mahar, "Three Wall Street Truths You Can't Trust," *Bloomberg Personal Finance*, November 2000.
3. Marc Faber provides compound annual rates of return on real assets in the seventies in *Tomorrow's Gold* (Hong Kong: CLSA Books, 2002), citing Salomon Inc. as his source.
4. Marc Faber, *Tomorrow's Gold*, 35.
5. Unless otherwise indicated, Faber's remarks are based on interviews with the author. See also Maggie Mahar, "Seeing the Future," *Bloomberg Personal Finance*, November 2001.
6. Maggie Mahar, "Seeing the Future."
7. Marc Faber, *Tomorrow's Gold*, 14.
8. Martin Barnes published the charts and analysis in *The Bank Credit Analyst*, March 2003. Kate Welling quoted Barnes's research in *welling@weeden*, 11 April 2003.
9. Martin Barnes, interview with the author; Barnes, *The Bank Credit Analyst*, March 2003; and see *welling@weeden*, 11 April 2003.
10. Peter Bernstein, interview with the author.
11. *welling@weeden*, 28 February 2003.

12. Greg Ip, Nicholas Kulish, and Jacob M. Schlesinger, "New Model: This Economic Slump Is Shaping Up to Be a Different Downturn," *The Wall Street Journal,* 5 January 2001. *The Journal* cited Bianco Research as its source for its numbers.

13. See Chapter 19 ("Insiders Sell; the Water Rises") for a discussion of how easy money leads to excess capacity.

14. Ralph Wanger, interview with the author.

15. Craig Torres, "Feldstein, Unlike Greenspan, Says Weak Economy Needs Tax Cuts," *Bloomberg News,* 13 March 2003.

16. Marc Faber quoted Richebächer in *The Gloom, Boom and Doom Report,* May 2003.

17. For a fuller explanation of Dow Theory, see Chapter 1 ("The Market's Cycles").

18. Ralph Wanger, interview with the author.

19. "Q&A with GMO's Jeremy Grantham," *Business Week,* 8 March 2002; "How Far Is Down?" *Barron's,* 22 July 2002; Barrie Dunstan, "Grin and Bear It, Says Grantham," *Australian Financial Review,* 13 June 2003, 35.

20. E. S. Browning, "Does Current Stock Rally Have More Room to Run?" *The Wall Street Journal,* 7 June 2003.

21. *Richard Russell's Dow Theory Letter,* 11 June 2003.

22. Ned Davis, interview with the author. See also Sandra Ward, "Bear's Pause—The Rally Is Just a Phase of a Long-Term Down Market, Researcher Says," *Barron's,* 16 June 2003.

23. Richard Russell, interview with the author; *Richard Russell's Dow Theory Letter,* 21 October 1998. Russell cites John Schott, a psychoanalyst and pioneer in the study of investor's emotions.

24. See Chapter 1 ("The Market's Cycles").

25. "Q&A with GMO's Jeremy Grantham," *Business Week,* 18 March 2002.

26. *welling@weeden,* 28 February 2003.

27. *Richard Russell's Dow Theory Letter,* 23 July 2003.

28. Sandra Ward, "Bear's Pause"; and Ned Davis, interview with the author.

29. Maggie Mahar, "Seeing the Future."

30. Andy Engel and Steve Leuthold, "How Long to Catch Up?" The Leuthold Group, May 2000. As Leuthold pointed out, not too many investors plow dividends back in once they realize that they are trapped in a long bear market. Most would eventually sell.

31. Ralph Wanger, interview with the author.

32. Nassim Nicholas Taleb, interview with the author. See also Maggie Mahar,

"No Such Thing," *Bloomberg Wealth Manager,* June 2003; and Nassim Nicholas Taleb, *Fooled by Randomness: The Hidden Role of Chance in the Markets and in Life* (Texere, 2001).

33. Peter Bernstein, Interview with the author. See also Maggie Mahar, "No Such Thing"; and Robert Prechter's *Conquer the Crash: You Can Survive and Prosper in a Deflationary Depression* (New York: John Wiley & Sons, 2002).

34. Nassim Nicholas Taleb, *Fooled by Randomness.*

35. Peter Bernstein, interview with the author. See also Maggie Mahar, "No Such Thing."

36. A columnist for *Forbes,* and later for *The New York Times,* Hulbert has written about Russell's success in his columns. (See, for example, "The Dow Theory Still Lives," *Forbes,* 6 April 1998, 153.) See also Chapter 1 ("The Market's Cycles").

    In an interview with the author, Hulbert explained: "We measure Russell's returns by keeping his subscriber in an index fund throughout those periods when Russell's theory signals buy or hold, then putting him into T-bills when Russell's Dow Theory sends a 'sell' signal," Hulbert explained, "and that's how we arrive at an average return of 11.9 percent."

    On paper, a theoretical investor who bought and held the S&P 500 throughout that period would have done even better—earning 14.1 percent annually—though very, very few investors actually got into the market of June of 1980 and held, without wavering, over the next 21 years. Moreover, the success of the buy-and-hold strategy depended on making a correct guess as to how long the bull market would continue. "This is why," Hulbert explained, "after adjusting for the risk involved in betting on the market's long-term direction, Russell's less risky advice actually beat a buy-and-hold strategy, on a risk-adjusted basis."

    For further evidence of the Dow Theory's effectiveness, see Chapter 1 ("The Market's Cycles").

37. Mark Hulbert, interview with the author. See also Maggie Mahar, " 'Buy-and-Hold' vs. 'Market Timing,' " *Bloomberg News,* reprinted in *The Journal Record,* 15 September 1998.

38. *Richard Russell's Dow Theory Letter,* 19 June 2002.

39. Jeremy Grantham, interview with the author. Grantham originally described his "feathers" analogy to Sandra Ward in a *Barron's* Q&A, "After the Deluge: An Elegant Thinker Deconstructs the Stock Market's Latest Bubble and Its Likely Aftermath," 6 August 2001, 34.

40. Bob Farrell, interview with the author.

41. Sandra Ward, "How Far Is Down? A Money Manager Explains How to Discover When the Market Finally Reaches Fair Value," *Barron's*, 22 July 2002, 21.

42. For the full text of Di Tomasso's commentary, see www.ditomassogroup.com.

43. Marc Faber, interview with the author. See also Maggie Mahar, "Seeing the Future."

44. "Robert Greer Discusses the Benefits of Commodity Investing," www.pimco.com, June 2003.

45. Michael R. Sesit, "Going Global: This Manager's Tips Travel Well," *The Wall Street Journal*, 11 April 2003 and "Mr. Rogers' Far-flung Neighborhood," *The Financial Times*, 29 May 2003.

46. Timothy Green, *The World of Gold: The Inside Story of Who Mines, Who Markets, Who Buys Gold* (London: Rosedale Press, 1993), 2–3.

47. For a full discussion on the Fed's efforts—first to keep the bubble afloat, and then to reflate the economy—see Chapter 19 ("Insiders Sell; the Water Rises").

48. Marc Faber, *The Gloom, Boom and Doom Report.*

49. On the debt that remained after the bubble burst, see Chapter 19 ("Insiders Sell; the Water Rises").

50. Interview with the author. Marc Faber, *Tomorrow's Gold*, 288. Gold mining shares do not necessarily track the price of gold, which is why investors such as Eveillard buy gold bullion as well as mining shares.

51. Marc Faber, interview with the author.

52. Gail Dudack, interview with the author.

53. Marc Faber, interview with the author.

54. Lee R. Thomas III, "Global Markets Watch," www.pimco.com, June 2003.

55. Maureen Allyn, interview with the author.

56. See Timothy Aeppel, "Goodyear Eliminates Dividend, Helping Push Shares Down 17%," *The Wall Street Journal*, 5 February 2003, for full description of Goodyear's woes.

57. Peter Bernstein, as quoted in *Richard Russell's Dow Theory Letter*, 2 January 2002.

58. Maggie Mahar, "Total Return," *Bloomberg Personal Finance*, January/February 2002.

59. "Q&A with GMO's Jeremy Grantham."

60. Faber quoted Richebächer in *The Boom, Gloom and Doom Report* of May 2003, and, in an interview with the author, he noted that an independent economist had confirmed Richebächer's numbers.

61. Richard Russell, "Rich Man, Poor Man (The Power of Compounding)," available at www.dowtheoryletters.com.

62. TIPS can present a tax problem. The inflation bonus is paid on the back end: when the bond matures it is added to the bond's principal. Along the way, the investor receives only the fixed dividend as income. Nonethelesss, if an investor buys TIPS for a taxable account, he is taxed as if he received the inflation each year. So he must pay the taxes on the inflation bonus before he receives the bonus. The easy solution is to buy TIPS only for a 401(k), an IRA, a Keogh, or any other tax-deferred retirement account. In that case, the TIPS are sheltered, along with the rest of his investments: he pays taxes only when he retires and begins withdrawing his savings. Alternatively, an investor can buy "I bonds," which are similar to TIPS but do not require him to pay taxes along the way.

APPENDIX

THE PROFILE OF A BUBBLE

"The classic profile is for the market to trade sideways for an extended period after the bubble bursts." —Martin Barnes, BCA Research 2003

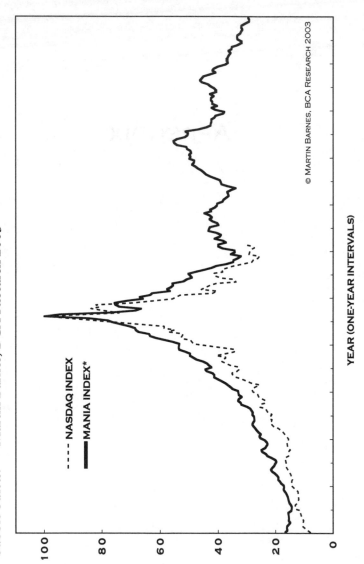

© MARTIN BARNES, BCA RESEARCH 2003

YEAR (ONE-YEAR INTERVALS)

* A COMPOSITE INDEX OF PEAKS IN GOLD AND SILVER (1973–86), JAPANESE NIKKEI (1982–95), AND DOW JONES (1922–35).
NOTE: BOTH SERIES ARE INDEXED TO 100 AT THEIR RESPECTIVE PEAKS.

STOCK FUNDS KEEP ONLY A SMALL CASH CUSHION

Equity Mutual Fund Cash Ratio

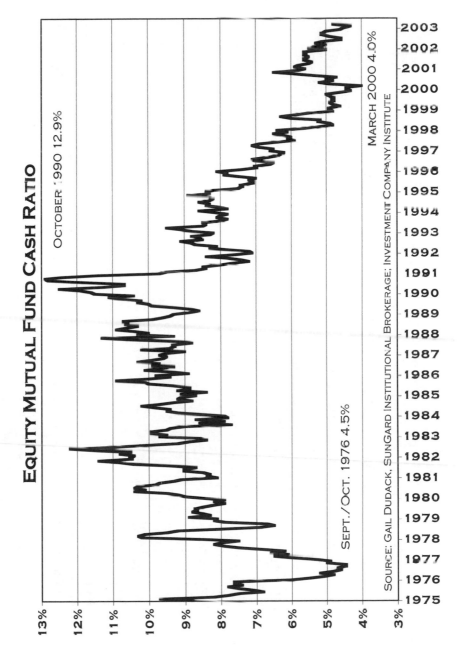

OCTOBER 1990 12.9%

MARCH 2000 4.0%

SEPT./OCT. 1976 4.5%

SOURCE: GAIL DUDACK, SUNGARD INSTITUTIONAL BROKERAGE; INVESTMENT COMPANY INSTITUTE

MUTUAL FUND INVESTORS HANG ON

"Since the beginning of 2002, net redemptions from equity funds have been tiny compared with total fund assets. The net cash outflow in the 12 months ending March 30, 2003, amounted to 3.6 percent of the sector's assets. In the past, by the time a bear market bottomed, outflows were much greater—as high as 8 percent a year." —Gail Dudack, SunGard Institutional Brokerage

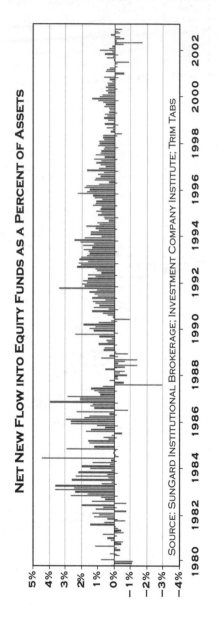

NET NEW FLOW INTO EQUITY FUNDS AS A PERCENT OF ASSETS

SOURCE: SUNGARD INSTITUTIONAL BROKERAGE; INVESTMENT COMPANY INSTITUTE; TRIM TABS

WHO OWNS STOCKS?

Less Affluent Households Began Buying Later—When Prices Were Highest

EQUITY OWNERSHIP CHARACTERISTICS BY HOUSEHOLD FINANCIAL ASSETS

	Household Financial Assets			
	Less than $25,000	$25,000 to $99,999	$100,000 to $499,999	$500,000 or more
Median				
Household financial assets in equities	$6,000	$25,000	$100,000	$497,200
Number of equities owned	3	4	6	11
Percent of Equity-Owning Households				
Own				
Individual stock (net)	33%	38%	53%	73%
Inside employer-sponsored retirement plans	10%	15%	20%	21%
Outside employer-sponsored retirement plans	25%	31%	44%	67%
Stock mutual funds (net)	89%	88%	92%	90%
Inside employer-sponsored retirement plans	68%	76%	72%	58%
Outside employer-sponsored retirement plans	38%	39%	60%	71%
Conducted equity transaction(s) during 2001	20%	33%	44%	60%
Year of first equity purchase:				
Before 1990	12%	27%	55%	78%
1990 to 1995	20%	33%	25%	12%
1996 to 1998	25% [68%]	27% [40%]	12% [20%]	9% [10%]
1999 or later	43%	13%	8%	1%
Source of first equity purchase:				
Inside employer-sponsored retirement plan	63%	60%	49%	30%
Outside employer-sponsored retirement plan	31%	33%	41%	64%
Both inside and outside employer-sponsored retirement plan in same year	6%	7%	10%	6%

(continued on next page)

	Household Financial Assets			
	Less than $25,000	$25,000 to $99,999	$100,000 to $499,999	$500,000 or more
Type of equity first purchased:				
Individual stock only	17%	19%	21%	31%
Stock mutual funds only	74%	72%	67%	51%
Both individual stock and stock mutual funds	9%	9%	12%	18%
Willing to take:				
Substantial risk for substantial gain	11%	10%	8%	10%
Above-average risk for above-average gain	25%	29%	27%	29%
Average risk for average gain	45%	47%	51%	50%
Below-average risk for below-average gain	11%	7%	9%	8%
Unwilling to take any risk	8%	7%	5%	3%
Primary financial goal:				
Retirement	63%	72%	68%	64%
Education	12%	9%	10%	8%
Other	25%	19%	22%	28%
Agree				
I am not concerned about short-term fluctuations in my investments	77%	77%	80%	80%
I tend to rely on advice from a professional financial advisor when making investment decisions	54%	54%	57%	56%

SOURCE: INVESTMENT COMPANY INSTITUTE; SECURITIES INDUSTRY ASSOCIATION

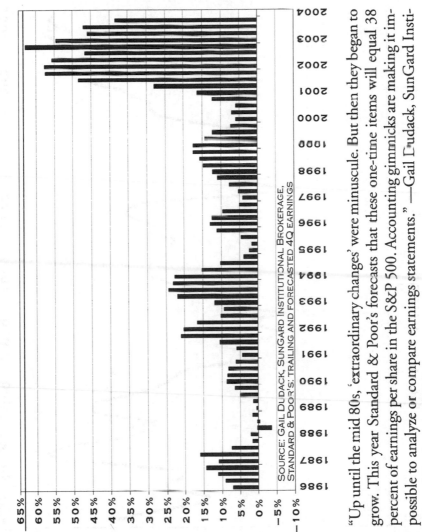

EXTRAORDINARY ITEMS AS A % OF REPORTED S&P EPS

SOURCE: GAIL DUDACK, SUNGARD INSTITUTIONAL BROKERAGE,
STANDARD & POOR'S: TRAILING AND FORECASTED 4Q EARNINGS

"Up until the mid 80s, 'extraordinary changes' were minuscule. But then they began to grow. This year Standard & Poor's forecasts that these one-time items will equal 38 percent of earnings per share in the S&P 500. Accounting gimmicks are making it impossible to analyze or compare earnings statements." —Gail Dudack, SunGard Institutional Brokerage, 2003

COMMODITIES NEAR ALL-TIME LOW

PRICE LEVELS
(1.00 = 1921
LEVELS)

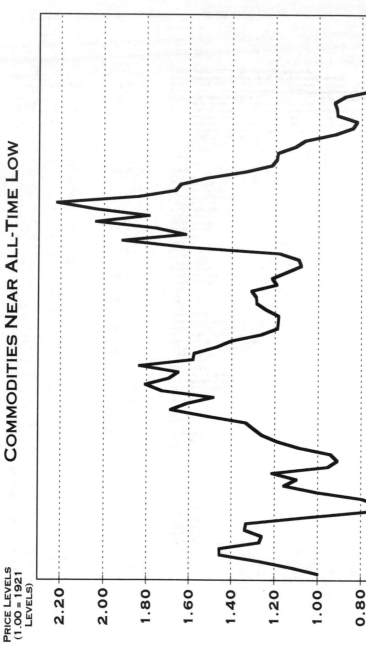

SOURCE: DI TOMASSO GROUP

BASKET CONSISTS OF INFLATION-ADJUSTED PRICES OF THE
17 COMMODITIES COMPRISING THE CRB INDEX

INDEX

Page numbers in *italics* indicate charts, graphs, or tables.

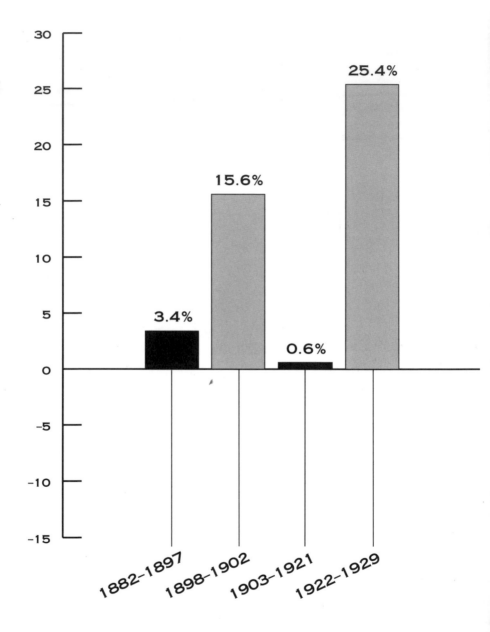